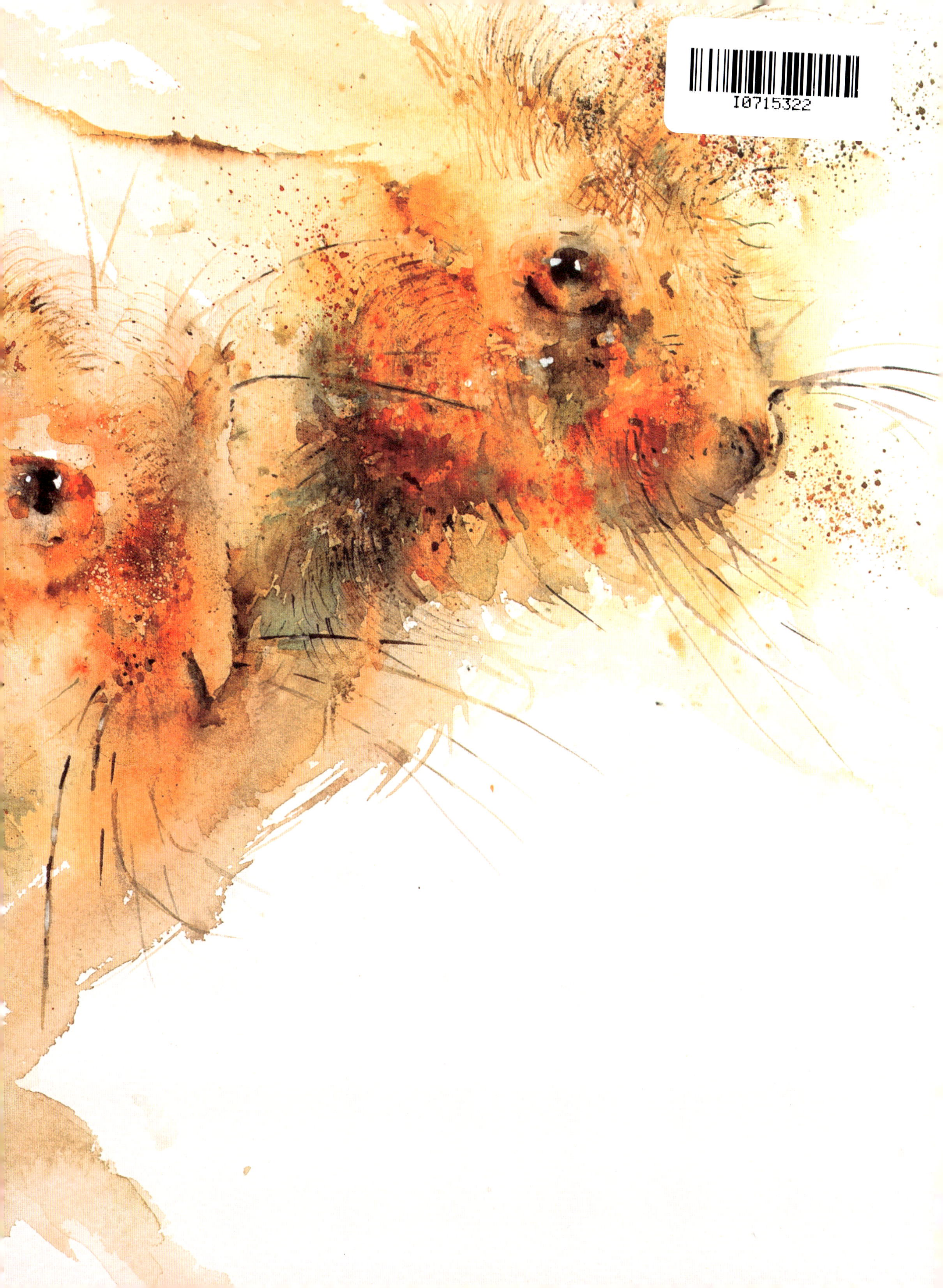

I0715322

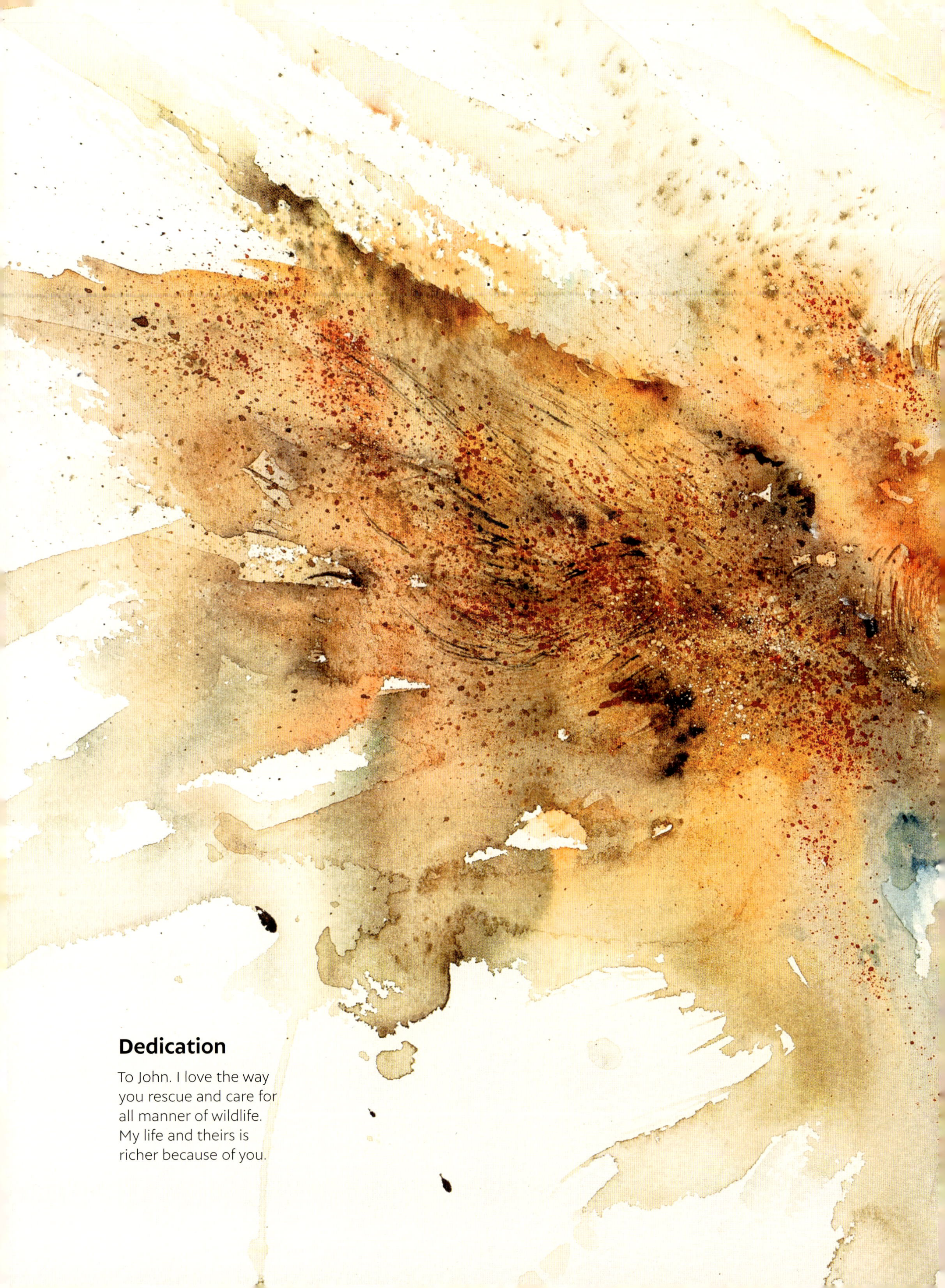

Dedication

To John. I love the way
you rescue and care for
all manner of wildlife.
My life and theirs is
richer because of you.

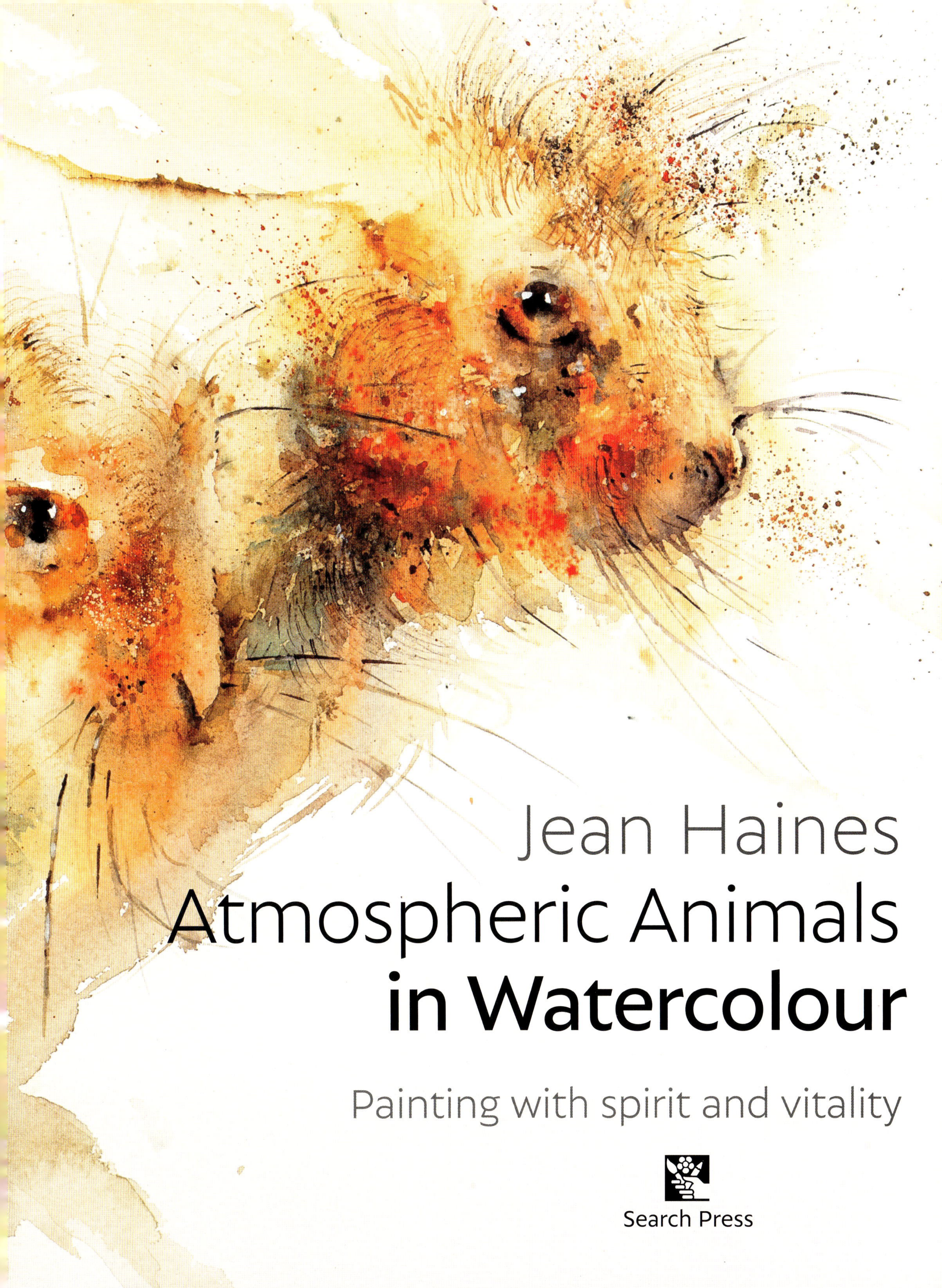

Jean Haines
Atmospheric Animals
in Watercolour
Painting with spirit and vitality
Search Press

First published in 2022

Search Press Limited
Wellwood, North Farm Road,
Tunbridge Wells, Kent TN2 3DR

5 6 7 8 9 10

Text copyright © Jean Haines, 2022
Photographs by Mark Davison at
Search Press Studios and on location at
the author's house, except for pages 12,
14, 15, 23, 88 and 122 by Kristy Peacock,
and pages 10, 11, 48 (three insets), 55,
61–63 (top right, bottom middle), 69, 78,
84 and 94, author's own.
Photographs and design copyright ©
Search Press Ltd. 2022

ISBN: 978-1-78221-959-0
ebook ISBN: 978-1-78126-954-1

Bookmarked Hub
For further ideas and inspiration, and to
join our free online community, visit
www.bookmarkedhub.com

Publishers' notes
The Publishers and author can accept
no responsibility for any consequences
arising from the information, advice or
instructions given in this publication.

For errata, please visit our website
(www.searchpress.com) or the
Bookmarked Hub
(www.bookmarkedhub.com).

GPSR information can be found at
www.searchpress.com

Printed in China, AP022026

Acknowledgements

The success of any publication
is not only down to the author
but also the support behind
them. For this special book I owe
huge thanks to so many people.
My enthusiasm for colour is
heightened by the wonderful
shades from Daniel Smith and
I thank them greatly for their
support. To Edward Ralph, an
exceptional editor, it's been
wonderful teaming up with you
again on this project.

Fantastic wildlife photographs
have been supplied by the
extremely talented Kristy Peacock
(@travel_momma) and they have
added soul. To the owners of the
fabulous animal models in my
book, thank you for allowing your
pets to be stars! For the hours,
days and months I've disappeared,
a huge thank-you to my
wonderful husband John, who has
missed me through yet another
writing experience.

Thank you, most of all, to you the
reader, who makes my dream of
being an author come true.

Finally, without a publisher who
has confidence in you, authors
couldn't exist. For this reason
I'd like to close by saying thank
you so much to Search Press for
yet again believing in me and for
encouraging my literary journey.

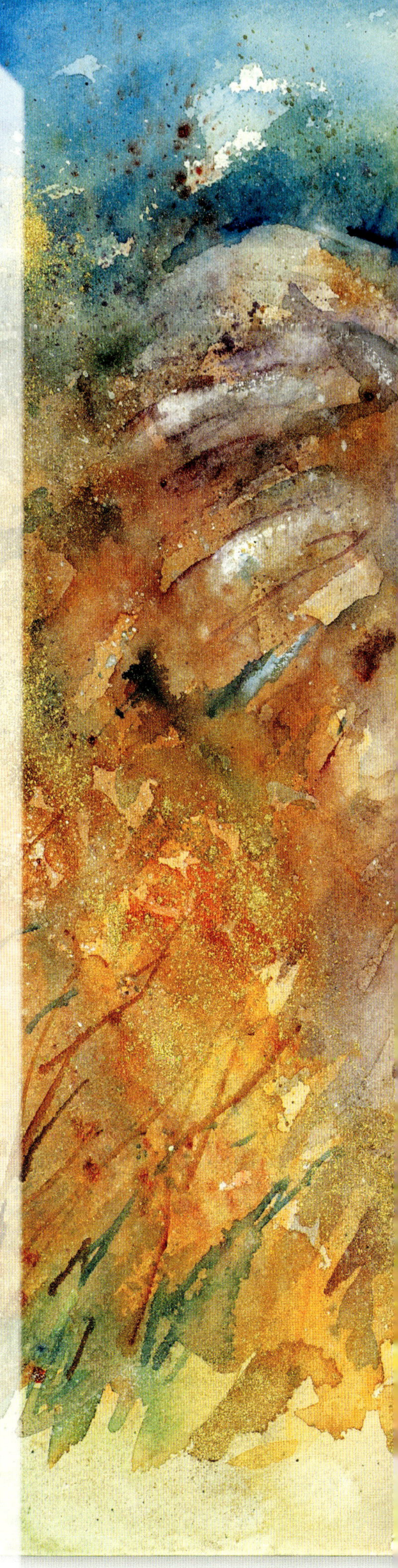

Page 1:
Piggled
28 x 38cm (11 x 15in)

Page 2:
Seeing Double
58 x 38cm (23 x 15in)

Opposite:
Out of Africa
58 x 38cm (23 x 15in)

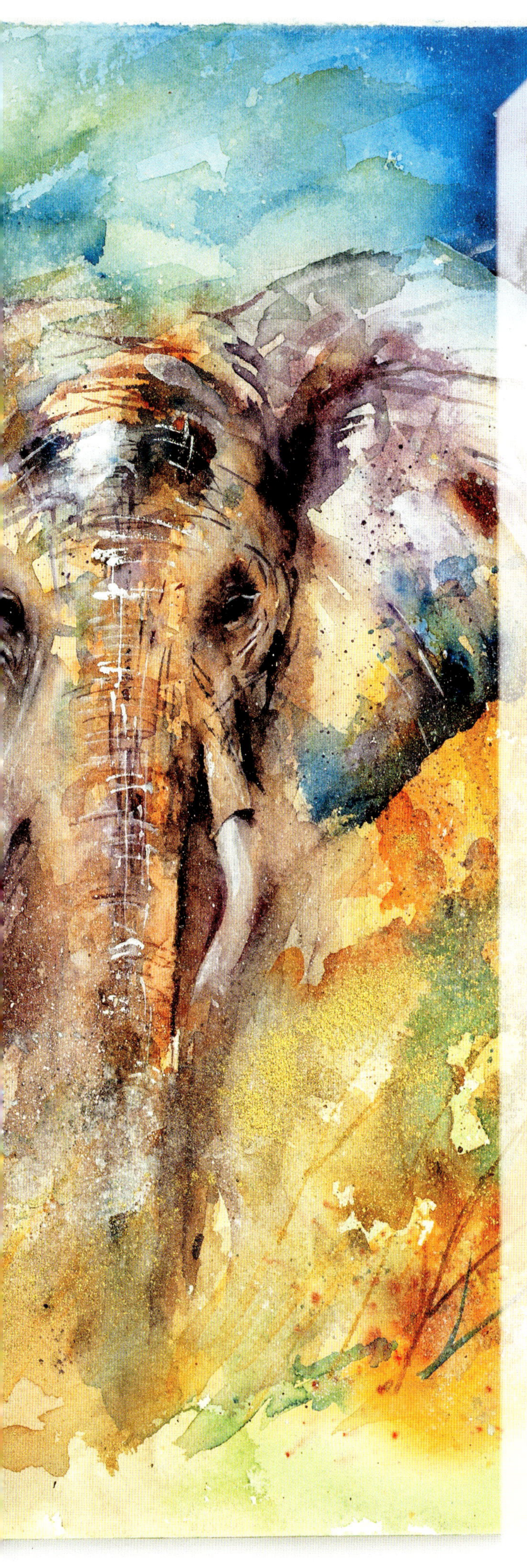

Contents

Author's welcome

TRAVELLING SO OFTEN HAS GIVEN me the opportunity to see many animals and birds in their natural habitat, and after one trip I found myself drawn to painting hummingbirds repeatedly. "Are you going through a change in your life?" I was asked. I was. And so began my fascination for meanings connected to animals. Hummingbirds represent change. Turtles carry a message of telling you to slow down; and I needed to when I was drawn to painting them. The tiny seahorse is said to carry a message of holding on.

There is so much to learn if you love animals as I do. From ancient folklore to the present-day stories around our favourite creatures, we enter a magical world when we are drawn to them. In this publication, I hope to enchant you not only with demonstrations on how to capture animals in watercolour in an atmospheric style; I also want to help you to connect with your subject.

As you move through the following chapters and turn each page maybe these three animal messages will help you as you evolve in your animal painting journey:

The hummingbird will help you change in your way of thinking and how you approach the creative process. Change can be a good thing: embrace it.

The turtle will remind you to slow down when you feel like racing to complete a painting; helping you to take your time and leading to far better results.

And the seahorse will wisely let you know that you need to hold on when you face the new challenges that I hope my projects will give you.

I hope you will absolutely love painting animals in a loose style, and I hope that my book leads you to creating unique art that you never realized you were capable of painting before.

Happy painting!

Jean Haines.

Animal meaning: hummingbird

It is said that the hummingbird carries a message reminding us to enjoy life. It has the ability to change direction at any given time. Related to art, embracing new ideas or changing direction in either style or choice of subject is a gift. Embrace change as a positive goal and enjoy every new adventure!

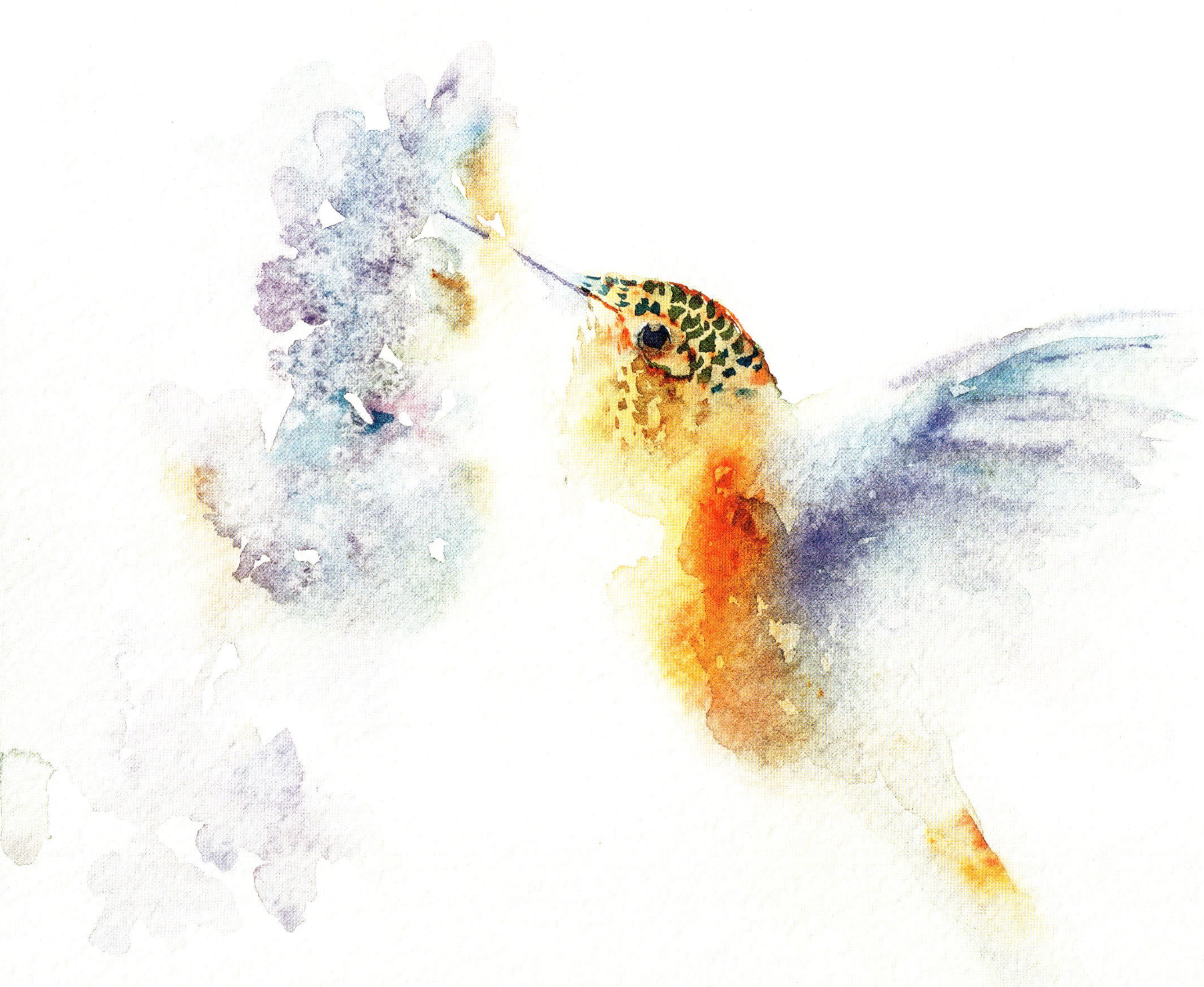

Taking Flight
28 x 38cm (11 x 15in)

Introduction

I ALWAYS FEEL A HUGE SENSE of excitement whenever I write the introduction to a new book, but this time my heart is literally beating fast. I can feel it. It is the most magical sensation; the kind you only get when something wonderful is about to happen, and it really is.

Why? Because I have longed to write a book on painting animals for years. They are my favourite subjects and have always been highly popular on my international workshops. I am about to begin the best of watercolour adventures with you by my side. Together we are heading on a journey that will be full of glorious colour, incredible watercolour techniques and, of course, fascinating subjects. Some of the animals in this book will pull at your heartstrings. Some may be familiar, some will bring out your curiosity, and others may be completely new subjects to you. My aim as the author of this special publication is to have you longing to paint every single animal on every colourful page.

As you enter each new chapter, I want you to feel that wonderful 'I can't wait to paint' thrill that is constantly with me. I want you to paint animals in a way that you may never have attempted before, or even felt possible. I want you to feel as though you are breathing life into each new subject you create in watercolour. And I want you to look at every blank piece of white paper as if it is a valuable treasure, with a fascinating story waiting to be told on it via your paintbrush.

You are an artist. You can paint anything you wish to, and I will be showing you how, guiding and encouraging you every step of the way. As well as painting animals in watercolour, we will be looking at their meanings and the folklore and stories connected with them.

There are many books available that show how to paint animals. My hope is that mine will inspire you to create in a unique style that is yours and yours alone.

We are about to embark on the most incredible watercolour journey of a lifetime, and I cannot wait to get started. Join me, explore, have fun and learn how to absolutely love painting animals from all over the world. The adventure begins the minute you turn the page.

Opposite:
Imagination
14 x 38cm (5½ x 15in)
The animal adventure begins.

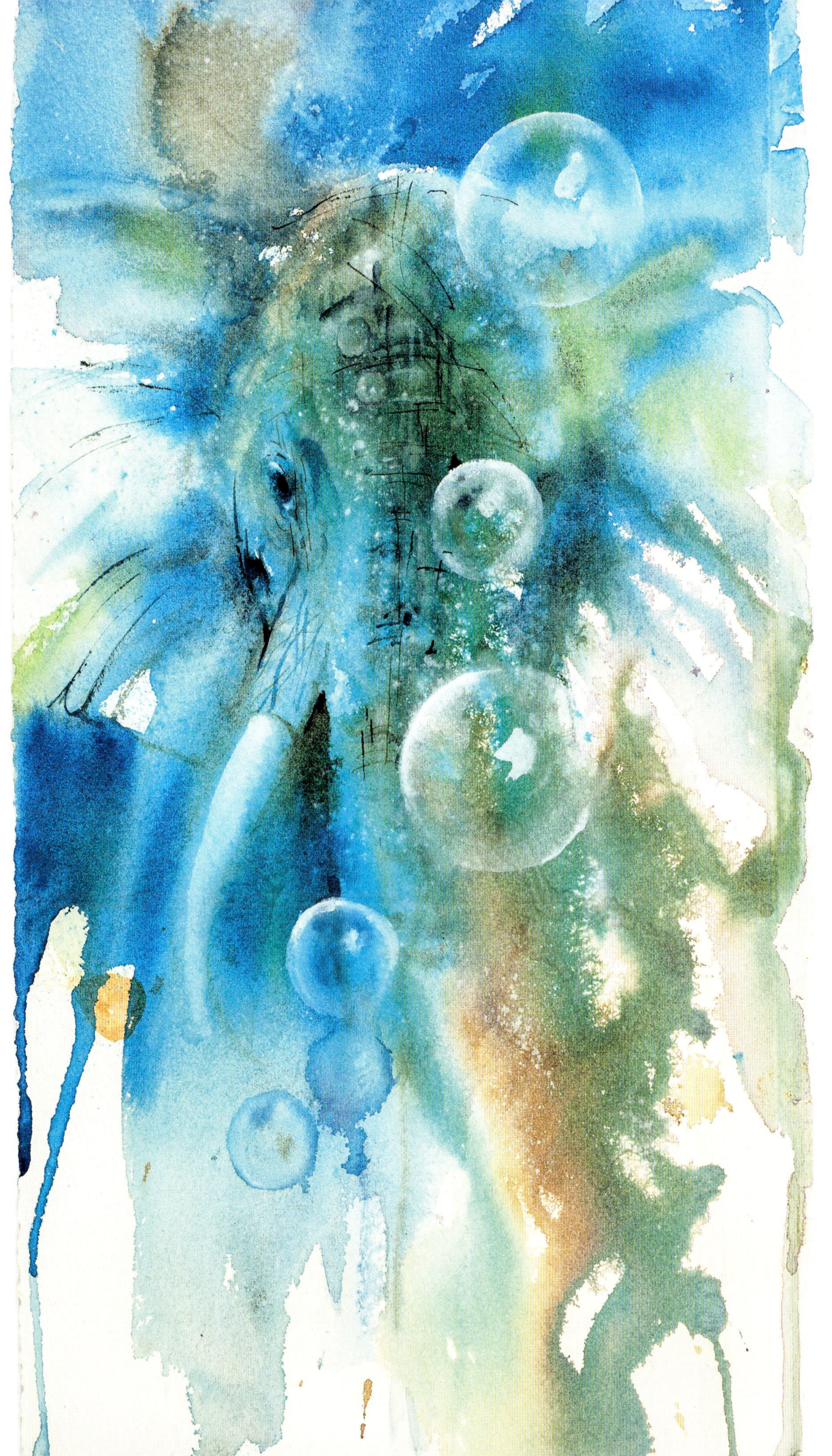

Igniting the passion
Why paint animals?

"Until one has loved an animal, a part of one's soul remains unawakened." Anatole France

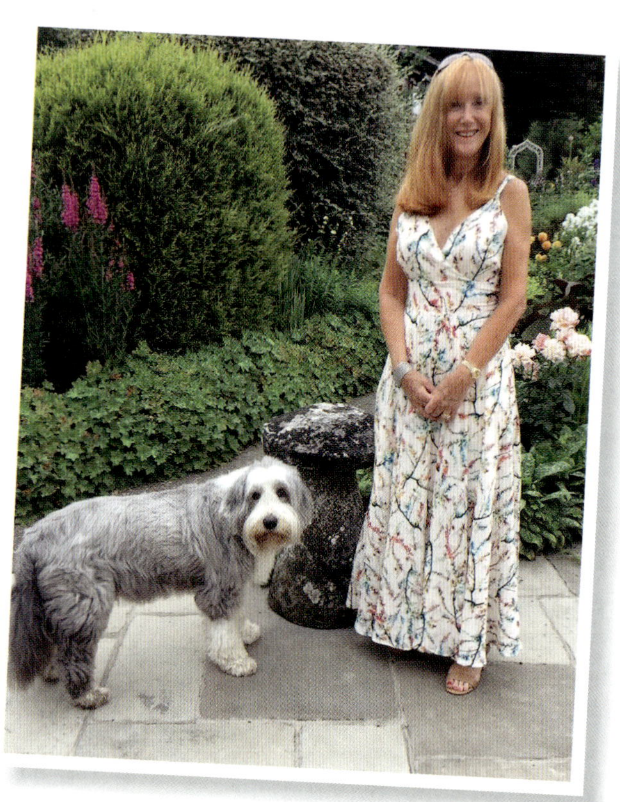

Early animal connections

Where does our fascination with the animal kingdom begin? My passion for animals started as a child with my love for teddy bears. Many of us have happy childhood memories of our favourite toys. This pleasant connection can often bring a smile to our faces, and for many of us this is where our love for animals first began. Can you remember your childhood animal connections? Your first toy? What was the first animal you fell in love with – and why?

Emotional relationships

Pets can greatly influence our lives with their special form of companionship, and there are many incredible true stories of indefinable love between them and their owners; especially dogs. I am fortunate enough to have been owned by many dogs over the years, each giving love in a way that is totally unique.

There is no doubt about it, animals can creep into our hearts and leave a gaping hole when the time comes to say goodbye. We can easily see that we are able to fall in love with animals from an early age.

Buddy and me

I am pictured here with Buddy, one of two dogs we rescued from our time living in China. Buddy became one of those very special dogs who was loved by everyone that came to visit us while we lived abroad. He travelled with us throughout Europe, the Middle East and Asia. He became my hero when he saved my life on an isolated walk in Hong Kong where I was attacked at knifepoint. This gentle giant moved between me and my attacker, forcing the man to back away from me. I never forgot Buddy's heroism.

The vet who saw him as a puppy said he would never live past four months as he was in such bad shape and had hip dysplasia. Amazingly, he went on to live a full healthy life, swimming daily; and died in my arms at the good age of thirteen years old. They say love conquers all.

He was a wonderful four-legged friend.

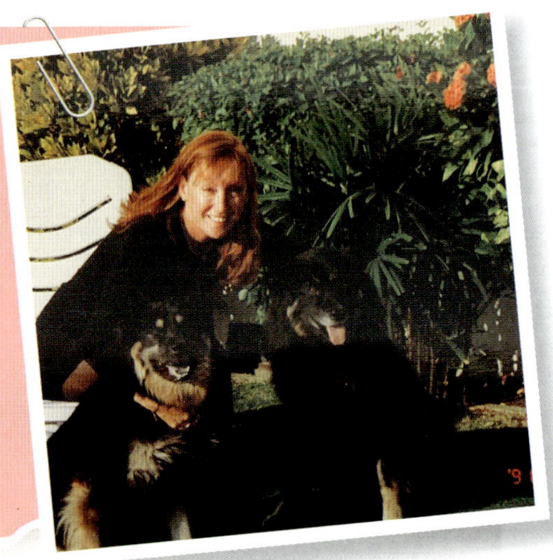

A growing passion

A passion for animals can also grow over time, particularly for those interested in painting them as part of their art journey. There are many successful wildlife or pet portrait artists. Animals are sheer joy to paint, and there are so many ways to paint them!

My love affair with animals first began with dogs. I was obsessed with them and studied every breed. I became engrossed in learning about them as a species and they were always in my earliest paintings. I painted my first dog when I was four years old. It was a boxer puppy, although I had no idea what the breed was at the time. I just knew I loved the look of that particular dog.

I have never stopped painting animals from that moment on. Over the years my passion grew and, from living in different countries, I've seen many animals. From feeding giraffes in Africa to holding a koala in Australia, each time I've seen an animal I have been in awe at how wonderful they are. I'm enthralled with the animal kingdom and always will be.

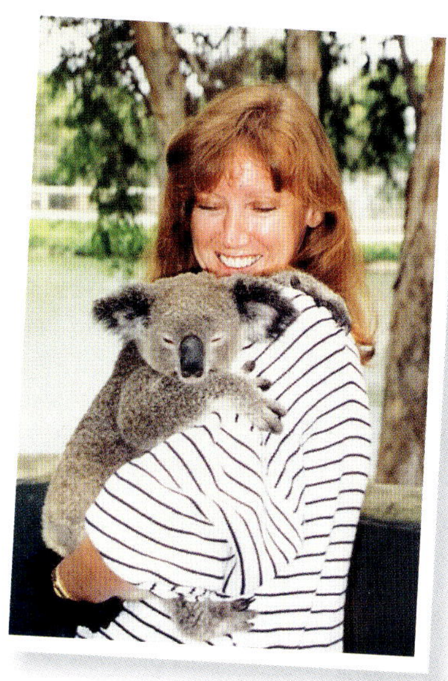

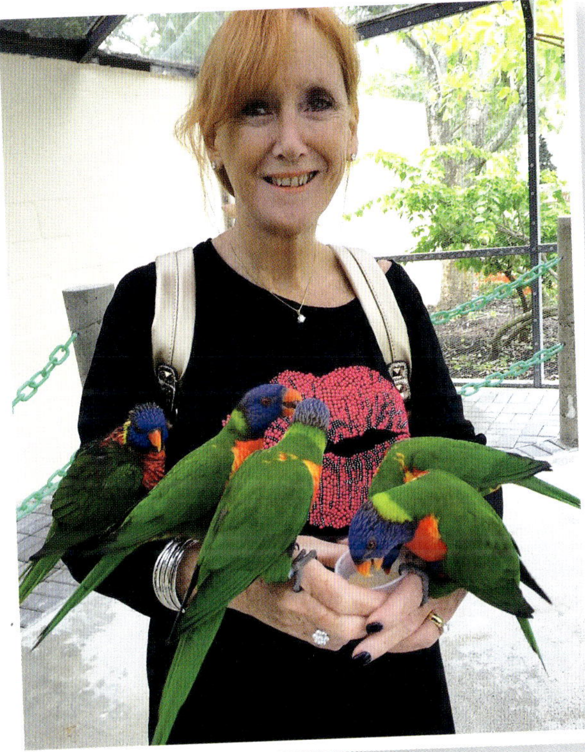

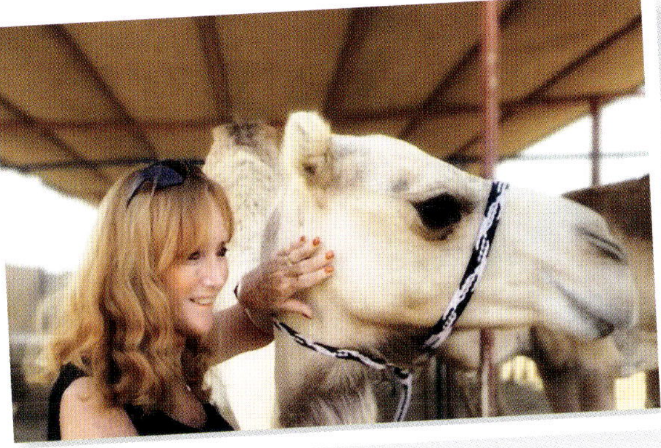

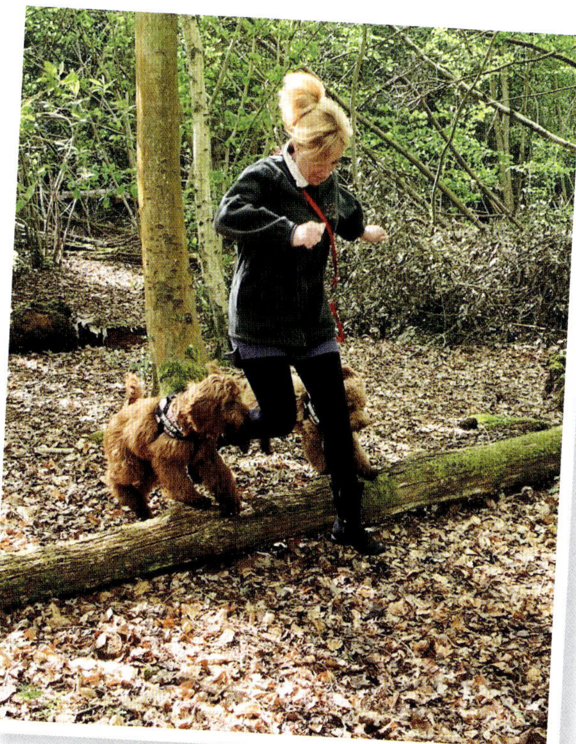

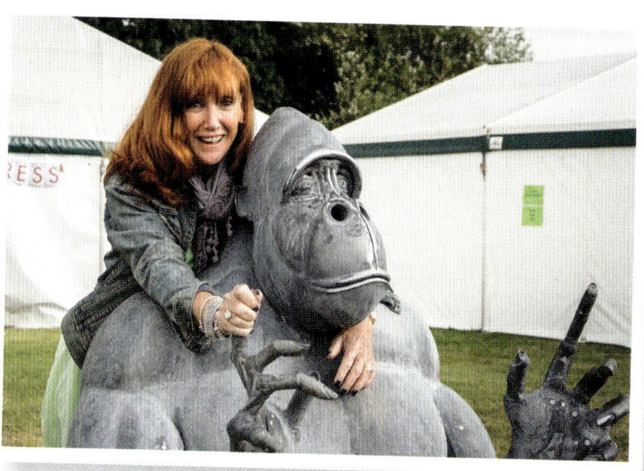

Intriguing communication

Animals are intriguing. They seem to have their own rules, codes of conduct and their own language. Their lifestyles are so different to ours and yet we can learn so much from them, as we will see through the pages of my book. There is much to explore, learn and enjoy by studying animals, whether you wish to paint them or not. There is no doubt that the animal kingdom is magical.

All over the world there are wonderful creatures that leave us in awe and quite rightly so. The film *The Lion King*, for example, comes to mind when I think about popular stories that have evolved over the years in versions of movies or stage plays.

Capturing soul

When we paint an animal as a subject, it is not enough just to sit and create a pretty picture. I think we need to feel the soul and the magic of each creature we paint in watercolour. We need to tell the story of where the animal is from, what country it could be living in, and how it feels to touch it, if we hope to capture their character. This is what I'm going to show you in the following pages.

I am passionate about animals and I'm sure, because you've purchased this book, that you are too. We are going to go on a journey together, learning how to paint animals in watercolour; but more than that we're going to absorb their energy and learn about their symbolism, which is so fascinating. I will explain more about this as we move through the chapters of my book.

Embrace the unknown

We all have our favourite animals, and we perhaps have some that we don't like. As you turn the pages of this publication, you might feel that you want to race to paint the animals which you know very well. But it is so much more fun if you embrace painting the subjects that you don't know alongside those that you do.

We need to master technique, study colour selection and observe shape and form. Most of all, we need time to paint our subjects.

I cannot wait to get started, so let's begin by looking at what we need to paint and then we'll move on to capturing our favourite animals in our favourite medium, which for me is watercolour.

Happy painting.

"Animals are such agreeable friends ~ they ask no questions; they pass no criticisms." George Eliot

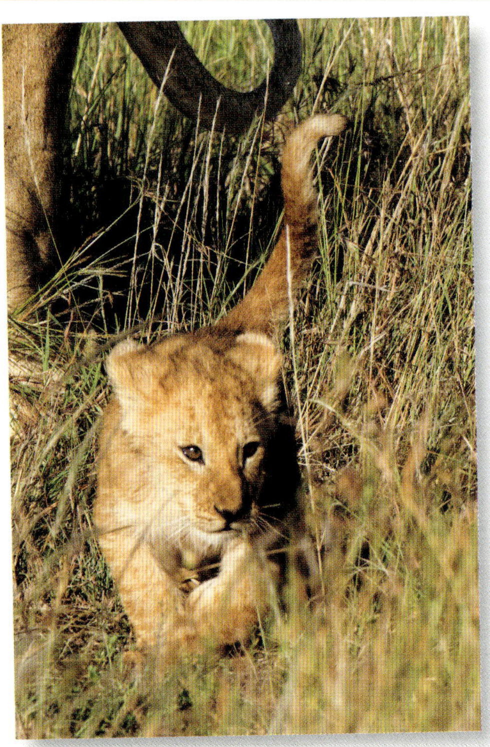

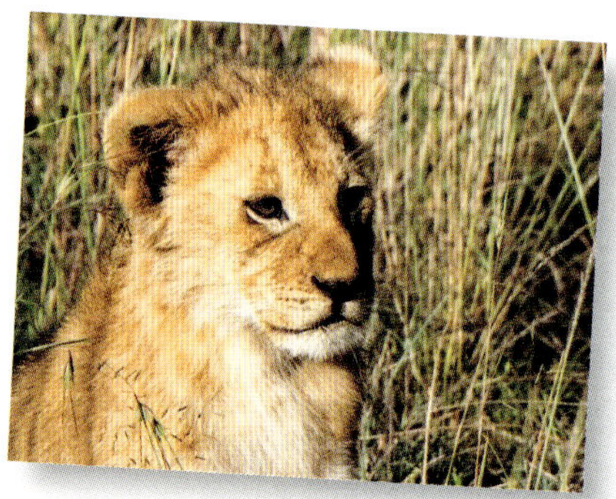

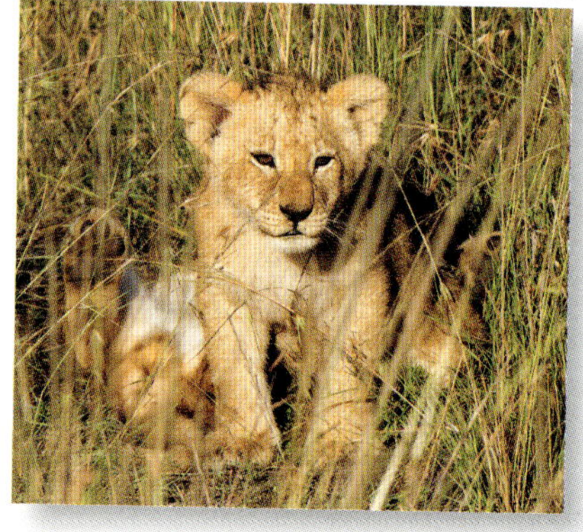

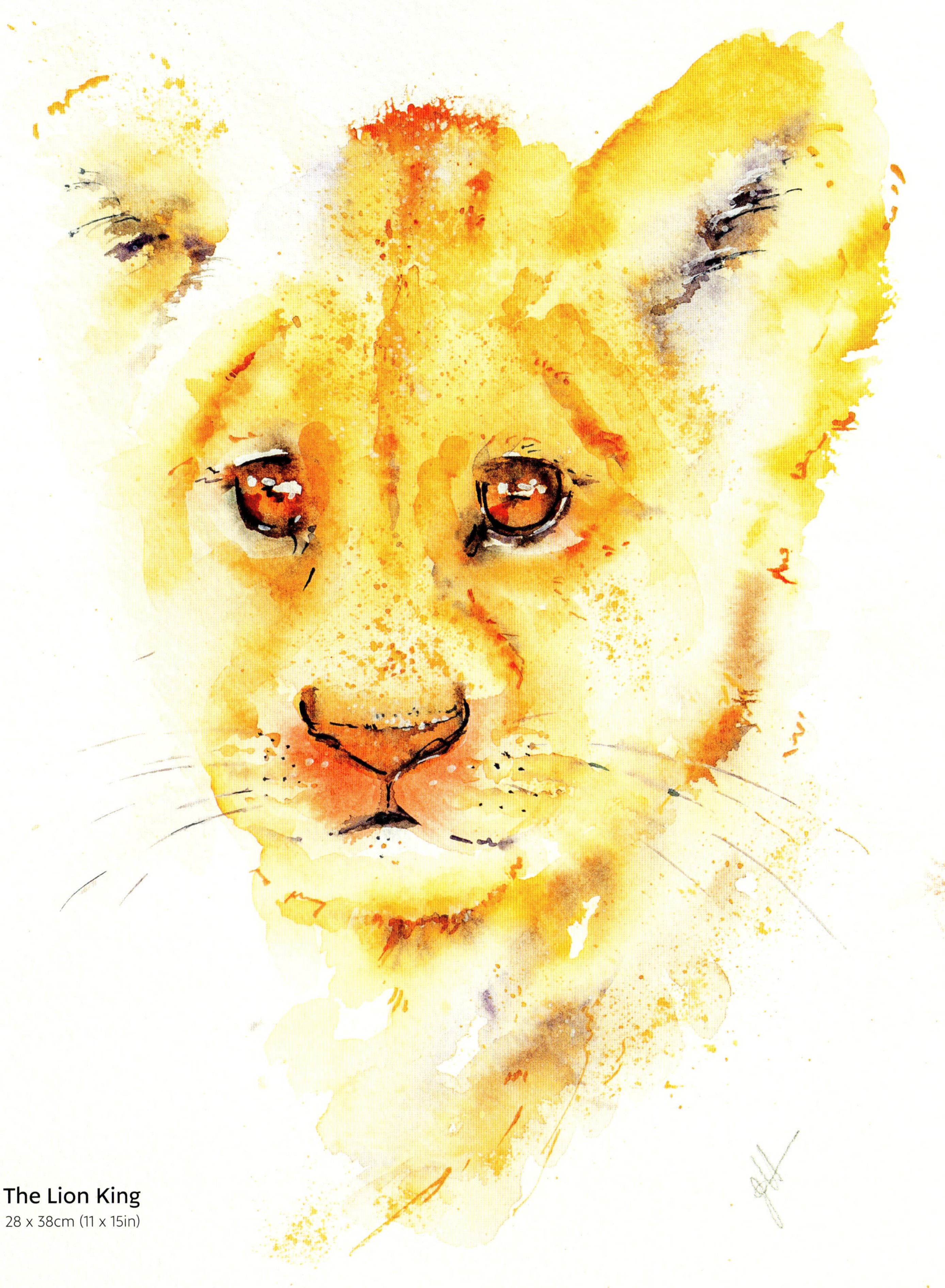

The Lion King
28 x 38cm (11 x 15in)

The bear necessities

"If you hear a voice within you say 'you cannot paint', then by all means paint, and that voice will be silenced." Vincent van Gogh

Materials and learning tools

I'm sure beginners to watercolour will be reading this section of my book concerned about what they need to buy to paint animals in watercolour. Let me reassure you that just the basic art materials will be fine to begin with. On these pages I want to share my tips to help you get the most out of your painting sessions. The materials we use when we create can make a huge difference to our results.

My collection of art materials has grown over the years and, if it hasn't already, I'm sure yours will too. I am constantly finding new things to paint with, which is as it should be if you are an artist always on the look-out for new techniques, new products and new subjects to paint.

As you move through my book, I will describe additional materials more fully with each demonstration. Some may be completely new to you; others will be very familiar. The main thing is to have fun when you are painting, rather than worry about what you have or have not got.

Great resource photographs

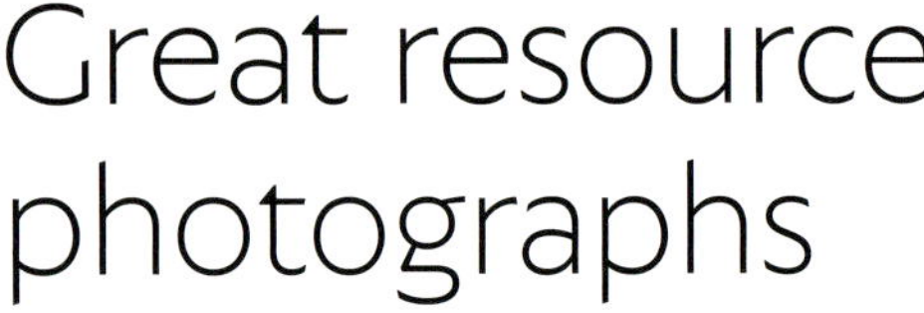

Great photographs are a must. Painting from life is wonderful but animals move, and you have to be quick to capture them in their natural habitat. Photographs are the next best thing and very valuable. However, they need to be great photographs, with all the information in them. If you can see your chosen subjects and take your own photographs, that is the best way to learn, but we aren't all able to travel to far-off lands or spend the time in the animal's environment.

If possible, you should not rely on just a single photograph of the animal in the position in which you would like to paint it, but have a supporting range of excellent close-ups of facial features and other details so that you can observe them and learn about them well.

Avoid images that have parts of animals missing that you have to make up! Have the full information right in front of you while you paint so that your depictions can be more accurate.

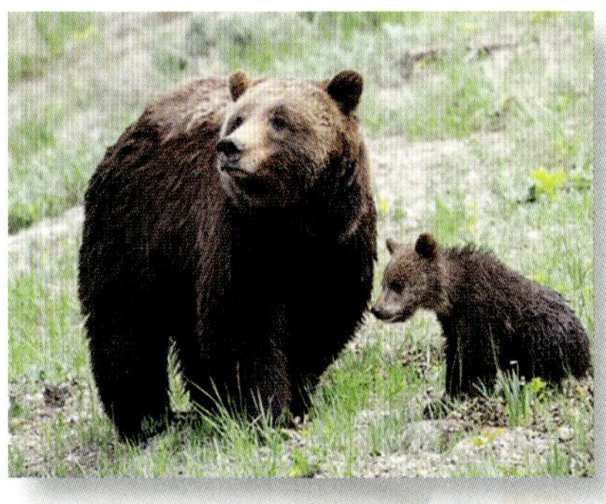

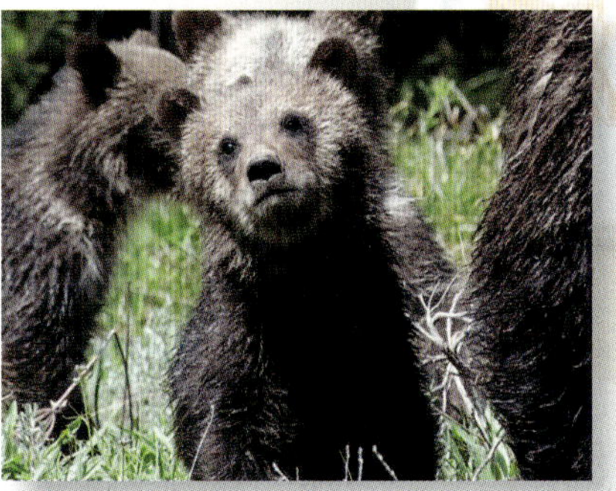

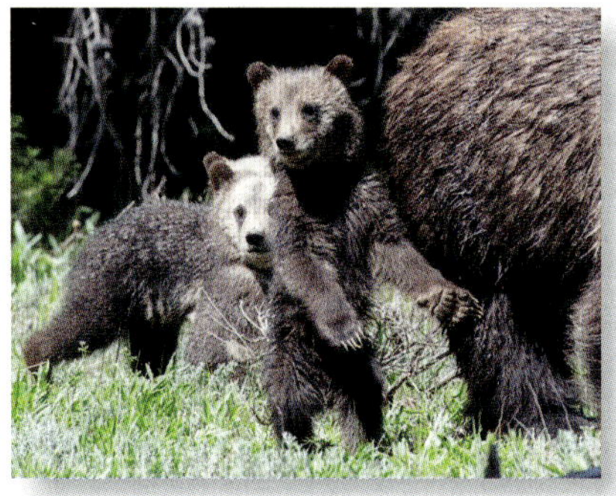

Falling in love
A good selection of source photographs includes shots of the whole animal along with close-up details of facial features, fur and other important elements.

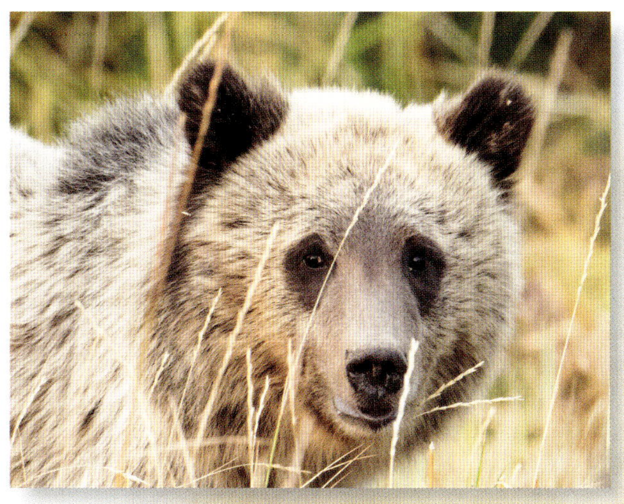 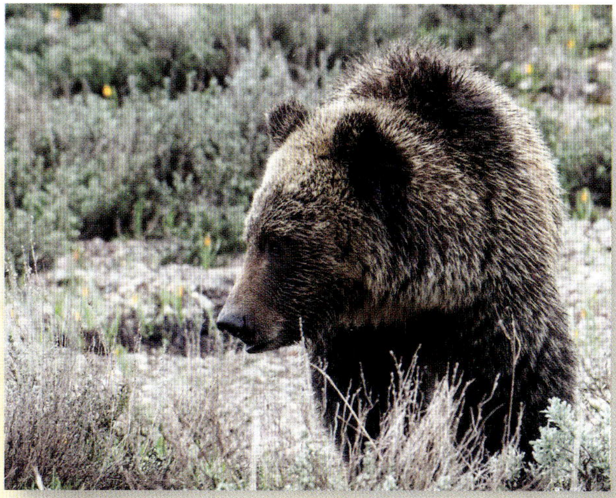

Plan and prepare

Gathering the paints and other tools you wish to use is essential to good results – and don't play it safe! You can see my unusual choice of the colour 'Wisteria' in the colour selection below.

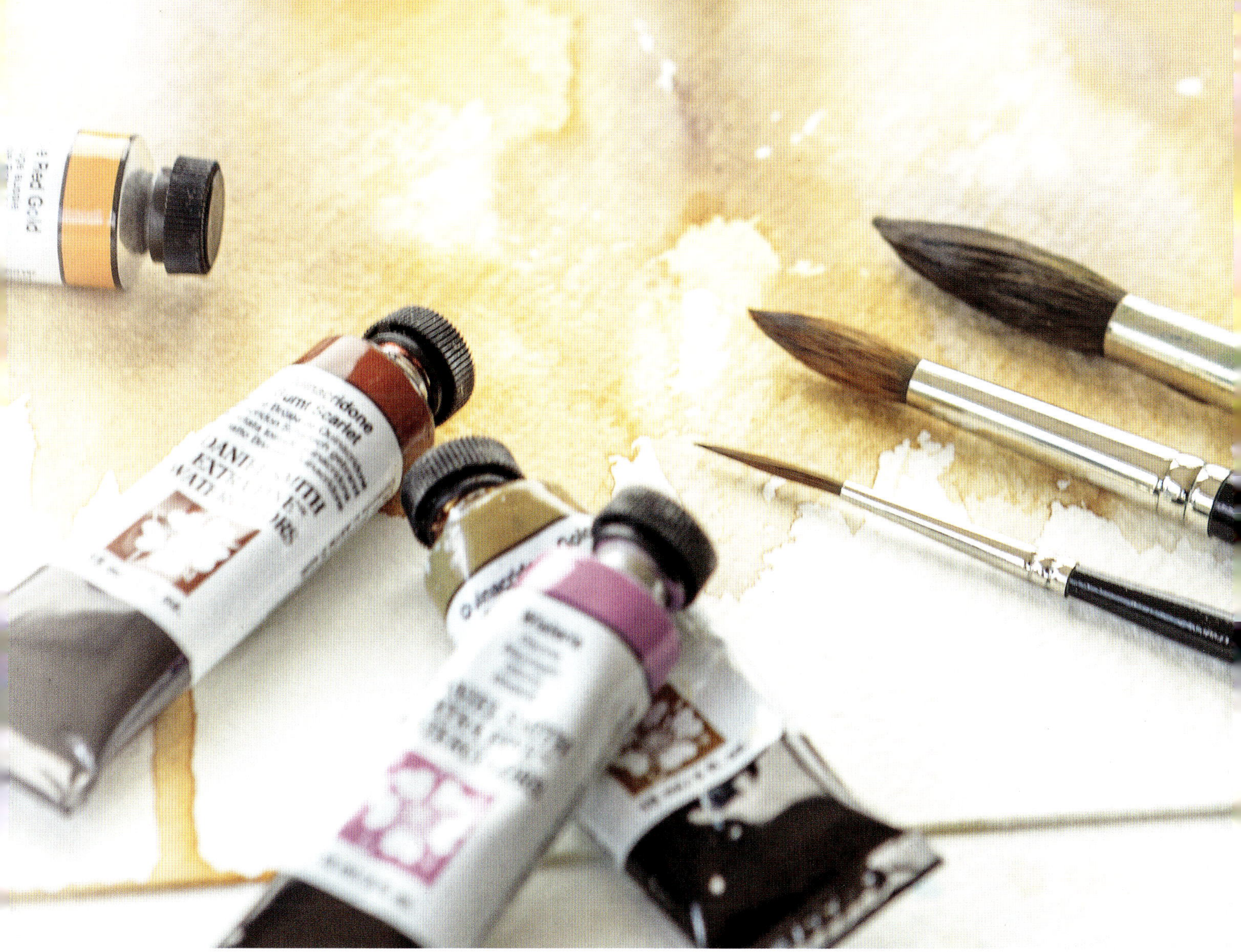

Watercolour shades

This is a very exciting area for all artists. No one can ever have too many watercolour shades. I used to have favourite colours that I would use all the time without fail. But now I have fallen in love with so many incredible Daniel Smith watercolour shades and their range is unbelievably stunning. Some of the pigments are so magical because they give unusual effects when dry.

I will be demonstrating my personal 'must-have' shades as we come to paint each individual subject. For now, I want to stress this: please use whatever colours from whatever manufacturer you are happy with, because we are all different in what we enjoy using and I appreciate that. We also have to look at what we can financially afford, so you choose what suits you best. I can't stress enough that the joy should be in creating every time that we pick up our brushes.

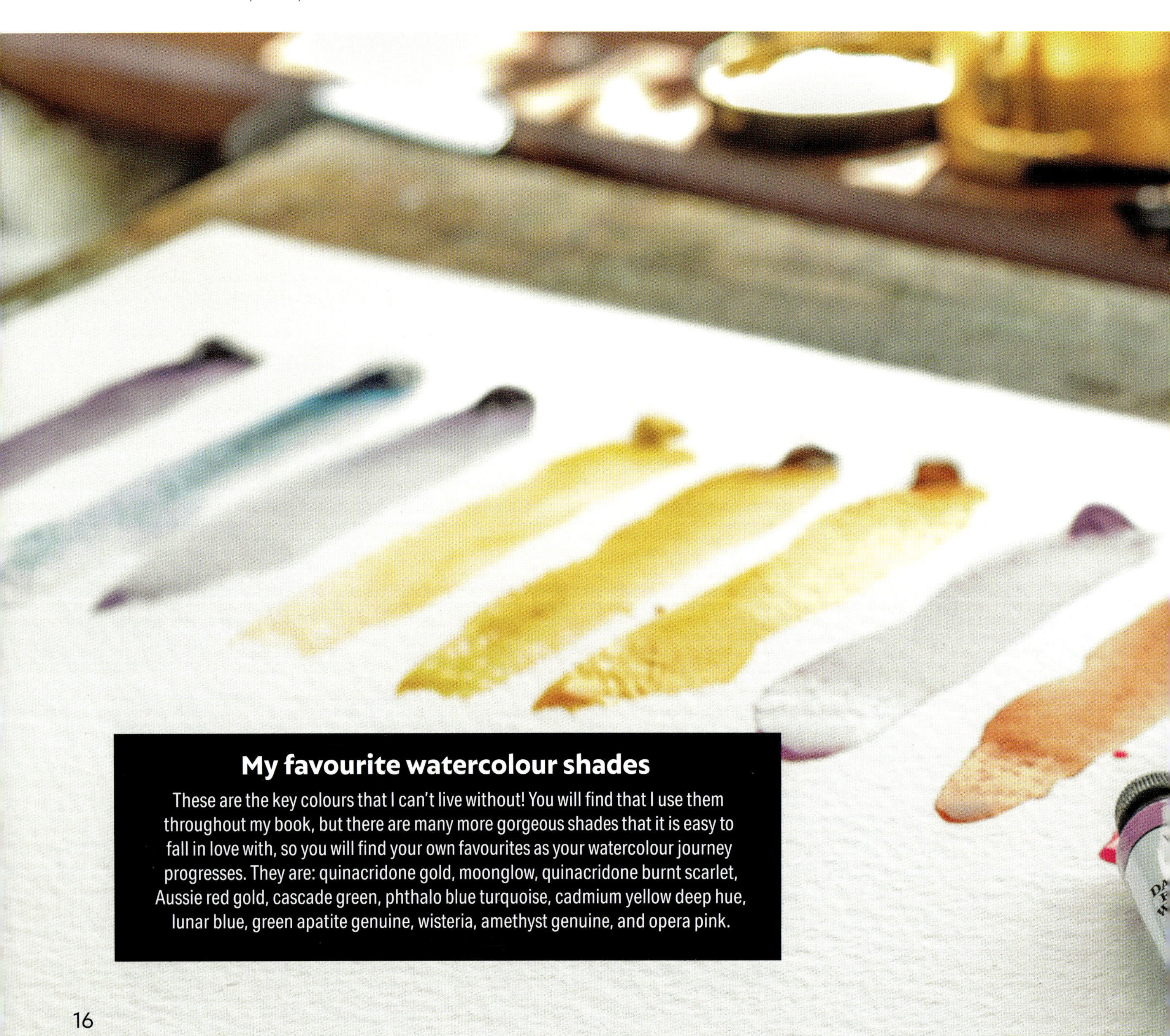

My favourite watercolour shades

These are the key colours that I can't live without! You will find that I use them throughout my book, but there are many more gorgeous shades that it is easy to fall in love with, so you will find your own favourites as your watercolour journey progresses. They are: quinacridone gold, moonglow, quinacridone burnt scarlet, Aussie red gold, cascade green, phthalo blue turquoise, cadmium yellow deep hue, lunar blue, green apatite genuine, wisteria, amethyst genuine, and opera pink.

White gouache

White gouache is invaluable for adding whites to your work to give you a highlight in a cat's eye or sheen on a dog's nose. It's certainly worth having a tube of this product!

Palette

This is an interesting area of discussion. Even though I'm working with watercolour, I often put my colour directly onto my paper, rather than pick it up from a palette, which is the usual way of creating with this medium.

I developed my own 'lose the palette' technique, which has become very popular with watercolourists of all levels, and we look at this technique alongside choosing colours on pages 26–27.

For now, though, I would like you to have a palette that holds plenty of colour. Make sure it has compartments that can hold enough colour in each, so you don't have to keep stopping and starting to refill each section.

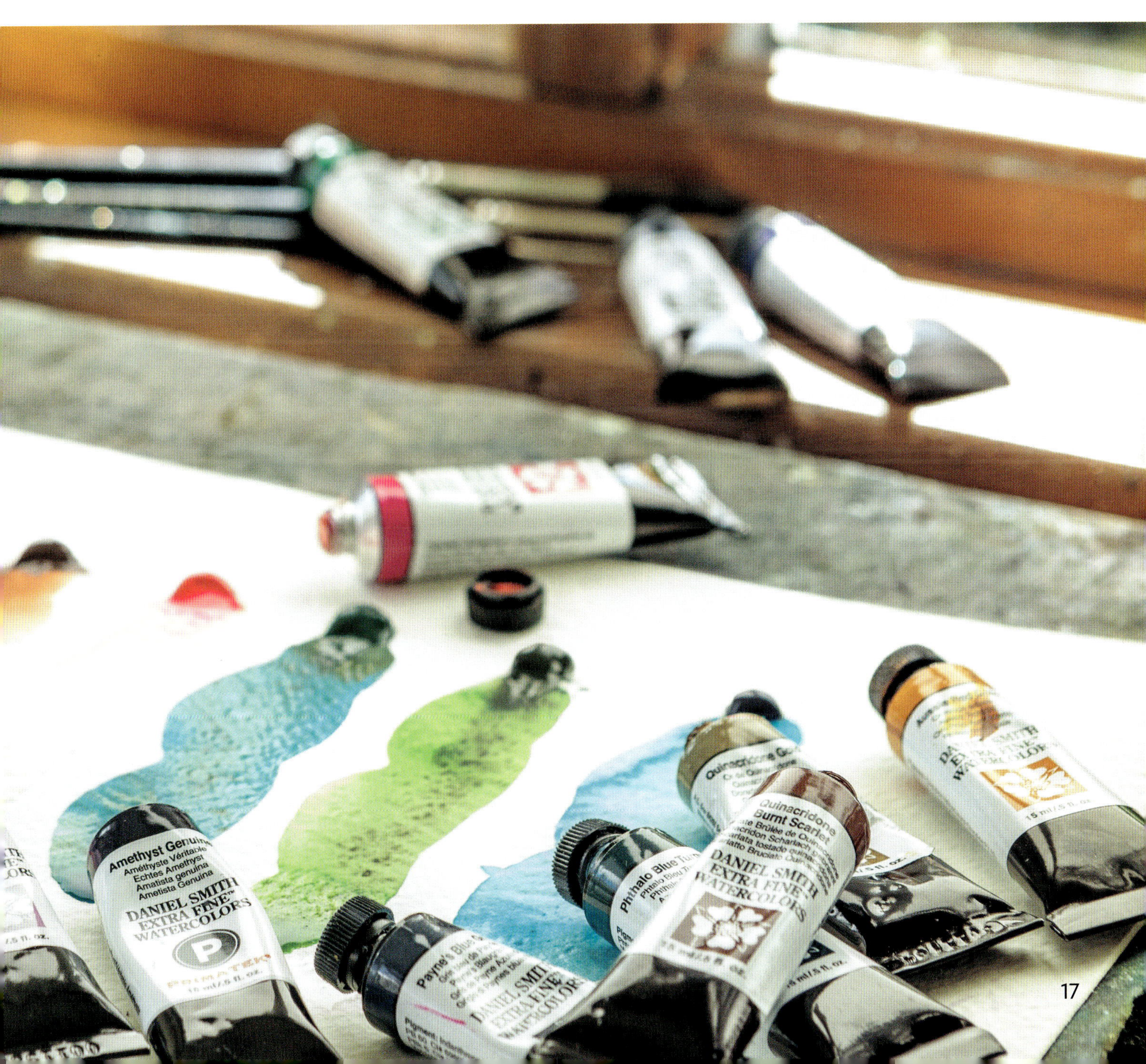

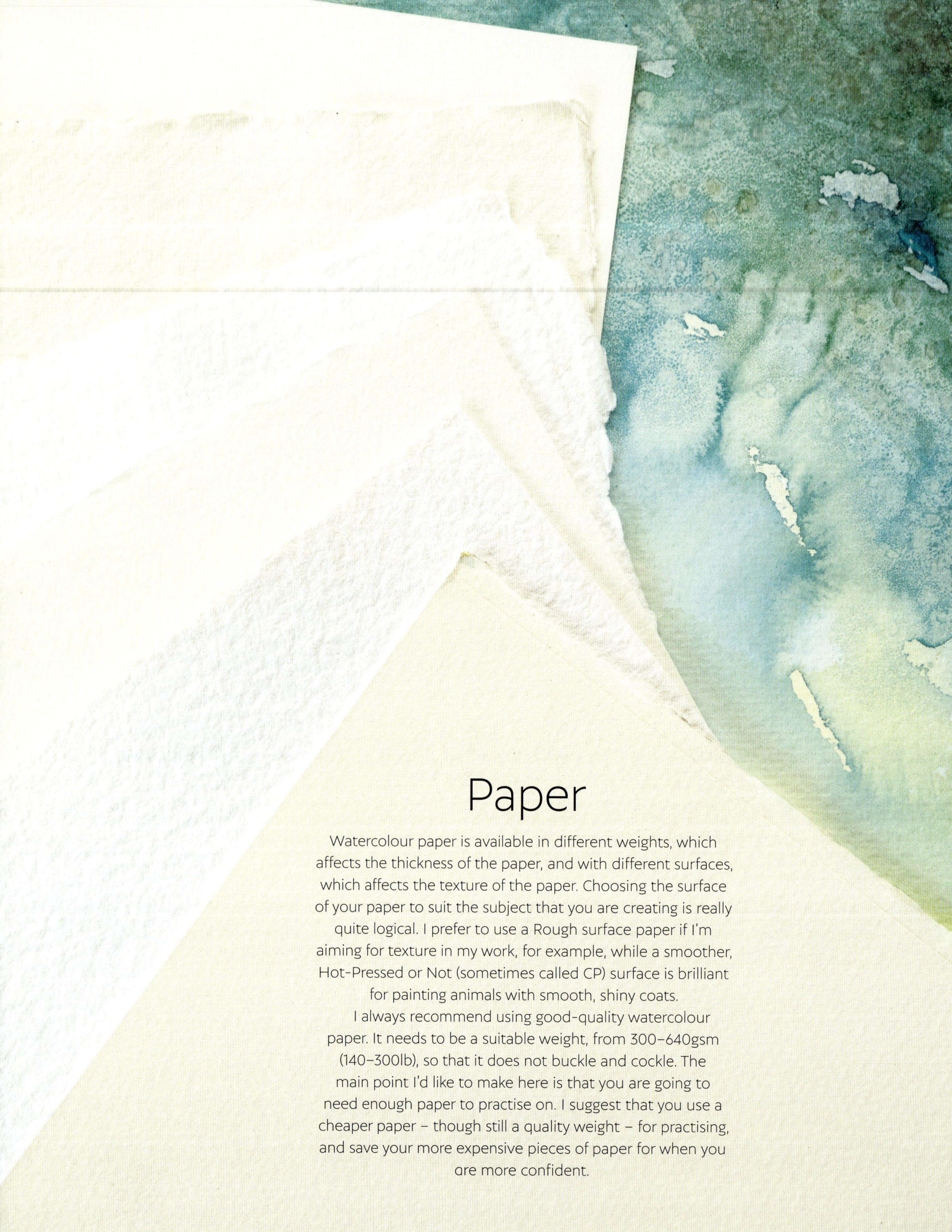

Paper

Watercolour paper is available in different weights, which affects the thickness of the paper, and with different surfaces, which affects the texture of the paper. Choosing the surface of your paper to suit the subject that you are creating is really quite logical. I prefer to use a Rough surface paper if I'm aiming for texture in my work, for example, while a smoother, Hot-Pressed or Not (sometimes called CP) surface is brilliant for painting animals with smooth, shiny coats.

I always recommend using good-quality watercolour paper. It needs to be a suitable weight, from 300–640gsm (140–300lb), so that it does not buckle and cockle. The main point I'd like to make here is that you are going to need enough paper to practise on. I suggest that you use a cheaper paper – though still a quality weight – for practising, and save your more expensive pieces of paper for when you are more confident.

Brushes

Every artist has their favourite brushes to use.
I certainly have mine, because I have designed my
own personalized set, which I love using to create my
watercolours. However, it took me a long time to find
brushes that I not only enjoyed using but loved the feel
of in my hand. I believe every single part of creating
should be a pleasant experience and having good tools
as an artist can make a huge difference to the way you
feel when painting.

The newcomer to watercolour could be completely
confused by the large number of brushes available
in art supply catalogues on- and off-line. My
recommendation is to buy the best brushes that you
can afford, but think about the sizes that you really
need. It's very easy to collect far too many brushes that
you will never use. In all honesty I tend to use the same
three brushes in all of my artwork. I will explain why
each is useful.

A size 12 round brush with a very good point is
extremely useful, especially if it loads well with water
and colour. I use this sort of brush for creating washes
or background shapes to which I can later add detail.

If I'm painting medium-sized detail or working
from a feature as a starting point, a technique you
will see me use throughout this book, I tend to use
my size 10 round, which has a beautiful point. I can
use this particular brush to create many different
brushstrokes and patterns. It is the ideal brush size to
paint eyes, noses and brushstrokes for fur. In fact, I'd
be lost without it. Once I have created a background
wash for my subject and created medium-sized detail,
I then move on to adding the finishing touches to my
paintings with a rigger (a brush with very long, fine
hairs). Such details include fine lines for hair or other
intricate marks that can help to bring my subject to life.

All three brushes should curve well when in use.
You can add paintbrushes to your collection as you
move forward in your art journey. There are many that
are useful for painting special effects, but these three
main brush sizes are really all I have ever used and
I have been painting for years.

Brush care

When buying brushes, check that the brush hair is soft to the touch so that you don't damage
the surface of your paper when you use them.

Most importantly, always clean your brushes well after use. This can be done by swirling
your brushes in clean water when you have finished painting. Remove excess water from your
brush, then use your fingers to gently tease the brush back into a nice tip so that you have a
beautiful point when you next start painting.

Remember this: If you look after your brushes well, they will last a very long time.

Texture products and additives

Because I am now working with many texture effect techniques, there are some new additions to my usual materials. These products, which may be new to you, will enhance your creative sessions, adding another element of excitement and your results from using them will be absolutely fascinating. Keep an open mind on this new animal kingdom adventure.

In particular, we will be looking at **watercolour ground**, which allows you to use watercolours on more unusual surfaces; **granulation fluid**, which creates grainy, mottled effects; and **crackle paste**, which allows you to achieve craquelure with watercolours; to name but a few products.

There will also be various examples that include **gold** and **bronze bronzing powder** and other interesting effects. We are going to have fun!

Mediums and additives used in this book

Matisse White watercolour ground and the following dry mediums: lang lang sand, pumice, microspheres, gel beads, small gel beads

Golden Fibre paste; bead paste

Jacquard Silk salt

Ranger Texture paste opaque crackle; Distress crackle paint 'clear rock candy'

Daniel Smith Watercolour grounds in white, black and buff

Schmincke Bronzing powders in rich gold and pure gold.

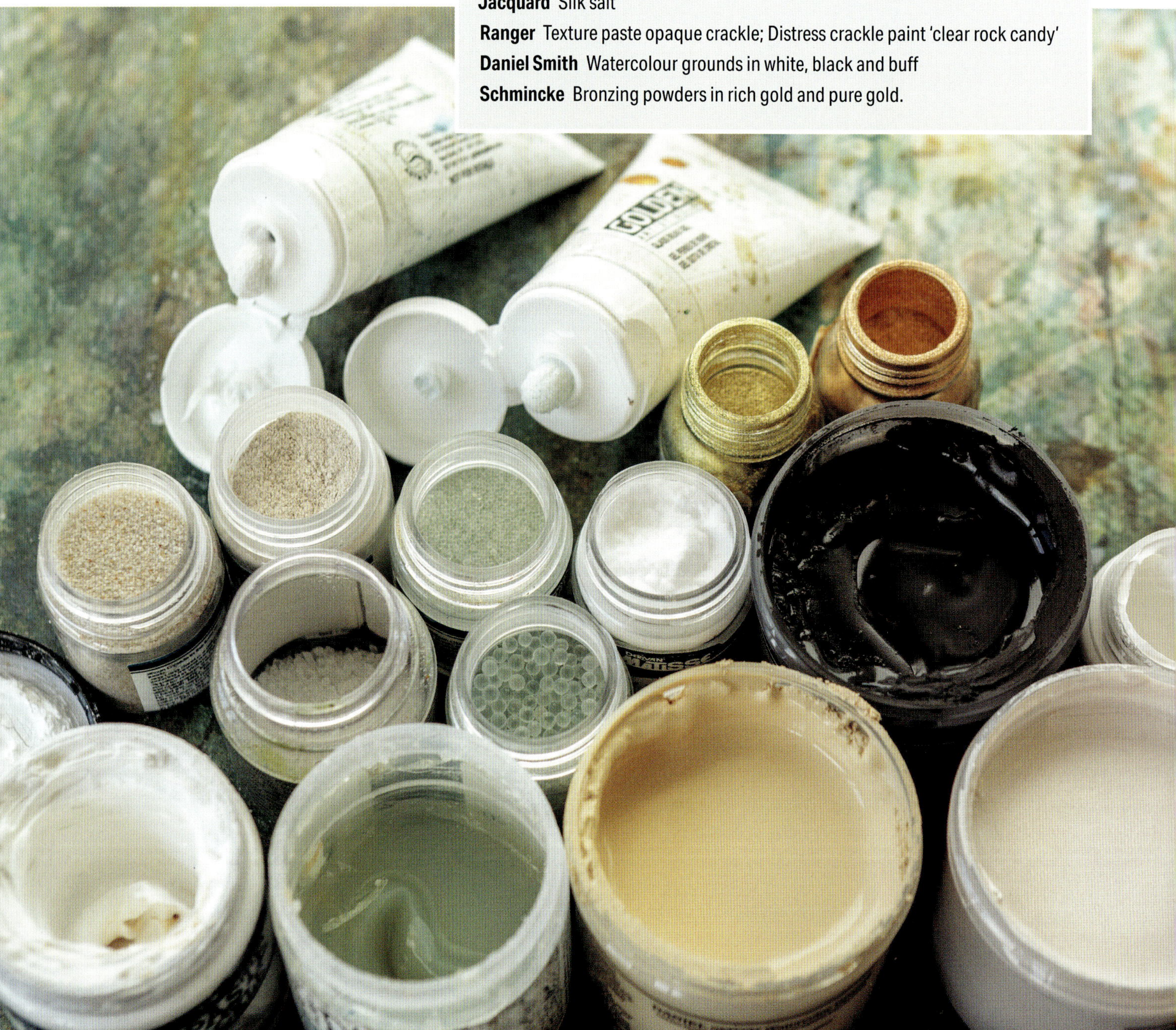

Other materials

Containers I use two: one for clean water to work with, and one to clean my brushes – it's as simple as that. I prefer large water pots over tiny ones because I use a lot of water. Do change your water frequently during a painting session so that you keep your colours fresh. Spare plastic pots are useful for experimenting with inks and mediums.

Easel I work either at a table easel or a standing easel depending on how large my painting is – and also how much energy I've got! The table easel is great to work on if you prefer to work from a sitting position. This is great for longer periods of painting.

For my larger compositions, particularly horse racing, I prefer to stand while painting, because I can add more intense energy while creating, through my movements as well as my brushstrokes. This sense of freedom and being able to move really does add impact to my results as it flows into my artwork. This is a personal choice, and in time you will decide which way of working is best for you.

Inks I am a firm believer in using only products that say the word 'watercolour' on them, in order that I can always say that my paintings are true watercolours. I love products that are made of natural dyes, such as Daniel Smith walnut ink, or homemade inks, both of which you will see me use later on, especially in the monochrome chapter.

Markmaking tools In addition to the brushes on page 19, it's useful to have a large mop brush for particularly large washes, an old brush to apply bronzing powders and mixing mediums, and a toothbrush for splattering.

Kitchen paper Used to dry and clean your brushes.

Spray bottles These are small plastic bottles that can be filled with prepared watercolour or inks to allow you to spray onto the surface.

These are the basic items we need and we will cover them more fully in the pages to come. I am eager to get started, so let's get to grips with this animal journey and move on!

"Only those who will risk going too far can possibly find out how far one can go." T. S. Eliot

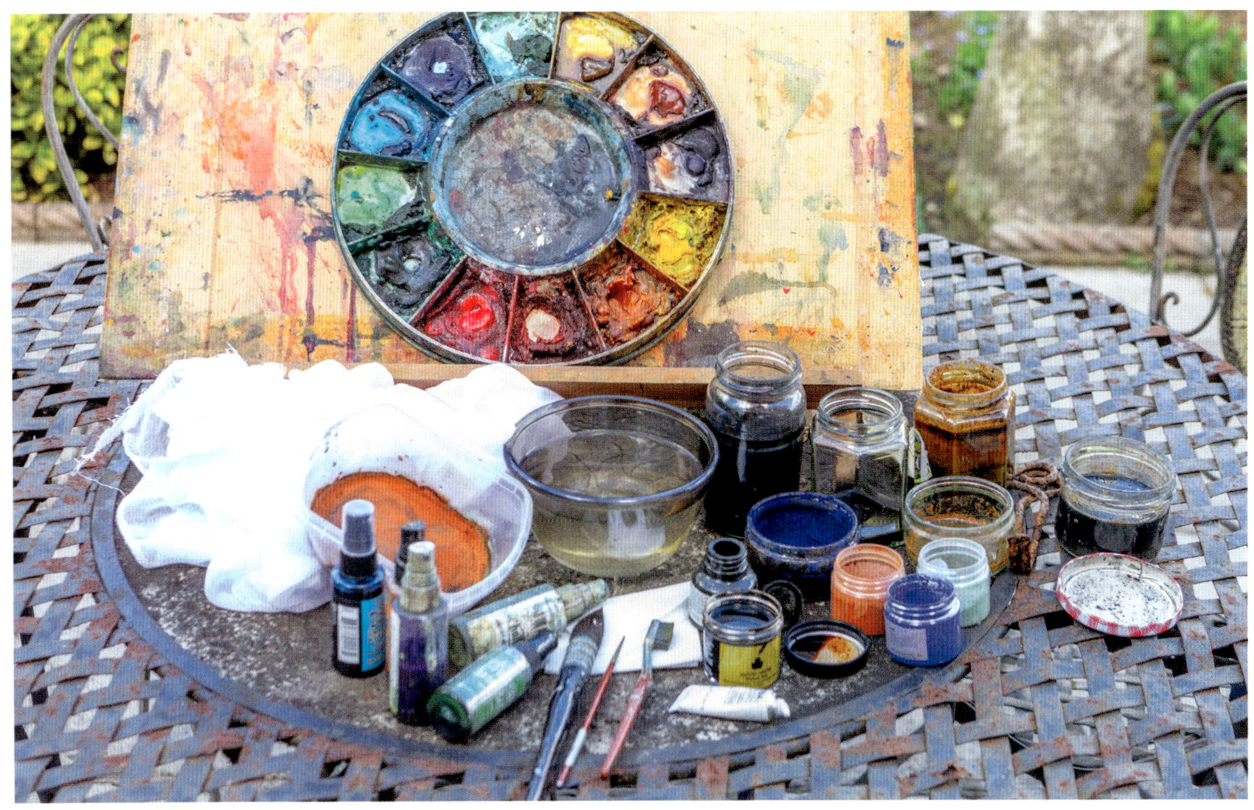

Bear basics summary

My approach to painting animals

Getting everything you need ready before you pick up your brushes will enable you to paint freely and without having to stop and start in the creative process. Try to avoid interruptions when painting. Being able to concentrate can lead to a terrific sense of connection to our subject as it gradually appears in front of our eyes.

Allow yourself set times to work that you know will be peaceful. Find a great resource photograph and collect the painting equipment that suits you and your financial situation. Once you have everything in place you are ready to create. My approach to painting animals has always been the following.

1 – Fall in love with a subject Find a great model or superb reference photo to work from. If you do not love your subject or know it well, your painting time could be less enjoyable, frustrating and possibly lead to unsatisfactory results.

2 – Plan and prepare Choose your paper surface and the watercolour shades before you start painting. I always trying to include at least one shade that is slightly unusual. The painting of a bear on page 25, for example, shows the use of Wisteria, a pink shade that you might not expect.

3 – Practise, practise, practise! Create a wash for your subject by simply placing colour in the shape of the whole animal until you almost see a ghost-like version of your subject, onto which details can then be added. This is a great technique for simplifying painting without the use of a preliminary sketch.

4 – Move from large to small I use different brush sizes during a painting's development. I use my larger size 12 brush for large background colour areas and move gradually to my size 10 brush, finally moving to my rigger for adding the fine details you see around the eyes in particular.

...And that's it. The basic 'bear necessities' that are all you need! Throughout my book I will be sharing tips on which products and techniques I use and why. Let's move on in our journey into painting atmospheric animals in watercolour.

Studying the masters

There are so many wonderful wildlife artists, and I have been fortunate to have studied in many countries over the years. I also have a vast collection of books on painting animals from my early learning years as an artist.

Do study books that show you how to draw animals. Admiring how other artists create can help us so much on our art journey. Although I paint in a loose atmospheric style, knowing how to sketch really does help. You will build your skills so that when you eventually choose to lose the pencil, you will find the process of creating without a sketch far easier.

My favourite books on painting animals in watercolour are my Chinese collection from my time living in Asia, and a beautiful gift from Hungarian artist Victor Ambrus, his book, *Drawing Animals*.

Animal meaning: fox

Quick-thinking, adaptable and clever, the fox can overcome all manner of obstacles. It is a wonderful animal to relate to as an artist because, when we are working with watercolour, we do at times need to be flexible. The fox reminds us that if we are faced with an artistic problem there is always, without fail, an ingeniously cunning way to solve it!

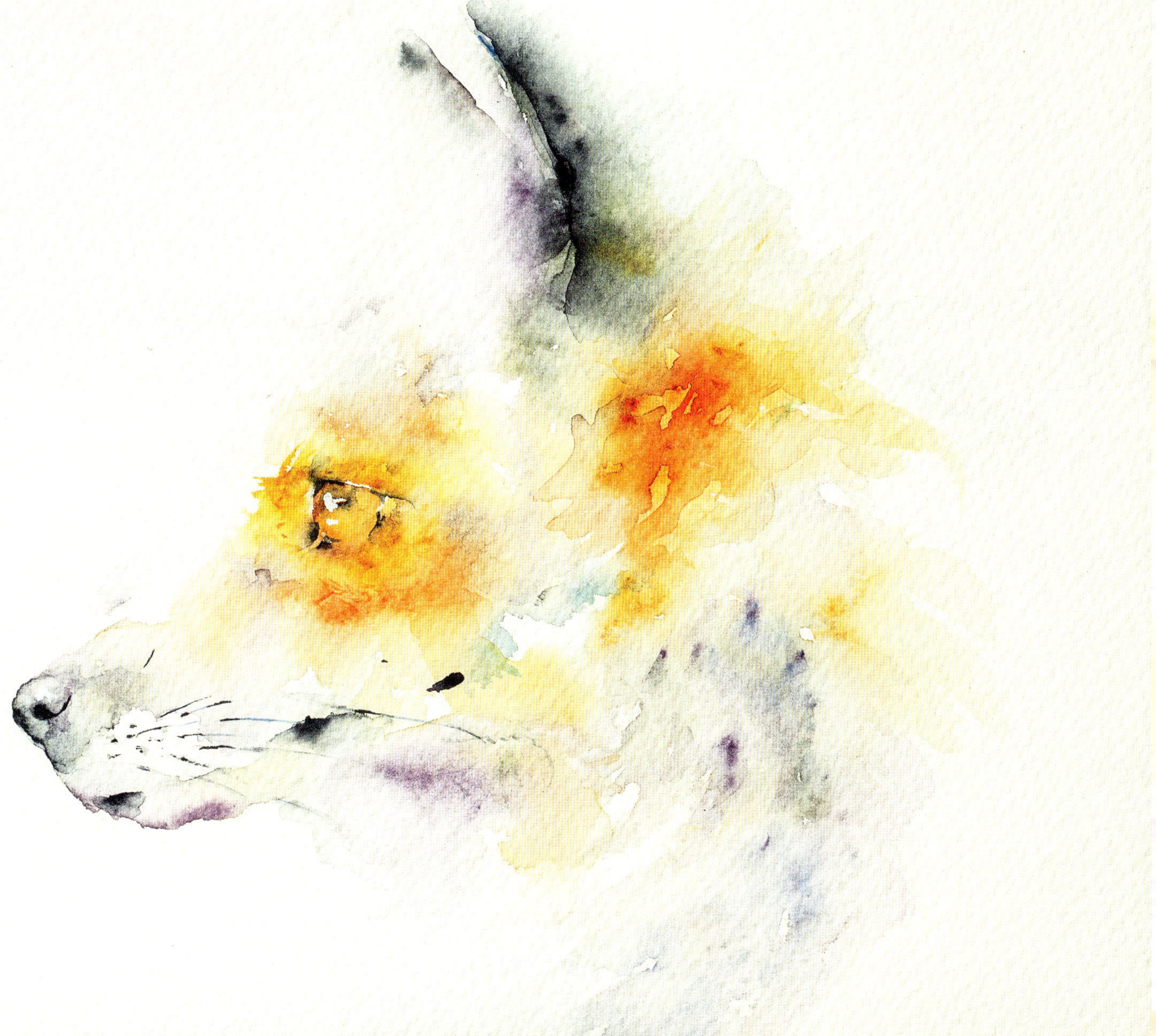

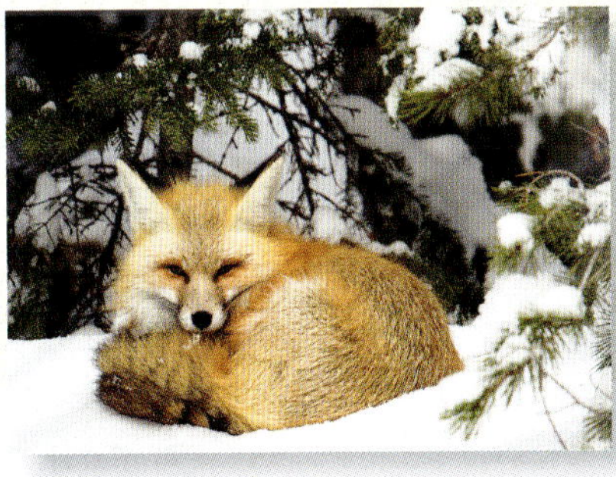

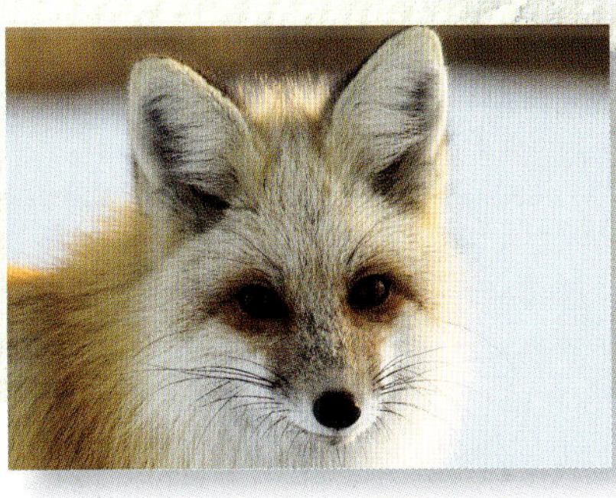

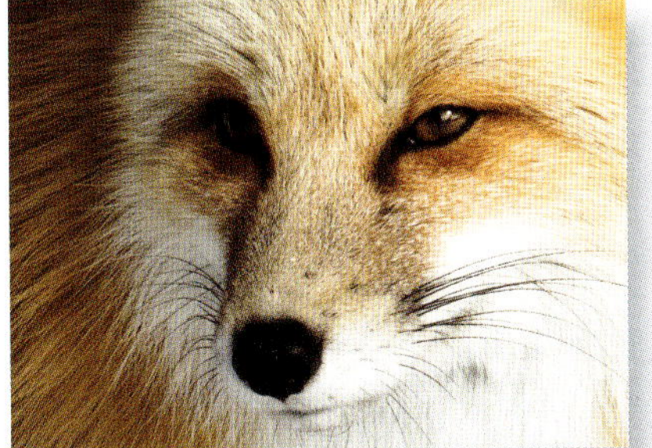

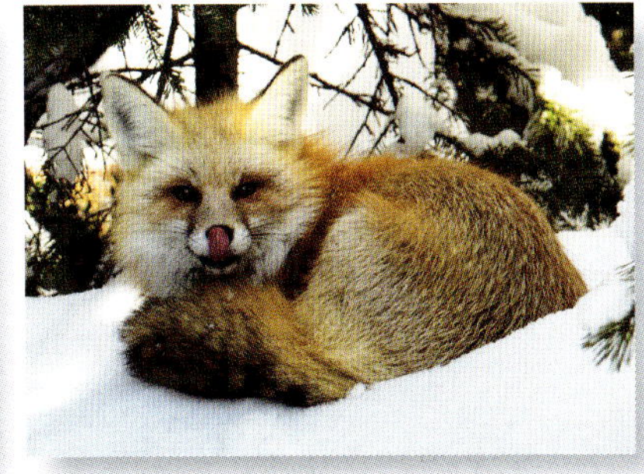

In Wait

38 x 38cm (15 x 15in)

Fox in watercolour. Capturing an animal with just a few brushstrokes telling the story can be a great way to introduce yourself to working without a pencil for the first time.

Animal meanings

When we are faced with painting any given subject for the very first time, it can be a really daunting experience. I want to make your art journey a fun and enjoyable adventure. To paint animals well, getting to know a little bit about each one before attempting to create them in watercolour is a really good idea.

While teaching international workshops I came to learn about spirit and totem animals. Throughout the book, I have added boxes to highlight what we, as artists, can learn from the animal we are painting – you will have seen one or two already, on the previous pages. Many animals have meanings associated with them by different cultures. This is a fascinating topic that I encourage you to research further.

Some people believe that particular animals appear when you need them to. You may be drawn to painting a subject at a time in your life when their message is quite strong. Bears are said to be great leaders. They nurture their young so have a strong connection with family ties. In the Chinese practice of *feng shui*, statues of bears were once placed in front of homes to act as guardians, due to the bears' protective instincts.

If you feel the need to paint a bear, for example, it could be that you need to take some time in your 'cave' resting and creating more! Whatever you believe, they are wonderful subjects and great fun to paint.

Animal meaning: bear

Due to their links with hibernation periods, bears remind us to greatly value rest, peaceful quality time and solitude. These are perfect attributes for the artist who likes to concentrate when they paint. And they give us a useful tip: to take breaks every now and then during the creative process of our work. A well-rested artist often achieves better results!

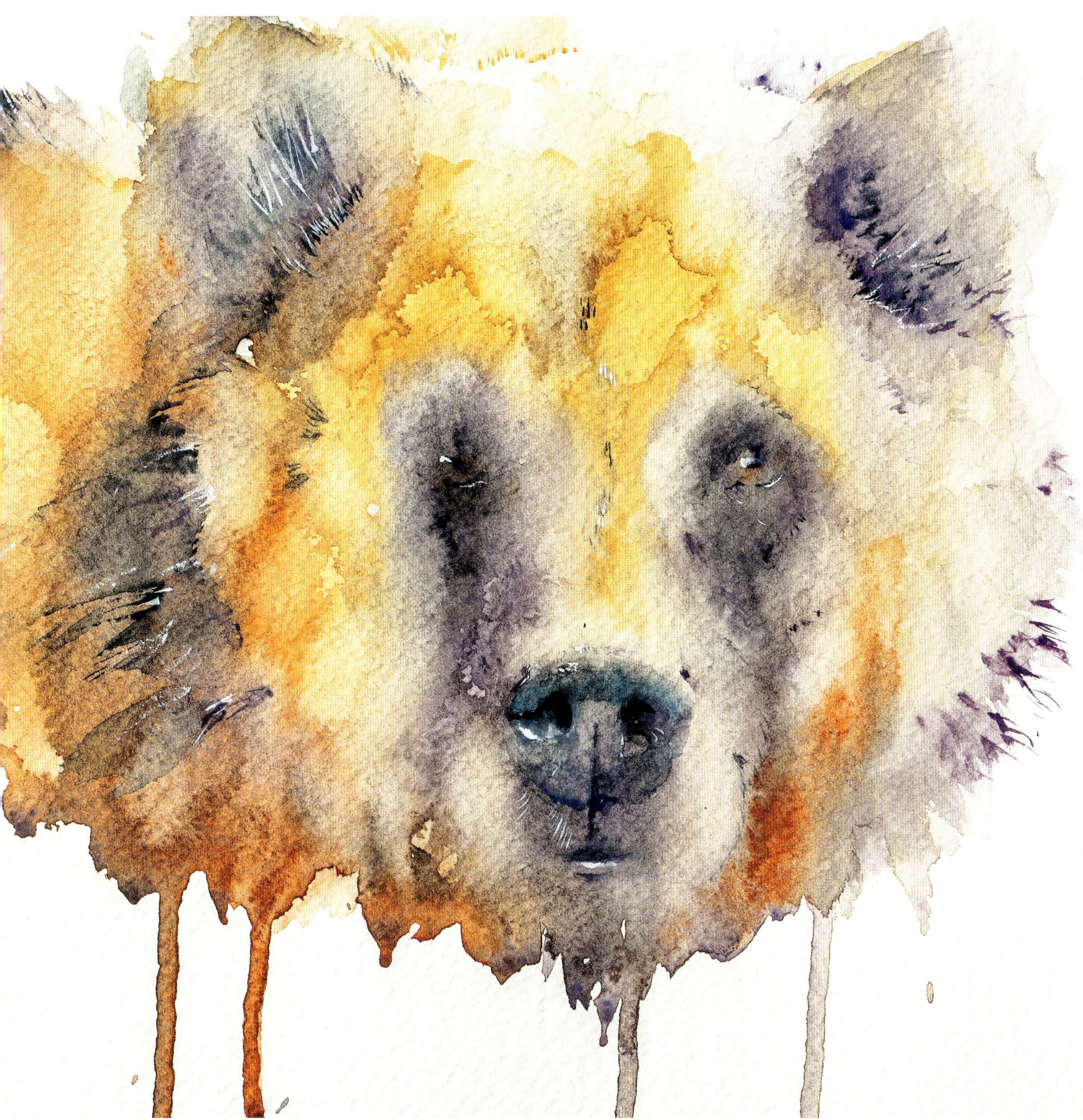

Barely There

58 x 38cm (23 x 15in)

To create this painting, I initially placed a colour block outline of my bear as a first
wash, because the subject was new to me. I then added the detail, highlighting the
nose, the eyes and fine lines for fur at the outer edges of the bear's face. I allowed
the watermarks from the first wash to show in my finished painting. Working in this
way helped to boost my confidence when painting this new subject.

Dancing ladies: colour selection

Over the years, while teaching, I have noticed that many artists often have problems choosing the right colours to depict their subjects. Even if they initially gain a great colour match for their subject, they can later find it difficult to select shades to act as an attractive background in their compositions. For this reason, I invented my now well-known dancing ladies exercise, which has become extremely popular. Why? Because this simple exercise eliminates many problems you could experience once you have started painting. It not only helps you choose the right colours to match your subject accurately, but it also has fantastic value in that the exercise teaches you about the qualities of each individual pigment.

You may be wondering why this exercise is called 'dancing ladies'. On one of my workshops, it was noted that the dots looked like a row of heads and the colours underneath looked like costumes.

Over time, the more dancing ladies you create, the better your knowledge of your watercolour pigments becomes. Let me explain with a simple demonstration. There will also be dancing ladies colour selections throughout my book, so you will soon see why they are so important.

Avoid using the same colours in every painting. Always keep an eye out for new shades that interest you, to add a sense of excitement to your work. It is only by regularly painting my dancing ladies exercises that I discovered that I preferred the vibrancy of Aussie red gold to cadmium orange. With practice, in time you will discover your absolutely favourite new shades too!

How-to select your colours

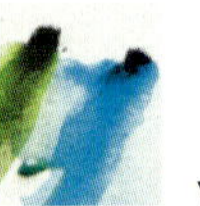

As I prepared to create *All That Glitters*, the goldfish painting seen on page 28, I carried out this exercise to create a dancing ladies swatch of colours. I looked at my photograph of the fish and selected shades that I felt would look great to bring my subject to life.

To carry out this exercise you need scraps of paper, a size 10 round brush and, of course, all your paints to choose from. For some subjects I will only use three colours, while for others – especially more complex compositions – I will choose up to six or seven shades. Usually this is enough.

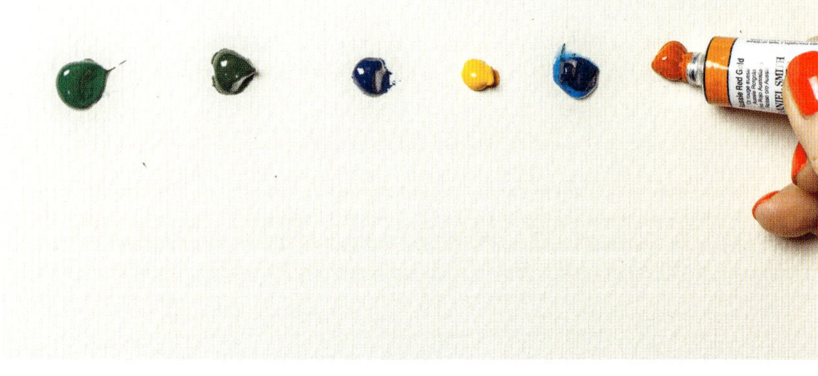

1 Start by choosing shades that you imagine would work well for your subject. Try to include a few shades that might enhance the other colours to increase their attractiveness. Place a dot of each selected shade in a row at the top of a long narrow scrap of paper. Here I chose phthalo blue turquoise and cascade green for my background. I felt the turquoise would add vibrancy and interest. I opted for cadmium yellow deep hue to add a sense of sunshine hitting my scene; and Aussie red gold, as it seemed perfect for the goldfish themselves. Lunar blue and moonglow were selected to enhance these main colour choices. The row looked pleasing, so I could move ahead with painting knowing my result would look stunning. Making these decisions before you pick up a brush is invaluable. It leads to painting with more confidence.

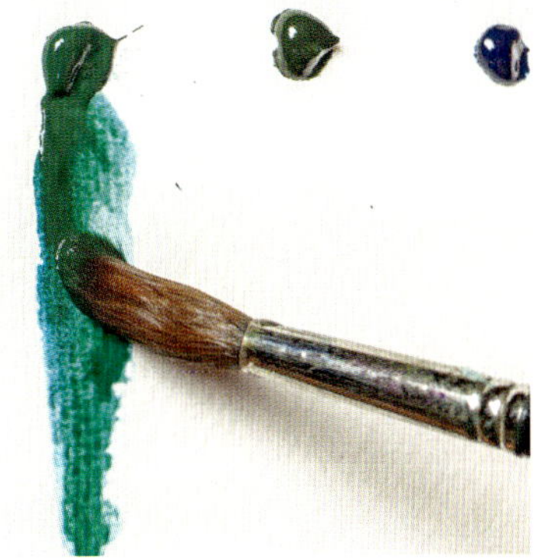

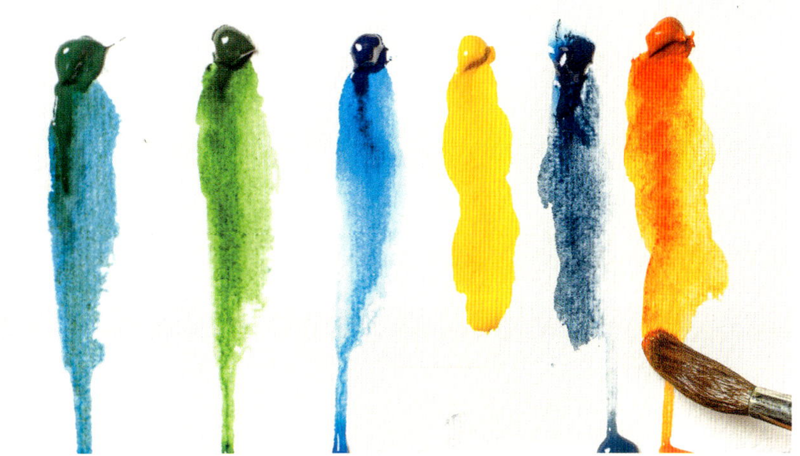

2 Wet your brush and place a clean brushstroke under each colour dot in a downwards direction. Be careful not to touch the colour itself at this point. Once you have a row of lines of water under each pigment dot, gently touch the first pigment with a clean brush and encourage the pigment to run into the wet line beneath it. Draw the paint out; the more water you add to the pigment, the lighter the result will be, and the nearer to the spot of pure paint, the darker.

3 Rinse your brush before moving on to touch each new pigment dot in turn. This action will teach you how to keep your colours clean and fresh. Observing each pigment as it acts is fascinating. Some pigments will granulate. Some pigments will move faster than others. Some pigments will give you more solid, opaque results while others will give you beautiful transparent effects. Studying each pigment will enable you to choose the best colours to paint animals beautifully. Do take your time on this exercise to gain maximum knowledge from each pigment as you work.

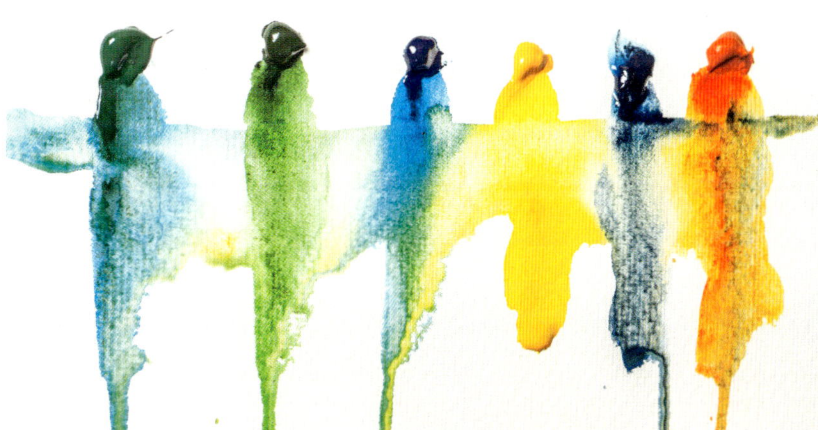

4 Once you have a clean row of shades and while the colours are still damp, run a horizontal brushstroke through every single colour in your row of dancing ladies. Watch how they interact. Some pigments will easily flow into the neighbouring shades. Some will completely overpower the pigment next to them, while others will allow strong bold pigments to take over. This knowledge will help you when you allow pigments to interact naturally in a composition. You will also learn how much water is needed to produce the right depth of colour in each shade; and learn how beautiful diluted colours can be.

Using your dancing ladies

When you have carried out your dancing ladies exercise, check to see which colours appeal to you most for your subject.

Importantly, please do not throw these scraps of paper away as they become your palette to paint from. Each pigment dot is exactly the same as the shades you see in watercolour pans. So nothing, not a drop of colour, should be wasted.

Now you have a fabulous way of choosing colours for your animal subjects.

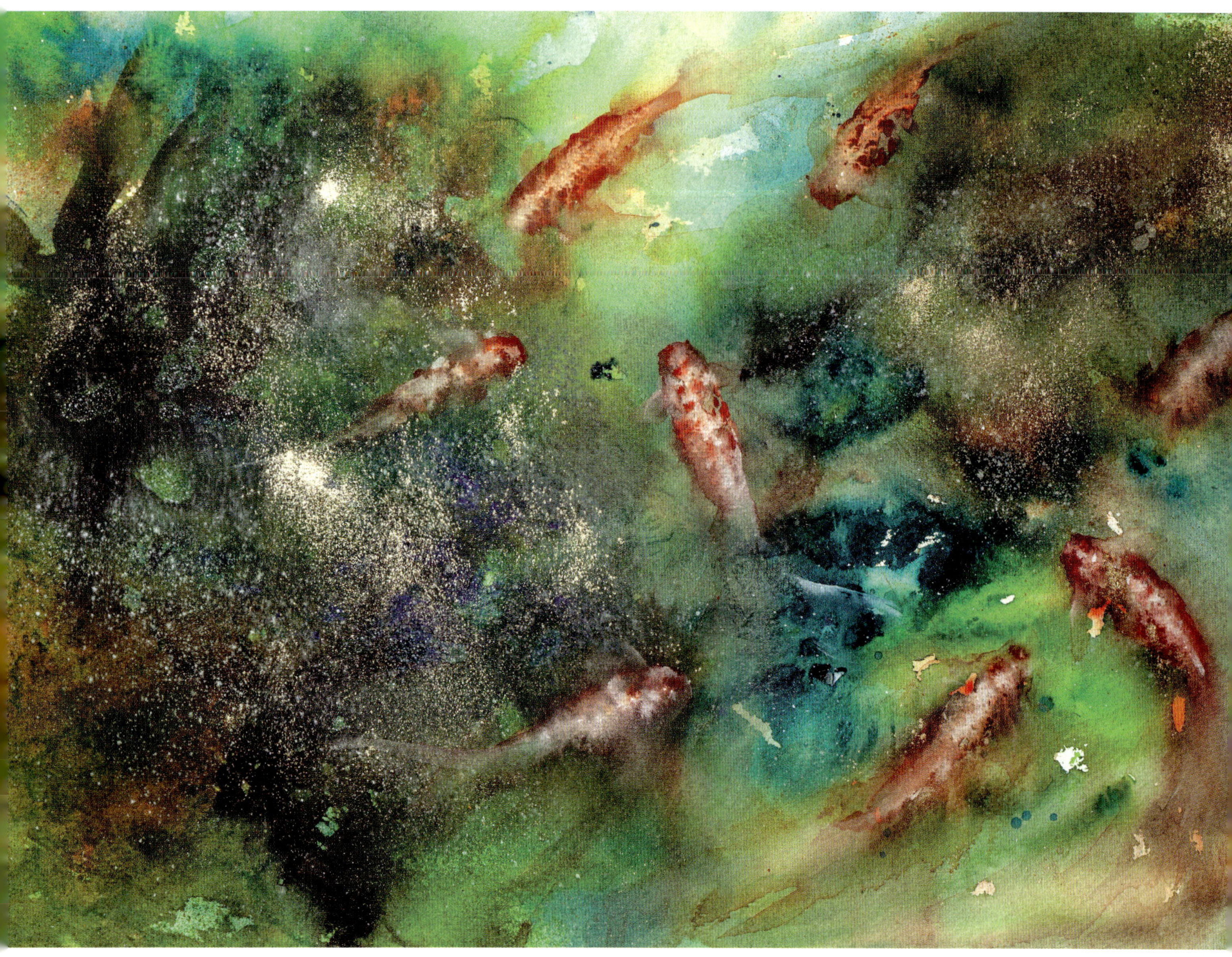

All That Glitters

58 x 38cm (23 x 15in)

Painted on top of an exciting creative wash, fish swimming in different directions here form a fascinating composition. I chose my colours for this painting using the dancing ladies exercise on the previous pages. My aim was to ensure that I gained a beautiful sense of harmony with intriguing colour combinations and effects throughout. I wanted my painting to be full of vibrant colour, life and energy with a fascinating sense of movement.

Due to my time living in Asia, I call this a feng shui piece; the addition of gold bronzing powder bringing good luck to the owner of my finished piece. We look at how to use bronzing powder in more detail on page 126, but for now I'd like you to concentrate on choosing colours for a variety of subjects with my dancing ladies exercises. Mastering colour selection will greatly improve your art.

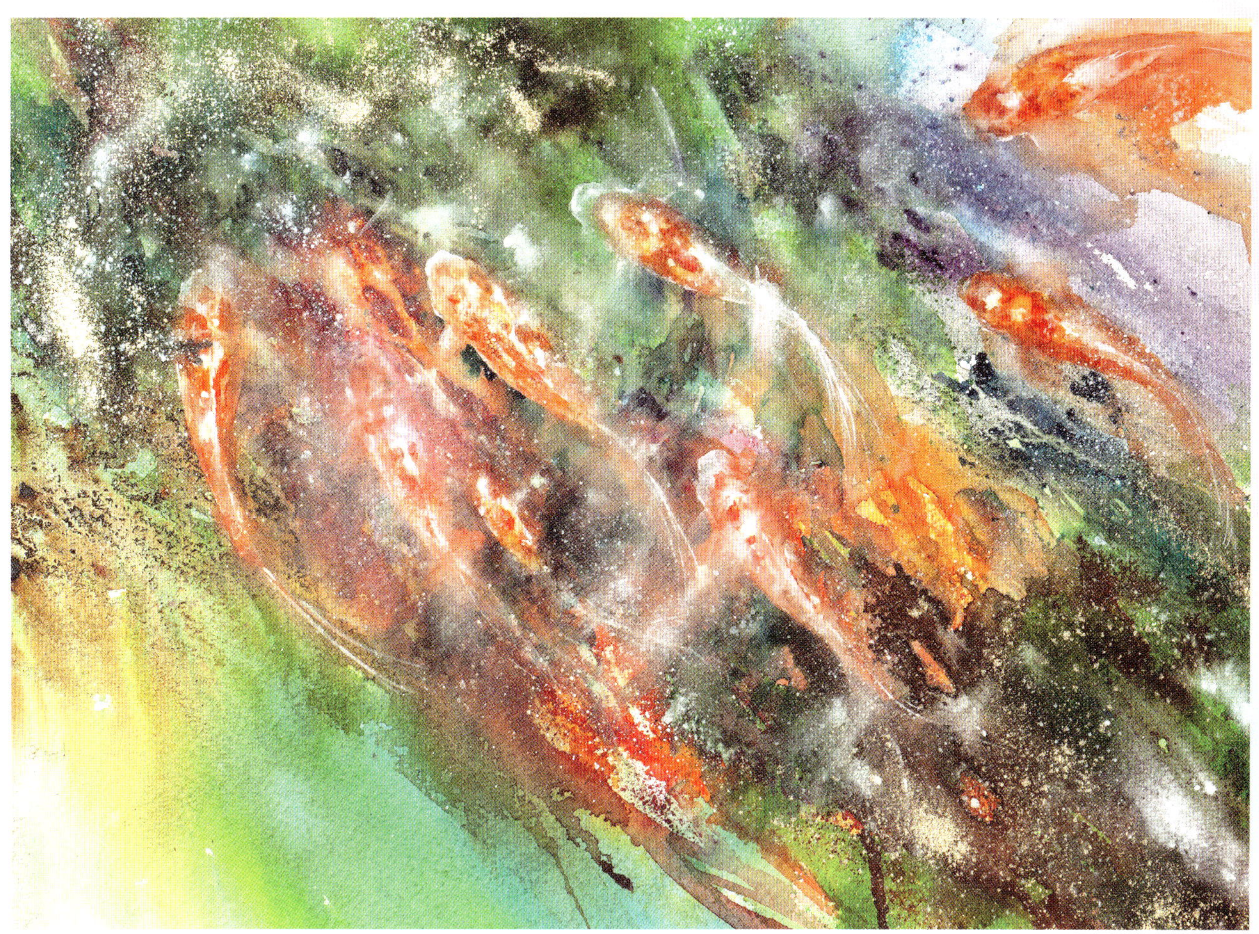

Going For Gold
58 x 38cm (23 x 15in)

Animal meaning: goldfish

Goldfish are said to be lucky omens, bringing health, wealth and prosperity. In certain cultures, their gold colouring represents wealth and if they are in your home it is believed that your fortune will be blessed. Watching fish swim gives us a peaceful feeling, which is why they are popular in parks and waiting rooms. They carry a sense of calm. They are also linked to creativity. Painting koi or goldfish could be a peaceful creative session for you to enjoy. And your finished koi paintings may bring you good luck.

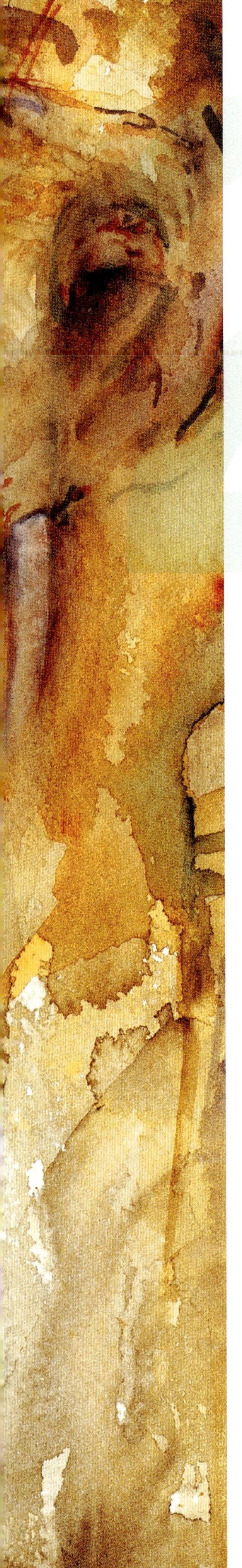

Getting started: simple studies

Reduce the pressure

When we were young, we often created small doodles. As adults, sketching in watercolour is the same thing: painting for pleasure and capturing a subject in a way that can lead to a more complex version. This is an ideal method of learning about animals, new subjects and how to paint them. Starting out by creating small studies to learn from gives us the confidence to approach a full painting, as we then understand our subject better. Also, any mistakes we make are on our practice pieces.

I am a firm believer in painting for the waste bin as we learn. Taking away the pressure to constantly produce, and instead placing the emphasis on enjoying the creative process, has improved my skill as an artist. It leaves me always eager to paint rather than dreading picking up my brushes. I want you to feel happy about painting each time you pick up your brush too. Painting should be fun, especially when we are painting a subject we love like animals.

To gain a loose atmospheric interpretation of a subject we still need to have some idea of proportion and accuracy to tell a believable story in our completed artwork. Enjoying learning about shape and form is important, as it enables us to achieve a more successful composition.

The value of monochrome

When learning as an artist, it is valuable to paint any subject in just one colour. This is known as monochrome painting. This is easier for the beginner as it dismisses the need for complex colour decisions or combinations.

To limit any feeling of intimidation when you lose your pencil and pick up your brush, I highly recommend working in monochrome regularly. It is a wonderful and simplistic way of understanding light and dark sections in a painting, and why they are so necessary. This easier way of working takes the pressure of having to think about colour selection off your shoulders. For each demonstration that follows in my book, I suggest you try a quick monochrome version before attempting to paint the real thing. You will be amazed at how much this way of learning improves your observational and brushwork skills.

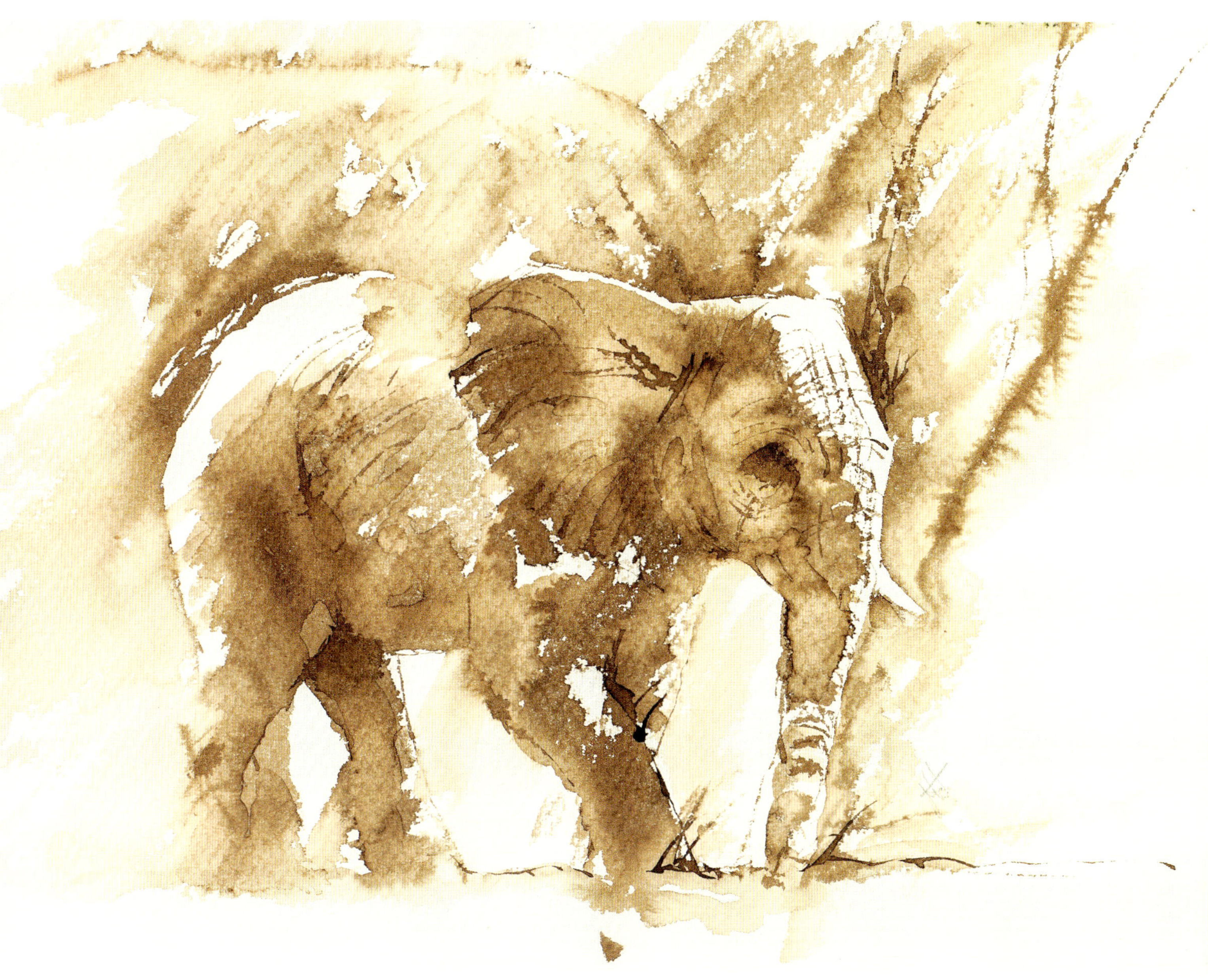

Out With Mother

38 x 28cm (15 x 11in)

Elephant in walnut ink. Trapping the light around the head of my ink study gave me a fabulous effect. White paper is vital to give 'oxygen', allowing the subject to breathe in a beautiful animal painting. We often forget this valuable tip.

Monochrome studies with inks and more

On these pages you can see examples that have been created using alternatives to watercolour pigment. It is a great idea to experiment with all kinds of products when working in monochrome including inks or even homemade materials to gain wonderful colours. If you look at my horse racing painting below, you will see I have left some of the sections missing for the viewer's imagination to complete. This is a fascinating way to gain a sense of life and movement. It's a great technique for gaining atmospheric results. This painting was created with a mixture of coffee and tea. Using coffee grounds with water can lead to a lovely variety of brown shades. The legs in my study are only suggestions of where they would be, heightening the sense of speed and movement here.

On the opposite page my elephant study has been created using walnut ink, which is a very soft beautiful colour. Unlike acrylic inks, walnut ink is more like watercolour as a medium in that it moves beautifully on paper, so that you can create wonderful watermarks which add to the atmosphere in a composition. I have added touches of quinacridone gold here to add warmth to my abstract painting. The paper was covered with colour first, and the subjects were then 'found' on top, within the wash. This technique is called working on a creative first wash, and we look at it in more detail on pages 88–93.

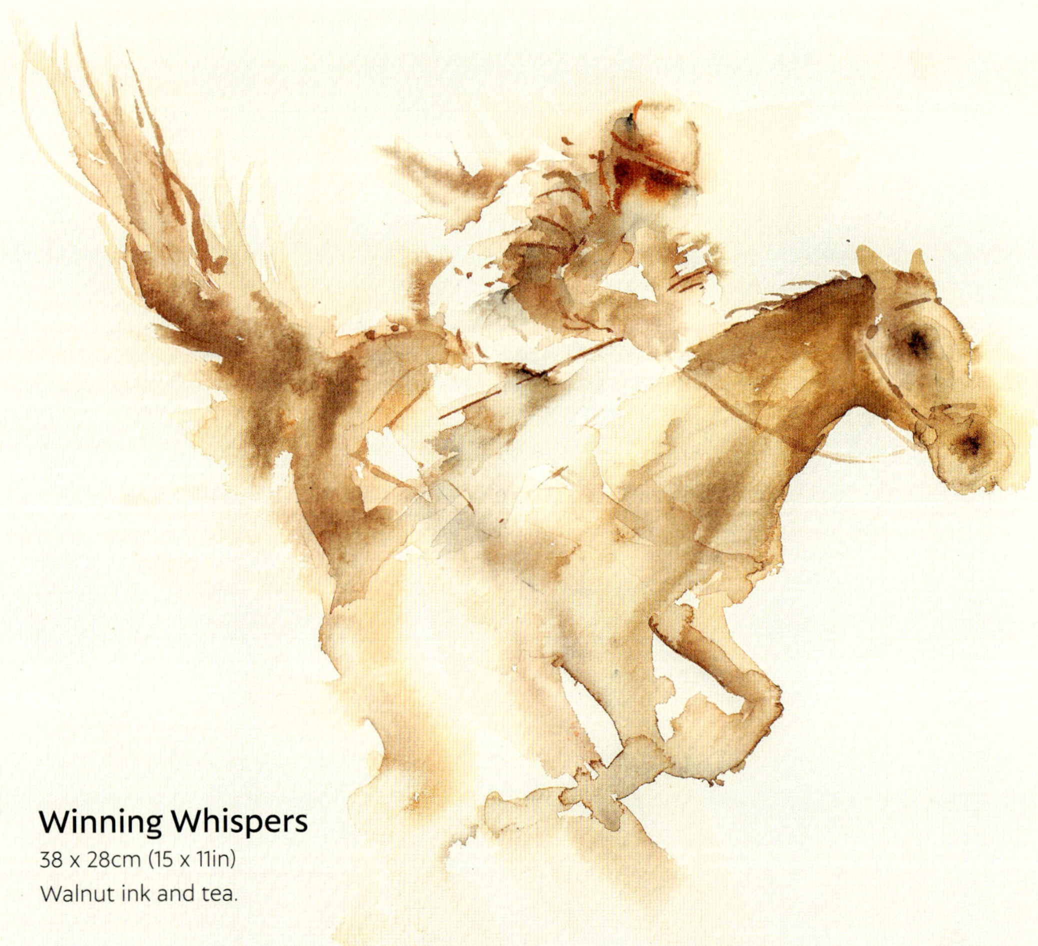

Winning Whispers
38 x 28cm (15 x 11in)
Walnut ink and tea.

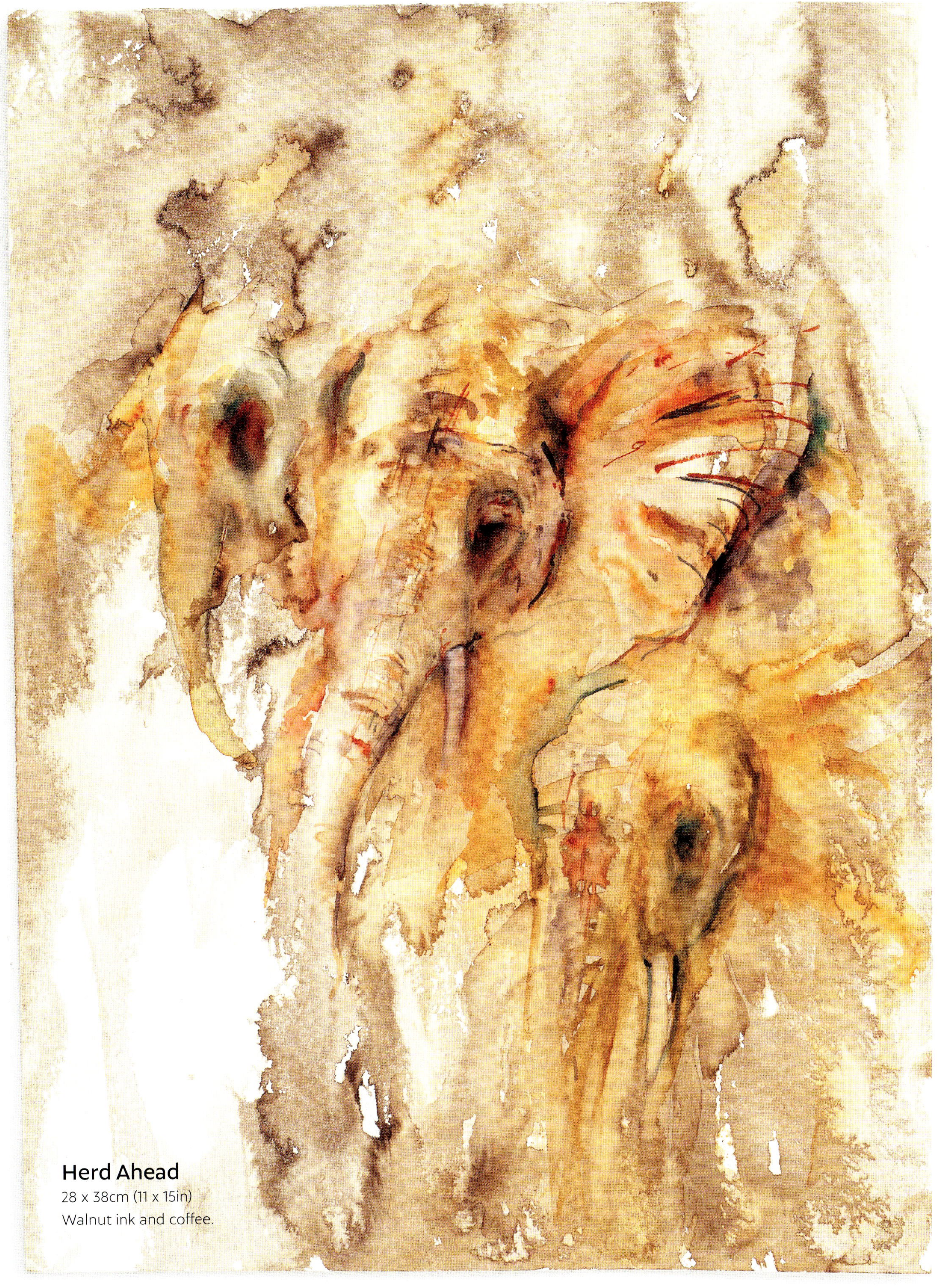

Herd Ahead
28 x 38cm (11 x 15in)
Walnut ink and coffee.

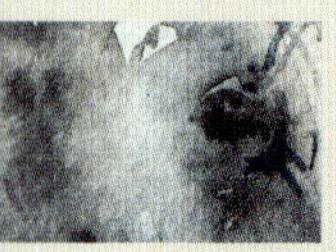

Step-by-step
Elephant in Monochrome

To get started with something very simple, here is a demonstration of an elephant head in just one colour. You need just a scrap of paper and one tube of paint. You can use any colour you like. I used Daniel Smith Payne's blue gray as it suited the subject.

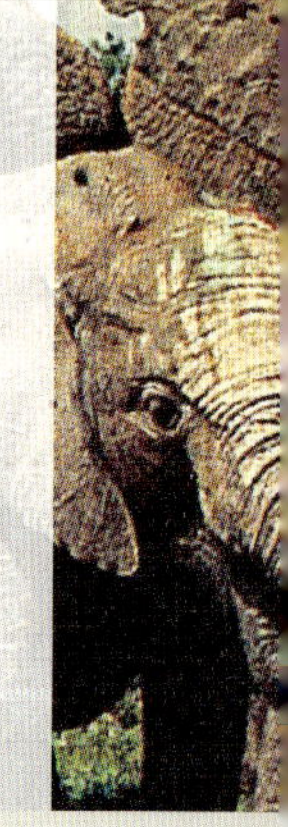

Materials

Surface: scrap of 300gsm (140lb) weight Not surface watercolour paper

Brushes: size 10 round, rigger

Watercolour paints: Payne's blue gray

Colour selection

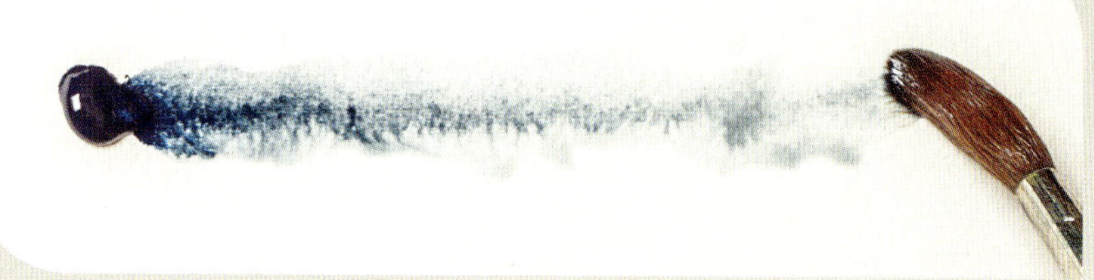

I usually create a set of dancing ladies to see which colours work best, but as we are concentrating on monochrome here, and using just one colour, this is not strictly necessary. If you are just starting out, it can still be helpful to practise adding water to achieve different tones, as shown here, and explained in step 1 below. You could also experiment with ink and use that for the project, if you prefer.

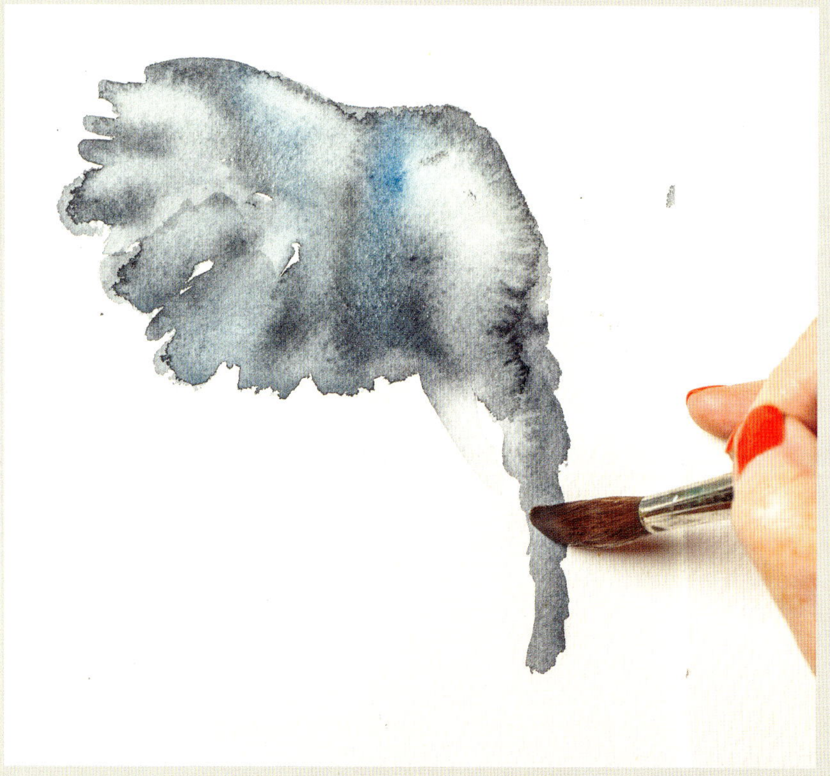

1 On a scrap of paper, use the size 10 brush to create a shape of colour that resembles an elephant's head; using sideways brushstrokes away from the head on the left-hand side to create the ear, and moving the colour downwards at the front to form a trunk on the right. With a clean, damp brush, make a brushmark dragging the wet colour downwards where you think a tusk could be and allow the colour to merge down into this new wet space. Try not to add too much definition at this stage: this is just an initial wash to suggest what the subject could be.

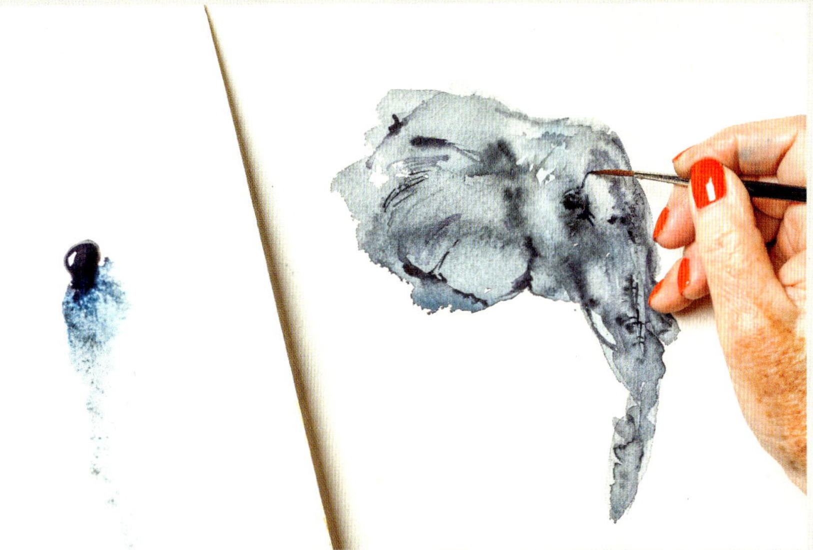

2 Once your wash is completely dry, you can begin to add details with the rigger brush such as the eye, lines or wrinkles on the elephant's head and trunk, and an outline of the ear. Use a slightly stronger mix of colour, by picking up the colour from nearer the spot of pure paint.

3 By using almost neat pigment, you can build up the details of a painting beautifully with the contrast of dark details against a lighter background. This is an important value we learn from creating studies in monochrome. Basically, we are learning how to add darks to a painting, which will help you throughout the rest of the projects in this book.

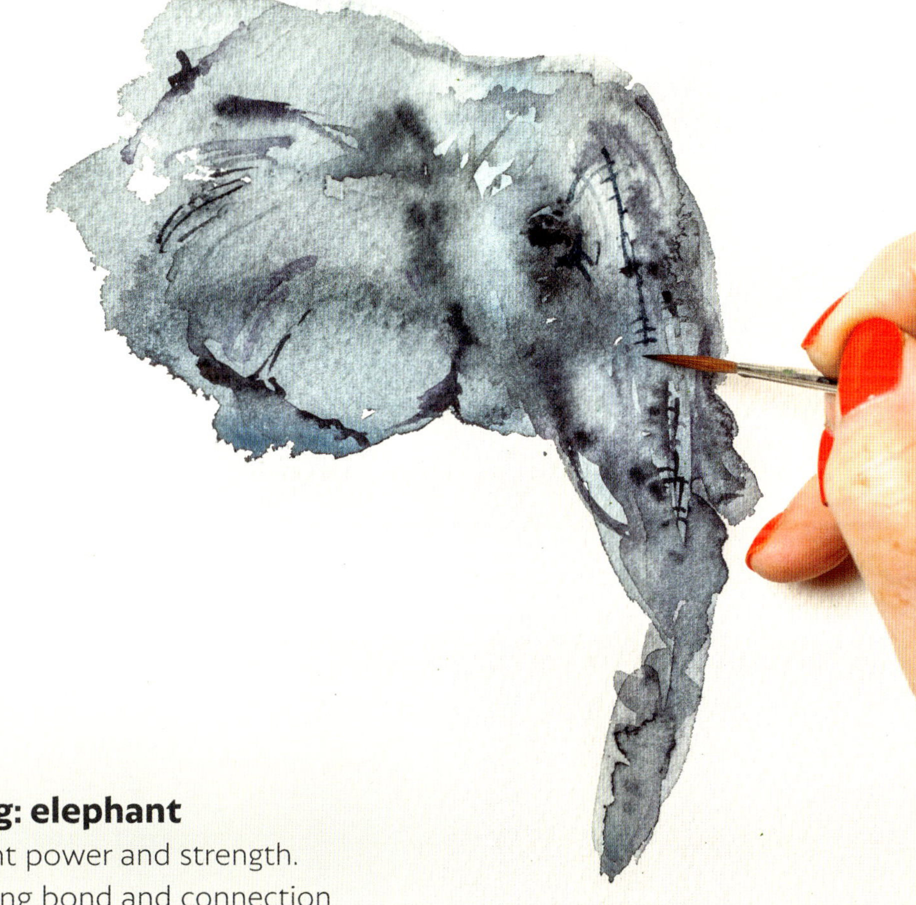

Animal meaning: elephant

Elephants are said to represent power and strength. A nurturing animal with a strong bond and connection to family, elephants represent good luck in some cultures. They are incredibly majestic beings and a favourite subject of many wildlife artists worldwide.

Moving to colour

Once you have mastered painting a subject in monochrome you can then begin to introduce colour to your paintings.

The value of working in only one colour helps you to see where you need to add darks to make your subject come to life in a less complex way, giving you what you need to introduce colour.

Simple demonstration

In my study called *In The Light*, you can see I have painted the same elephant head as on the previous page. *In the Light* was initially painted in one simple brown shade. Random touches of turquoise were then added to create interest. This is an example of how I would use a contrasting, unusual additional colour. Using the same additional colour in the background as well as in the elephant's head gives a new, wonderful form of harmony throughout the composition.

This study and the examples on the previous pages were created very simply, using natural products such as walnut ink, coffee and tea, or a combination of these materials along with watercolour pigment. The goal of this is to get used to moving our brushes to create an easy, simple head shape of an animal.

Simplifying our approach to painting is a wonderful way to learn about painting animals without the use of a preliminary sketch. However, eventually and with enough practice, there will come the urge to move on to more complex ways of painting. If you look at my painting *African Dream* on the opposite page, the result is far more dramatic because here I have used texture techniques to bring the same elephant head study to life. If you compare the two elephant paintings on these pages I'm sure you can see there is a huge difference. We talk about finding your style in a future chapter in my book, but for now we're going to move onwards with our animal adventure looking at how nature can influence our art.

Every single demonstration I share will hold many magical tips and techniques that will improve your art, leading you to a whole new level as an artist. Let's move on!

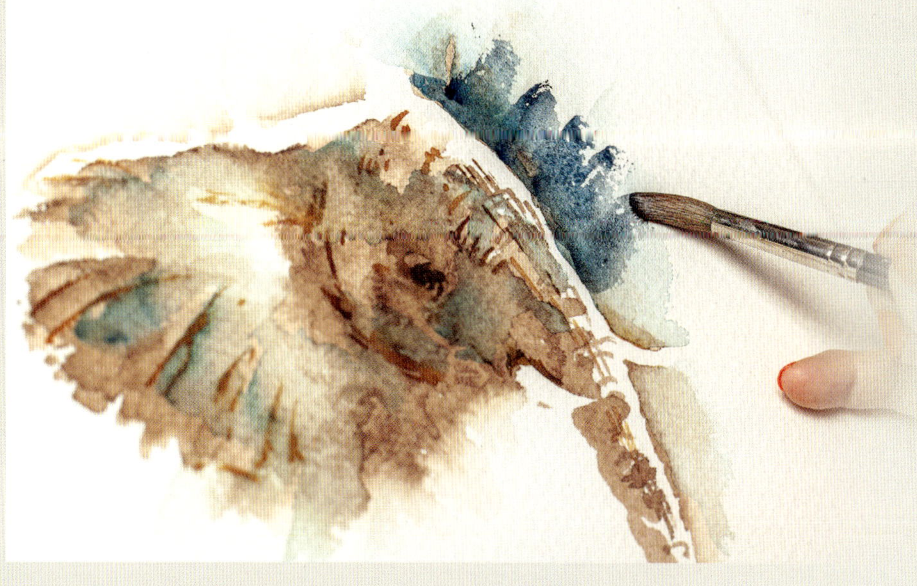

In the Light

In this study I used a technique called 'trapping the light'. To do this, create a new outline along the outer edge of the elephant's head by bleeding colour away into the new background area and leaving white space. This space, between the previous colour application and the new background gives a beautiful illusion of sunlight hitting the animal's head.

Tip

Glazing is a great technique which you can use in so many ways. You can glaze over any colour by placing a layer of another colour over your painting when it is completely dry. Practise this technique on your monochrome elephant head study.

Opposite
African Dream
28 x 38cm (11 x 15in)
Created using an interesting background wash and texture effects, particularly crackle paste, which you can read about on pages 100–101.

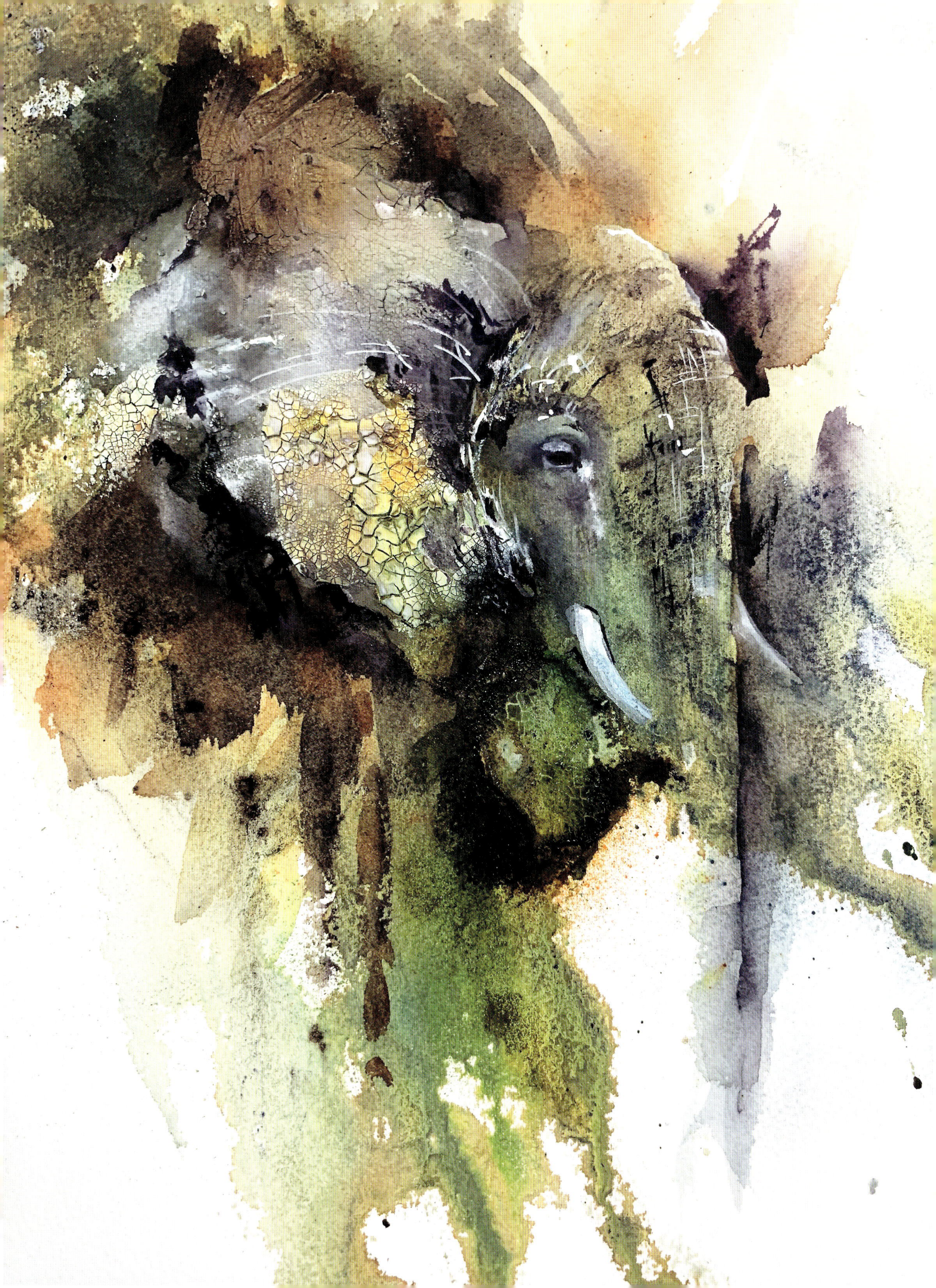

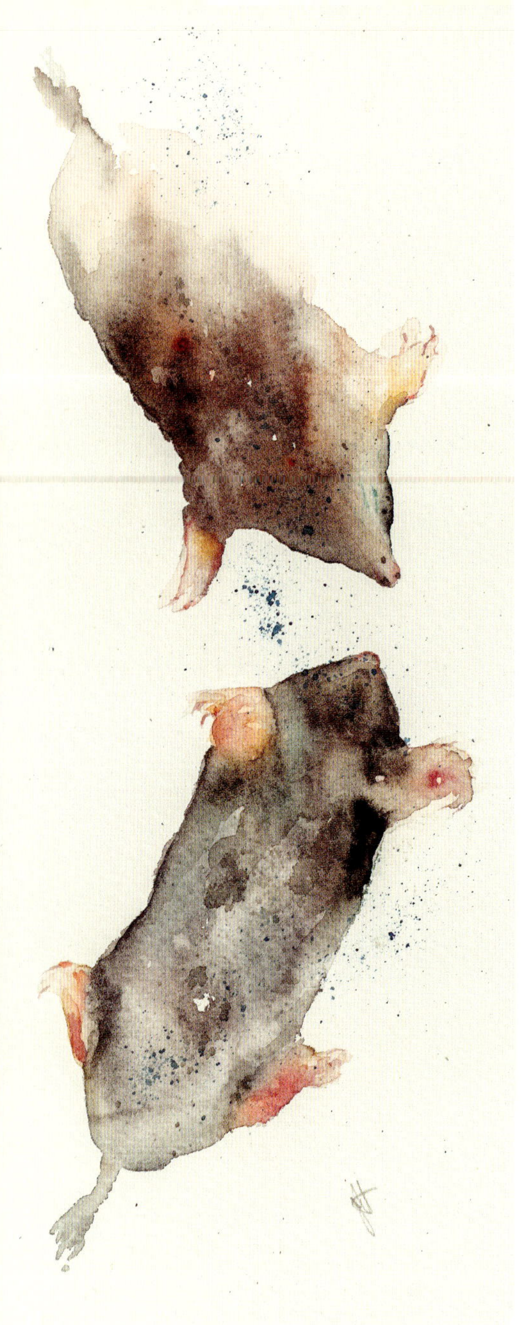

Learning from animals

"Humankind must learn to understand that the life of an animal is in no way less precious than our own." *Paul Oxton*

AS WITH ANY PAINTING SUBJECT, in order to create a good watercolour of an animal it is wise to learn about the subject first, studying the animal's shape, characteristics and colouring. I know from experience that painting animals with which we are familiar is far easier and often more enjoyable than aiming to paint one that we have never seen in real life.

To begin this adventure, I recommend painting subjects that are familiar to you as often as possible. You can use my watercolour techniques on any animal you wish to, as each demonstration in my book can be adapted to an animal of your choice. We will be covering domestic pets in this section. I am beginning with the wildlife from my garden.

Diggers
14 x 38cm (5½ x 15in)
Moles in watercolour.

Animal meaning: mole

Moles are nearly blind yet form amazing tunnels underground to reach new destinations. They don't hesitate. They go for it. Their message is 'Let go of doubt': it does nothing for you. To artists new and old, letting go of doubts and forging forward in a new art adventure can only be a great positive!

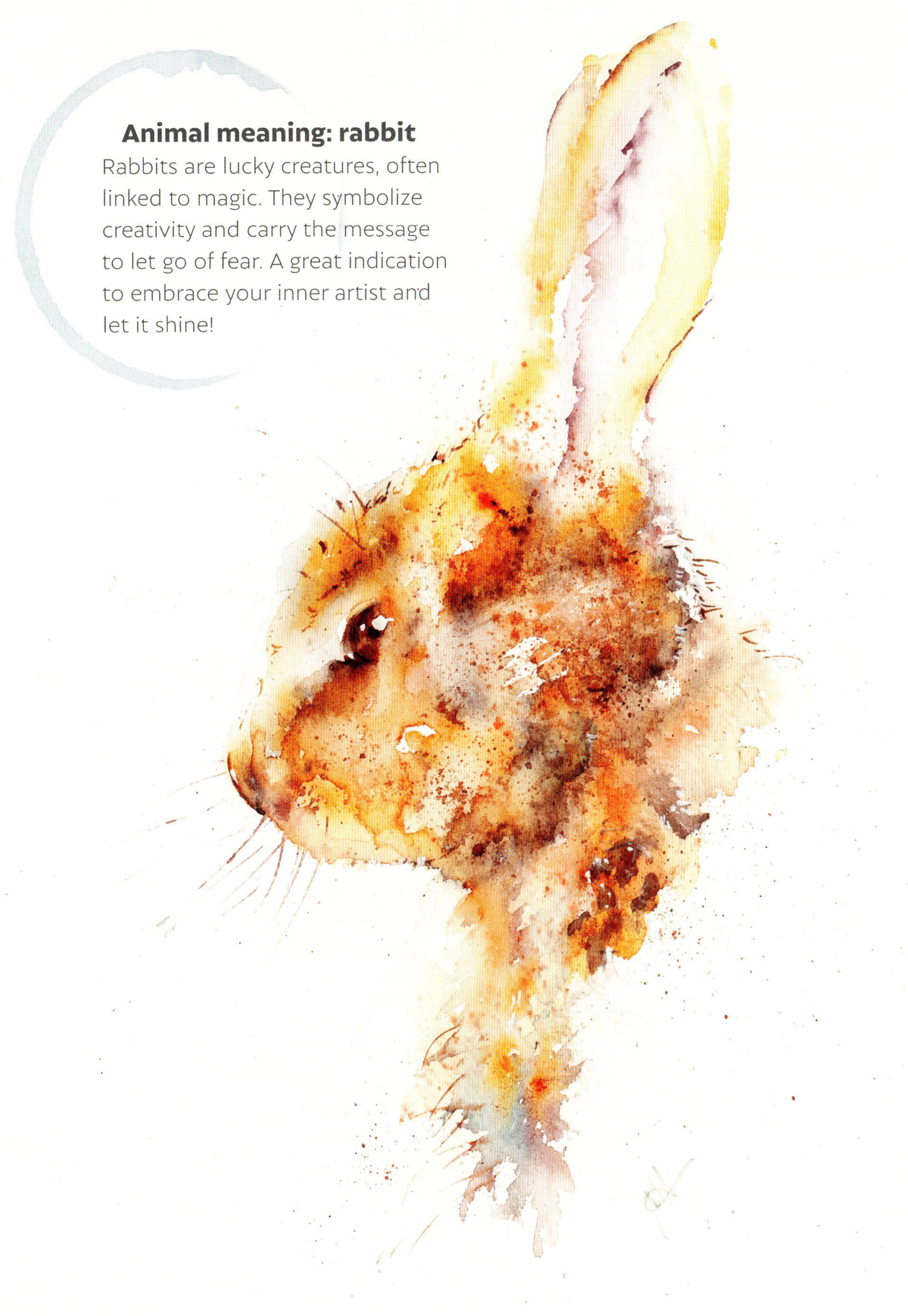

Animal meaning: rabbit

Rabbits are lucky creatures, often linked to magic. They symbolize creativity and carry the message to let go of fear. A great indication to embrace your inner artist and let it shine!

Garden Guest
28 x 38cm (11 x 15in)

Approaching art in simple stages

I am lucky, as I see many wild animals in our cottage garden. Some are more welcome than others... Moles, for example, consistently burrow under our flower borders while also leaving molehills all over our lawn. Rabbits regularly nibble on our beloved plants. But all are welcome. I believe we need to learn to live with nature rather than fight against it. And we can learn so much from our animal friends.

Animal characteristics

As explained on page 24, I discovered that there is more to painting animals some time ago when I came across animal symbolism during my international workshop tours. I heard many fascinating tales connected with each creature, which encouraged me to study the meanings, folklore and the spiritual side of animals. These I share with you in this publication, hoping they will fascinate and intrigue you too.

For example, moles are creatures that depend heavily on their senses: touch is really important to them. As a digger, a mole is always searching for treasure. While on this watercolour journey into the animal kingdom, we will be searching for treasure in our quest to improve our art. The mole is also said to teach us to trust our instincts. I will be asking you to trust yours at times, because the nagging feeling of self-doubt when we create can definitely hold us back in our art journey.

While the rabbit is an extremely popular animal to paint, it too has a wonderful spiritual meaning, in that it symbolizes rebirth. Right now, I would like you to consider the messages of both the mole and the rabbit. Whether you are new to painting animals in watercolour or have painted them previously, see this as is a new beginning in your watercolour journey. Now is the time to move ahead, trying new approaches to creating.

Begin painting animals from this minute on with an open mind, taking enthusiastic steps on a fabulous adventure, creating animals in watercolour in many different ways. Our aim is to create atmospheric paintings. Let go of any fears that you may be holding regarding your capability to paint. As the mole says, lose all doubt and move ahead with confidence and the eagerness to find treasures, whether it is through new techniques or new subjects. The goal of my book is to inspire you in many ways. Learning not only to paint animals, but to study them; gaining insights and a little bit more information with each brushstroke.

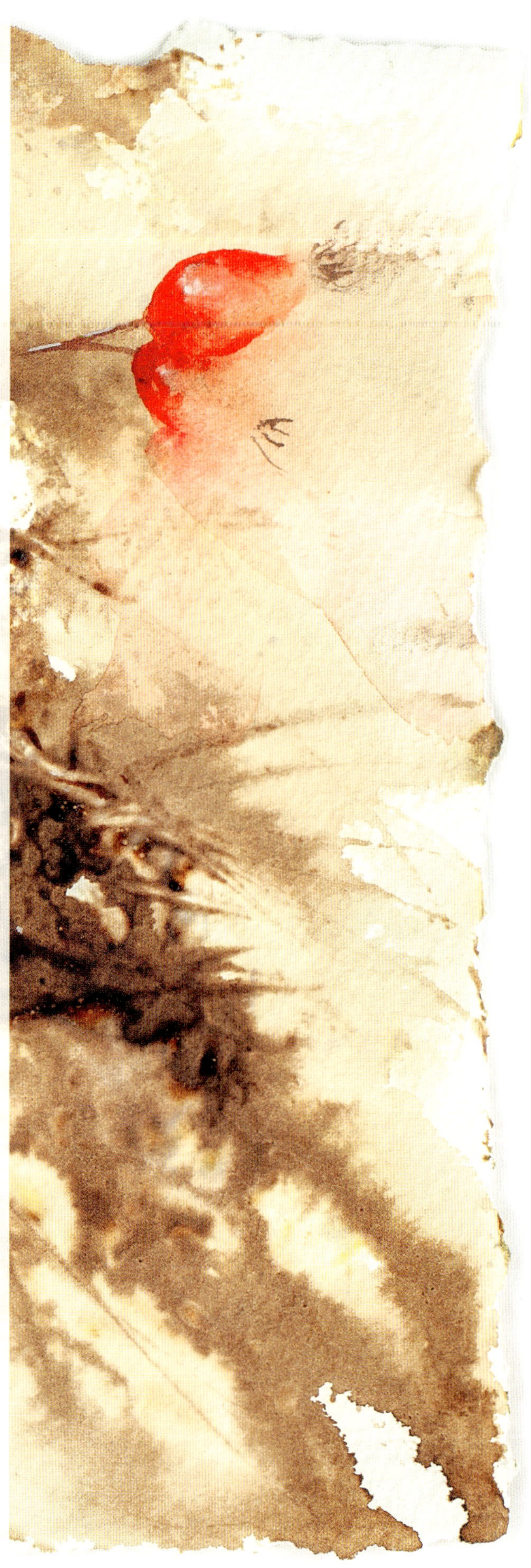

Simple to complex

Three approaches to painting hedgehogs

As we work through the chapters of my book, I will be guiding you from easy studies to more complicated compositions. The idea is that you can work at your own pace to discover what style of painting suits you the best. Please remember that we are all very different in our preferences, and when it comes to art it is these differences that make us unique. While I will be showing you how I approach painting animals in watercolour, there are many other options: enjoy my ideas, then build your own. It makes painting so much more fun if we personalize our artwork.

Shown here are two versions of hedgehogs painted in watercolour. The first a very simple study. The second shows the same hedgehog blending into a setting of autumnal leaves.

Overleaf is a third, larger composition, which shows the same animal in a full painting, where it harmonizes with the background in colour and style – we will learn how to do this later on in the book. For now, we will close the chapter with a simple step-by-step exercise to show you how to get started without the use of a preliminary sketch.

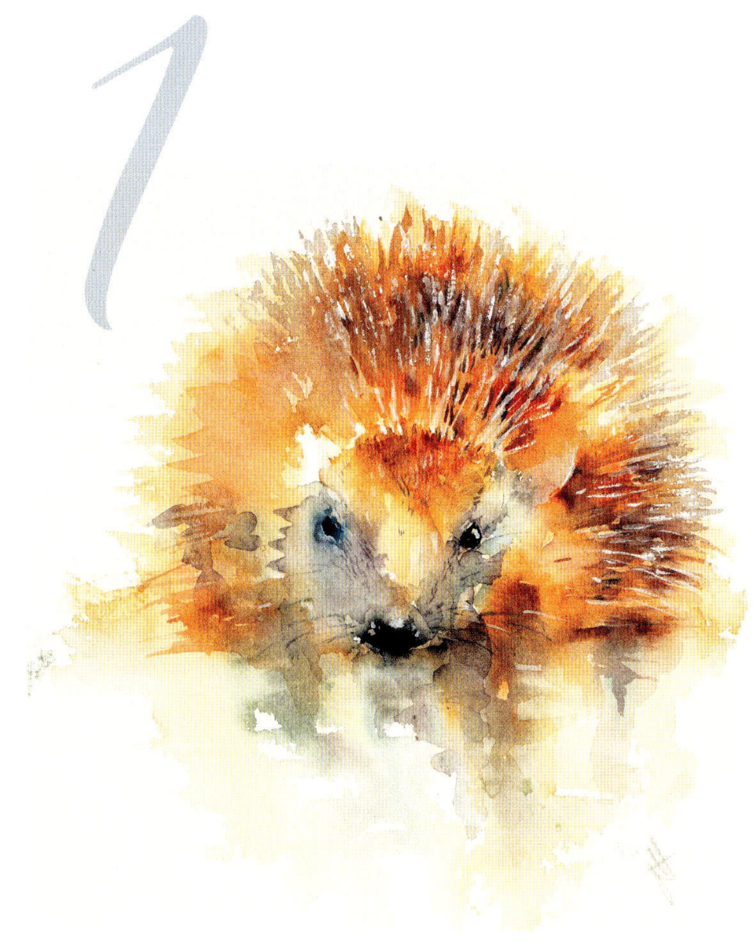

Hedgehog Reflection
28 x 28cm (11 x 11in)

Rustle
58 x 38cm (23 x 15in)

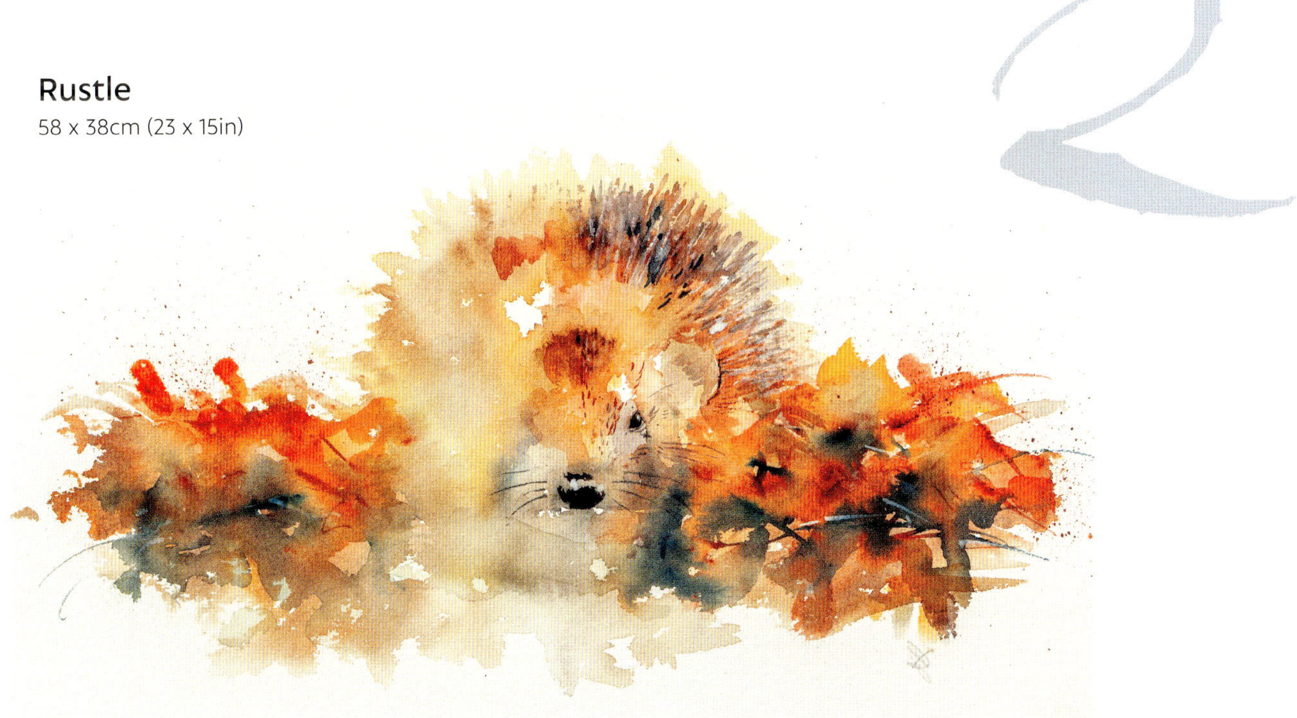

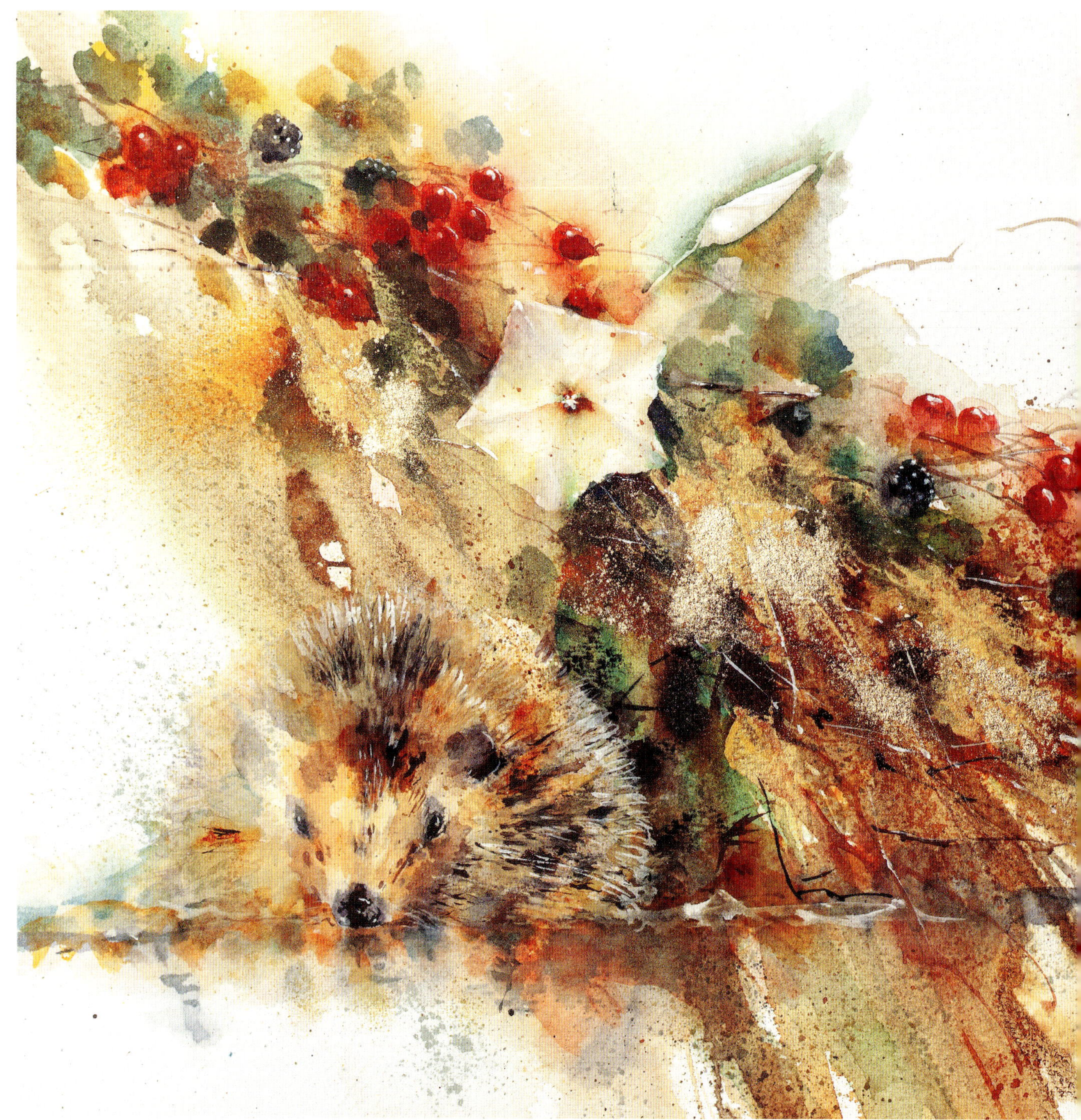

Thinking of Hibernation

58 x 38cm (23 x 15in)

Autumnal composition. The details to the right show the textural effects I have used in this larger painting to add interest. The details show the use of crackle paste (top); leaf sculpting using real leaves in watercolour ground (middle) and sprinklings of gold bronzing powder (bottom). I will be showing you how to use these textural additions later in my book.

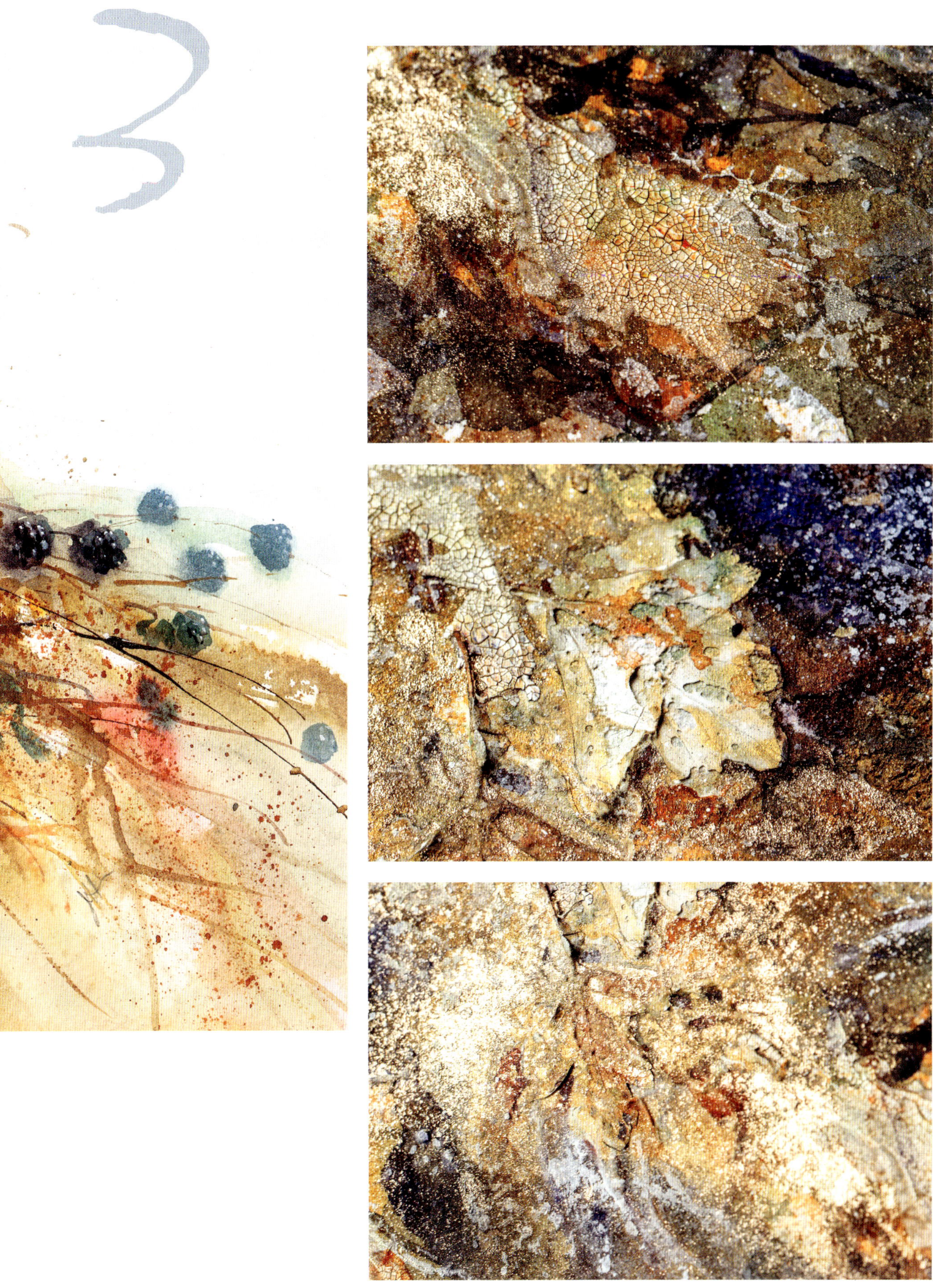

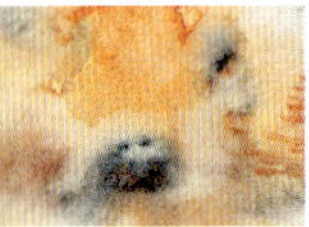

Step-by-step Hedgehog

From nose to prickles! I will demonstrate in this simple step-by-step how to mix colours on the paper, for vibrant results. For this simple hedgehog demonstration, you need just four watercolour shades and two brushes.

Materials

Surface: 300gsm (140lb) weight Not surface watercolour paper, 28 x 28cm (11 x 11in)

Brushes: size 10 round, rigger

Watercolour paints: quinacridone gold, quinacridone scarlet, Payne's blue gray, amethyst genuine

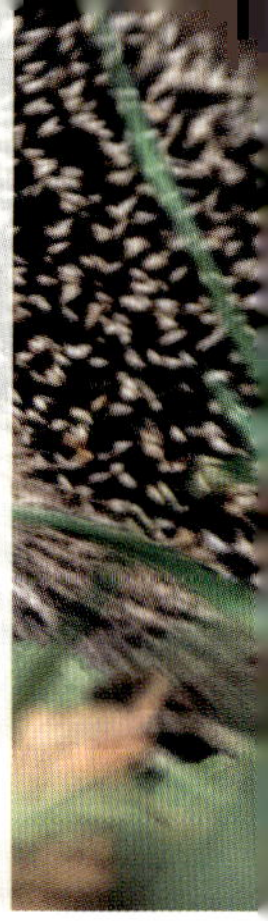

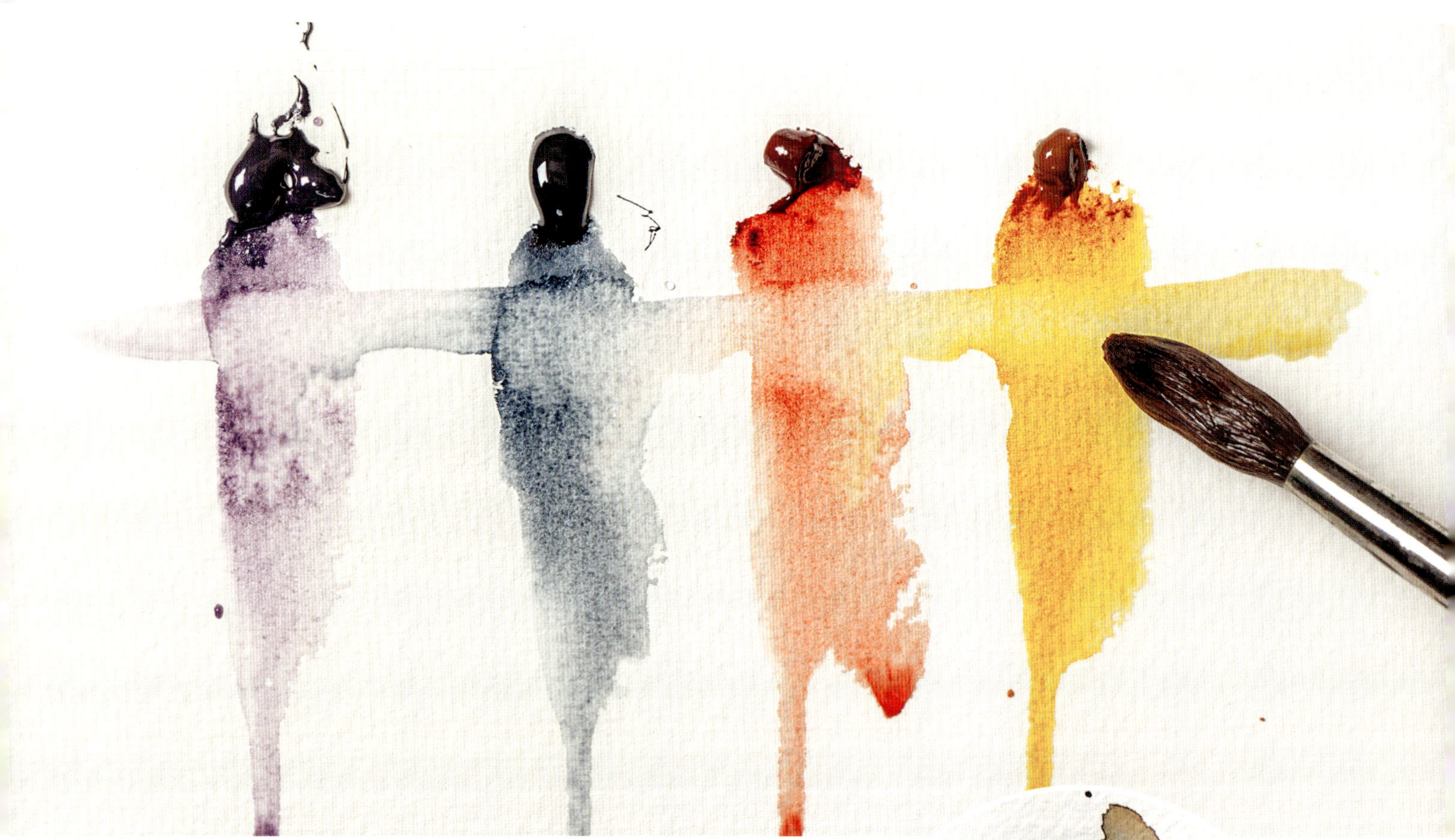

Dancing ladies: colour selection

For this hedgehog, I chose quinacridone gold and quinacridone scarlet to give me a variety of warm browns. I chose Payne's blue gray for the nose and dark eye sections and amethyst genuine as a purple to give me stunningly unique shadows.

Out of interest, I allowed all the colours to mix on my paper palette to show you how they create what is known as 'mud' when used this way! The last thing you want when working with watercolour is dull, flat, uninteresting colours, so always aim to allow your colours to mingle on your paper working surface naturally rather than trying to premix them.

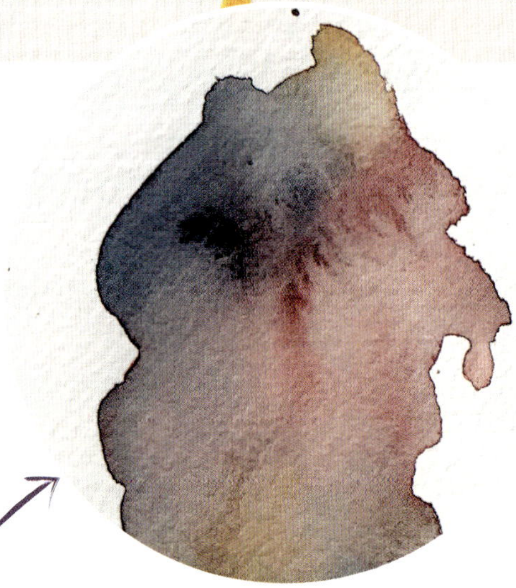

Horrid mud!

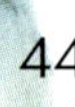

The face and nose

1 I start by painting a face shape for my hedgehog. This will be my starting point to work from. Using the size 10 round brush, I placed both the quinacridone gold and quinacridone burnt scarlet on the paper and allowed them to fuse – that is, to merge together naturally on paper.

2 While my pigment was still wet on my paper, I added a touch of Payne's blue gray to the base of the face to create the little nose. I deliberately add this colour while the paper is wet so that it will fuse with the previously applied colours and look soft, rather than as a hard, placed detail. Living things need to look as though they can move, so right from the beginning of this book, aiming to keep your work loose and atmospheric is so important.

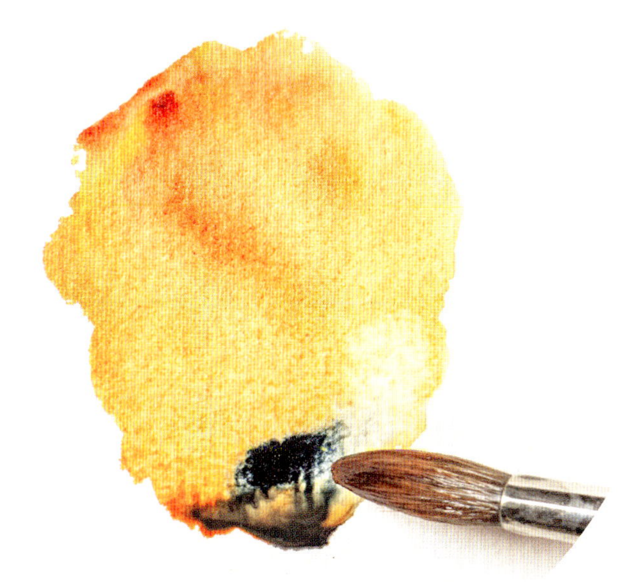

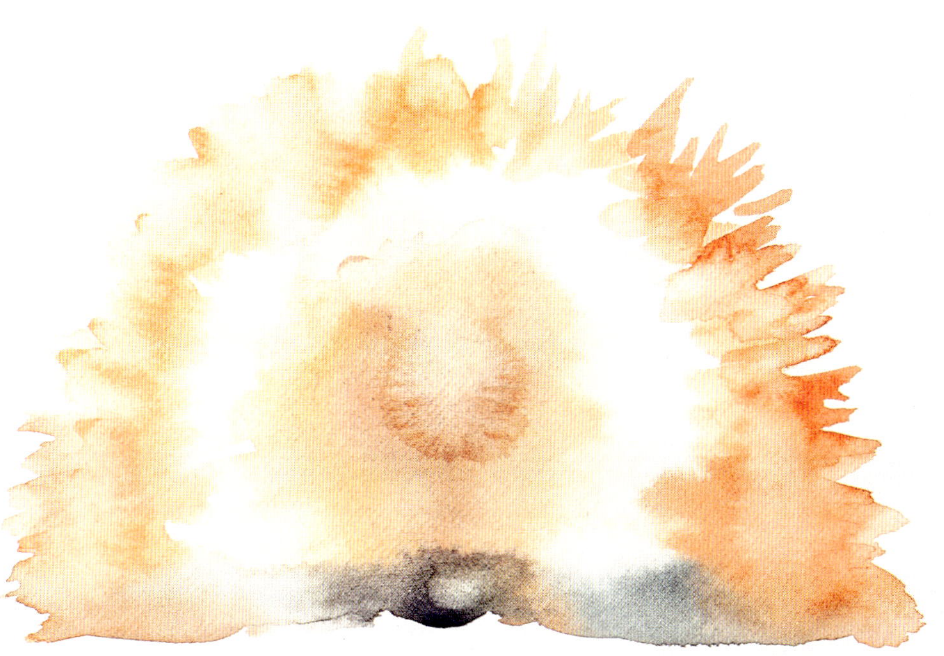

Adding the body

3 You can add the body to your hedgehog while the face section is still damp by bleeding colour away from the face. Use the side of the brush flat-on to the paper to drag colour in a direction; wherever you wish. Getting this initial shape right will be a huge asset as you progress further. Try to avoid adding detail at this early stage because this is just the foundation of your subject; the first base. These early soft stages will benefit you as an animal artist in that they can be adapted in future work as a technique for painting all kinds of animals. To recap: work from a starting point first and then build up your subject in a soft first wash shape.

Adding eyes, ears and grounding your subject

4 As your pigment starts to dry, add the eye and the ear using the point of the size 10 round brush and Payne's blue gray. Carefully study your source photographs of the animal when adding the facial features to ensure that they are in the correct places, and allow these newly added details to remain soft.

5 Next, place colour at the base of your subject and bleed it into the area below the hedgehog. This will create the illusion of it being a reflection. More importantly, it avoids having your subject looking as though it is floating on white paper.

6 Use your rigger to make sure that prickles are showing along the outline of your hedgehog. You will find that if you start painting the prickles on the body and lift your brush so that the tip leaves the paper last at the outer edge of the prickles, your lines will gradually taper to a fine point, as they should.

Hedgehog facts

Did you know that the hedgehog can eat poisonous plants? They are immune to certain flora and fauna, eating them to create a frothy saliva which they use to coat their spines by licking them. It is thought that this helps the hedgehog to hide its scent from predators and thus helps to keep it safe from harm!

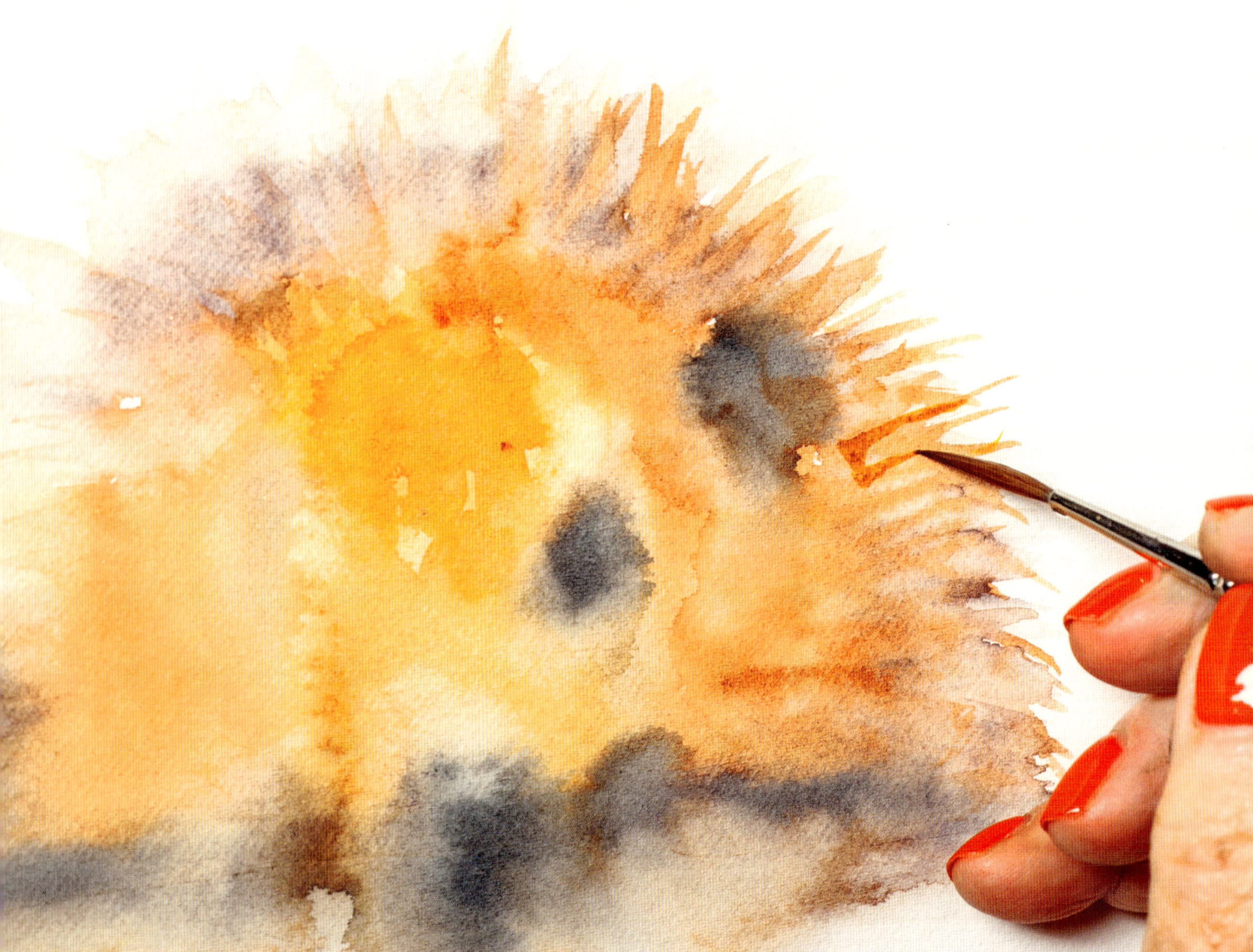

Putting it all together

Once you have experimented on scraps of paper, try using your newfound experience to paint another complete hedgehog. Allow watermarks to develop, as they will add interest to your completed painting. Leave sections missing, as these will give a sense of mystery and atmosphere to your work.

On this new painting go further with detail. In the example below, I strengthened the nose by adding more dark pigment. I added dark to the eye too but kept it soft rather than heavily detailed. I also added defined prickles.

On the next pages I will be looking at ways to use texture products to create patterns, but this very soft result is pleasing and a great start to painting in a loose style. Indeed, I prefer this image to the hedgehog paintings shown on the previous pages. We are all different and our tastes in art are unique. So, when you are creating, always paint in a way that pleases you. You are an artist and your choices on what to do next, how much detail to add (or how little) really are your own decision.

The more you paint, the more confidence you will have when making these choices. Remember that the hedgehog protects itself from negative forces. You too can learn to ignore doubts in your artistic ability, and you will then love painting animals still more. Have fun painting your hedgehogs and look for other spiny creatures to enjoy as new subjects.

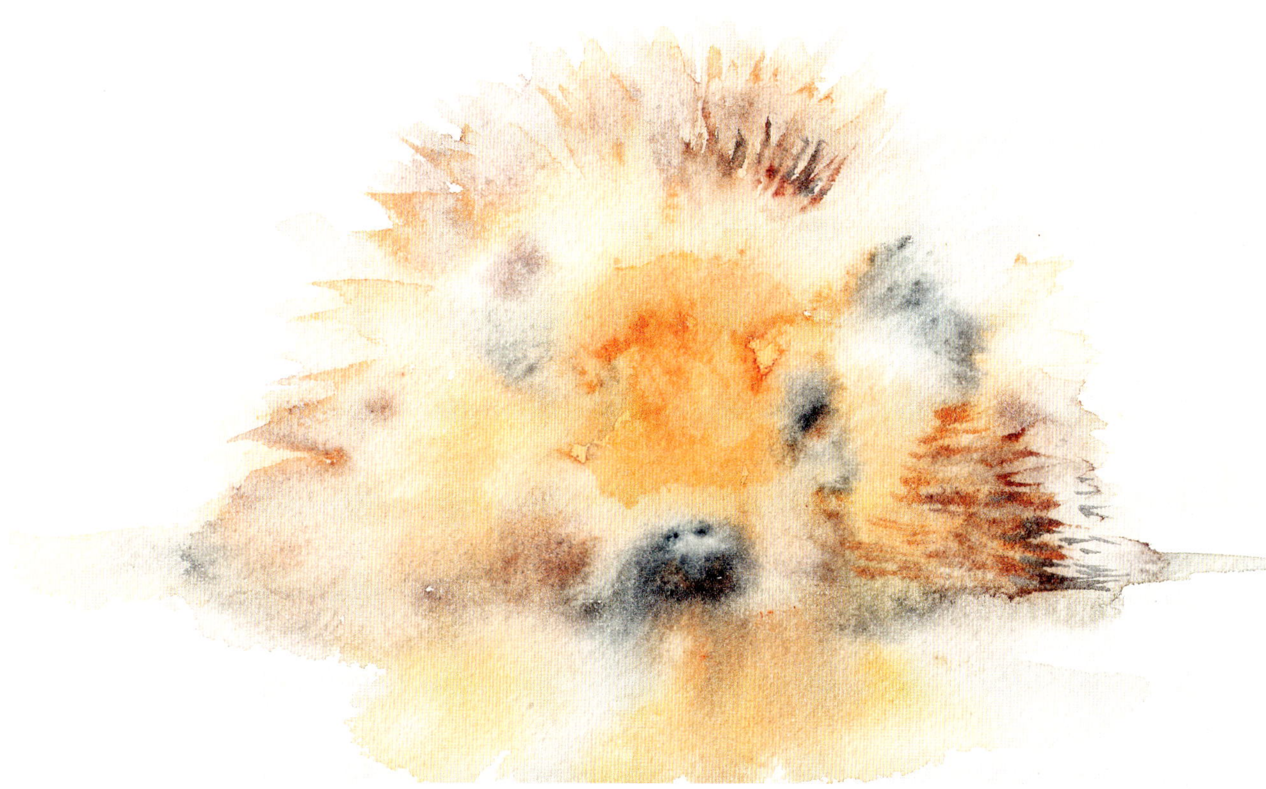

Hampshire Hog
38 x 38cm (15 x 15in)

Animal meaning: hedgehog
Appreciate the little things in life. Take time to enjoy life and always look for the positive with a calm approach.

Inspiration from nature

Homemade inks

I am constantly inspired by nature. Not just by finding subjects to paint, but also by the amazing range of textures and colour combinations that I see daily, and which influences my art; such as the ink cap mushrooms that grow in the autumn in the woodland section of our cottage garden.

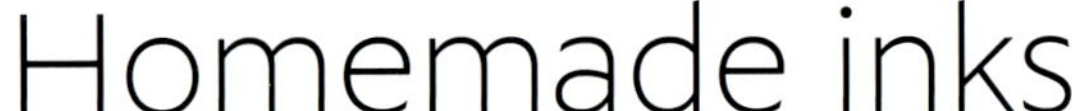

Reading about this variety of fungus led me to the magical value of homemade inks in art. This particular fungus, when left in a glass jar, will disintegrate to form a beautiful ink; an ink that was used for calligraphy purposes by monks in the past. I have now created my own mushroom ink very successfully and have enjoyed using it combined with my watercolour shades.

These homemade inks can be created using acorns, oak galls and many other treasures from nature. You can also create homemade inks from household ingredients such as turmeric, as seen on page 80, tea or coffee, and a variety of nuts. The list seems endless!

Mushroom ink is fascinating in that, when combined with other homemade products such as my homemade granulation fluid, amazing patterns occur. I give details on how to make my homemade granulation fluid on page 105 and the results from using it can be seen in my octopus and giraffe paintings in my book. However, what I have found the most fascinating is that the patterns that I'm creating now are very different from anything I have ever seen in any form of watercolour before.

This was all purely by experimenting, not accepting that everything has been discovered, and playing with natural ingredients.

Autumn Treasure
28 x 38cm (11 x 15in)

Be safe

Please remember that some fungus varieties are toxic and can make you extremely ill. Use gloves or wash your hands thoroughly after touching them.

Homemade ink recipes

I appreciate that not everyone has access to wild fungi, but shop-bought mushrooms can be useful in creating inks as they still give you great colour. Many homemade ink recipes simply involve boiling the selected ingredients in a small amount of water until the natural colour appears – as seen in the image of oak galls in an old saucepan here.

Rust ink can be made by filling a jar with rusty nails and similar iron objects, topping it up with a little vinegar, and leaving it to develop. You can try making colours from staining fruits too.

Once made, I leave my homemade ink substances to develop for a period of months, as the colours seem to intensify the longer they are left before use.

I cannot recommend highly enough the value of taking time out to unearth your own discoveries. It's worth noting that all these colours are staining, so need to be used with caution. Some are not lightfast when used alone in paper. I find ink and granulation combinations work best.

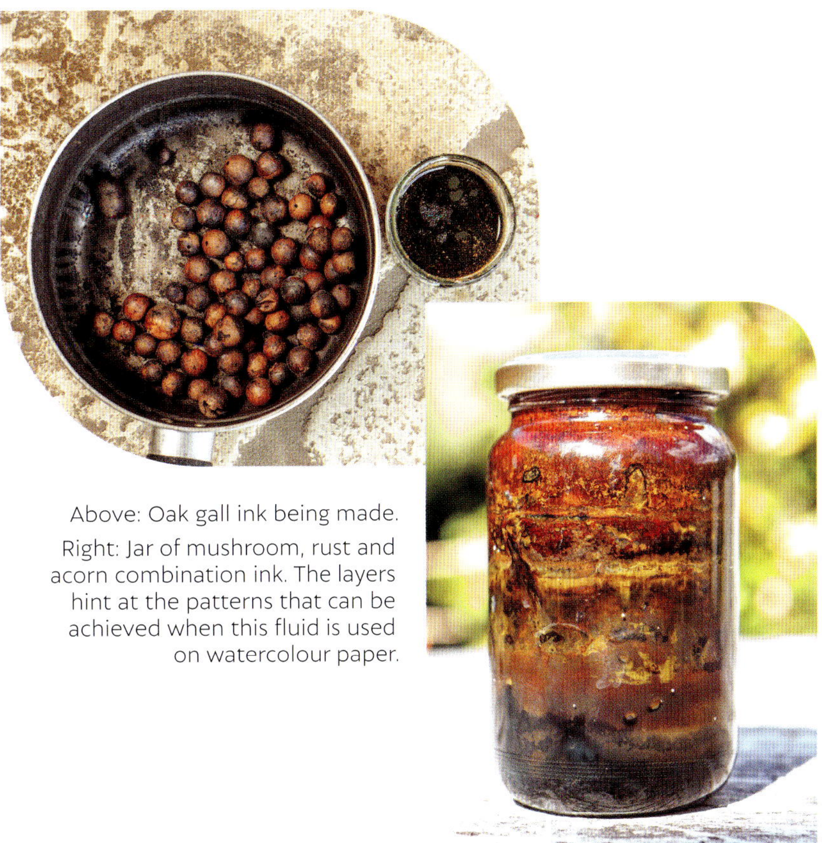

Above: Oak gall ink being made.

Right: Jar of mushroom, rust and acorn combination ink. The layers hint at the patterns that can be achieved when this fluid is used on watercolour paper.

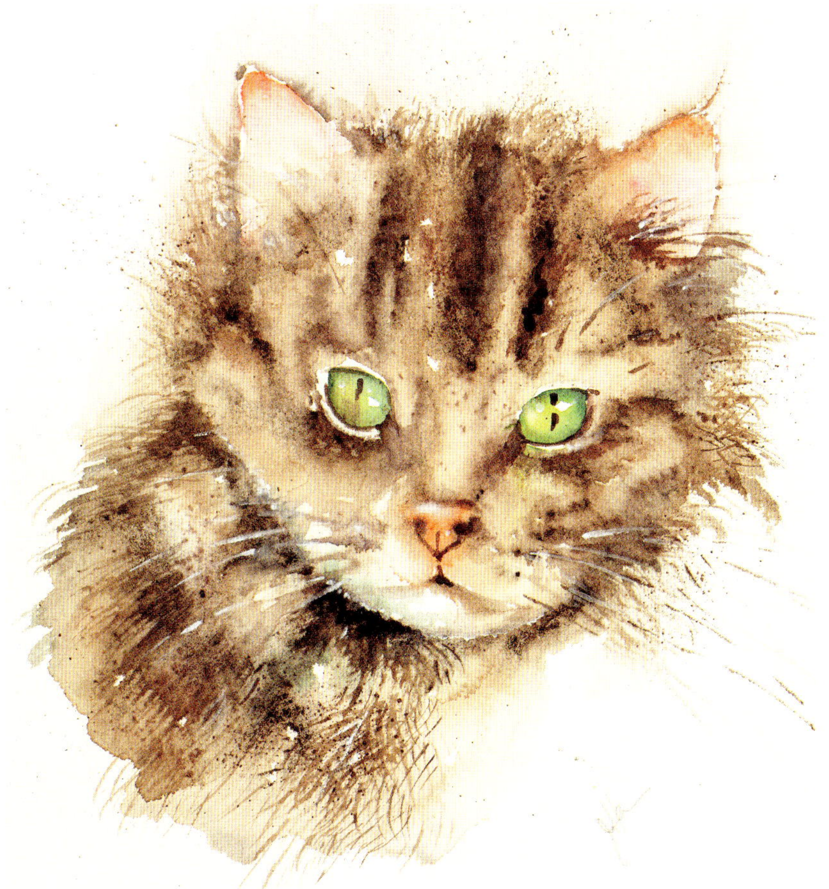

Green Eyes
38 x 38cm (15 x 15in)

Making your own inks and colours is far easier than it sounds. Mushrooms gathered from my garden gave me this beautiful colour, which was perfect for my subject.

Texture effects from nature

The texture on the ink cap mushrooms fascinated me so much that I was puzzled as to how to recreate this appearance in my art. After experimenting first, I developed a way to apply watercolour ground and then work with cocktail sticks to form the patterns that I could see in the fungi. Once I had created this pattern, I quickly realized that it could be used for fur and many other animals, as seen in my demonstration below.

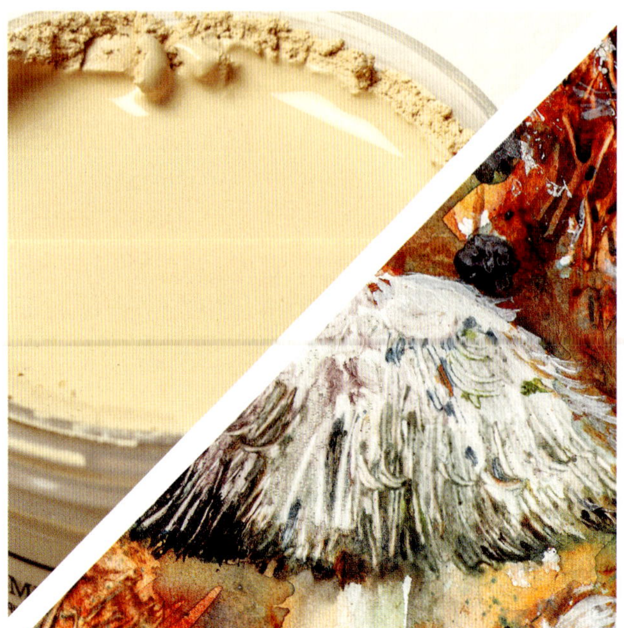

Watercolour ground

Watercolour ground is a fluid paste that can be applied to almost any surface to make it suitable to paint upon with watercolours. As it dries, it can be subtly shaped. Watercolour ground is available in different colours.

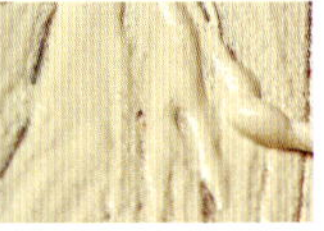

How-to use cocktail sticks and watercolour ground

By using items to create patterns in the surface of the watercolour ground once it has been applied, you can create amazing patterns. You can use any small sticks or even the handle of an old brush. You can pull string through the surface if you wish. Below is just one suggestion of how to create texture effects for animals.

Materials

Surface: scrap of 300gsm (140lb) weight Not surface watercolour paper

Other: buff titanium watercolour ground, palette knife, cocktail stick, burnt umber ink

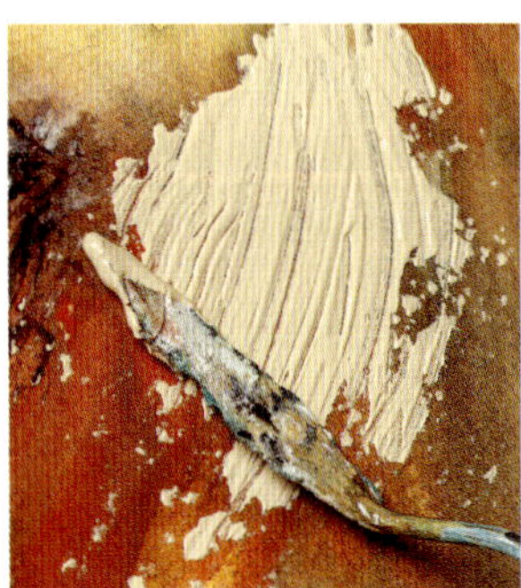

1 Use a palette knife to apply the watercolour ground straight from the pot. Apply it in curving strokes to represent longer fur.

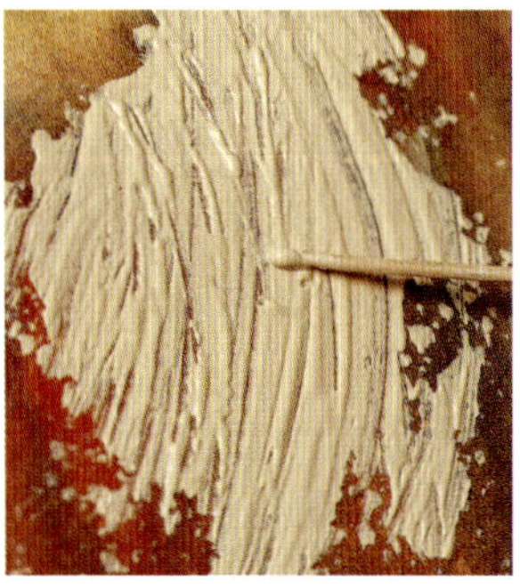

2 While it is wet, draw a cocktail stick through the ground, re-emphasizing the curve and adding the suggestion of detail.

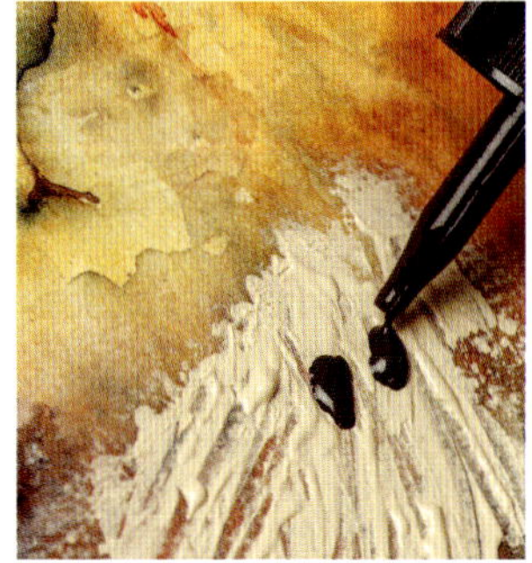

3 Use the dropper in the lid of the ink bottle to apply ink near the top of the curved area.

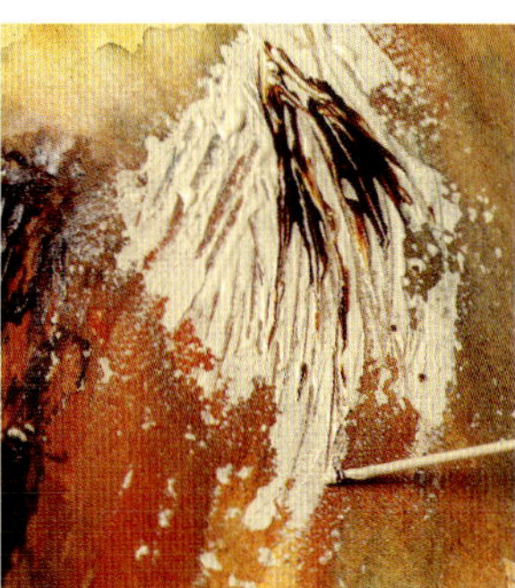

4 Draw the ink through the ground with the cocktail stick to encourage the ink and ground to interact, then leave to dry.

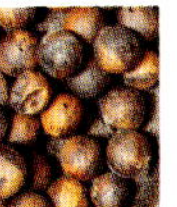
How-to use ink as watercolour

Homemade inks can be great fun to use, especially for the artist who likes to explore and experiment. You do need to be aware that your results will vary each time you use homemade products – but this makes using them far more exciting.

Materials

Surface: scrap of 300gsm (140lb) weight Not surface watercolour paper
Brushes: size 10 round
Other: homemade inks

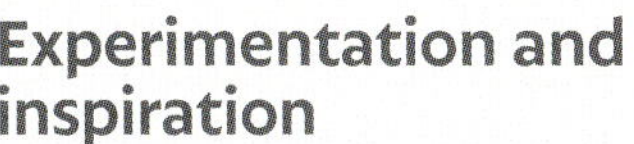

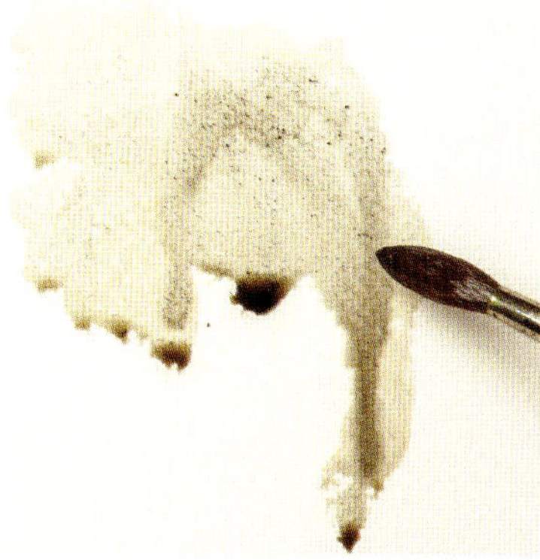

Inks can be applied with a brush, exactly like watercolours. Try the elephant in monochrome exercise on pages 34–35 again, this time using your own homemade ink.

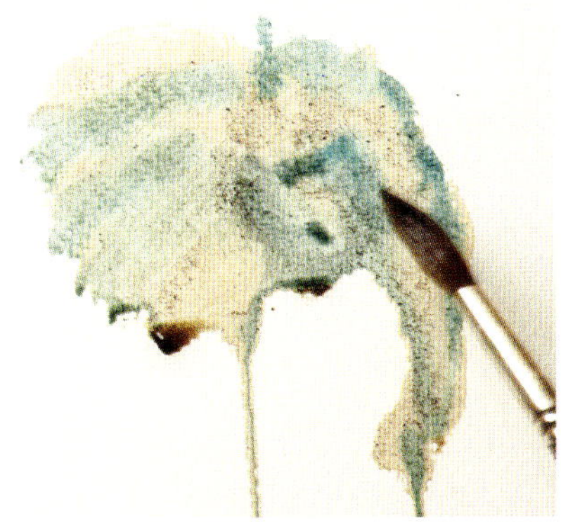

Inks can also be combined safely with watercolours. In fact, this will often create wonderful new effects to explore.

Experimentation and inspiration

So many animals have beautiful patterns and texture effects that intrigue us as artists. Throughout my book I hope to inspire you to find different ways of creating them.

Lionfish study

28 x 28cm (11 x 11in)

Homemade ink and watercolour. This study was inspired by the lionfish's incredible patterns.

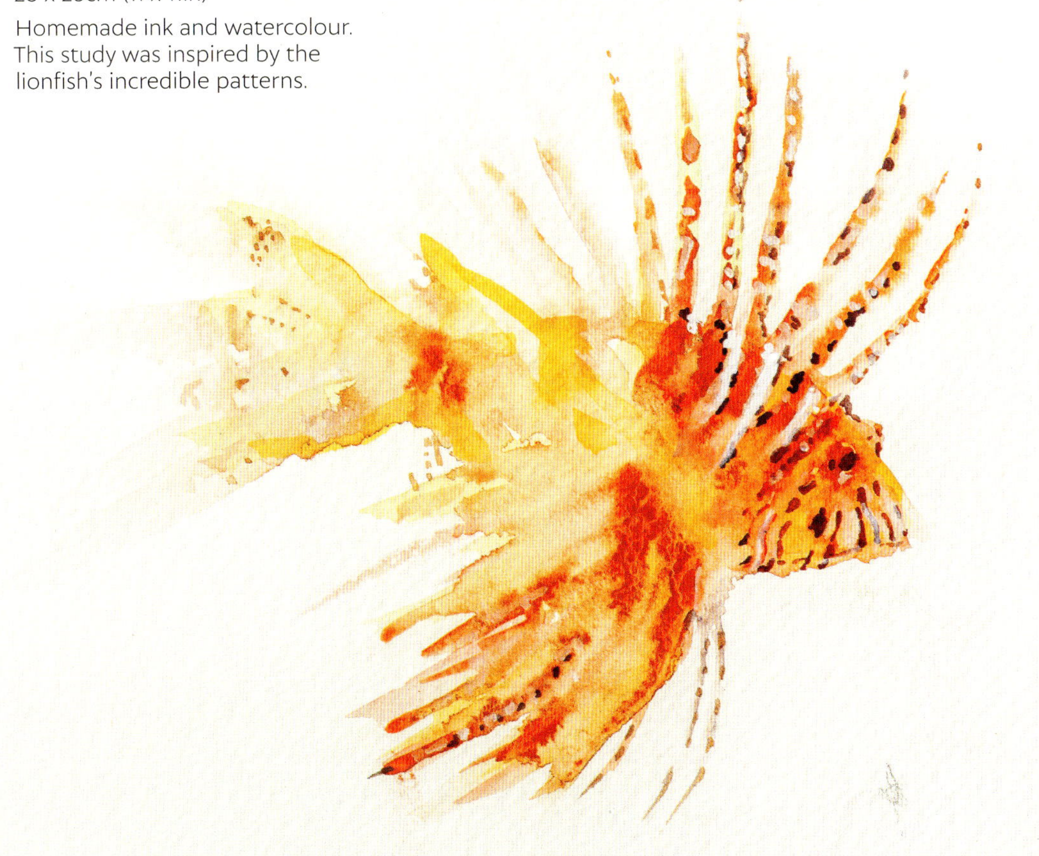

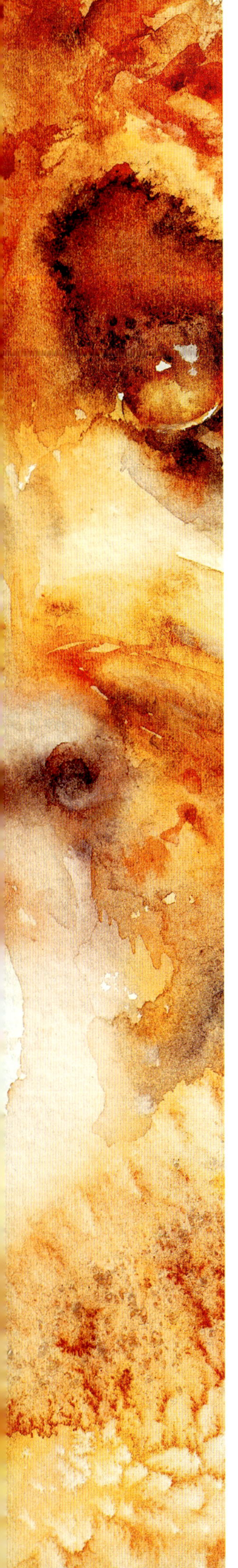

For the love of dogs

I COULDN'T POSSIBLY WRITE A BOOK about painting animals in watercolour and not include a section on painting our four-legged best friends. The problem for me is that there are so many delightful breeds and rescues that painting them all really requires a whole new book on this subject alone! Here, then, I will show you some great tips to painting our tail-wagging best friends and you can adapt my techniques to creating as many special fur friends as you wish.

Small stages: noses

Let's start by explaining that when painting animals, we are trying to convey their personality and character. The eyes are particularly important for this, and we are covering those in the next chapter. For now, however, I want you to consider breaking down each subject into tiny segments that you get right first before attempting to paint the whole thing. From the minute you start painting animals from my book, consider what sections you will be leaving out, and I will guide you with each animal we cover in each new chapter.

For dogs, I would like you to begin by studying their noses. Studying the nose of any animal is very valuable, so try to get a collection of pictures of noses in different sizes and colours, and begin painting a few to get them right.

Animal meaning: dog

Dogs are said to represent love, loyalty, faithfulness and reliability. In many ways they remind us to be true to ourselves and to connect with our inner feelings when we create: to love what we are doing and be passionate about it.

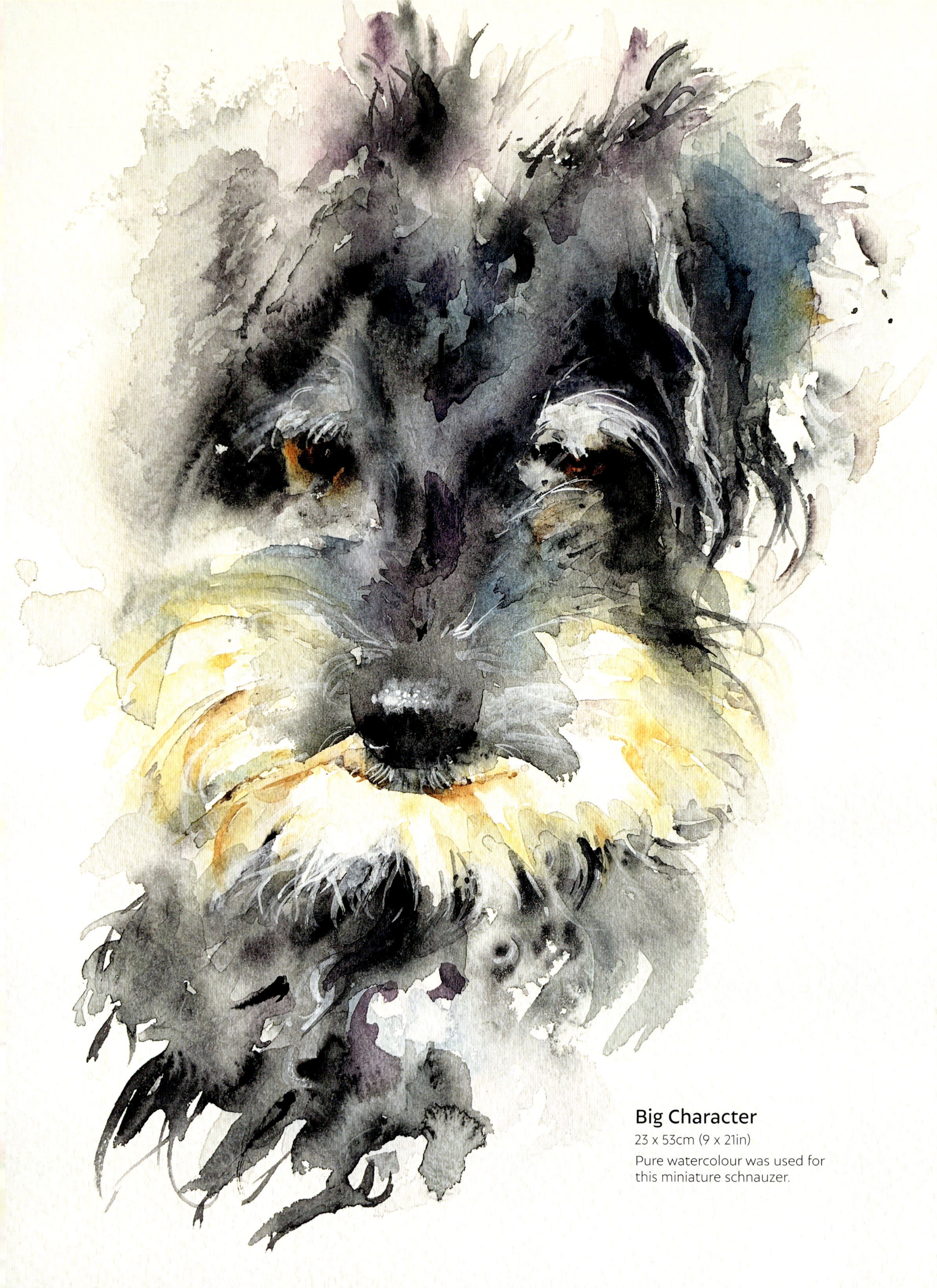

Big Character
23 x 53cm (9 x 21in)
Pure watercolour was used for
this miniature schnauzer.

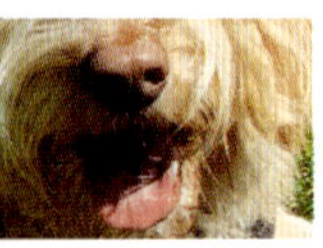

How-to paint a dog's nose

As explained on the previous page, I always find a starting point in all my subjects and practise until I get it absolutely right before I move on to paint the whole subject. Here we look at the shape, colour and detail to capture a good dog's nose.

Dogs' noses are very varied in colour, but a very good tip is to avoid using black, which can give you a very flat, dull result. I always opt for a shade such as Payne's blue gray (as in this example) to add a sense of life to my work and youth to my painted subject.

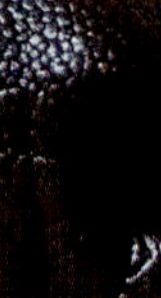

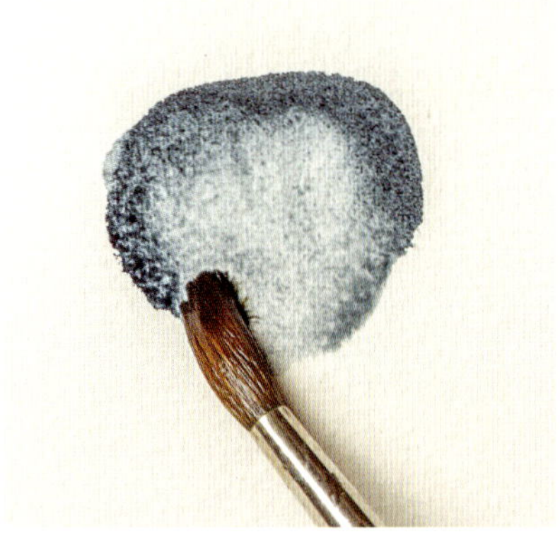

1 I begin by painting a rough heart shape with the size 10 round brush, and Payne's blue gray paint. Use plenty of water to ensure that the inside is lighter in tone than the edges.

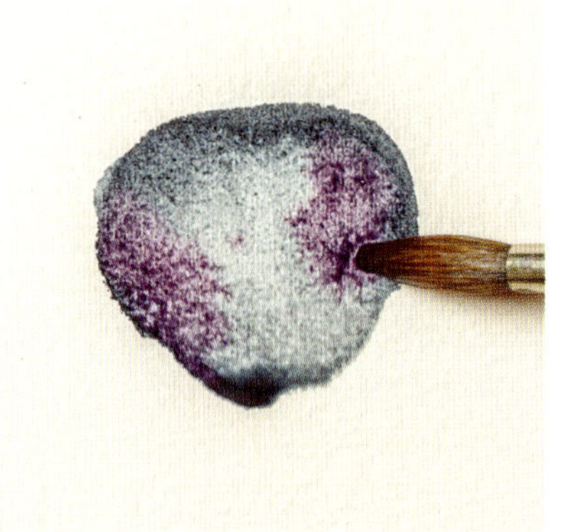

2 Add a second colour for interest if you wish. Here I added amethyst genuine to develop the sense of tone and shape.

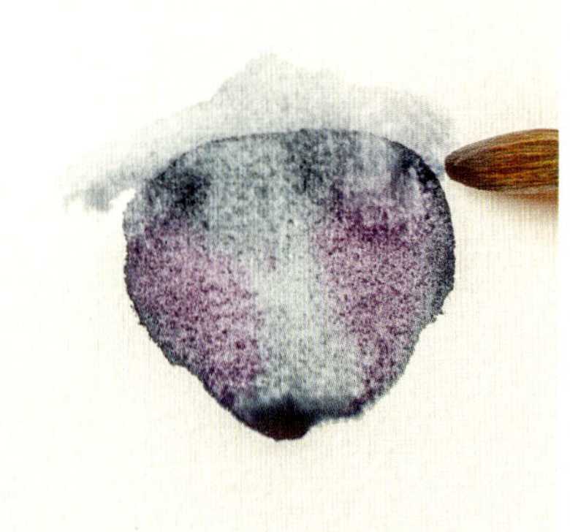

3 While the paint remains wet, soften the top middle section of the nose – where soft fur separates the nose from the face – by adding clean water.

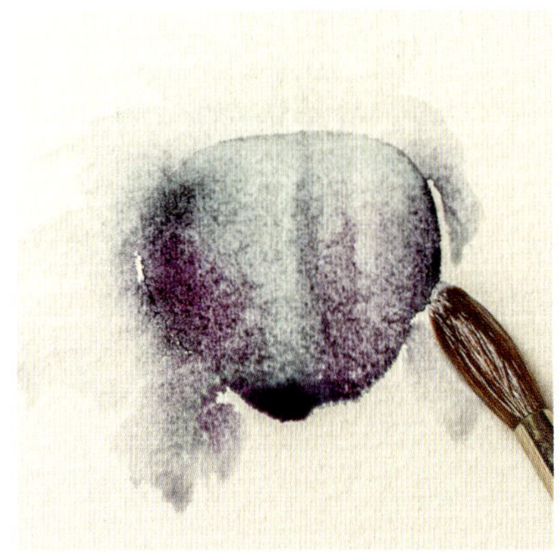

4 Using clean water, soften sections around the nose to hint at the surrounding fur. Leave some gaps of dry paper to ensure that the shape is not completely lost.

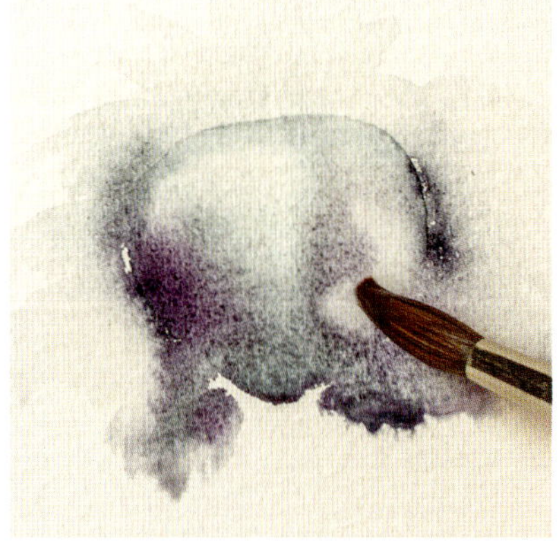

5 With a curved stroke of the brush, lift out some of the paint from the lower right, to suggest a soft highlight.

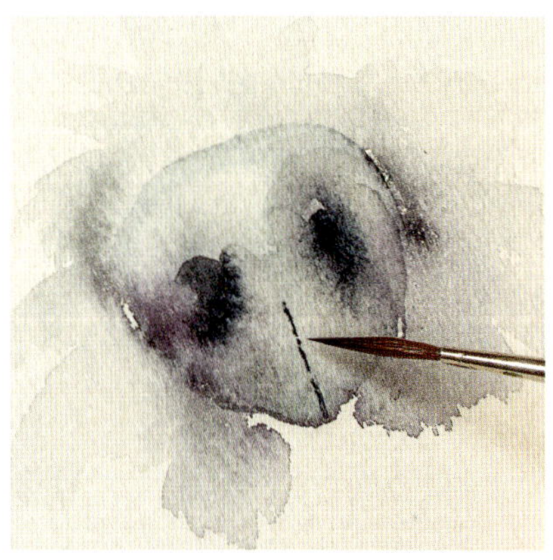

6 Once the initial wash is dry, add detail with the rigger – but not too much. Leaving out sections is what gives us a gorgeous atmospheric result.

Painting from close-up images

The collection of dogs' noses to the right highlights how different from each other they are in shape and colouring. The images are so clear that it is easy for me to paint from them. These are the kind of images you need for all your animal subjects to create great paintings. Collect great eyes, noses and fur close-ups as often as you can and build a great variety, so that your work is always improving over time.

By trying out different colours I can gain a more interesting result, as you can see in the studies below right. From the very beginning of your journey in painting animals, take this tip and remember it well: always add tiny touches of unexpected colours to bring your paintings to life. The hints of turquoise and pink certainly liven up what could be a dull, plain black or pink nose. And the aim of my book isn't for you to paint boring watercolours!

Note how I haven't painted defined outlines around any of the noses in the studies. Colours are allowed to merge and form patterns as they do so. Watermarks give me the best effects. Rather than trying to control watercolour as a medium, I work with it, giving it the freedom to form as many patterns as it wishes to. To me, this is the beauty of working in watercolour.

Dog nose studies

These examples of dogs' noses in watercolour are all painted on Rough surface paper, which gives me an added textural effect.

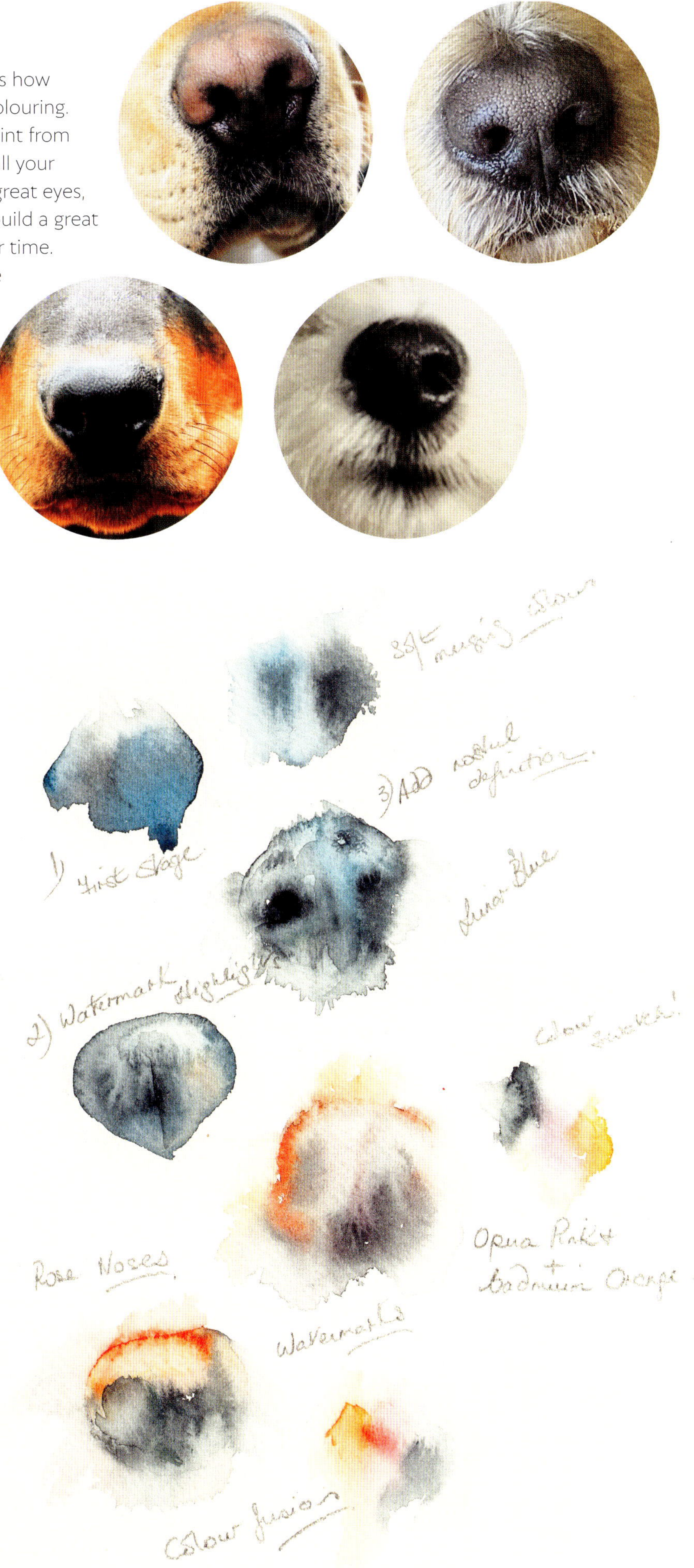

Finding the right subject

Sniffing out the perfect subject for you

As said earlier, before you even consider painting any animal, you need to completely fall in love with your subject. Look for a dog that really appeals to you for your painting. I have created a very simplified portrait to help you get started.

Simplify

If you look at the image on this page, you will see my very loose interpretation of a bearded collie puppy. This is my dog Bailey, who was with us for over thirteen years and was a very well-loved character.

To begin this painting, I began by painting the nose as described earlier. I then measured the distance around the nose to start adding black fur around one side of his cute face. I worked in a diagonal line to create the ear next and left some white fur under the chin to hint at the chest segment.

There is very little in this painting. It definitely carries the 'less is more' motto of my style very well. When aiming to create atmospheric animals in watercolour it is vital to lose as much detail as possible. Only paint enough to show what the subject is – and stop as soon as you feel you can see your chosen dog appearing.

The final details here included adding white gouache on the nose to give it a feeling of being shiny and wet. This is, after all, a healthy young pup! If you look closely at the grey pigment in this painting, you should see beautiful granulation. This is created by the shade I used, Daniel Smith's moonglow. There are many pigments that form patterns this way and they can really add impact to your results, so do take time to learn about them.

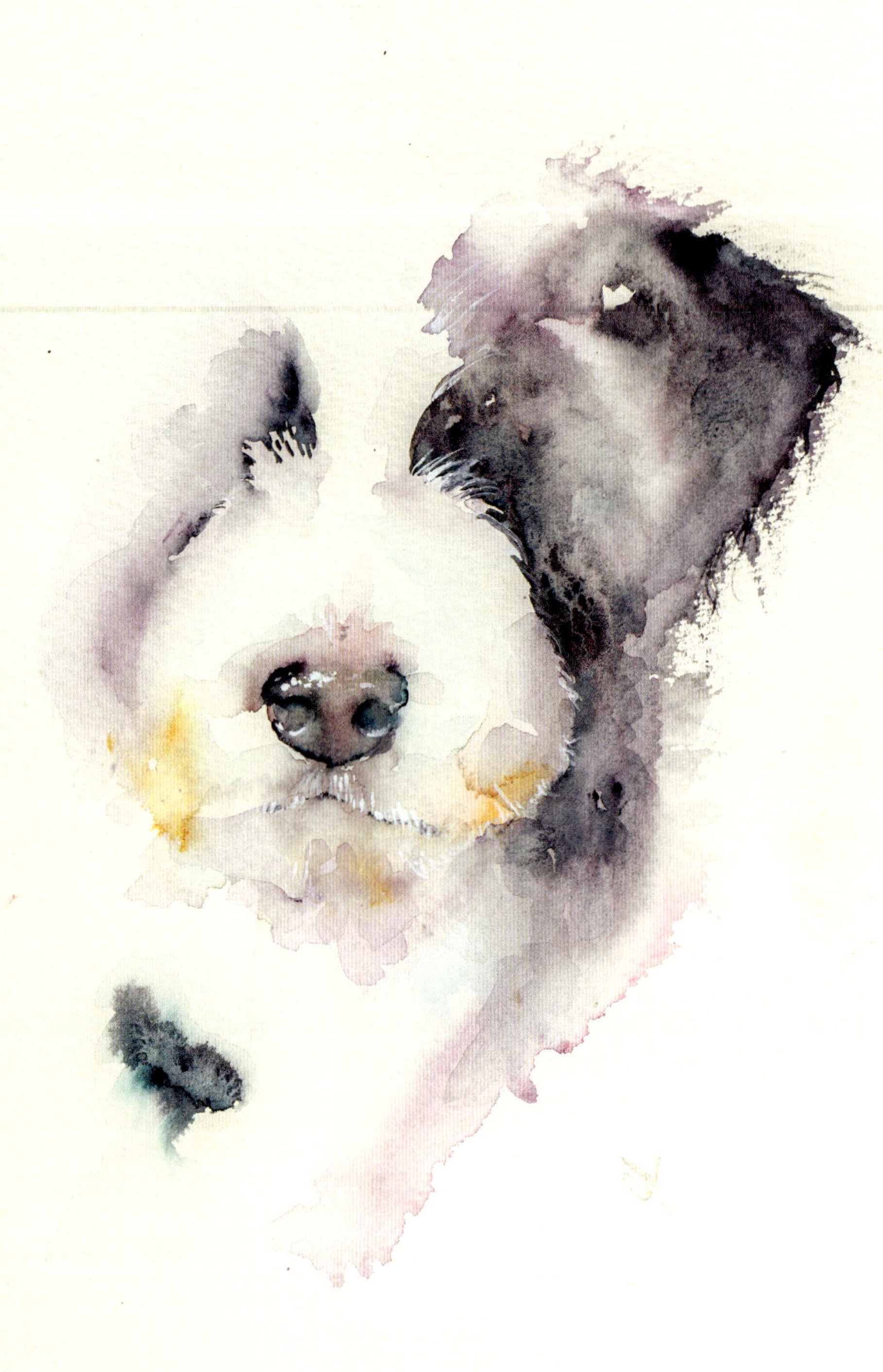

Sweet Pup
28 x 38cm (11 x 15in)

Missing information

Experiment by painting half a face, starting with a dog's nose and then adding the ear on one side of the face as seen in my image, *Sweet Pup*. This will help you to begin to see how leaving sections out of a painting can create interest in your work.

Once you have painted several half faces of different breeds try adding a body to your subject, as shown below, while leaving sections to the viewer's imagination. I call this my disconnection technique.

Building up to a full painting

Once you have painted several half faces of different breeds, you can move on to painting a whole dog. Stay focussed on painting only half of a dog. The idea is to lose the pencil gradually, so that you aren't working with a preliminary sketch.

As before, begin by painting the nose first. Next, add the fur around the muzzle section, taking it up to the ears. Keep one ear darker in tone so it looks as though the pup could move its head at any moment. Lose some outline edges by applying clean water while the paint is wet, to keep the edges soft and interesting.

Once the face is complete you can begin to add hints of the body. Here, I took the dark fur down towards the white legs, hinted at one hind leg and left the remainder to the viewer's imagination.

Also consider this. In a good painting that is created in a loose style, often an impressionistic approach leads to amazing and unique results.

It takes time to create a really good dog in watercolour. Learning how to use watercolour as a medium and learning about the colours available enhances our work, so do take time to study your subjects, your selected materials and your techniques. Take small steps to begin with and in no time at all you will be painting characters like those seen here and on the following pages.

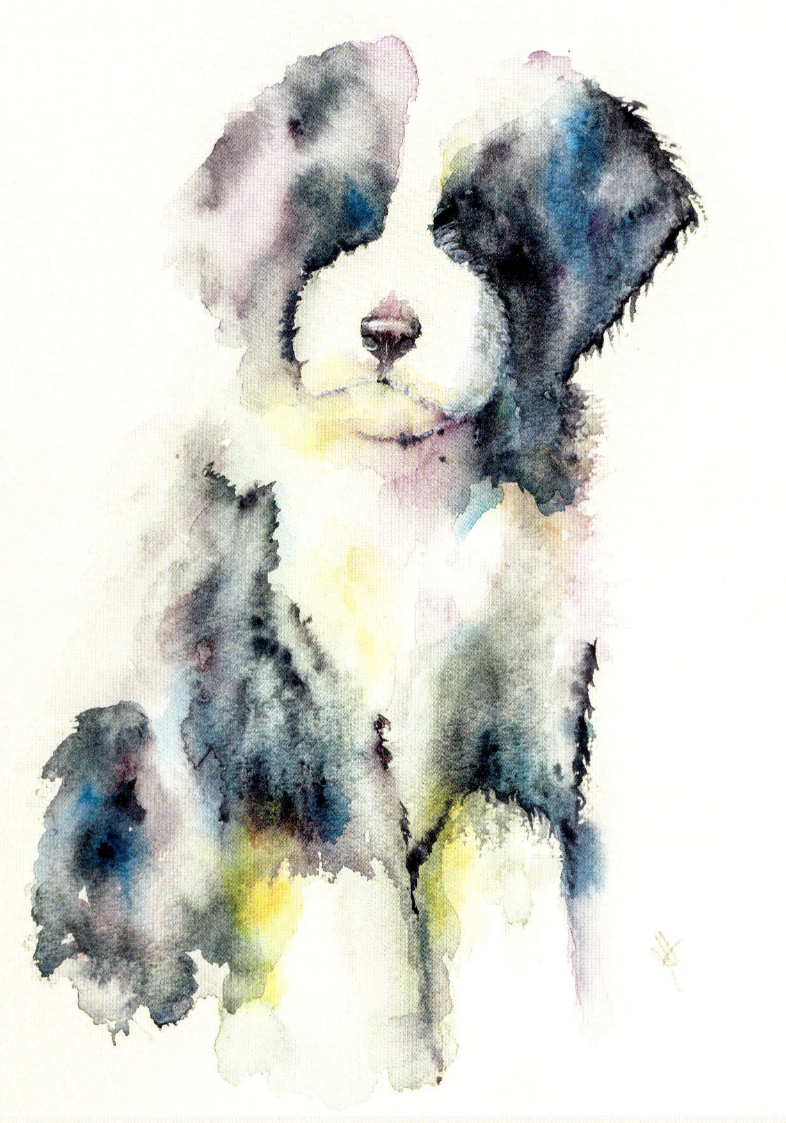

Good Boy

28 x 38cm (11 x 15in)

Bailey in watercolour. Notice the outlines of my sitting pup. Many sections are blurred or missing. This adds to the sense of this being an atmospheric painting.

Black and white simplicity

Following the theme of painting in black and white, now is a great time to introduce another favourite animal subject in watercolour: the giant panda. My painting was created in exactly the same way as my bearded collie puppy (see page 56), although here I began with the eye rather than the nose. I worked around my starting point and gradually built up my painting. I stopped as soon as I could see a soft impressionistic panda emerging.

Animal meaning: panda

Besides representing good luck, the panda is said to have connections with positivity and patience, which are both wonderful assets if we wish to be successful artists. It's also said to represent peace. What better subject could there be to paint in the animal kingdom? We all need patience when learning new skills and a positive approach when painting new subjects.

Simply Black and White
38 x 38cm (15 x 15in)

Capturing mood, personality and movement

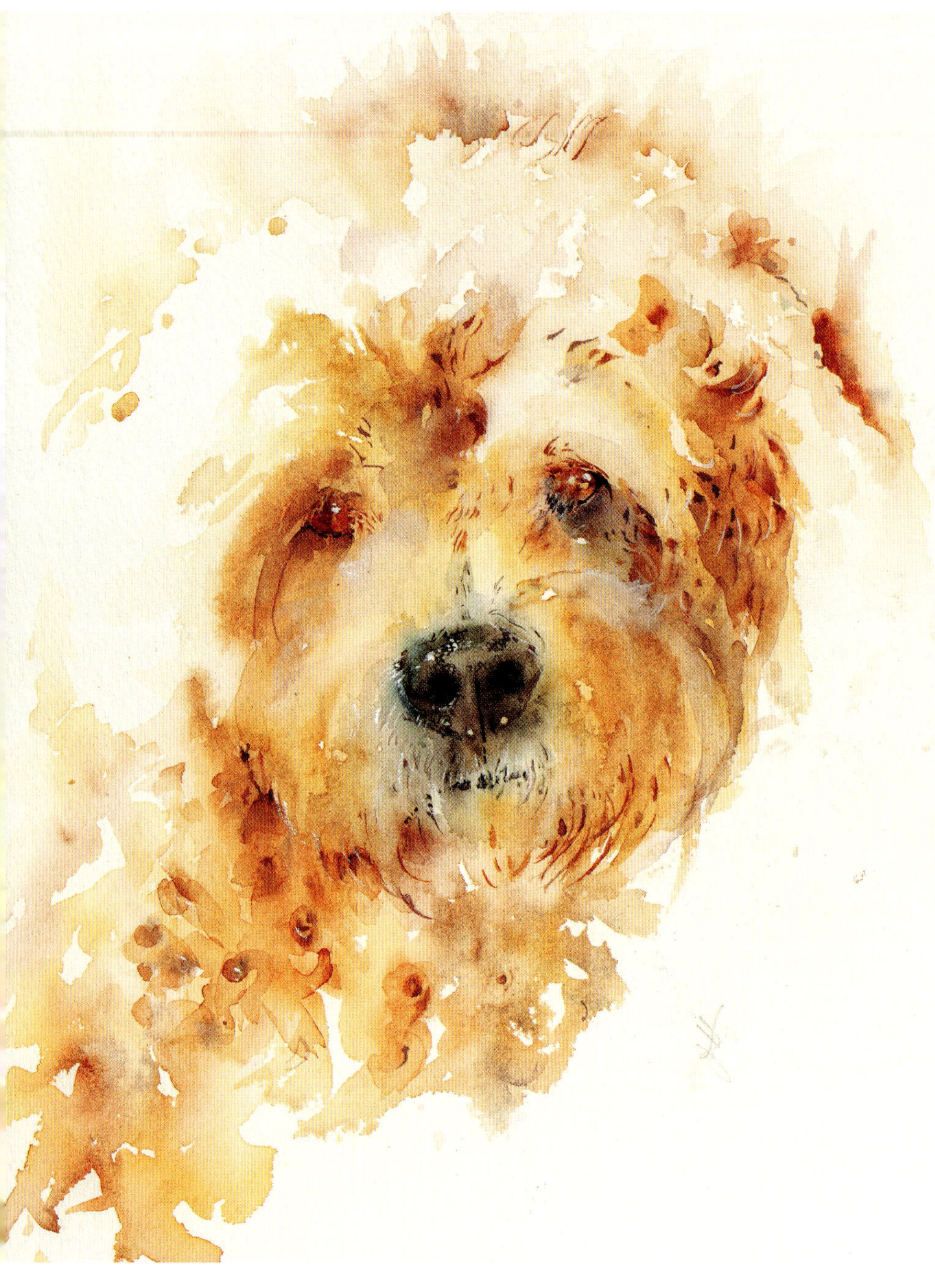

In these two dog portraits you can see examples of very different poses. The golden doodle is sitting patiently looking at its owner. I have used circular brushwork to hint at the curly fur in places. I have painted a negative edge around the outline of the head and over one ear, on one side only. White paper acts as oxygen to a composition, allowing the subject to breathe. Always aim to leave some white space in your work if you really want to gain a great atmospheric result.

Compare the brushwork of the two dogs. One dog has windswept hair as it has been racing around energetically. It is a very happy dog and its expression shows that it is enjoying life to the full. It's an active dog compared with the beautiful and very much adored doodle dog.

Coda
38 x 58cm (15 x 23in)
Golden doodle.

"A dog is the only thing on earth that loves you more than he loves himself." Josh Billings

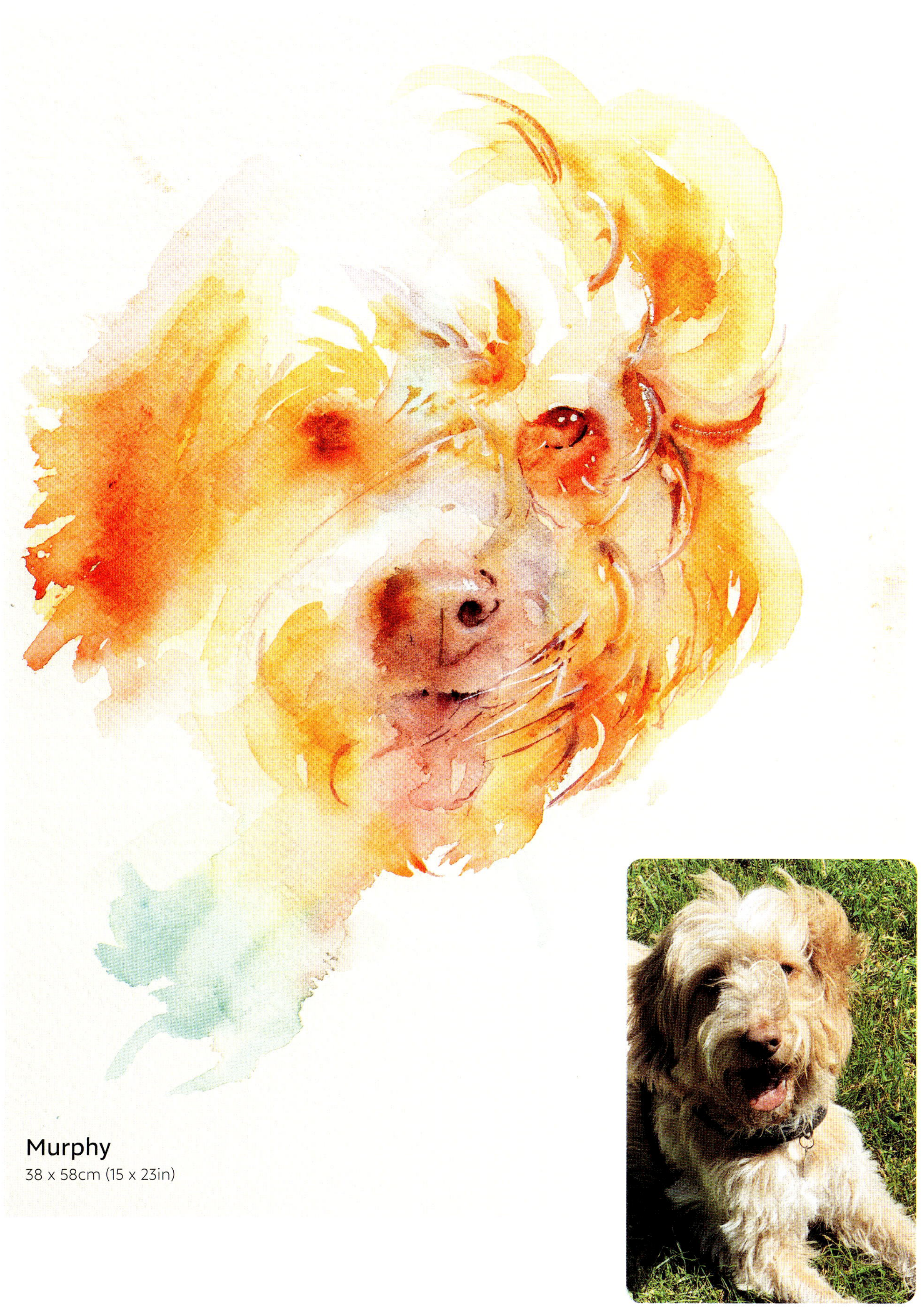

Murphy
38 x 58cm (15 x 23in)

Capturing expression

To close this chapter, I want to share an example of how 'less is more' in an atmospheric painting. This can be seen in my watercolour of Bryn, a working Welsh spaniel that was looking intently at treats when I took his photograph. His concentration shines in my result.

"Be the person your dog thinks you are." C.J. Frick

Dogs are fun to paint. They are lovable, trusting and so enriching to our lives as companions. Try to get all those feelings across when you paint your dogs. Take your time getting every feature in the right place: practise noses, eyes and then half faces before attempting whole dogs.

On the facing page are a selection of my dog paintings and photographs, to show what is possible, and to serve as inspiration for your own paintings.

The tips that you see over the next few chapters will have you creating gorgeous watercolours very soon. Read on to the chapter on cats, where we look at the importance of eyes to an animal painting – but before we do, let's paint a beautiful dog portrait using what we've learnt so far.

Bryn
38 x 58cm (15 x 23in)

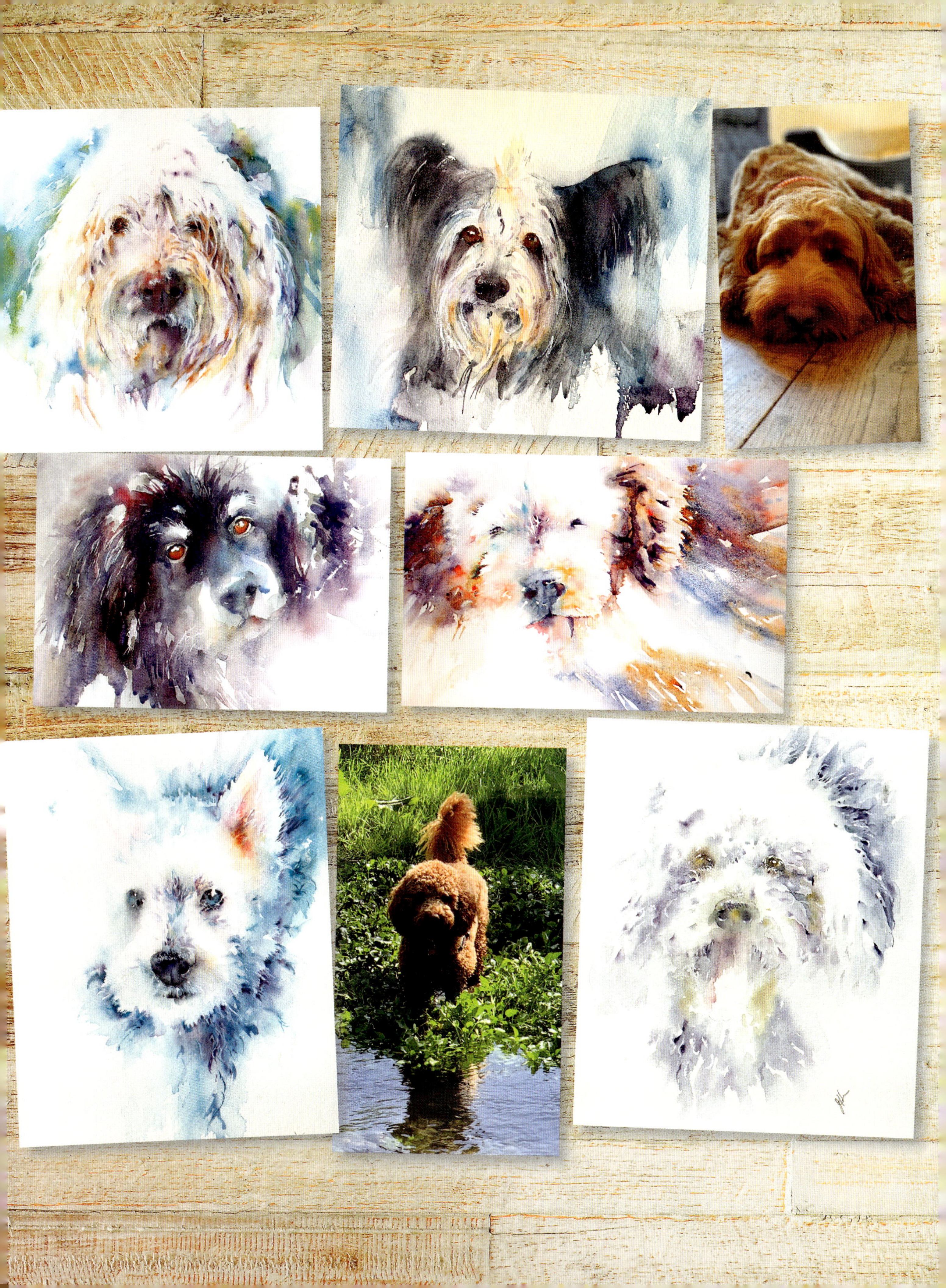

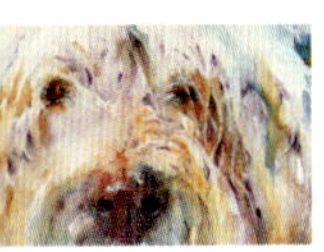

Step-by-step Italian Spinone: Humphrey

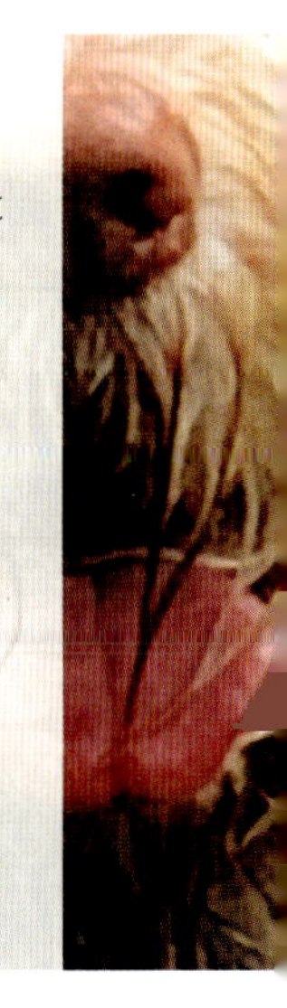

I have chosen this charming subject for my step-by-step because this dog has so much character. Choose a breed that captures your heart when painting dogs and always try to paint from a superb resource photograph. I always take my own photographs of pets so that I can get to know the animal before I attempt capturing them in watercolour. Once you have chosen your model, work through a dancing ladies exercise to help you choose the colours you feel would be the most suitable.

Working from a starting point without a preliminary sketch is a fabulous technique, and one we explore in this project. For this subject a wonderful large nose was the main focal point for my attention, and this is where I started.

Materials

Surface: 300gsm (140lb) weight Not surface watercolour paper, 28 x 28cm (11 x 11in)

Brushes: size 10 round, rigger

Watercolour paints: quinacridone gold, amethyst genuine, moonglow, Payne's blue gray, phthalo blue-turquoise, opera pink, lunar blue, quinacridone burnt scarlet

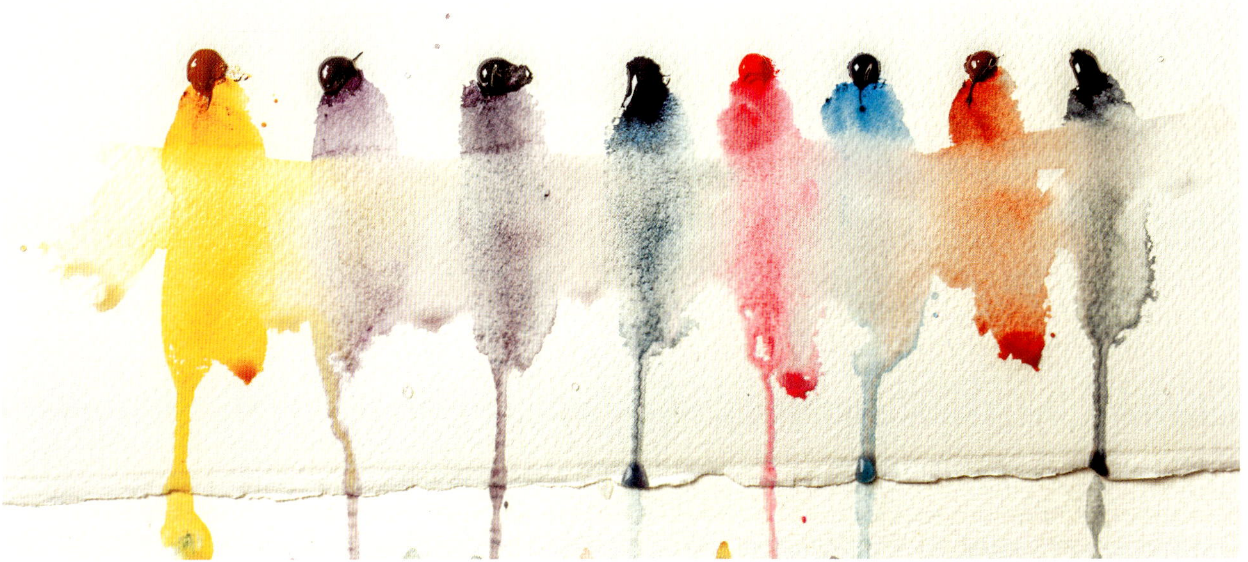

Dancing ladies: colour selection

I studied my model before choosing these colours. I chose quinacridone gold to add warmth to the fur and quinacridone burnt scarlet gave me a glowing dark for the eyes. Amethyst genuine was perfect to add shadows. Phthalo blue turquoise was perfect as a background colour for a white subject. Supporting these, I added opera pink, moonglow, and lunar blue. Think about your whole composition when preselecting your shades.

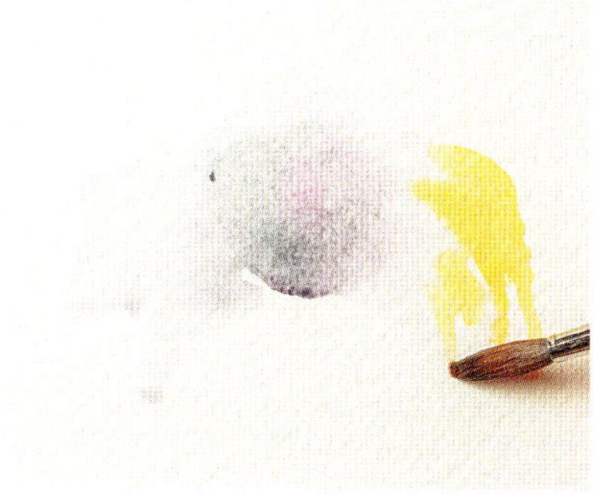

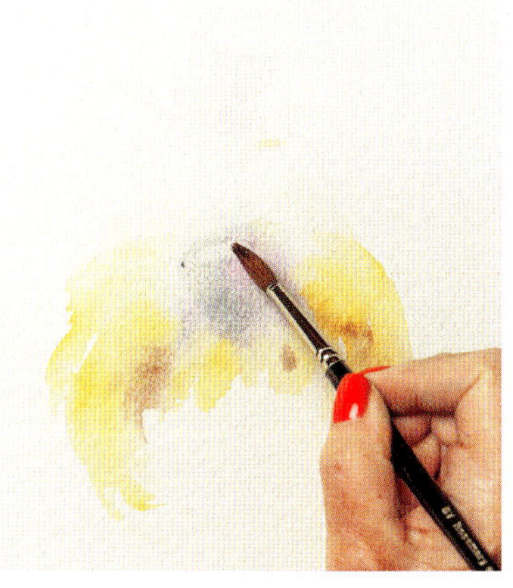

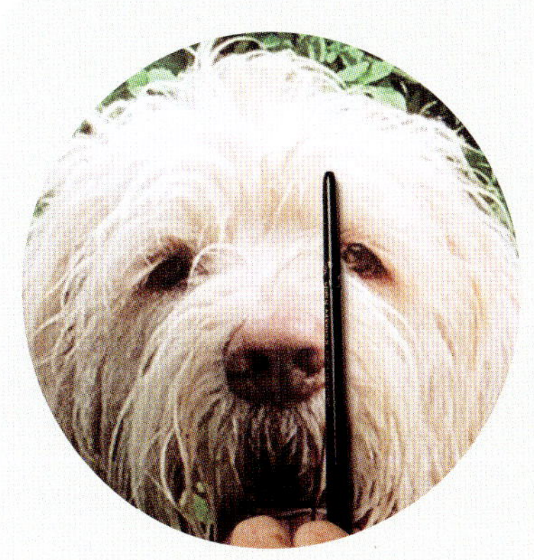

1 Following the instructions from my demonstration on page 54, I used a size 10 round to apply Payne's blue gray and opera pink. Once the nose was in place I began to use quinacridone gold to start to develop the fur on the muzzle.

2 Working outwards, I changed to a very dilute mix of Payne's blue gray and hint of alizarin burnt scarlet to add a few subtle darks. Next, I painted the top of the muzzle area (between the eyes) with very dilute amethyst genuine. While the paint was wet, I added highlights to the nose by lifting out.

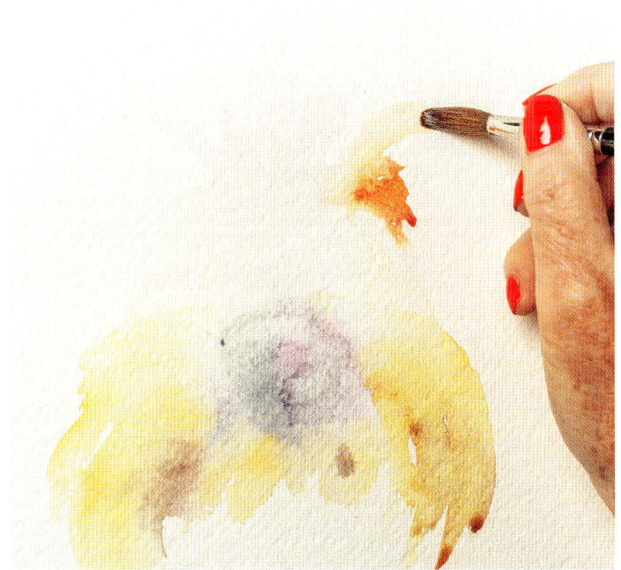

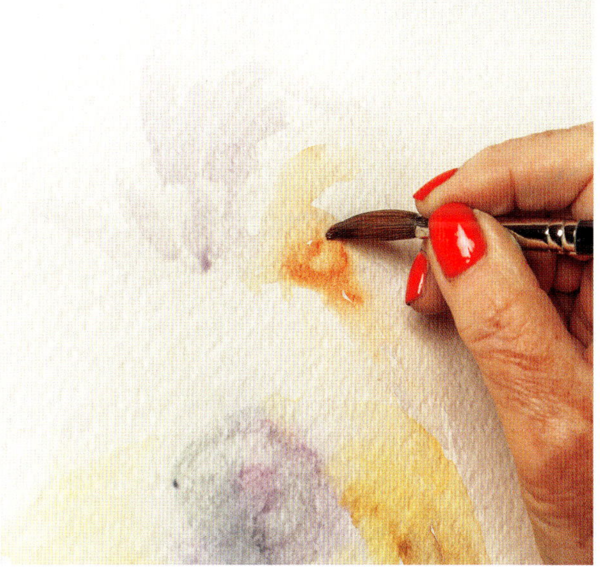

3 Once my starting point, the nose section, was in place, I used my brush to measure where to add the eye (see tip, above right). Connecting sections one stage at a time builds up the painting gradually. Taking time to accurately place each new additional feature is important. I used a mix of quinacridone gold and quinacridone burnt scarlet to place the eye, then began to soften the edge away with clean water.

4 I work away from the eye, building up the light fur with very dilute amethyst genuine. I keep my work soft in the initial stages. Lift out a highlight on the eye with a clean damp brush. With the eye in place, I could then look to find the next facial features: the ear and outline of the head.

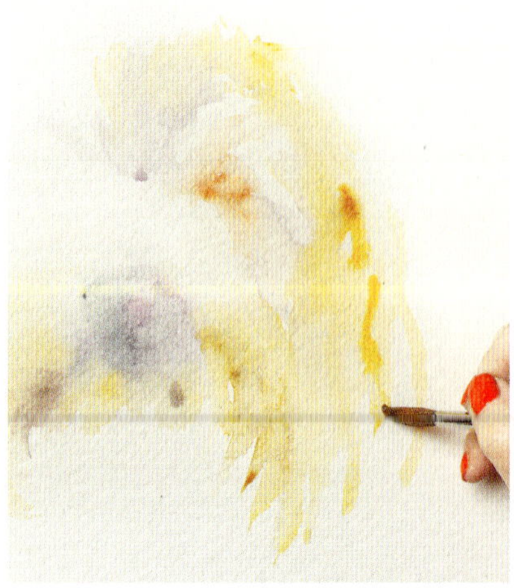  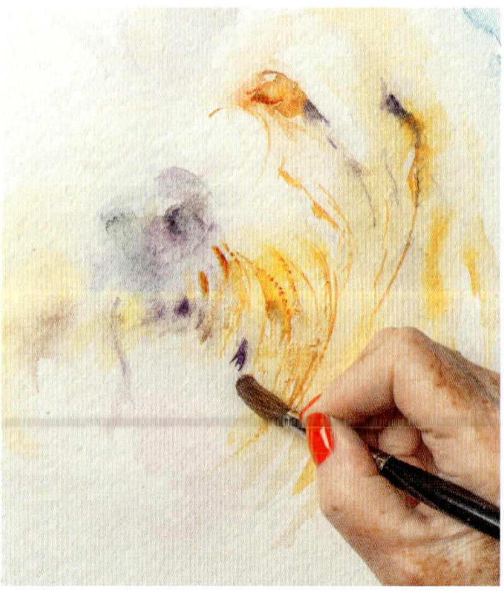

5 I build up the outside edge of the head on the right-hand side with quinacridone gold, using curved brushstrokes to reflect the shagginess and length of the fur. Once this first wash stage is completely dry, I can then add gradually darker details to complete my painting.

6 I add the outline with phthalo blue turquoise, then bleed the colour away from the head with clean water, keeping the outline undefined, as the breed calls for a loose edge here.

7 I now strengthen the details of the fur, painting finer lines with the rigger as well as shapes with the size 10 to indicate the wavy appearance of this breed's coat. You can use salt to create texture patterns for curly-coated dogs. A great tip is to always use your brush in the direction in which the fur is growing and feel as though you are stroking the dog with each new brushstroke.

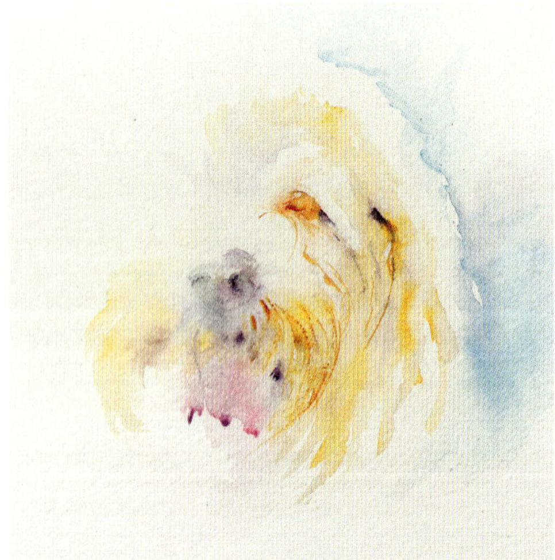 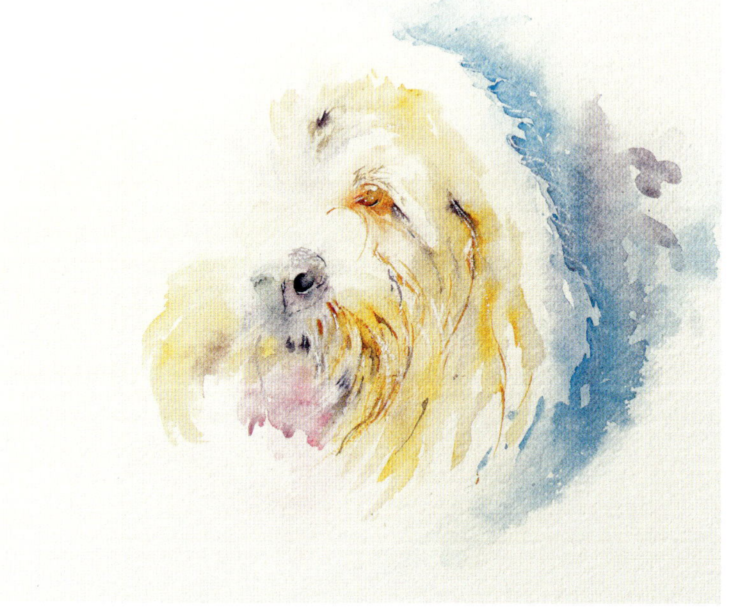

8 Use very dilute opera pink to paint the tongue, adding amethyst genuine wet in wet. As a beginner, it is easier to stop at just half a face. In fact, I recommend stopping as soon as you first begin to see your dog's face appearing.

Half face study

As you become more confident with this technique of losing the pencil, you can move on to painting dogs in a more advanced style and learn to gently bring a dog's character to life. Here I have used Payne's blue gray for the nostril detailing, and added shadow detailing to the fur with amethyst genuine. I often add small touches of white gouache to the nose or as highlights in the eyes to give an additional sense of life to my subject; but this is optional.

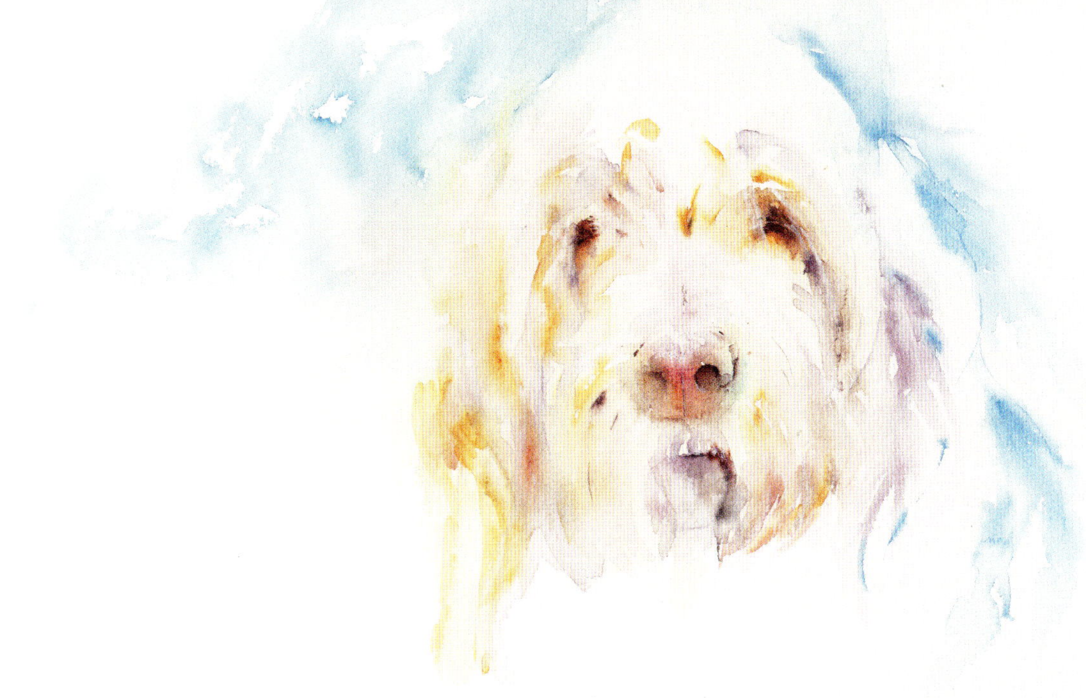

Moving to full paintings

Every painting we create is different. Here I have two more images of Humphrey. The one above is warm in colour and a softer interpretation. It is more advanced than the beginner's step-by-step due to the strength in colour and amount of detail added.

The painting below is even bolder, as the pigment application is both really strong and more boldly applied. You will find that the more animals you paint, the more aware you will become of your own personal preferences in style. Softer or darker in colour; looser or more detailed in style. Discover which kind of artist you are!

For homework, find a fabulous dog subject and paint it working from a starting point. Choose beautiful colours and use fabulous brushwork to create winning dog pet portraits.

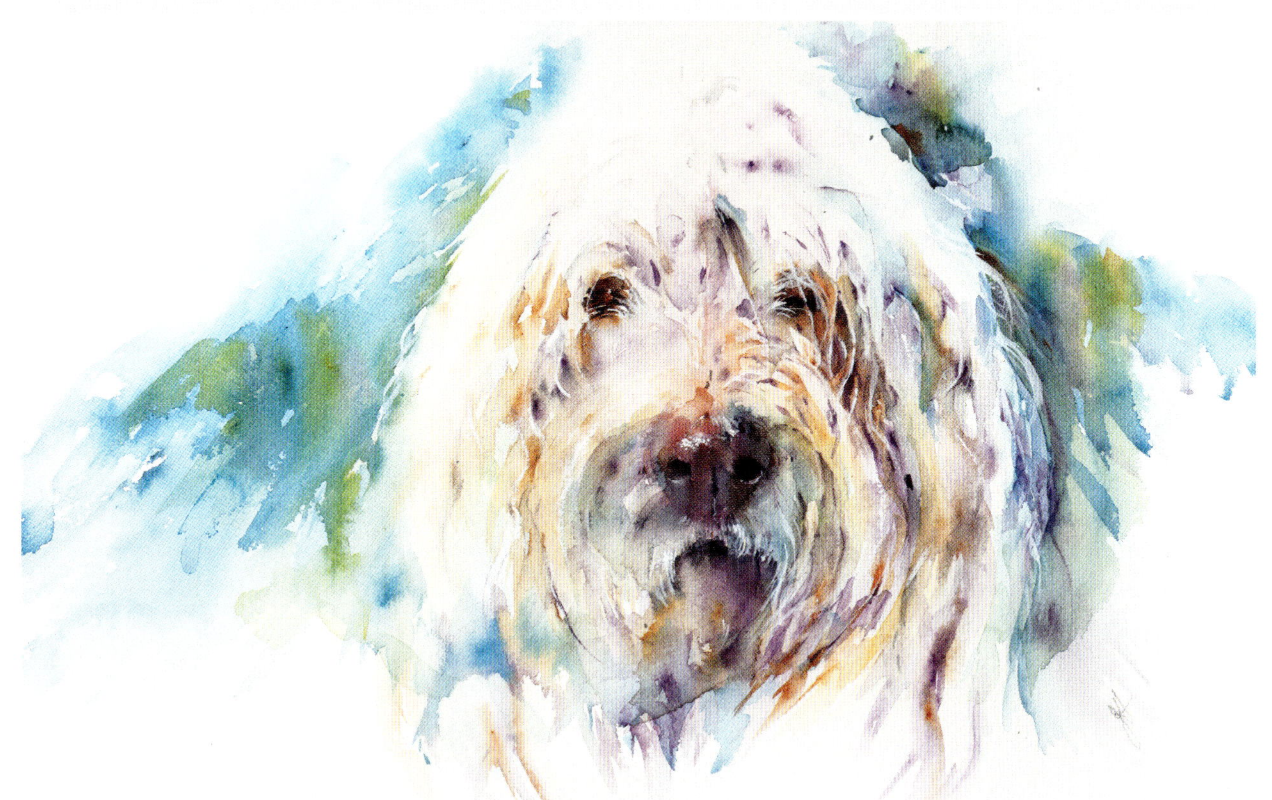

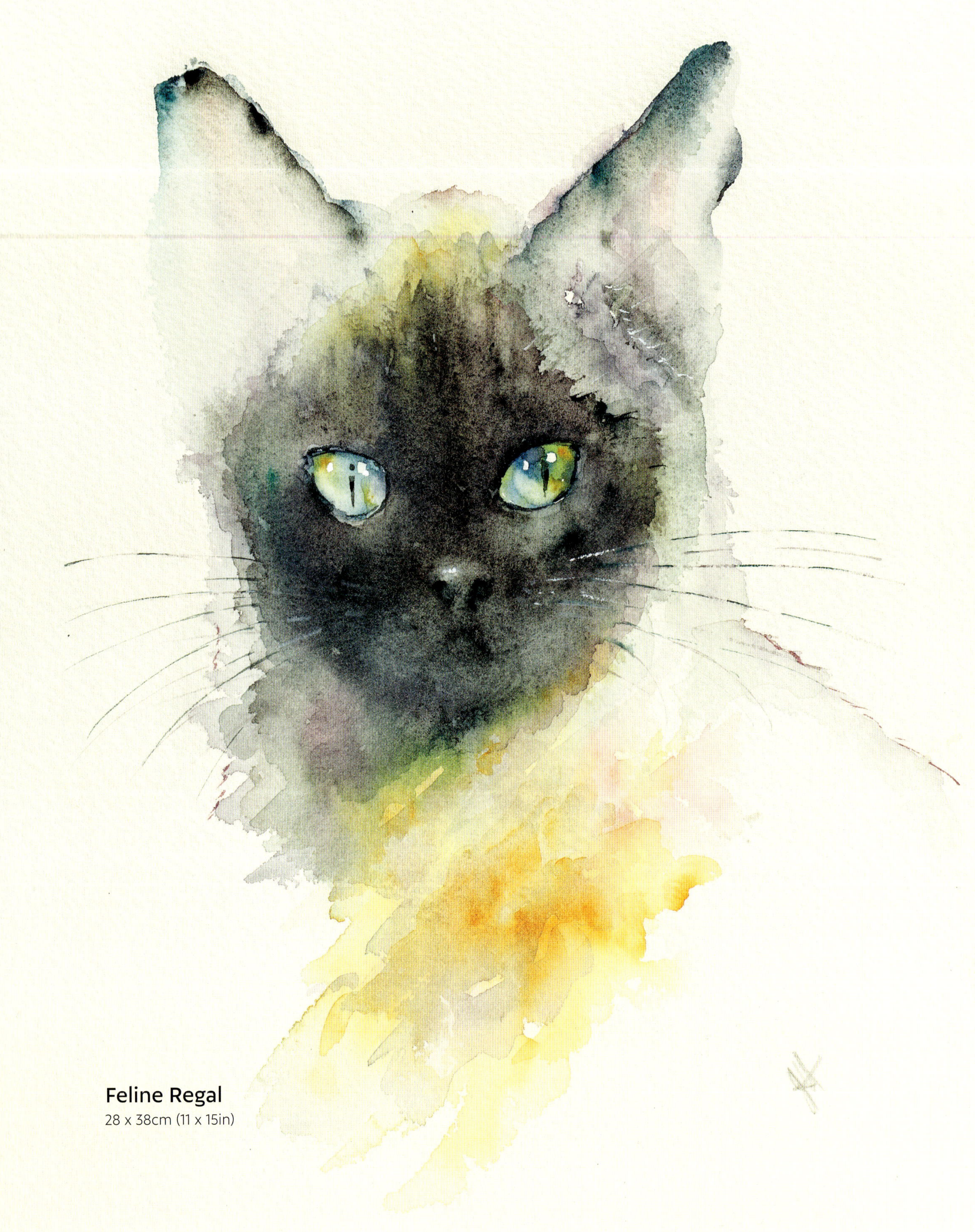

Feline Regal
28 x 38cm (11 x 15in)

Feline fine

"What greater gift than the love of a cat?" Charles Dickens

FOLLOWING ON FROM PAINTING DOGS on the previous pages, I am leading you into painting a new subject, cats, using exactly the same approach. Start by painting small features first, then the face and then the body. It's an easy way to build up your confidence and art skills by taking each new project a stage at a time. Breaking up the creative process means that each segment of your animal paintings becomes easier for you over time. For this subject the main focus is the eyes.

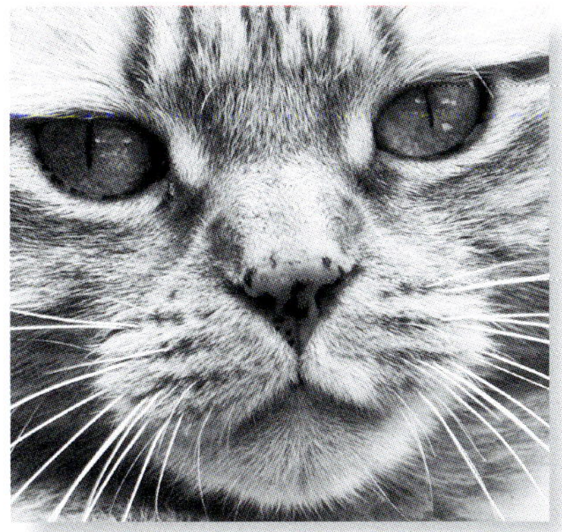

Small stages: eyes

Many artists realize that if you get the eye right on any animal subject, you have almost won the battle. The eyes are the life and soul of what you are creating. They can make the difference to whether your painting will look alive or flat. The eyes are definitely the most important feature to get perfect and, as such, they require time to practise painting them. To move forward in painting animals, this is where our focus for now will lie.

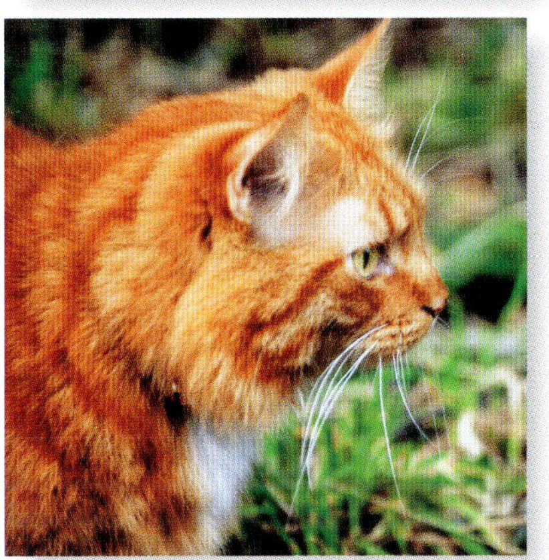

Animal meaning: cat

There are many meanings and spiritual connections related to cats. With their sense of adventure, they are said to represent patience and wisdom in knowing the right time to take action. Because of this wisdom they also represent patience. To many they simply represent the ability to be loved. They are deeply relaxed beings from whom we can learn a great deal.

Cats' eyes

Collect as many photographs of animals' eyes as you can and spend time painting them. These exercises will be invaluable for all your animal paintings. I can't stress highly enough the importance of gaining the ability to paint great animal eyes. They genuinely can make or break your animal artwork.

The colours I have used for the examples on this page are cadmium yellow, phthalo blue turquoise, green apatite genuine and Aussie red gold. I painted each eye as described opposite, but here you will notice I have painted green cats' eyes using a touch of orange to bring them to life.

You can use up to a three-colour combination in eyes such as yellow, blue and a touch of orange. Be careful not to use too many colours, though. Simplify. Keep your colours fresh. Animal eyes should be painted so that they carry a great sense of life and vitality!

Colour matching

Match your colours to the eyes of the cat that you are painting. Aim to have at least a two-colour combination, as this adds a beautiful sense of life and energy to your work. Using one colour alone can often lead to results that look flat and uninteresting. So, for example, when painting blue eyes I often add a touch of yellow as my second colour choice. When painting green eyes you can also add yellow. Brown eyes look terrific if a touch of orange is added. Experiment with unique colour combinations.

Lifting for life effects

This technique is my own that I created years ago. I realized that leaving white paper alone for highlights in an eye didn't give me the outcome I was searching for. I needed more light. If you look at the blue-green eye, just off-centre in the studies below, you will be able to see that it looks far more realistic than the others. This is because when the eye colour was still wet, I placed a curved clean, damp brushstroke in a circular movement to match the outline edge, lifting colour gently to create a new lighter section in the eye. The curved brushstroke is important. A straight line in the eye wouldn't look as believable.

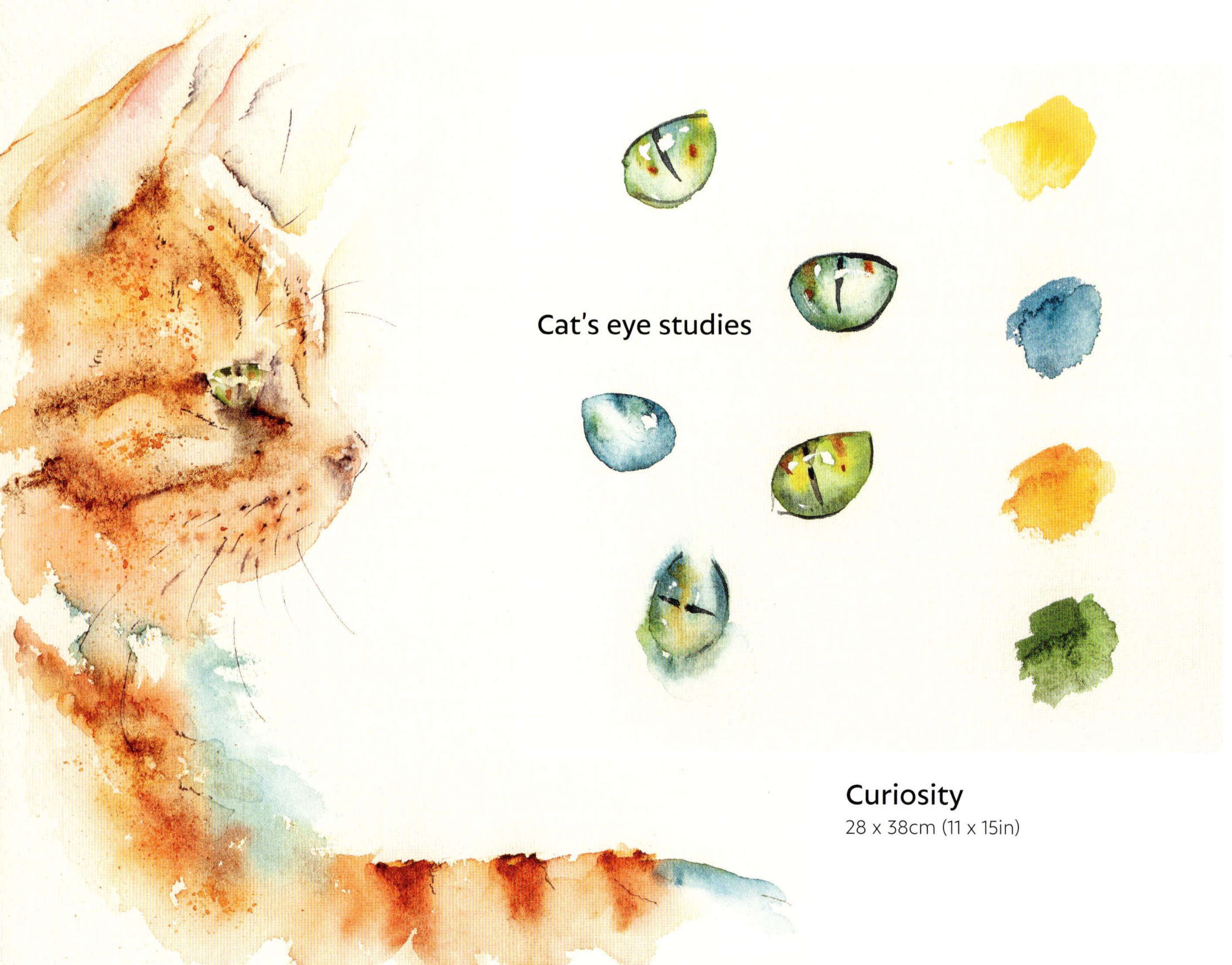

Curiosity
28 x 38cm (11 x 15in)

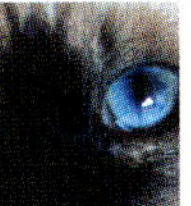

How-to paint a cat's eyes

Once you have mastered painting cats' eyes you can then move on to creating a cat's face in exactly the same way that we created the dog in the previous chapter: starting with one feature and then gradually building up your painting. For this exercise, study the real cat's eye before you begin, to gain the best painted interpretation as possible.

To master painting beautiful eyes, you need really great models or resource photographs. It is an excellent idea to paint as many different eye shapes and colours too. Try to look at different angles of the cat's face to practise as many different shapes as possible. Here are the important stages to follow to begin learning how to paint cats' eyes.

Materials

Surface: Scrap of 300gsm (140lb) weight Not surface watercolour paper

Brushes: size 10 round, rigger

Watercolour paints: cadmium yellow, phthalo blue turquoise, Payne's blue gray

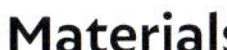
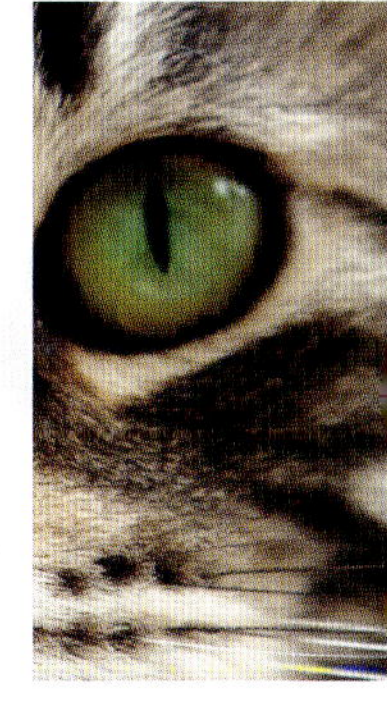

Tip

Please don't mix the colours with your brush beforehand. Allowing them to merge naturally on the paper will look far more interesting.

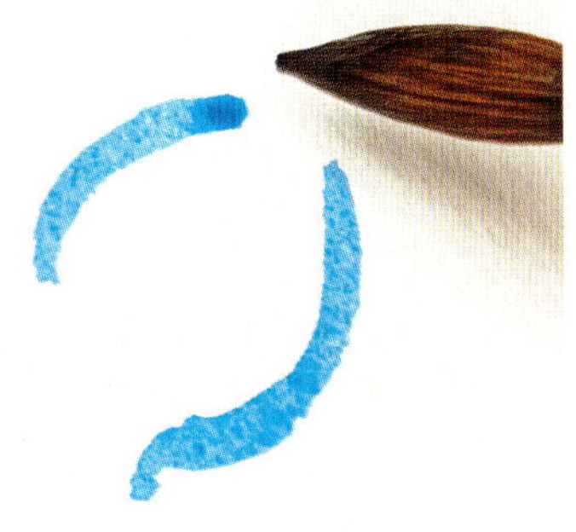

1 Paint the outline shape of the eye with a size 10 round. I use the dominant colour to create this outline. So if I am painting blue eyes, as here, I would use my selected blue shade (phthalo blue turquoise) to paint this outer edge.

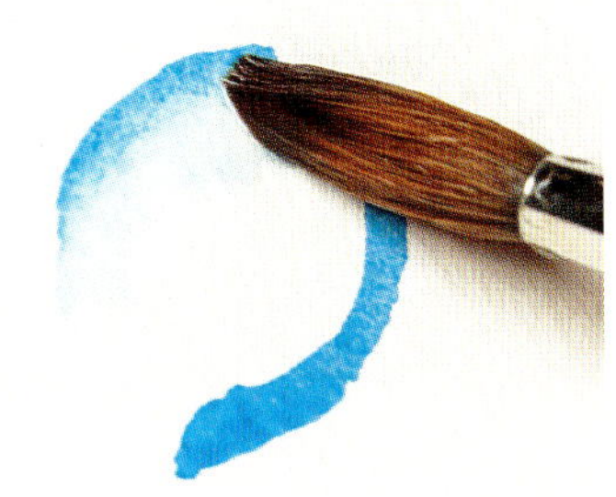

2 Use a damp brush to soften the inside edges of the outline.

3 Next I fill in the central section with colour, by dropping dilute quinacridone gold into my initial blue application. Always leave a white space of paper where the highlight of the eye will be.

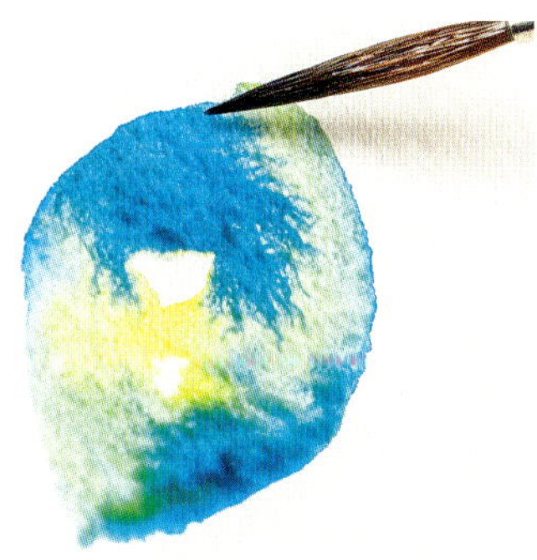

4 While this colour is still damp I use my rigger to pick up a dot of phthalo blue turquoise to drop into the eye shape, allowing it to merge with the colour on the paper.

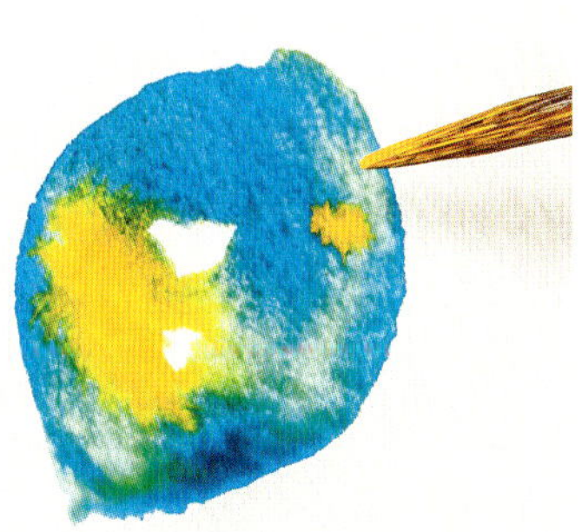

5 I use my rigger to pick up a tiny dot of quinacridone gold to drop into the eye shape. I allow this new application of colour to merge with the outer edge of the first shade.

6 Use a dry brush to make a curved brushstroke to lift out a highlight.

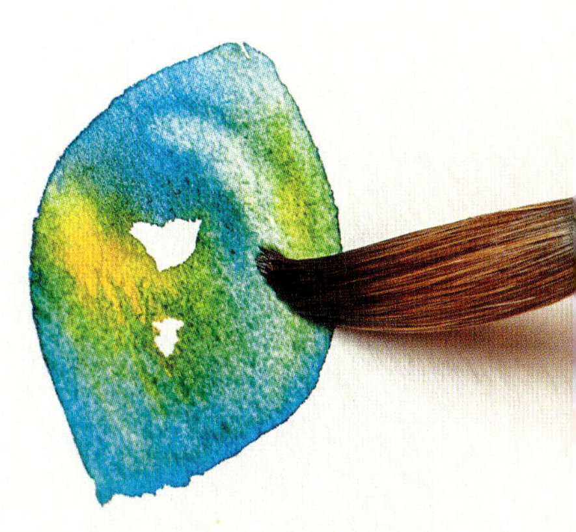

Adding details

Once you have created the foundation of your cat's eye with a great shape, beautiful colour, stunning highlights and lifted highlight sections, you can move on to adding the detail of the pupil. I avoid painting pure black pupils. Black as a shade can overpower fresh colour, especially in the iris. Instead, I tend to use indigo or Payne's blue gray, which gives far softer results.

The shape of the pupil can vary depending on the model. Some pupils are merely a fine line, others are larger and more pronounced. A great tip is to try to avoid painting a solid line. See my examples on page 70, where I have omitted sections of the pupil. These could be hints as to where light is hitting the eye. I also recommend painting lines for the pupil on a scrap of paper first, until you get used to painting fine details. I have seen many gorgeous animal paintings ruined because an artist has leapt in eagerly to add the black pupil too soon and too heavily. Practise every step and build your skills wisely!

I aim for three highlights in all of my animal eyes: the white paper highlight, the curved lifted highlight and the final touch of white gouache highlight. These contrast amazingly and really do look very effective together.

Always paint both eyes at the same time, to ensure you keep the colours absolutely perfectly matching.

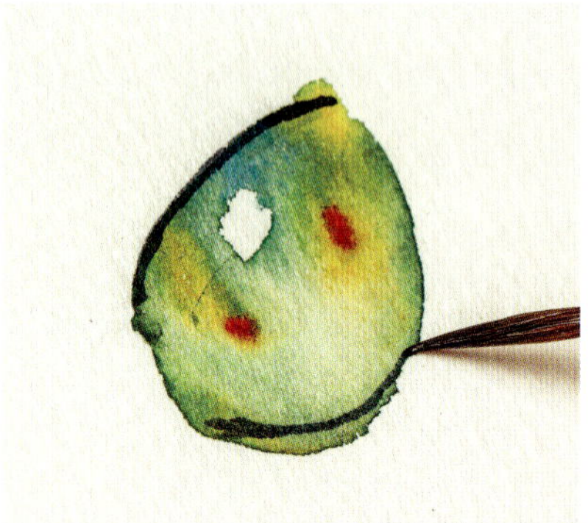

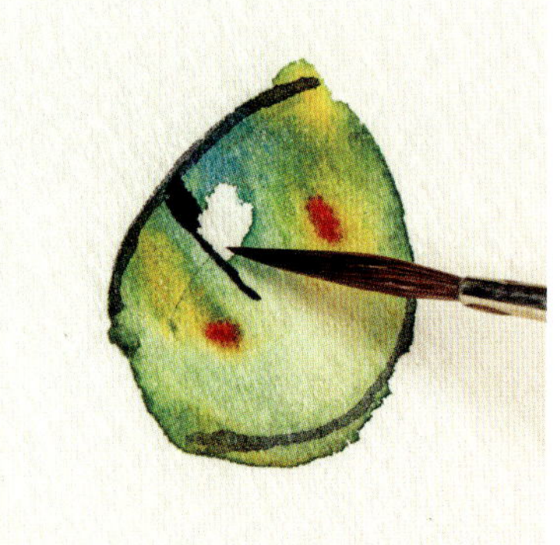

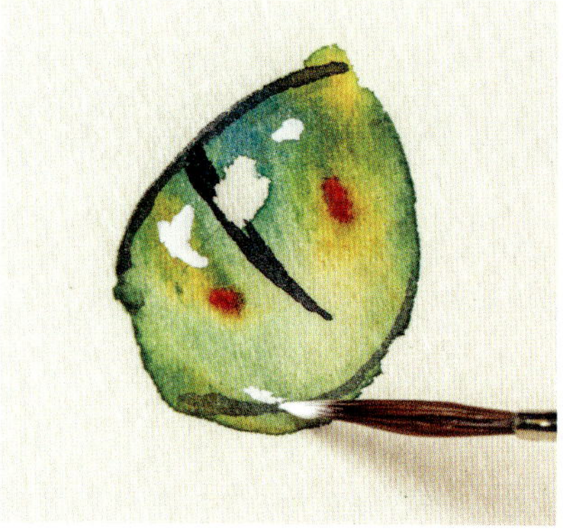

1 Some cats (and other animals) look as though they are wearing eye liner. They appear to have a black outline around the eyes. Do not paint this heavy outline too dark. In art, the dark black ring we see around the eyes can sometimes kill the 'life' in painted eyes. Instead, use a rigger and a softer brown or dark blue shade such as Payne's blue gray.

2 Study your model or resource photograph and, using your rigger, place a fine line where appropriate to match the shadow of your model's eyelid. Paint carefully around the highlight area.

3 The more varied the highlights are in your painted eyes, the better your animal paintings will be. When your painted eye is completely dry, add a tiny touch of white gouache where the strongest highlight should be. It adds sparkle and energy!

Homework

Collect as many animal eye photographs as possible and spend time just painting eyes. Bear in mind that many artists have successfully painted compositions solely on eyes. No face or other features, just eyes – and they are beautiful. Take time to get to know your subjects and make your animal eyes shine!

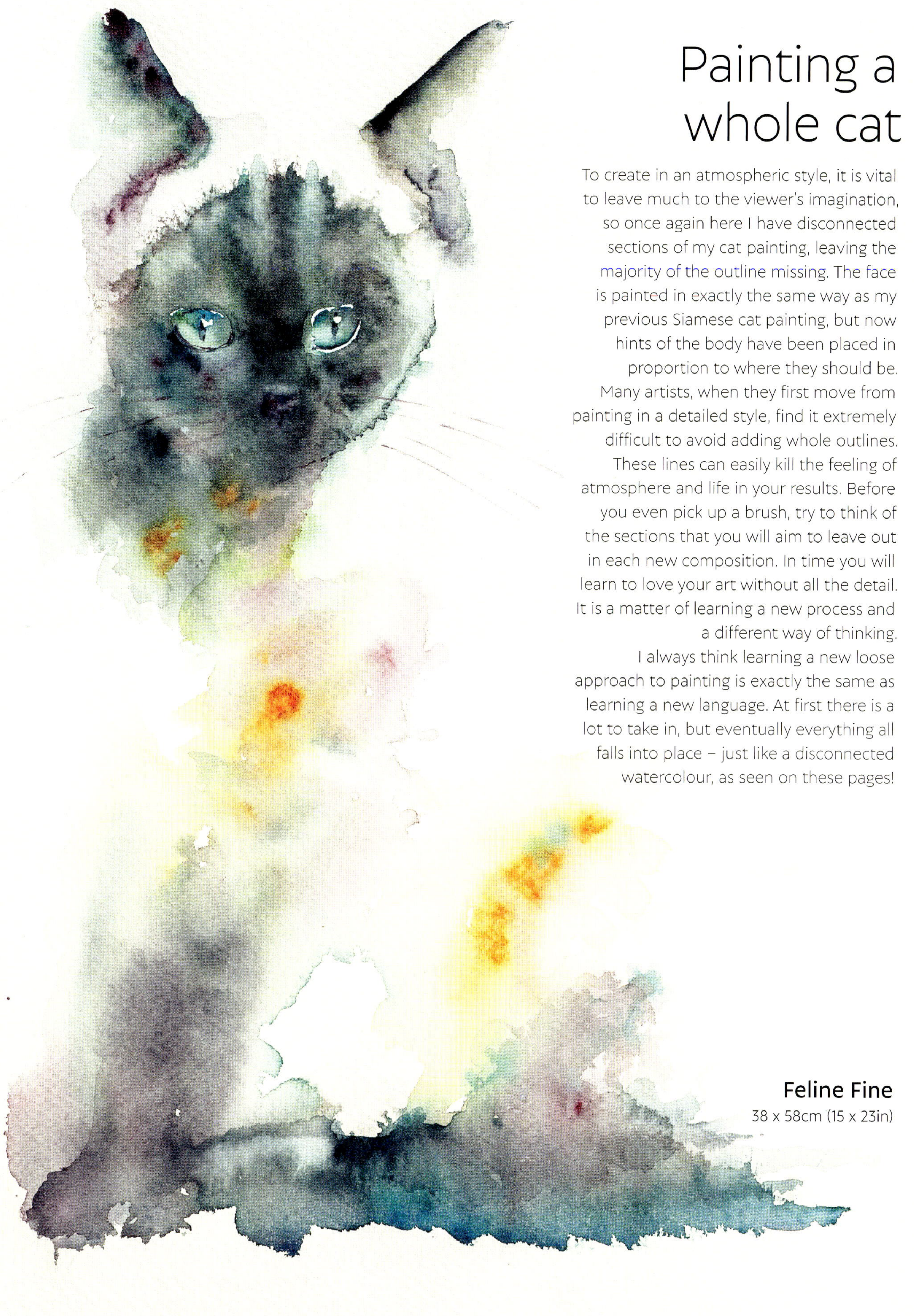

Painting a whole cat

To create in an atmospheric style, it is vital to leave much to the viewer's imagination, so once again here I have disconnected sections of my cat painting, leaving the majority of the outline missing. The face is painted in exactly the same way as my previous Siamese cat painting, but now hints of the body have been placed in proportion to where they should be. Many artists, when they first move from painting in a detailed style, find it extremely difficult to avoid adding whole outlines. These lines can easily kill the feeling of atmosphere and life in your results. Before you even pick up a brush, try to think of the sections that you will aim to leave out in each new composition. In time you will learn to love your art without all the detail. It is a matter of learning a new process and a different way of thinking.

I always think learning a new loose approach to painting is exactly the same as learning a new language. At first there is a lot to take in, but eventually everything all falls into place – just like a disconnected watercolour, as seen on these pages!

Feline Fine
38 x 58cm (15 x 23in)

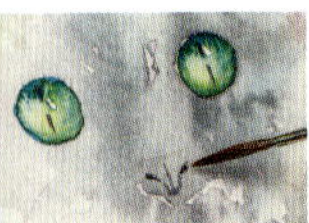

Step-by-step Socks

The importance of having vibrant eye colour for younger animals should never be underestimated. Choose bright colours for painting young animals and slightly duller shades for older pets. Here I demonstrate how to paint a young kitten, while leaving sections to the viewer's imagination.

Materials

Surface: 300gsm (140lb) weight
   Not surface watercolour paper,
   28 x 38cm (11 x 15in)
Brushes: size 10 round, rigger
Watercolour paints: cadmium yellow, phthalo blue turquoise, Payne's blue gray, quinacridone gold, amethyst genuine

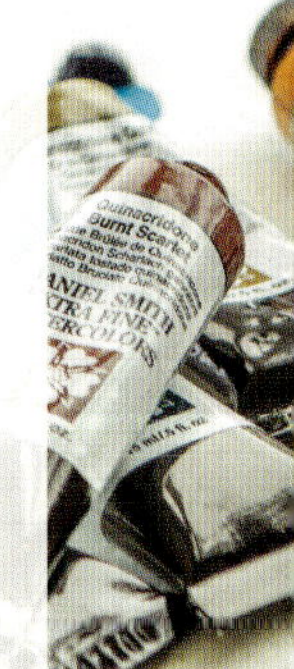

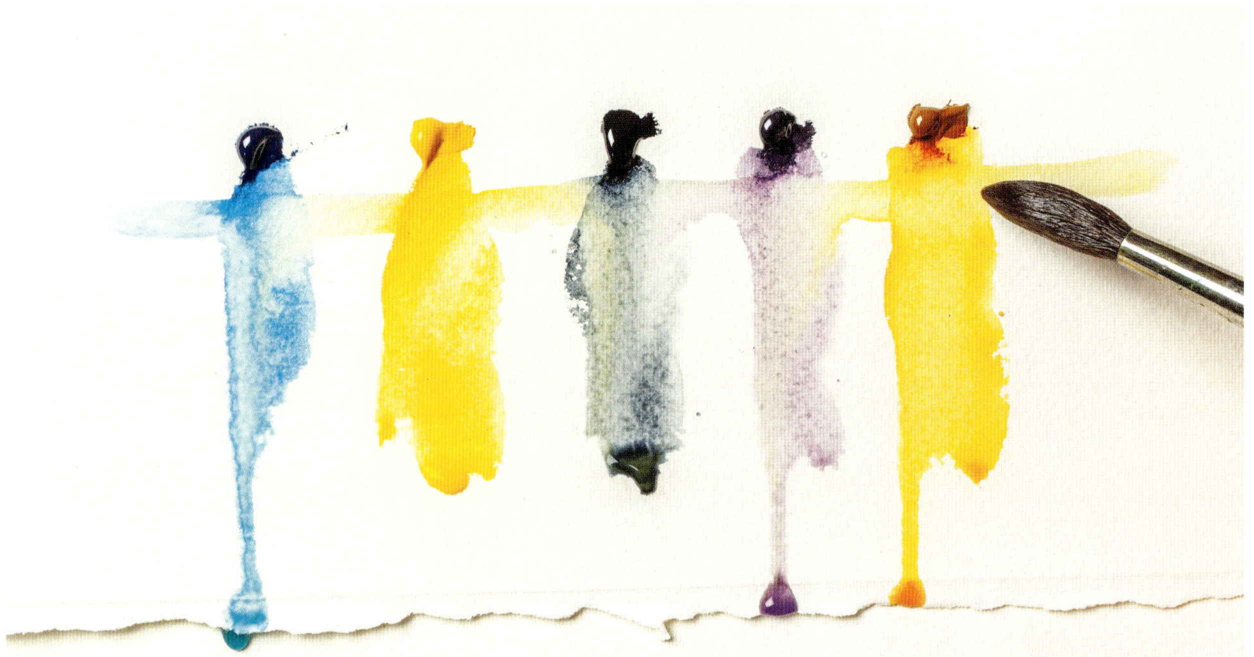

Dancing ladies: colour selection

Phthalo blue turquoise combined on paper with cadmium yellow gives me a stunning fresh green. Payne's blue gray is wonderful as a shade or for dark markings, while amethyst genuine can be added where necessary for shadows. Finally, a touch of quinacridone gold adds warmth. White paper will act as the backdrop to this gorgeous colour selection

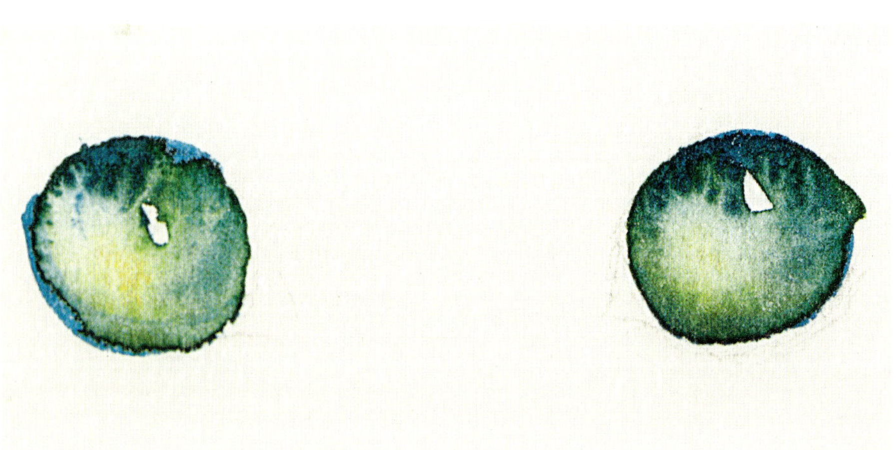

1 Using a size 10 round brush with phthalo blue turquoise and cadmium yellow, paint the eyes as explained on page 71. When painting two eyes of a subject, always paint them at the same time so that your colours match perfectly. Measure the distance between the two eyes to ensure they are placed correctly.

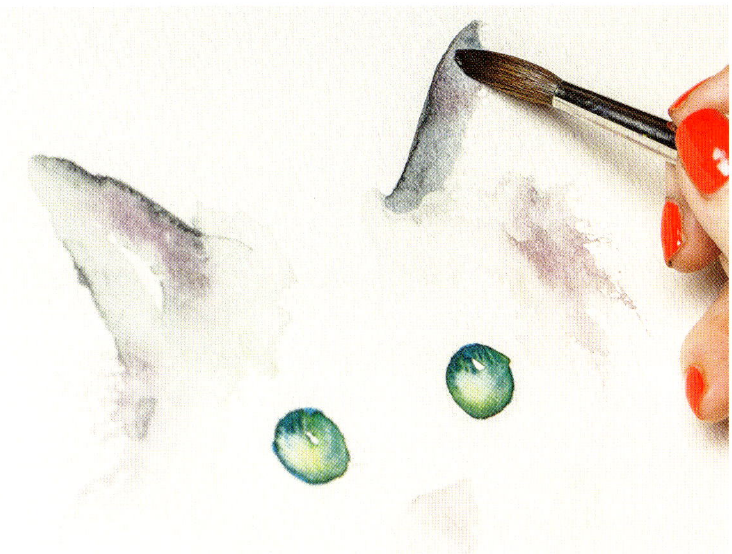

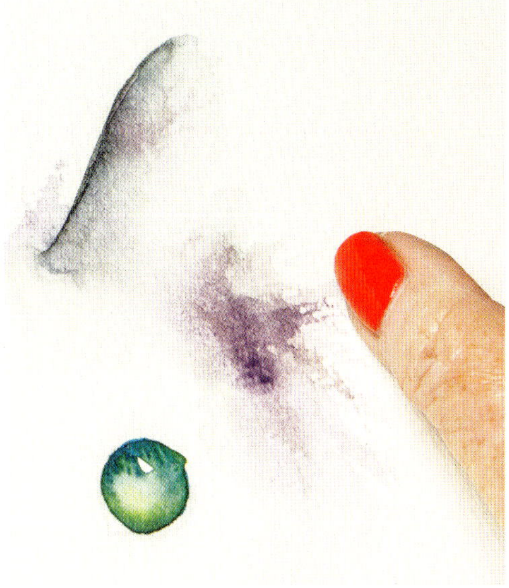

2 Hint at the first stage of the nose with dilute amethyst genuine, then start to create the fur at the edges of the head, by applying dilute Payne's blue gray with soft brushstrokes and adding a little amethyst genuine. Follow the direction of the fur with each new colour application. From here find the position of the ears, using your brush to measure the angles for placing each additional facial feature.

3 As you add the fur by the side of the face, use your thumb or fingers to gently stroke colour away. This will automatically give you a soft furry outline edge.

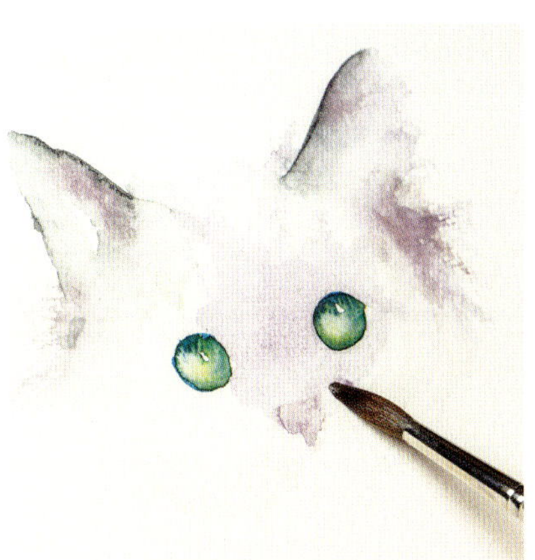

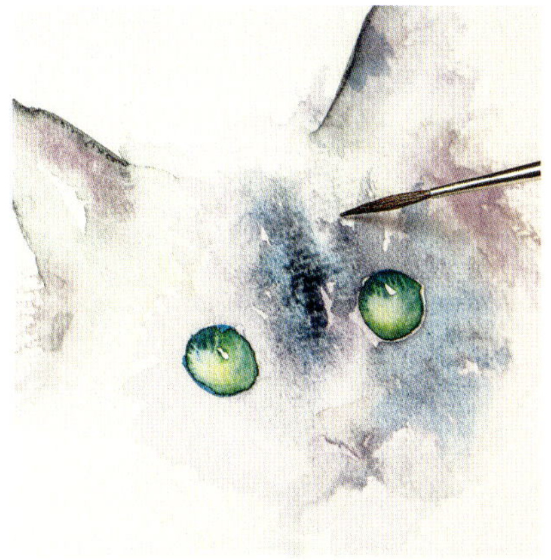

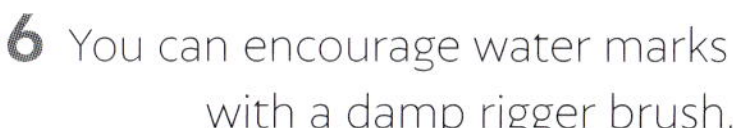

6 You can encourage water marks with a damp rigger brush.

4 Once the features are dry, begin to build up the face by painting the 'mask' on the cat with the size 10 round and dilute amethyst genuine.

5 Once dry, develop the area with Payne's blue gray, then add hints of phthalo blue turquoise with the rigger while it is still wet.

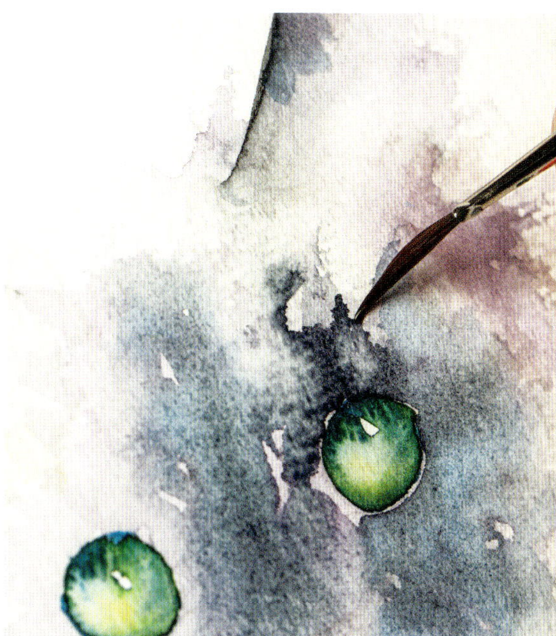

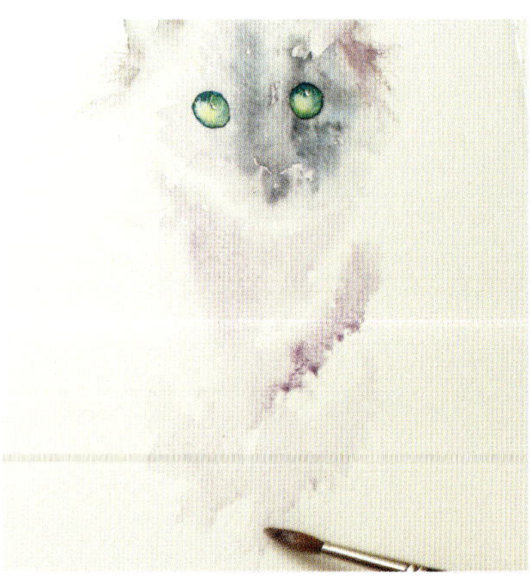

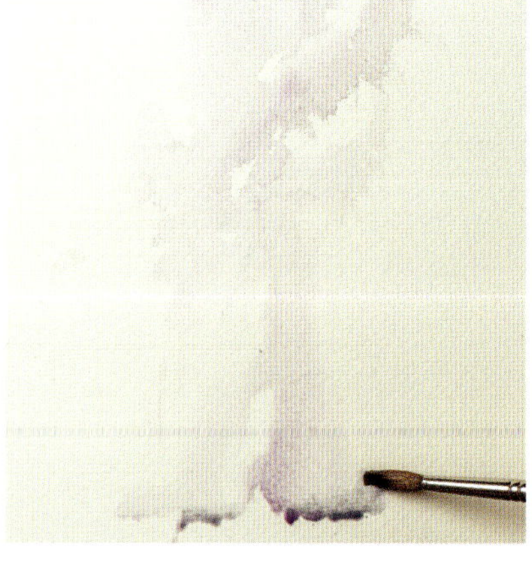

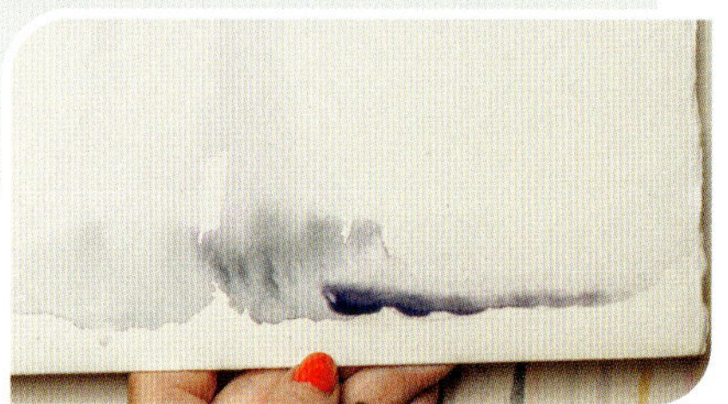

7 Using a size 10 round brush, dampen the area beneath the head and gradually add the body to the cat with dilute amethyst genuine, leaving sections to the viewer's imagination.

8 Draw the colour downwards, introducing Payne's blue gray wet in wet. As you add hints of the legs, allow colour to form at the base of your colour application. This puddle will act as a 'run back', creating fascinating hints of paws in an unusual way.

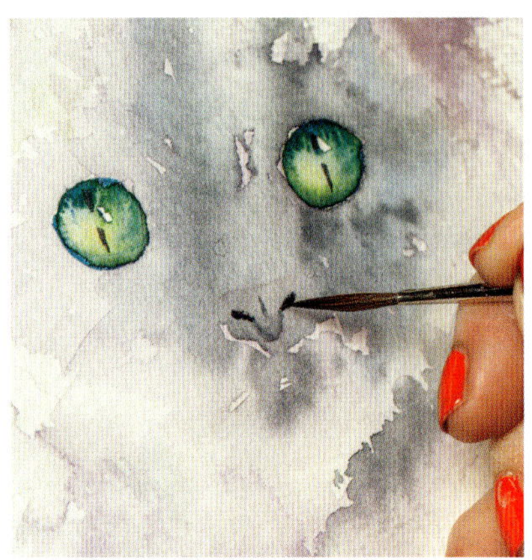

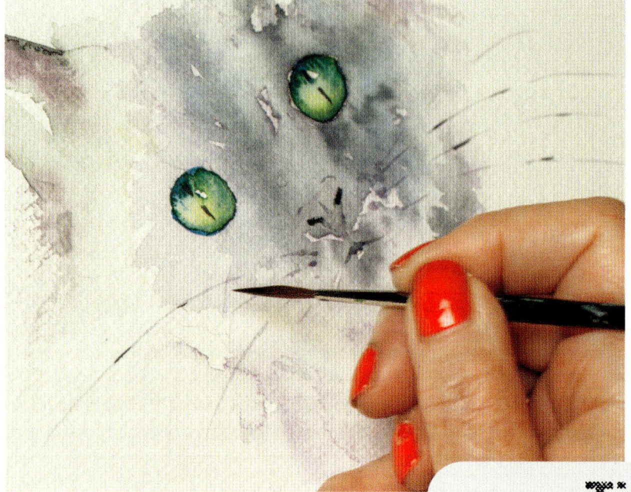

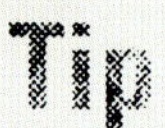

9 When my initial wash was completely dry, I began to add detail with the rigger to complete my painting. I added pupils and a soft outline to the eyes with Payne's blue gray.

10 I added the whiskers using a fine rigger. Breaking up the whisker lines leaving intermittent gaps gives an illusion of light hitting each whisker. I paint soft violet whiskers for most of my cat compositions and add touches of white gouache on top if needed when the cat's whiskers are white in reality.

Tip

Remember, avoid painting hard outlines around the eyes as this can often look like heavy eyeliner. Some cats do have these markings but in art they can kill the softness of your subject.

Tip

Practise painting whiskers on a scrap of paper before adding them to your full cat painting. This ensures you gain a soft, fine line (as on the left of the image below) rather than one that is too heavy (see right), which could ruin your work.

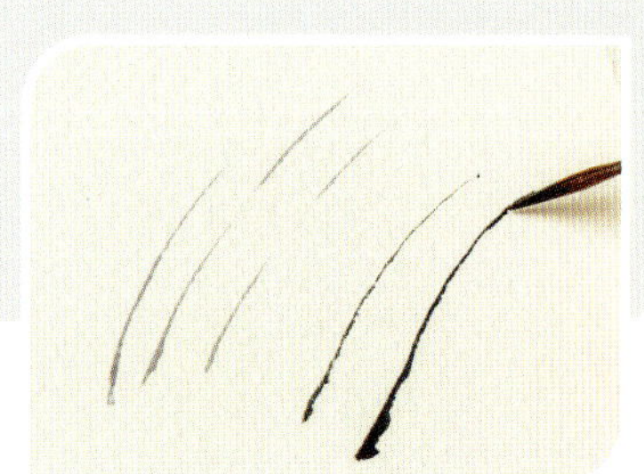

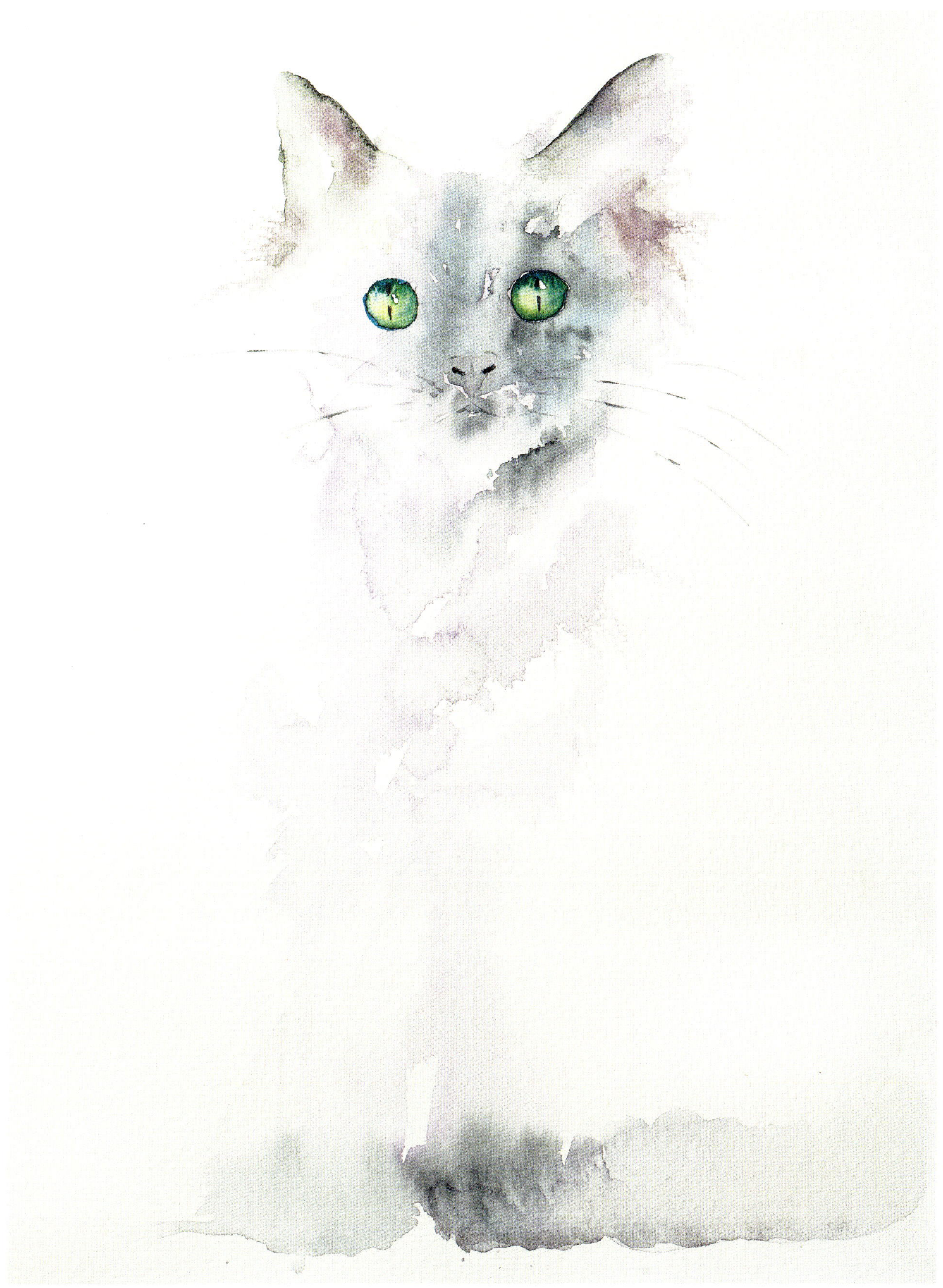

The finished painting

A touch of white gouache on the eyes and nose, for highlights, finishes off my painting.

Cat poses

Find a number of cat photographs in different colours and poses and try painting them working from a starting point. Practise the eyes alone first and then create your full cat paintings.

If you find painting eyes difficult, it is fortunate that cats have a wonderful habit of sleeping a lot. Painting a cat with its eyes shut is quite acceptable and great fun. In my painting *Catnap*, my own cat, Buster, is captured in watercolour quite simply. The first stage was to create an initial shape of colour on paper to match Buster's face shape; an almost circular application of colour. I then used a damp brush to lift out lines of pigment to form the striped pattern in his fur. I allowed this first wash to dry before adding the eye and nose detail. Buster had huge whiskers – and many – so I added quite a few in this piece.

Cats sleep in stunning poses that can delight an artist. In my painting, *Sleeping Cat*, I created a study in the form of a smaller painting before painting the larger composition. Why? When faced with a new subject or pose it is always a good idea to paint a small study first. This way you can ensure your colour selection and your chosen techniques work well to create a pleasing composition. This pose is very easy to create.

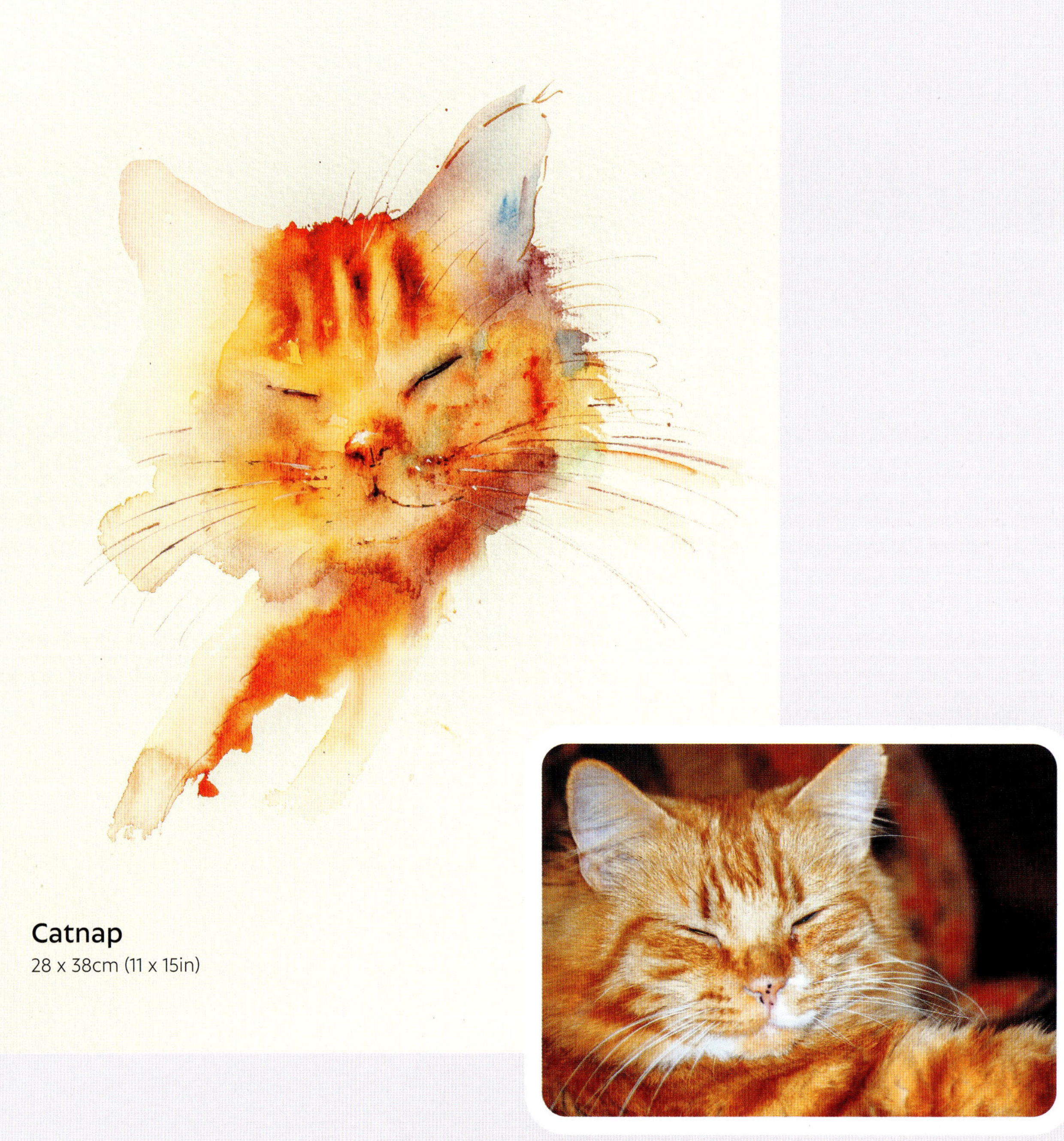

Catnap
28 x 38cm (11 x 15in)

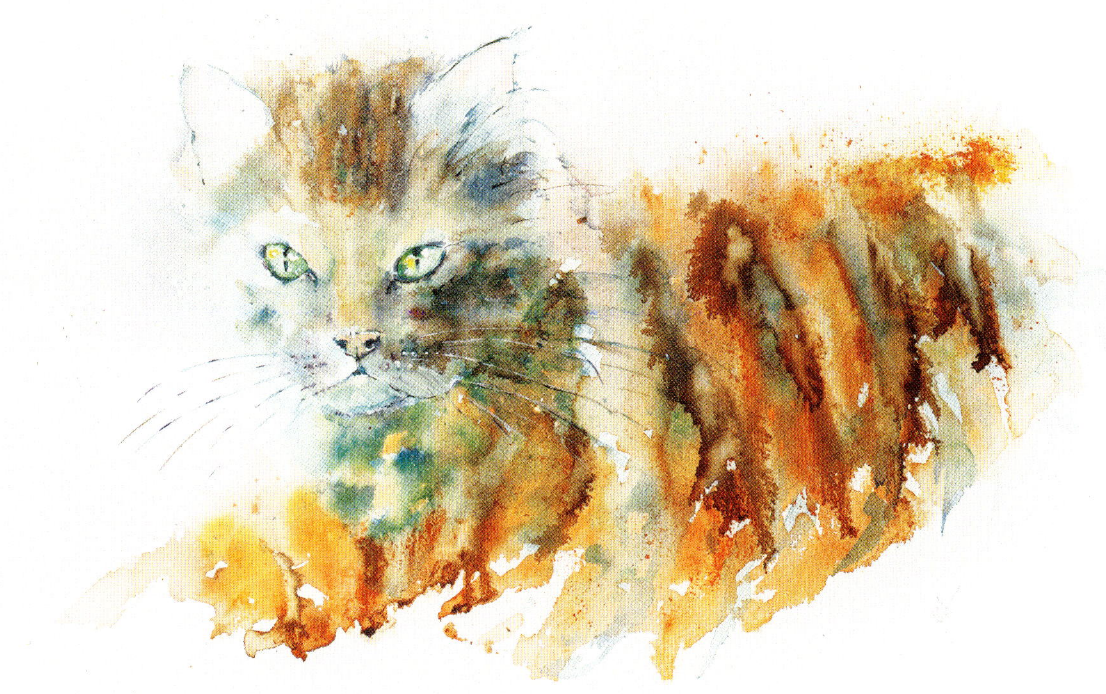

Cattitude
76 x 58cm (30 x 23in)

"A cat has absolute emotional honesty: human beings, for one reason or another, may hide their feelings, but a cat does not." *Ernest Hemingway*

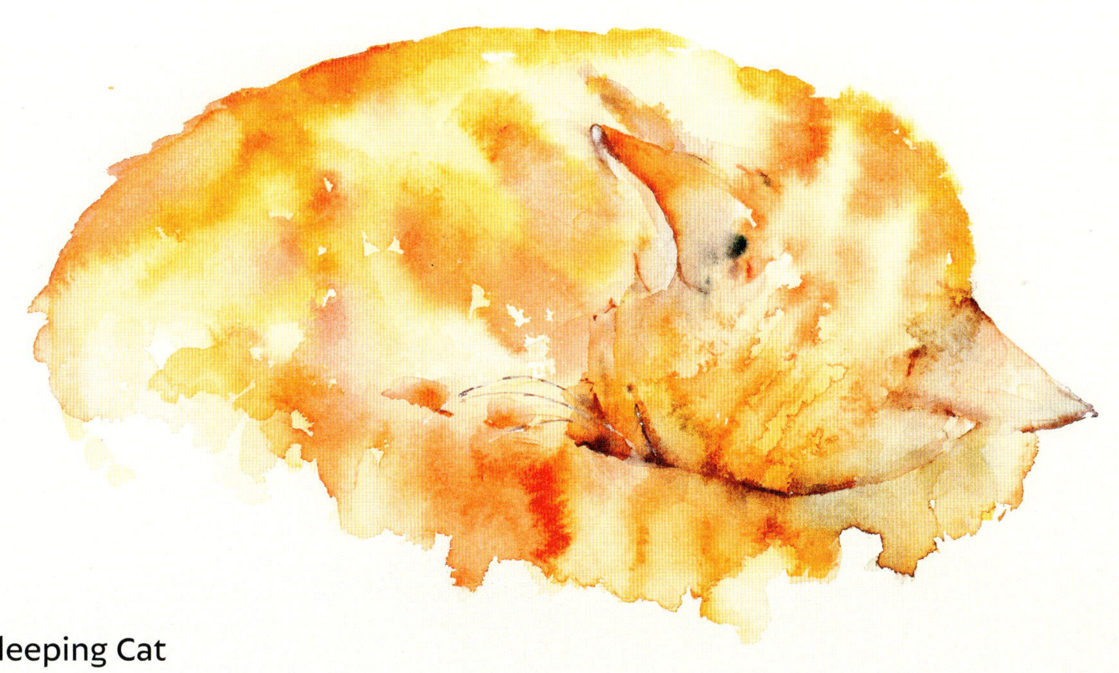

Sleeping Cat
58 x 38cm (23 x 15in)

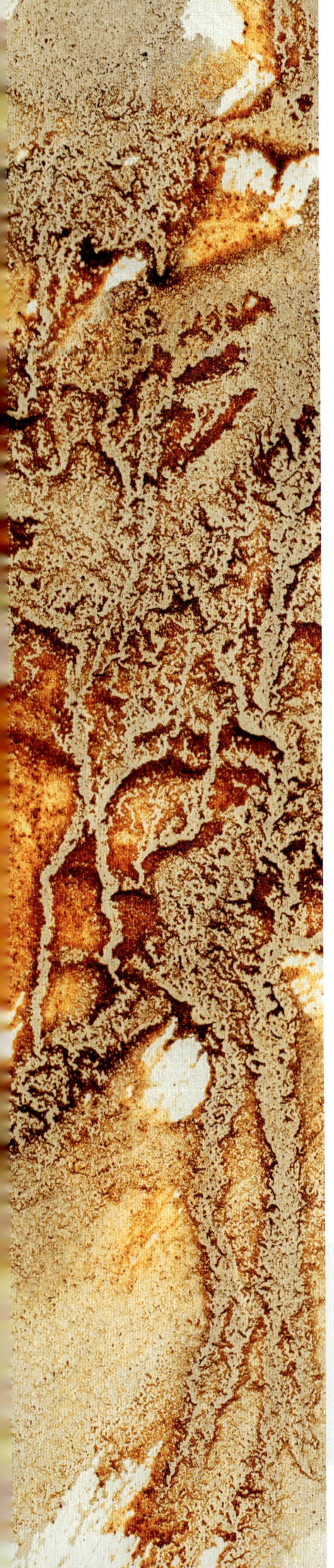

A walk on the wild side

"*Each species is a masterpiece, a creation assembled with extreme care and genius.*" E. O. Wilson

I HAVE ALWAYS LOVED SEEING ANIMALS in their natural surroundings, so being on safari in Africa was one of the highlights of my life. The colours, the sights and the majestic beings there took my breath away. I do believe once you have visited Africa you fall in love. I certainly did, and can fully understand why so many artists are completely mesmerized and drawn to painting African wildlife.

For me of course the passion is to capture each animal in a loose, interpretative and impressionistic style, capturing its essence rather than every single detail. An example of my atmospheric whispering interpretation can be seen in my image of a half-painted lion. Just enough is here to tell the story – but the tale is told. From the previous chapters we have learned how to paint eyes and noses which are vital to this suggestive painting. Now we move on to using patterns and texture in watercolour which is an absorbing part of creating. Learn as much as you can about texture techniques and products that will lead you to unique results. I aim to help and encourage you in this chapter.

Texture with turmeric ink

You will often see unusual patterns in my artwork as I experiment regularly to achieve them. All of my experiments are then combined to enhance my watercolours.

Many household items can be used to create fabulous colours and effects. This pattern was created with turmeric ink, which I make simply by making a strong mix of the spice with hot water. This I leave in a sealed jar and use occasionally to add texture to my art.

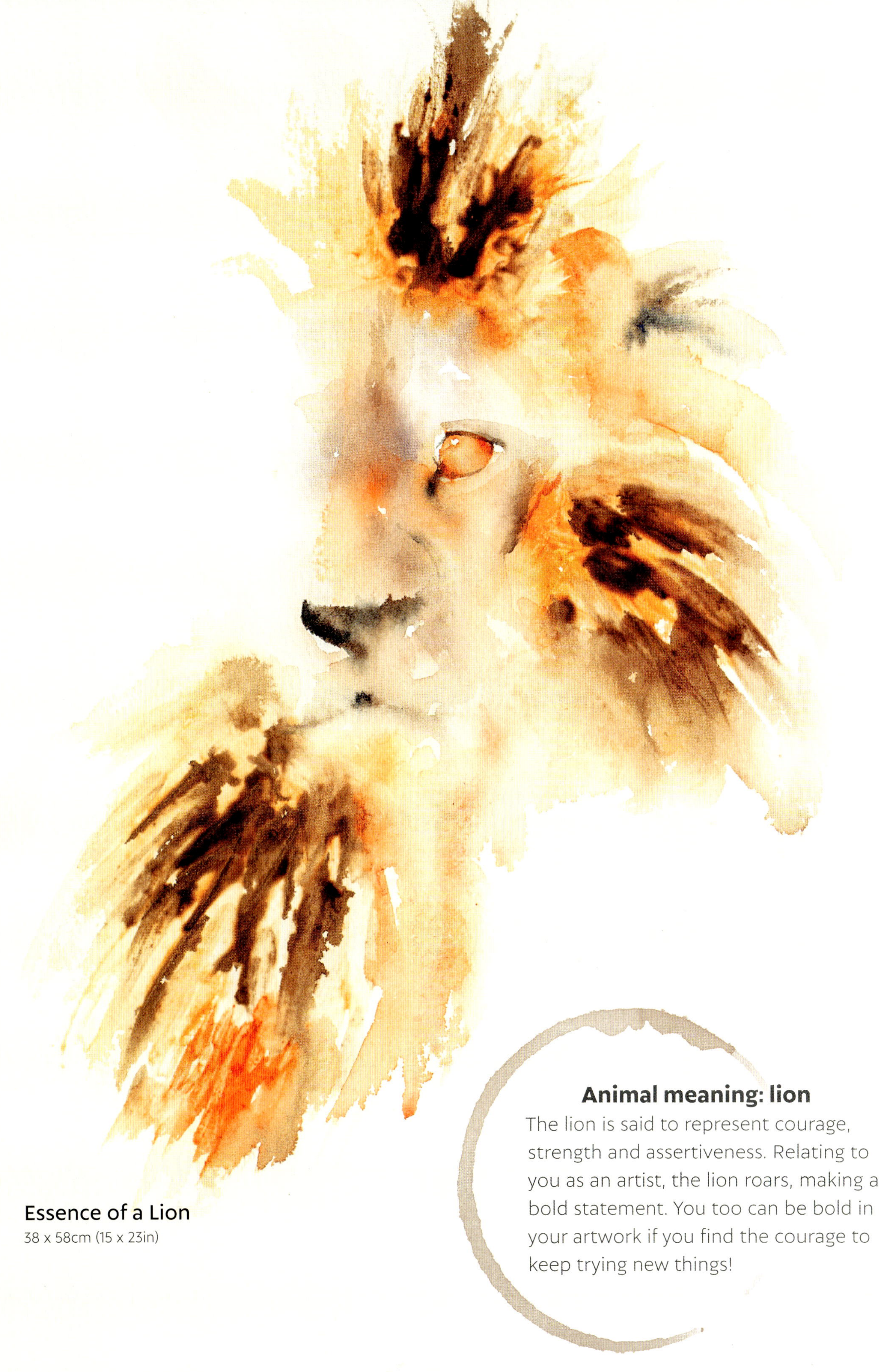

Essence of a Lion
38 x 58cm (15 x 23in)

Animal meaning: lion

The lion is said to represent courage, strength and assertiveness. Relating to you as an artist, the lion roars, making a bold statement. You too can be bold in your artwork if you find the courage to keep trying new things!

Different interpretations

Consider the interpretative, soft, half-complete face of my lion study on the previous page and compare it with the lion compositions here. In the painting below, *King*, I have used many products to bring this painting of a lion to life.

- In one section of the mane I have used **homemade mushroom ink** (see page 48) as a base, which leads to beautiful and unique granulation effects.

- The texture effects in the mane were created by using a spatula to apply **watercolour ground**. Once applied to the area, I held a rag in my hand and pulled it on and off the still-damp ground product, which gave me more charismatic and uneven patterns.

- Salt patterns in the background were created using **Himalayan salt**, sprinkling it on while the paint was wet and brushing it away once it had dried. The salt absorbs a little of the water and results in the pigment being deposited in interesting patterns. The kind of salt you use will determine the size and pattern it gives in your results.

This painting was formed by placing colour all over my paper in an interesting first wash, allowing it to dry, and then adding the lion. Now compare the two paintings with the one opposite, *Pride*, which is different again. The difference between the three lion paintings is vast. And you may find you prefer one style to the others. This will help you understand the style you are aiming for – quiet, bold or experimental?

When learning I highly recommend trying everything at least once. You may be surprised to discover that you enjoy experimental work far more than you thought you would.

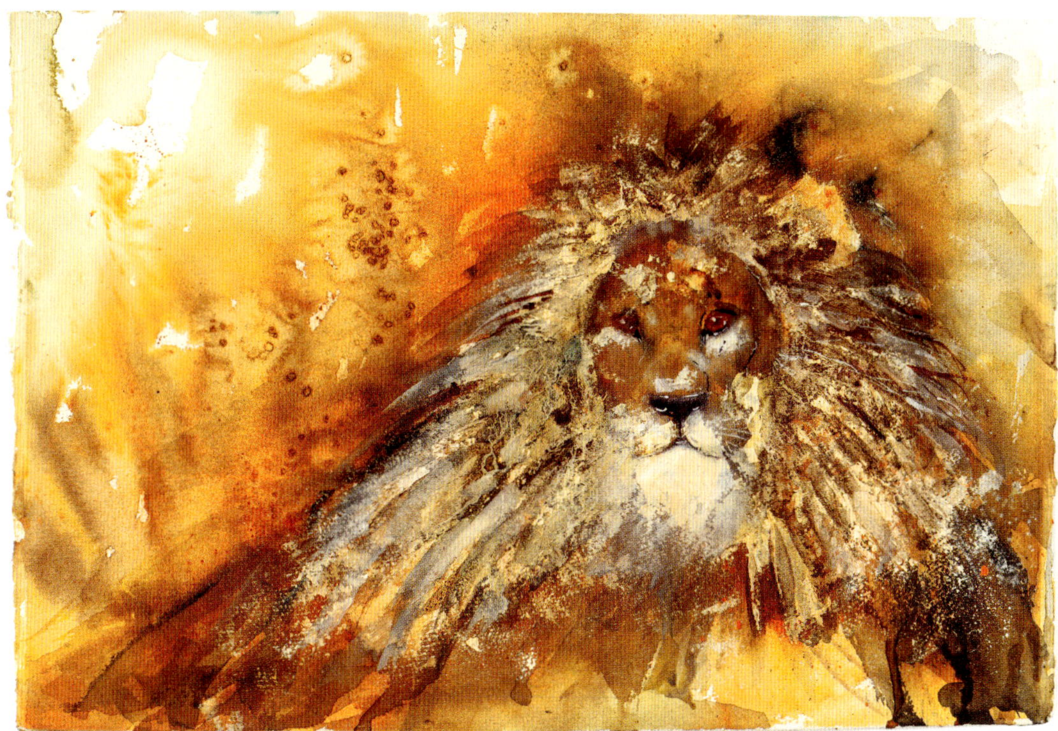

King

53 x 23cm (21 x 9in)

Lion created using Daniel Smith watercolour ground, homemade mushroom ink and salt for texture effects. The main colours used here are quinacridone gold, quinacridone burnt scarlet and cadmium orange.

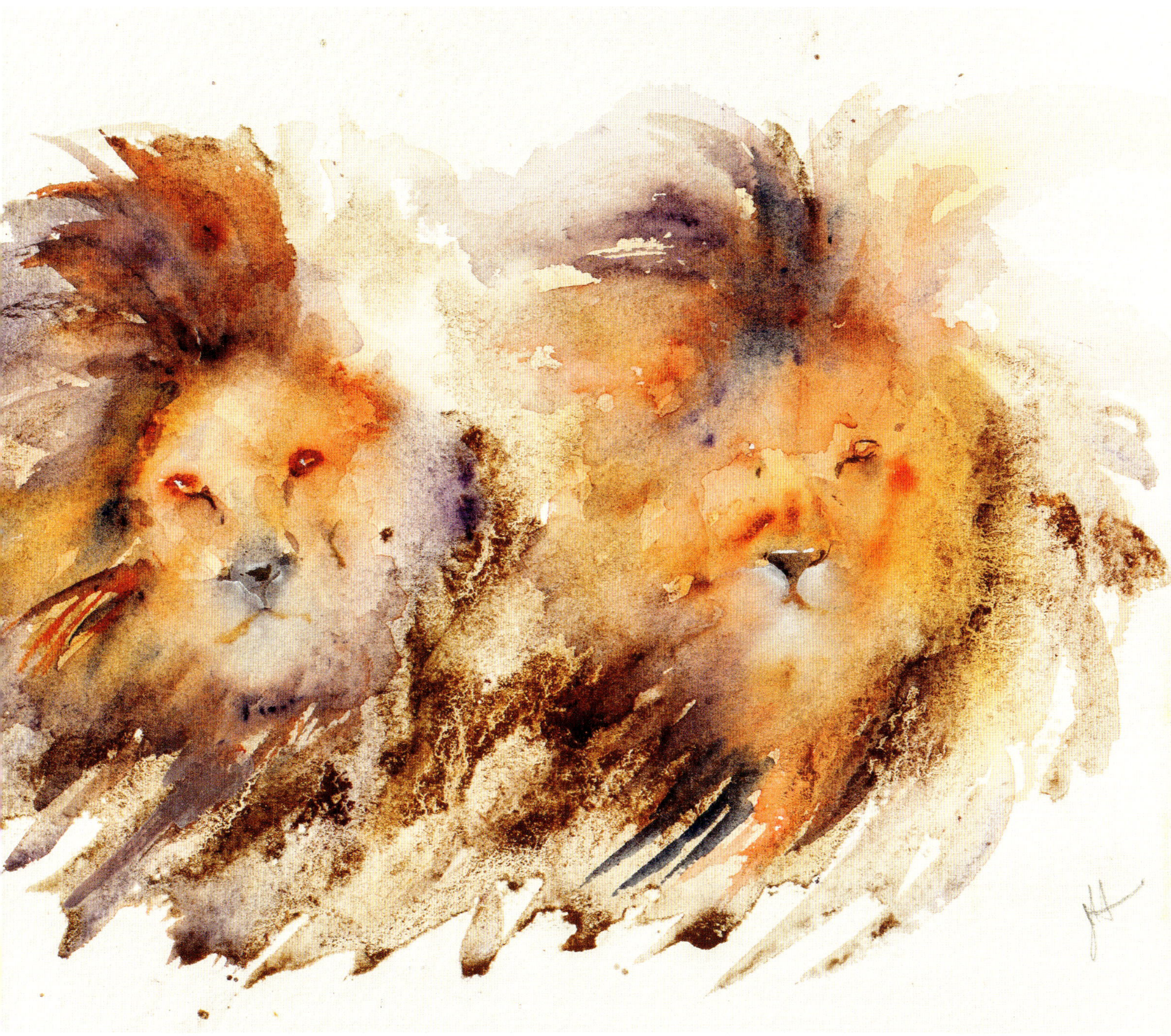

Pride

58 x 38cm (23 x 15in)

The two lions are connected by colour and directional brushwork. Granulation effects are created, adding interest to the manes, and there are sections where information is missing, which adds a sense of atmosphere to the piece.

Tip

Keep your colours appropriate to hint at the country your animals are from when painting, because this can really aid the storytelling in your results.

Animal patterns

The importance of experimentation

Patterns and texture effects on animals are amazing. It's worth taking time to study them. If you are really keen to improve your art skills, take time to paint just the patterns you see in different animals.

We so often place our focus on painting a whole subject in a full composition. We can then be extremely disappointed in our results because some particular element isn't quite right. Having the patience to experiment, creating small sections of an animal, before we paint the whole thing really can lead to the most magical of results; rather than frustration at not having achieved anything we feel is successful as a painting.

Painting a small study first helps you understand the animal's features, where they are placed and how the different sections of the animal connect. Connection in any painting is vitally important. In my painting, the colours on the neck connect through the granulation pattern. My colours harmonize throughout.

These paintings are both interpretations of my own photograph seen below. Try painting patterns using colours that you feel would bring a giraffe to life. Quinacridone gold is invaluable for this animal, along with quinacridone burnt scarlet.

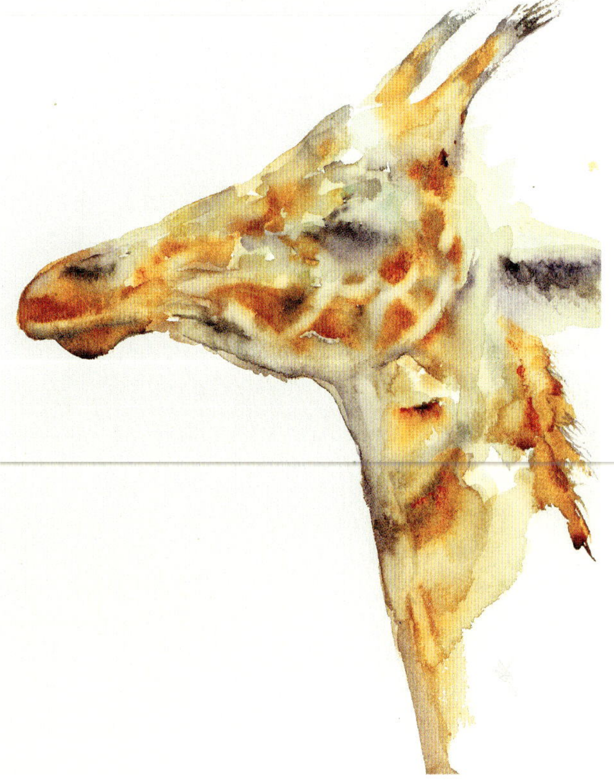

Giraffe study

28 x 38cm (11 x 15in)

Compare this study, created with pure watercolour, and the giraffe on the opposite page, where the use of my homemade granulation fluid has added interest to the animal's markings.

How I start experimenting

Only after falling in love with a subject will I even begin to consider picking up a brush and painting it. I will work on studies of the eyes and the nose, and then the exciting part for me: the colour and texture effects I could use to bring my animal to life.

Compare the two giraffe paintings. The smaller study was painted first so that I could get a feel for my animal. A giraffe's mouth is very different from those of other animals and of course it has a long neck. But what is really unique about the giraffe is its magnificent markings. They are worth taking time to paint – and paint well! In my study I didn't use any texture effects; it is a simple watercolour using pure products.

In the large painting of a giraffe, opposite, I have used my own homemade granulation fluid which I describe on page 105. My advice is always to experiment to see what effects you can come up with on your own. No one has ever shared or shown me how to create my own granulation recipe. But from trial and error I now have an amazing formula that works so well on many subjects, as you will see!

Have fun painting your giraffe!

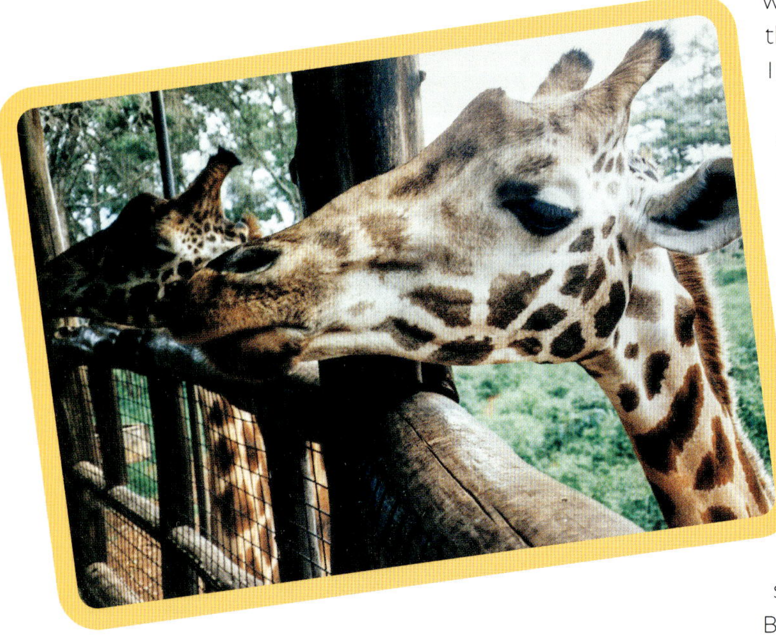

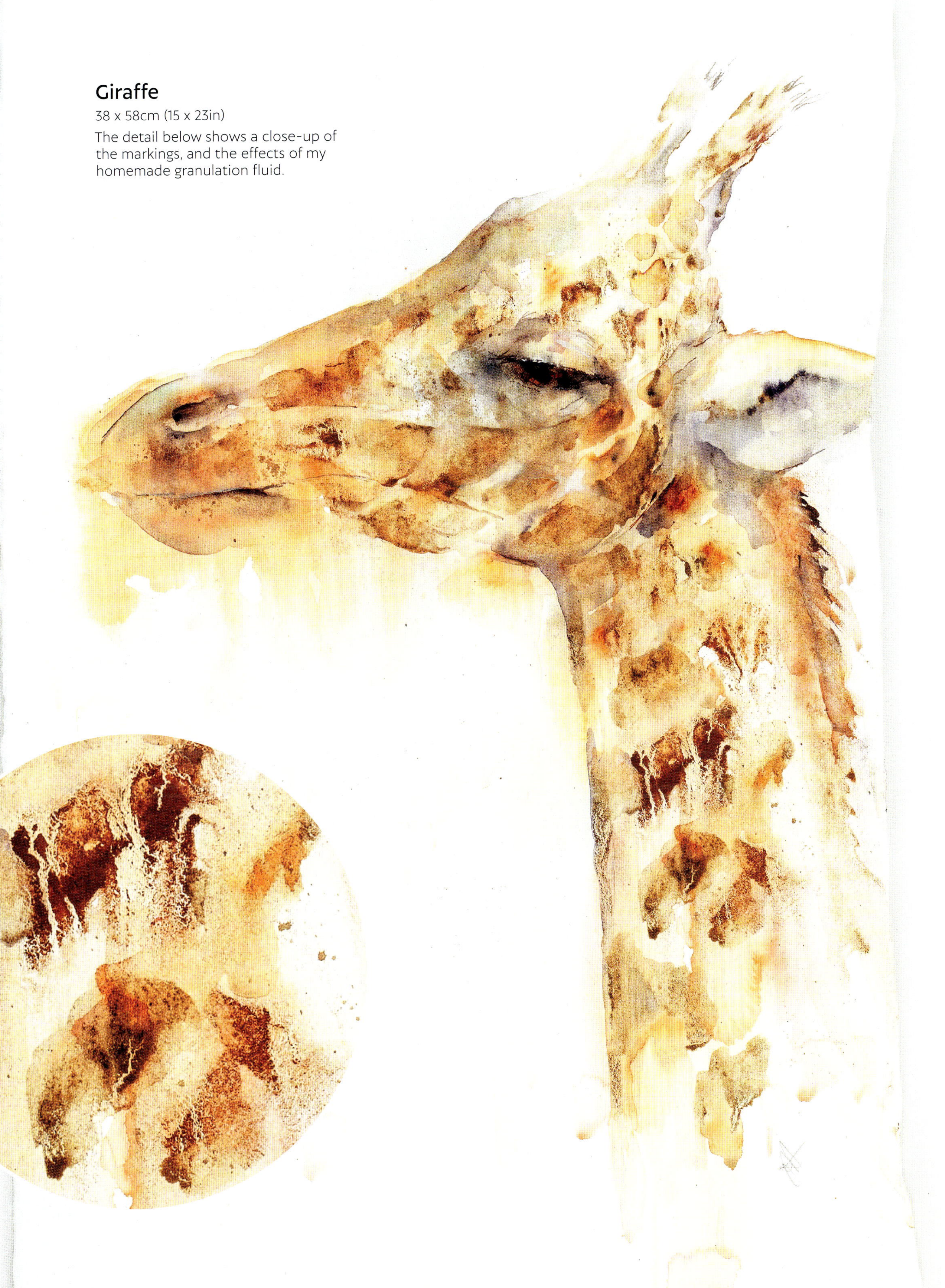

Giraffe

38 x 58cm (15 x 23in)
The detail below shows a close-up of the markings, and the effects of my homemade granulation fluid.

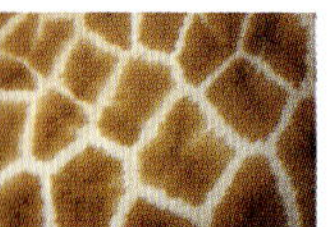

How-to create a giraffe's pattern

Materials

Surface: Scrap of 300gsm (140lb) weight Not surface watercolour paper
Brushes: Size 10 round
Watercolour paints: Aussie red gold, quinacridone gold, quinacridone burnt scarlet, amethyst genuine

Animal markings are an incredible part of wildlife art. Learning how to create them in any medium is enjoyable, but in watercolour they can dramatically come to life in amazing ways, especially if you are aiming for wonderfully unique results. I find when painting animals, no two compositions look alike because of the way pigments wonderfully interact, as we see in this simple exercise.

Choose any animal and study the colour markings. Create your dancing ladies to match the subject well and then practise creating small studies of the markings as seen below in my giraffe colour experiment.

1 Start by selecting appropriate colours. I always avoid just painting the colours I actually see. A unique colour addition, in this case amethyst genuine, can often work wonders!

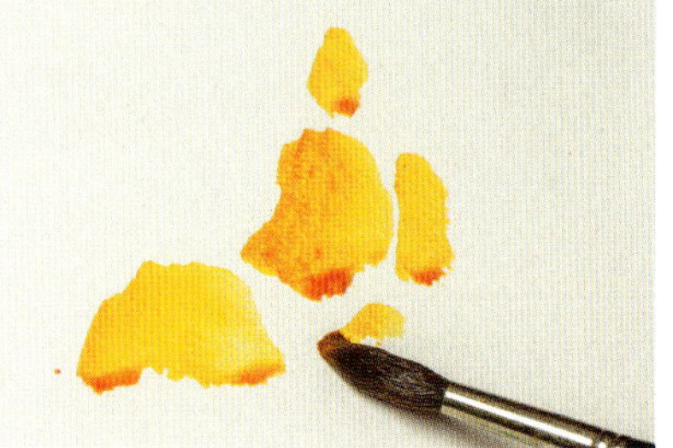

2 I begin by painting squares of the markings I see on the giraffe's face and neck in my resource photograph. My colour placement is guided by my observation of the real subject. Here I am using the size 10 to paint the squares with a mix of Aussie red gold and quinacridone gold.

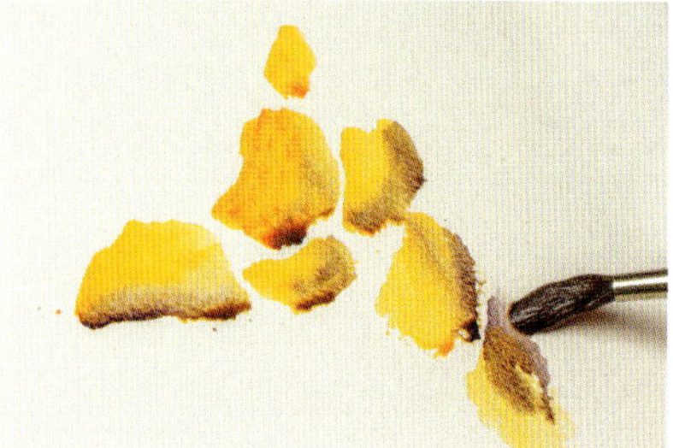

3 I add a second colour, in this case amethyst genuine, to enhance the colouring of the animal. This makes my art look more original and totally fascinating.

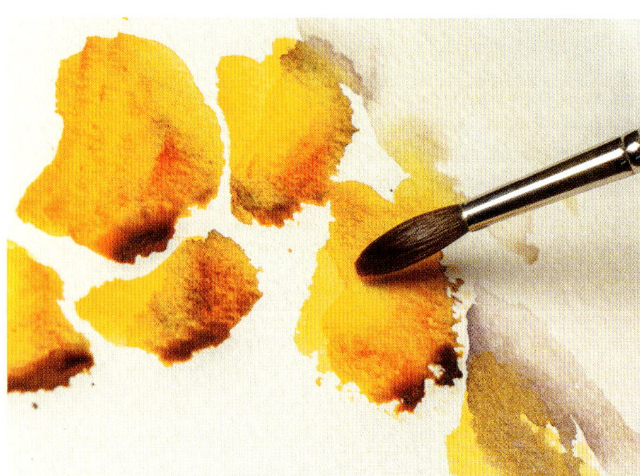

4 I soften the edges of some of the squares of colour, sometimes allowing the pigments to flow in the space between the squares. I use a clean, damp brush to gently touch the centre of some squares to create watermarks in each section. The patterns created by the mix of water and pigment naturally interacting can superbly boost an atmospheric painting, often giving you unique patterns that cannot be repeated.

Homework

Try selecting a collection of animal resource photographs and practise just painting the patterns that you see. Use your dancing ladies exercises to gain a good colour match before you begin painting and experiment with watermark effects to gain a variety of effects that will be useful when painting a whole variety of animals.

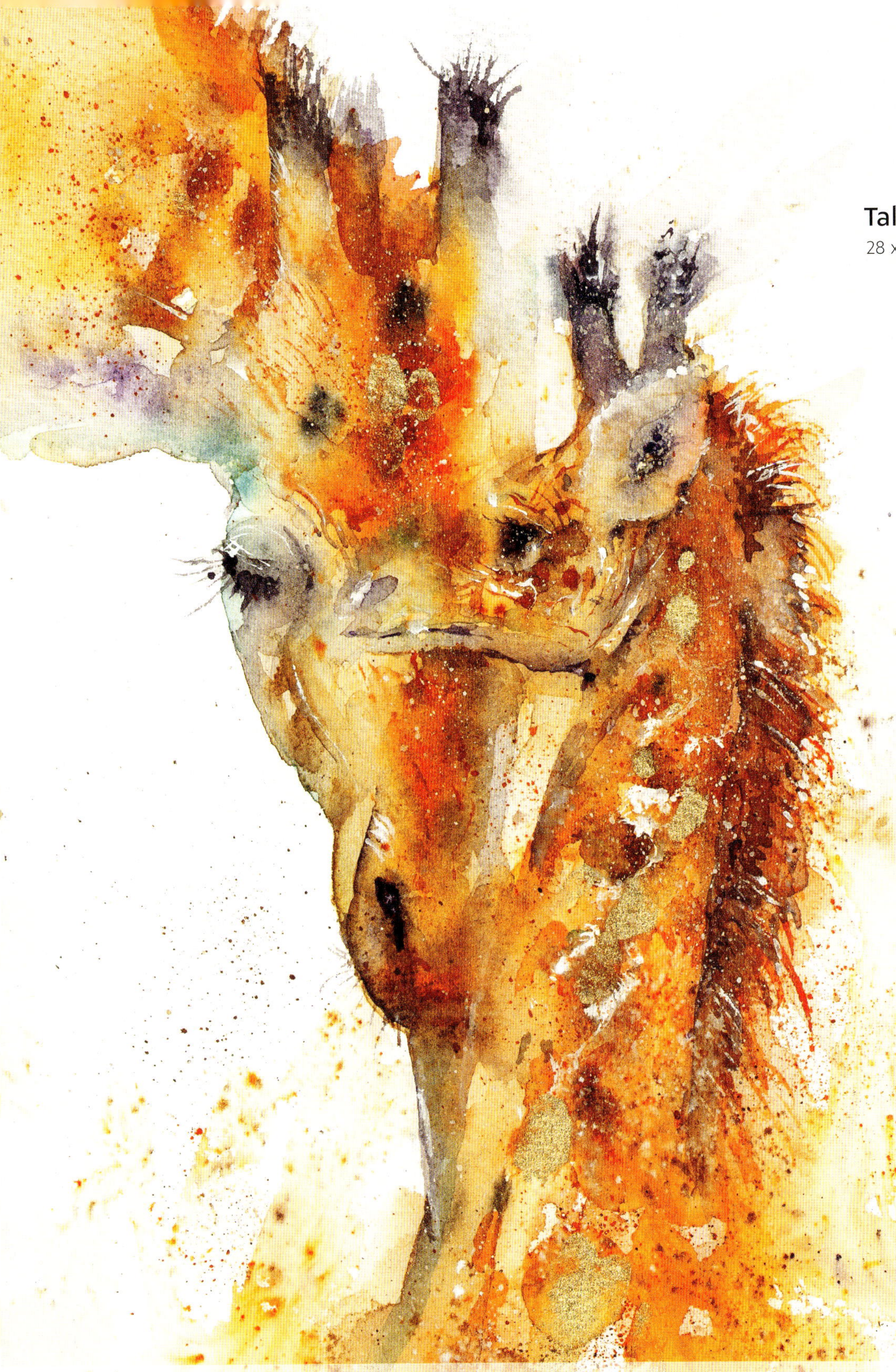

Animal meaning: giraffe

The giraffe has a wonderful meaning. When your life becomes impossible due to circumstances out of your control, this beautiful animal reminds us to hold our heads up. They symbolize grace, peace and individuality.

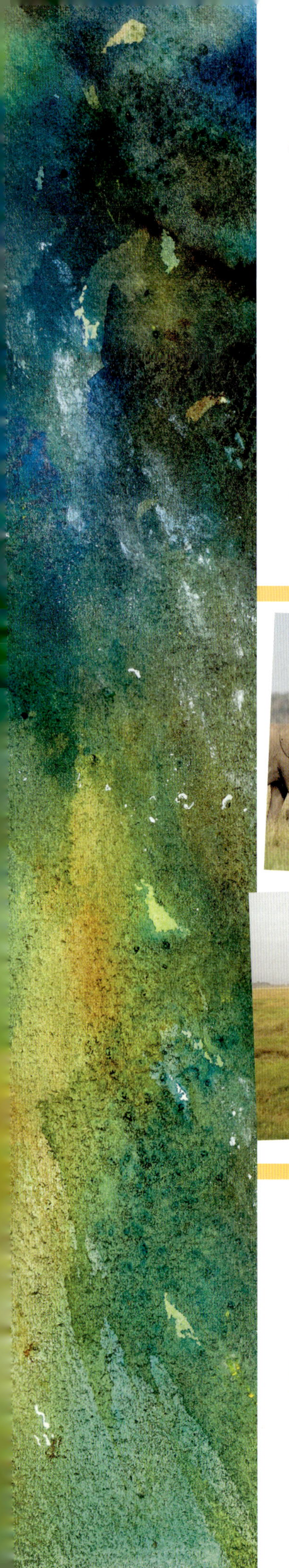

Animals and creative washes

Patterns for background washes

I am known for painting fascinating background washes – how to do so is explained overleaf. These creative washes can be used as a technique in different ways. I either work spontaneously, laying down the wash and then finding a subject on top of it, or more deliberately; painting a wash, knowing what my subject will be before I pick up the colour.

On pages 34–35, we looked at how to paint an elephant's head. The painting here was created in exactly the same way, except that it was painted on top of a coloured background, made with a creative wash instead of white paper. This is where painting animals becomes even more exciting. By developing creative washes using the colours and patterns of your selected animal, the surface will help to guide you in your subsequent choice of colours and texture effects, leading you to the most fantastic art – and with each painting you create being totally unique.

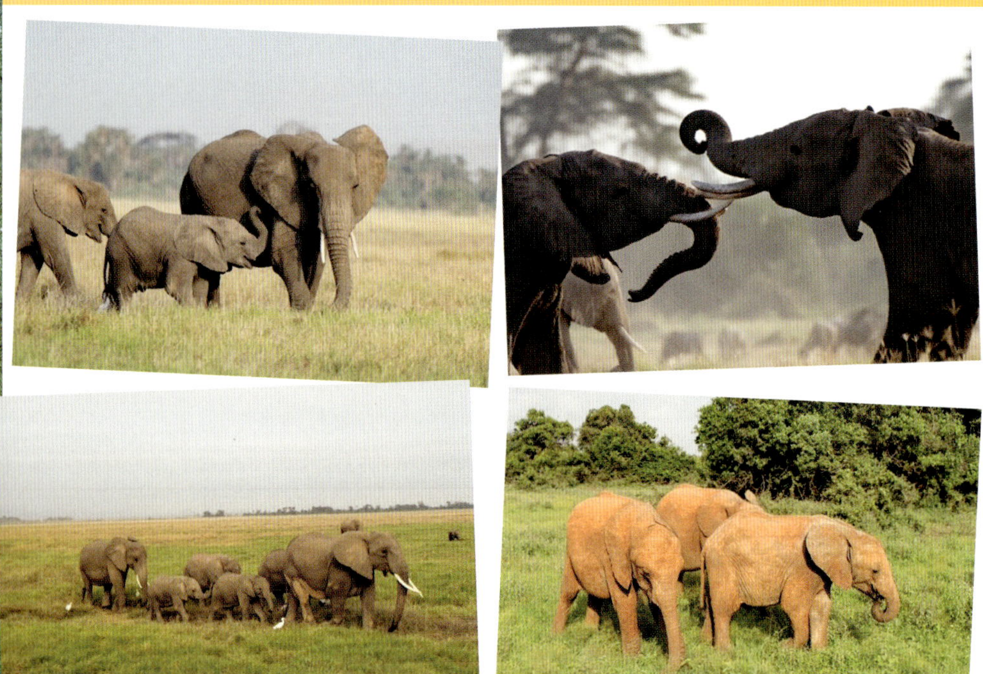

Animal meaning: elephant

Did you know that elephants are traditionally seen as symbols of good luck? Wearing an elephant charm with its trunk facing upwards is thought to bring good fortune to the wearer. So you could try hanging your elephant art in your home to see if it brings you good fortune!

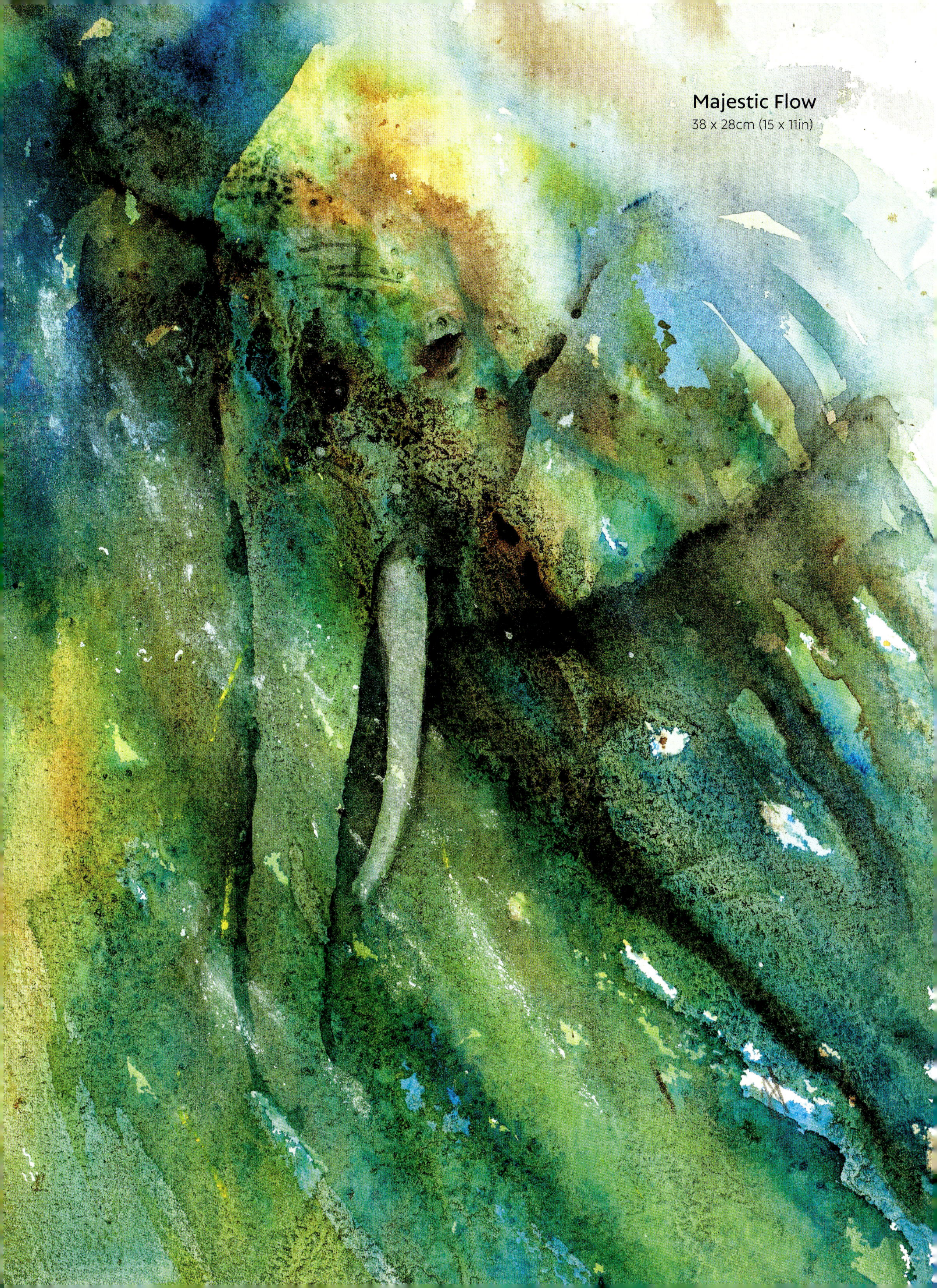
Majestic Flow
38 x 28cm (15 x 11in)

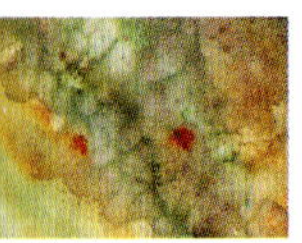

How-to work over creative background washes

Creating an exciting background to suit a subject can be so fascinating as a technique. You have options of adding texture: I have used a combination of salt and splattering here. The more intriguing your background, the more interesting your subject will appear.

Materials

Surface: 300gsm (140lb) weight Not surface watercolour paper, 28 x 38cm (11 x 15in)

Brushes: size 10 and 12 round, rigger

Watercolour paints: quinacridone gold, Aussie red gold, cascade green, cadmium yellow, phthalo blue turquoise, Payne's blue gray

Other: silk salt, white gouache

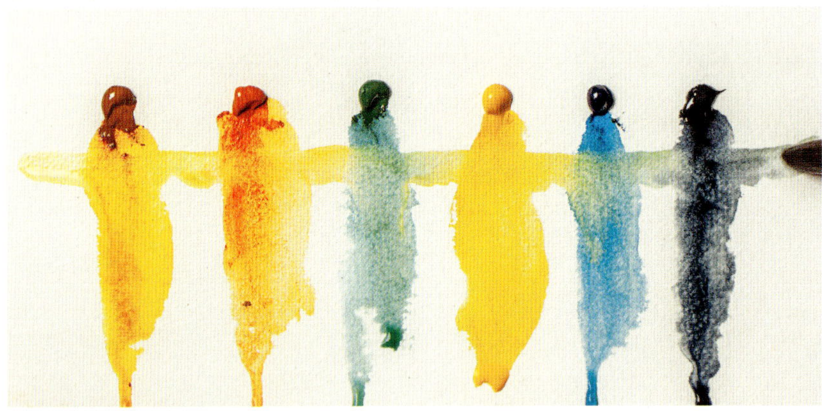

Dancing ladies: colour selection

I've chosen slightly unusual colours so that my result will be more unique, including warm shades to set off my elephant beautifully.

1 To create my first wash, I tipped the paper at a diagonal and used a size 12 round brush to add water, from the top left to the bottom right. I then used the brush to begin adding phthalo blue turquoise.

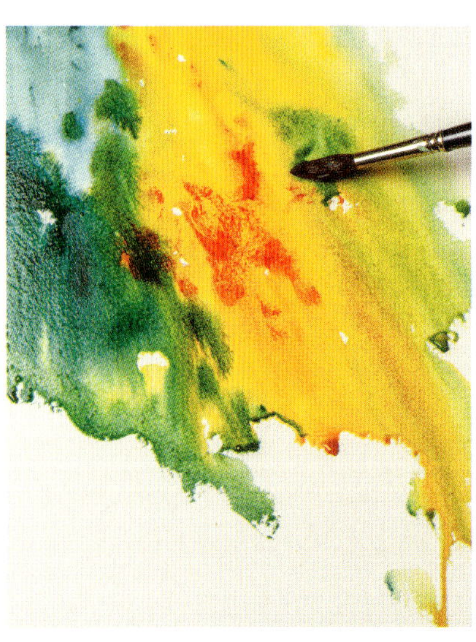

2 Working down from top left to bottom right, I continued adding quinacridone gold, cadmium yellow and cascade green in turn to create a loose wash.

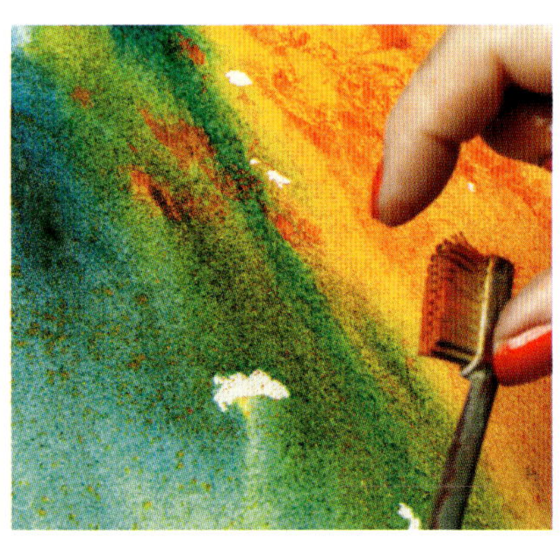

3 While the wash was wet, I suggested texture by dipping a toothbrush in a pool of paint, then holding it near the surface and drawing my finger across it to flick the paint onto the surface.

Tip

This technique is called splattering, and we look at how to use it for different effects later on.

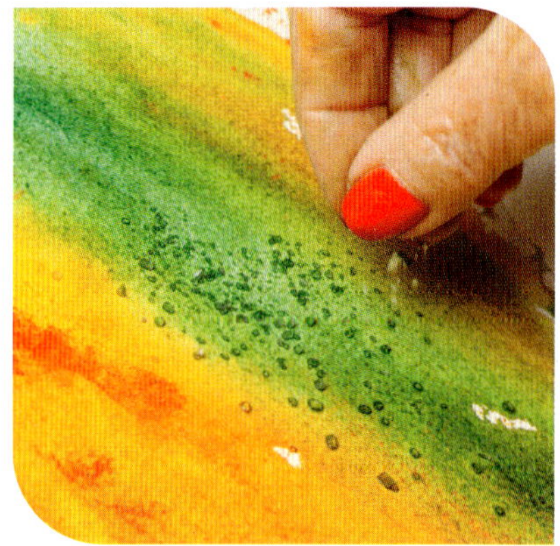

4 Laying the paper flat, I carefully dropped in a few granules of silk salt. It was then left to dry.

5 Gently brush away the salt, then look at the wash, and look for a space that has interesting marks and patterns that you can develop into the animal. Here, I used the rigger to paint an eye with Payne's blue gray, before softening the colour away with a damp size 10 brush. Next, I used a mix of quinacridone gold and Payne's blue gray to paint a line at the front edge of the elephant's head, before softening it away into the background, leaving a negative edge. You can add Payne's blue gray to the edge near the head for added impact.

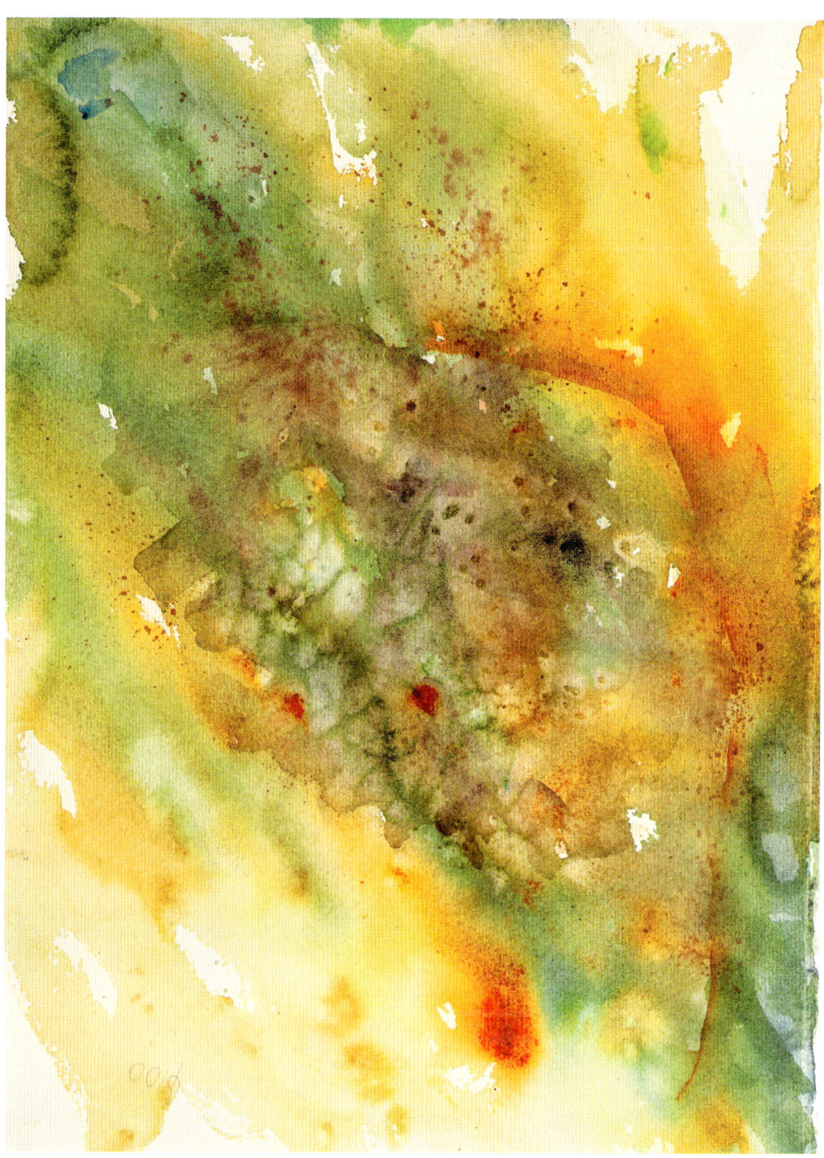

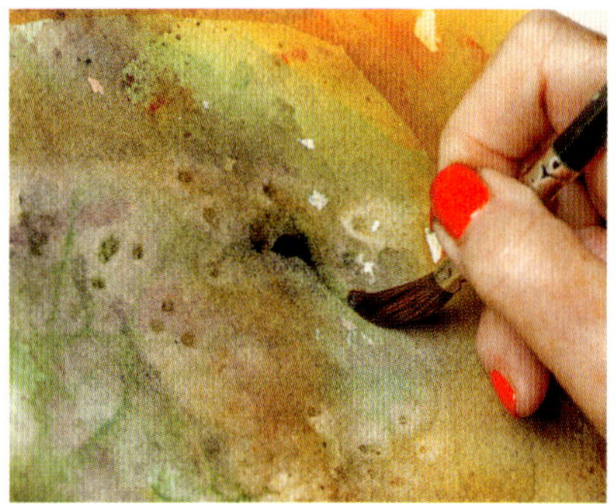

Softening

Detail of the wet paint being drawn away from the eye with the size 10 round brush.

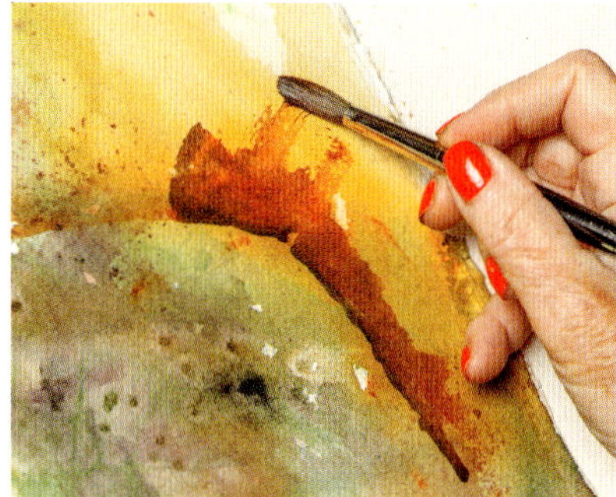

Negative painting

Softening the paint away while leaving a line suggests an edge to a shape. This negative painting technique is useful for keeping the freshness of the creative wash in the area you want as the focus.

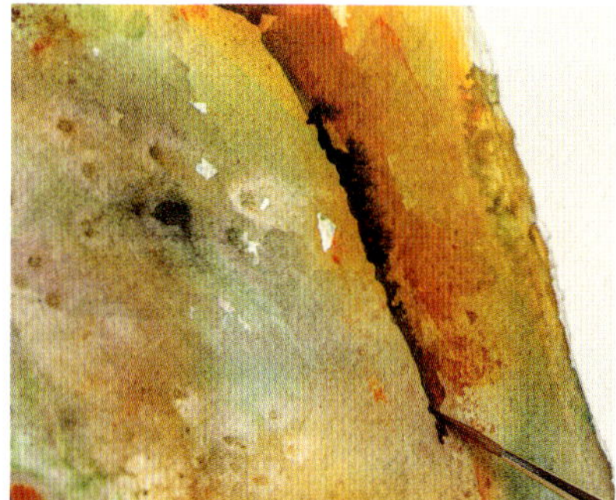

Adding impact

Reinforcing the line near the elephant increases the contrast; just be sure to apply the darker colour while the paint is still wet, and soften it away from the edge.

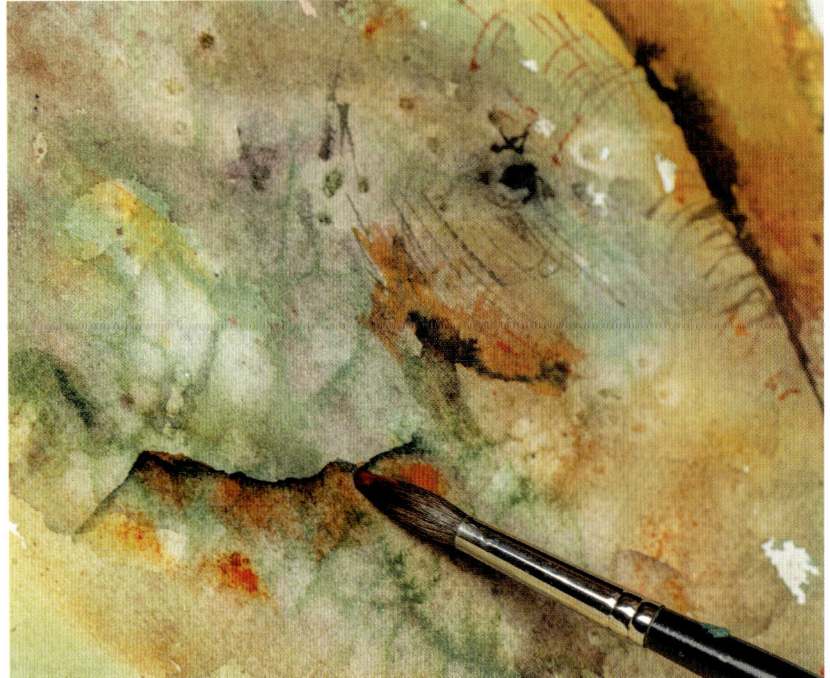

6 I now use the rigger with Payne's blue gray to add fine lines and wrinkles to the trunk and head. Suggest the elephant's jawline and ear with negative painting, looking to keep the beautiful patterns created in the initial creative wash by the salt.

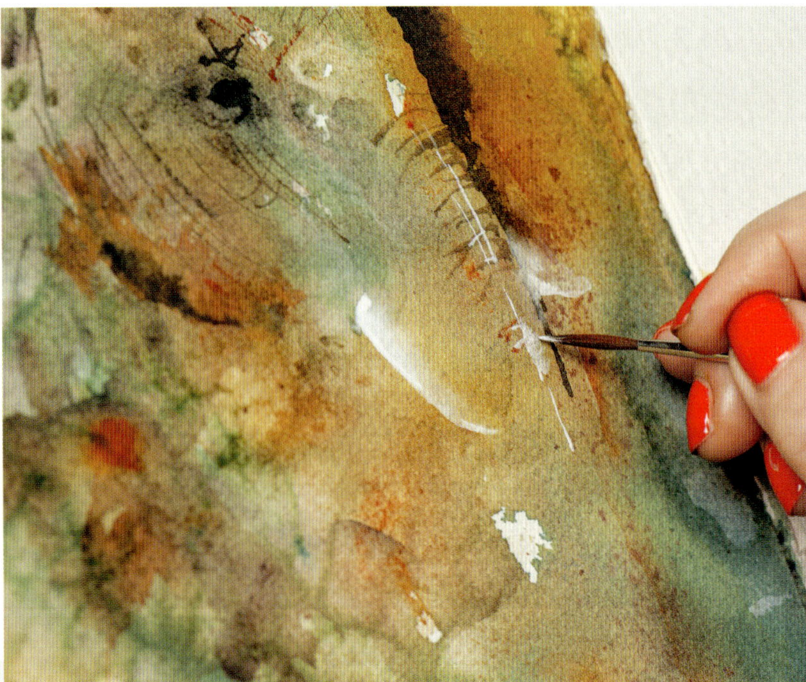

7 To finish, use the rigger and white gouache to paint a line for the tusk, softening it into the surface with clean water. Pick out a few highlights on the skin to accentuate the wrinkles.

Adventures in painting

There is no end to the possibilities in ways to paint animals in watercolour. You can paint from a starting point like the eye or nose. You can paint an animal on a white background or you can paint it on top of a fabulous first wash.

The point is, you can have fun creating, improve your art skills and allow your imagination to awaken. To think, we have more excitement to come in the following pages. Are you loving the thought of painting animals in watercolour yet? I hope you are. Let's continue our atmospheric animals in watercolour adventure.

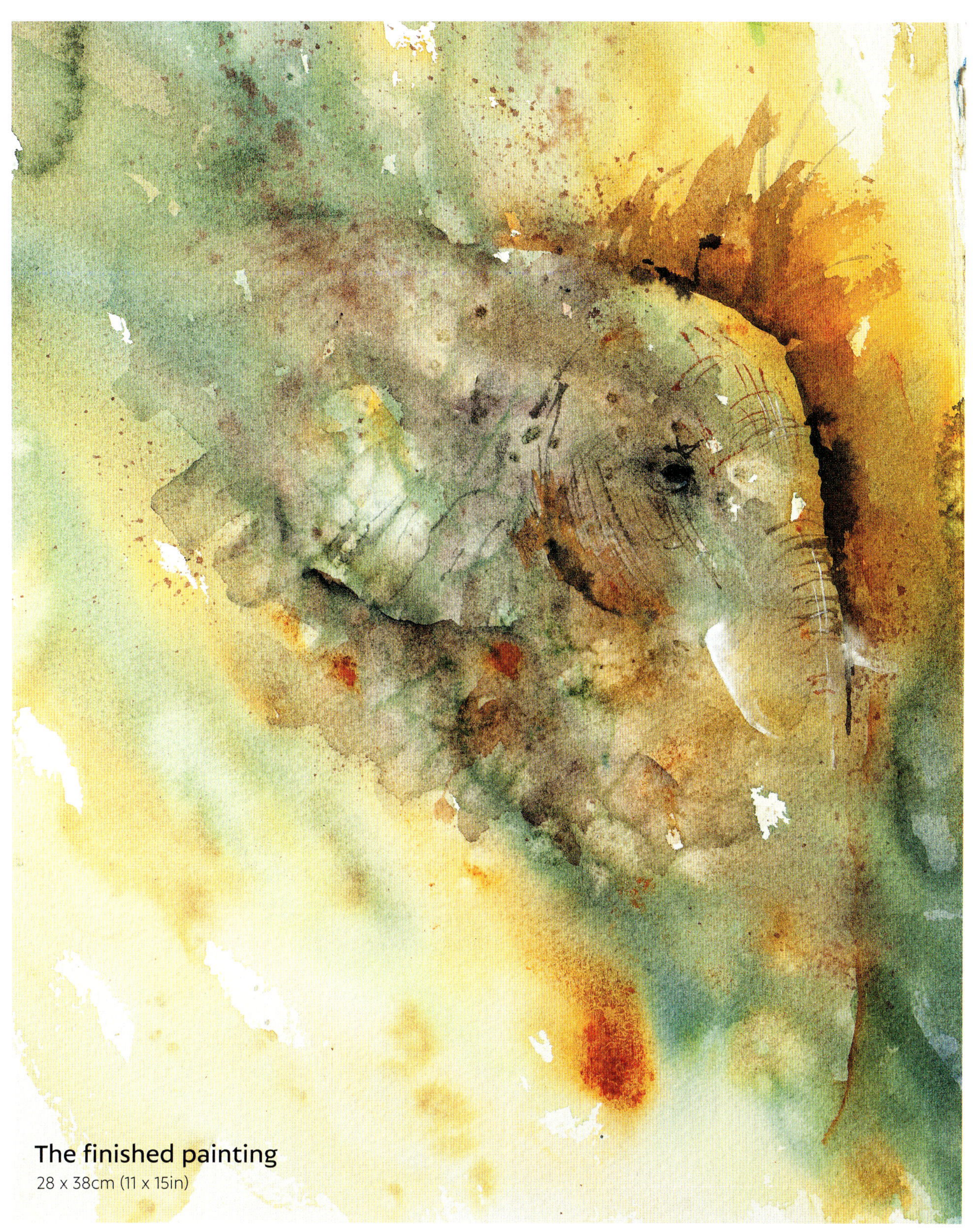

The finished painting
28 x 38cm (11 x 15in)

"If you can reach out and touch and love and be with wildlife, you will forever be changed, and you will want to make the world a better place." *Terri Irwin*

Down under

FROM CHILDHOOD I ALWAYS LONGED TO see a real koala. The story behind this longing is shared in another of my books, but since writing it I have now painted many beautiful koalas and still have that wonderful happy feeling when I create them in watercolour.

Admiring animals' textures

Koalas give the illusion of being sleepy, cuddly creatures. Sleepy they may be, but cuddly really isn't one of their best attributes! They do look adorable though, and there is no question that their fur is both a fascinating texture to create and an interesting challenge to a wildlife artist. This is exactly what we are now looking at: more fabulous texture effects.

There are now many products available to artists which you can use to easily create incredible patterns in your art, even watercolour. I have painted two koalas in this chapter to show you the difference that adding texture products to your work can make.

I should explain here that I regard myself as a purist when it comes to watercolour. I love working with watercolour pigment alone but I am still intrigued by patterns and experimenting. I aim to always be on the lookout for something new, and this is a huge part of my daily painting routine.

First we need great subjects. Here I have a selection of images. One is of me holding a koala in Australia. The brochure is of a sanctuary I visited, which really fuelled my passion for these cute little beings.

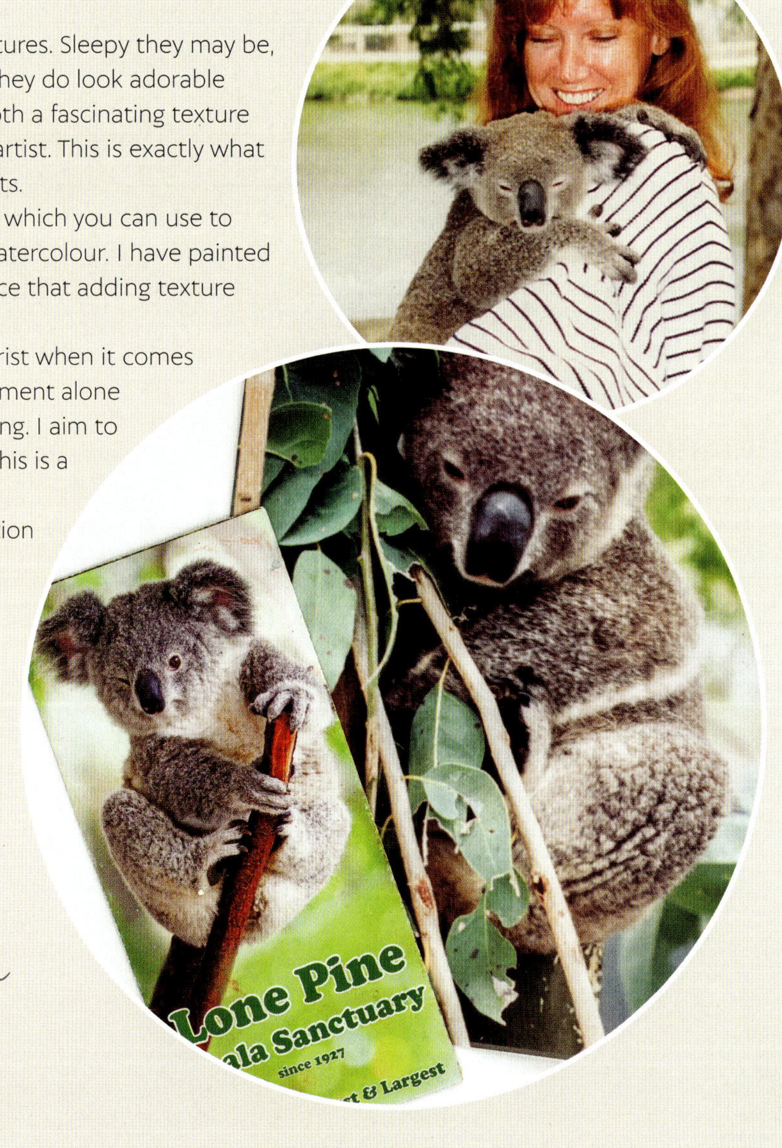

"

From study to painting

In the simple study below, I began with the left eye. From here I built up the face, before adding the ears and body, leaving several sections to the viewer's imagination. As usual, we don't need to add every part of an animal when aiming for atmospheric results. When complete, I added a touch of opera pink to the ear, exaggerating the colour purely for effect.

For the later, full painting (right) I used a toothbrush to splatter the fur sections of my koala painting, in order to intensify the appearance of the fur. I used Payne's blue gray for my first splatter application and when this was completely dry, I used white gouache to splatter on top. The combination of the two colours led to a very pleasing koala fur pattern. There are also other ways to create texture with watercolour. Read on and let's see them.

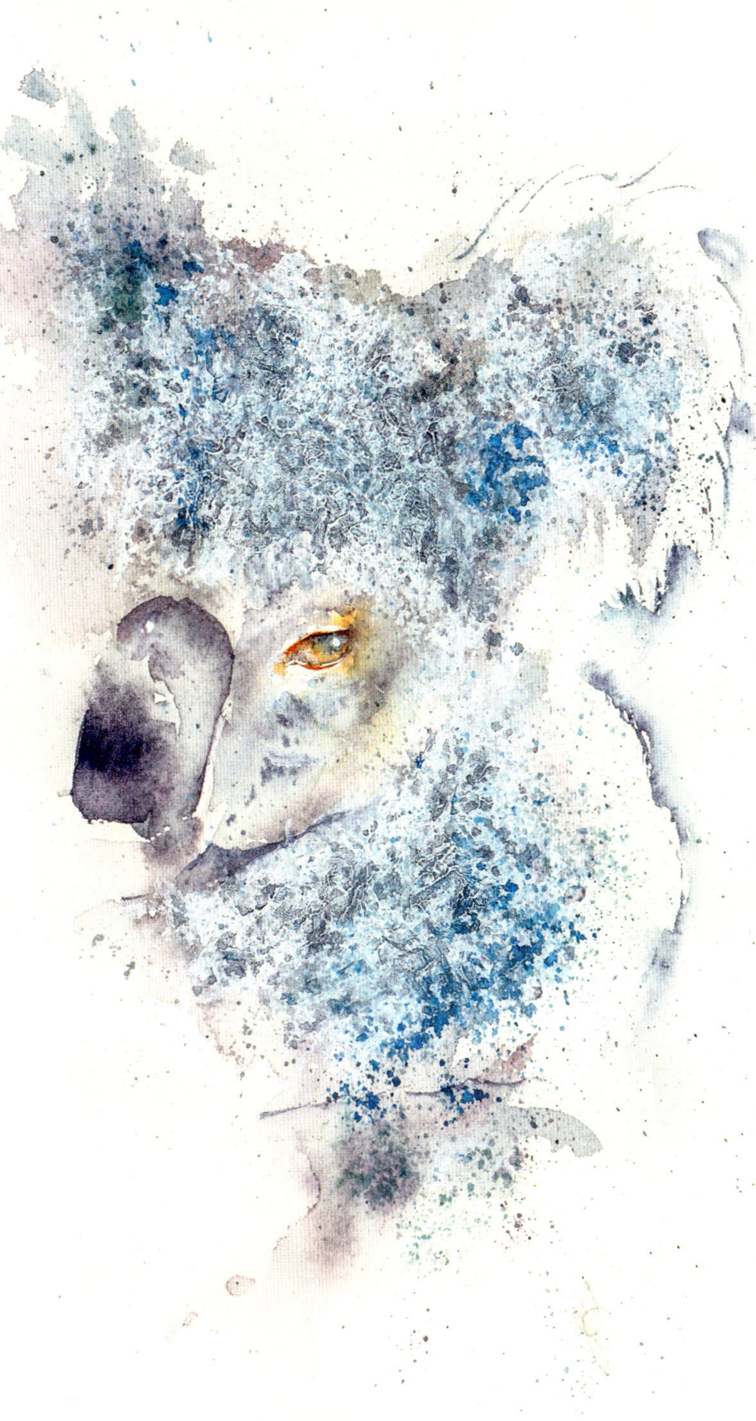

Sleepy Koala
28 x 38cm (11 x 15in)

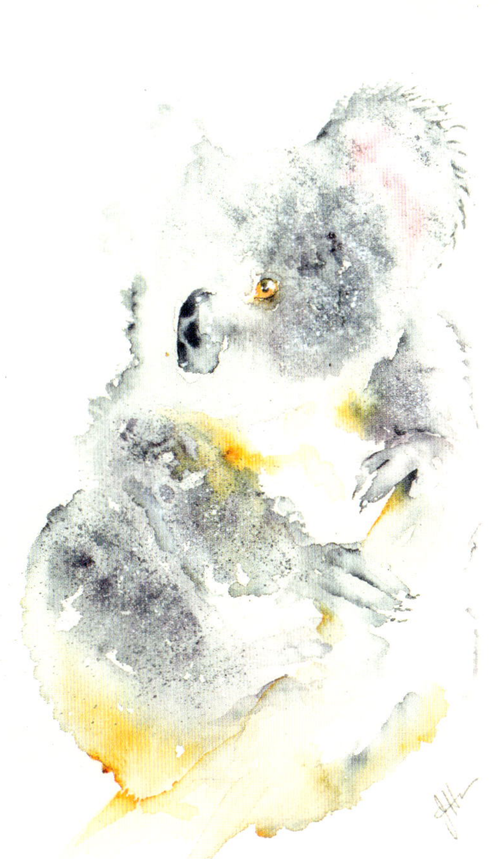

Koala study
28 x 38cm (11 x 15in)

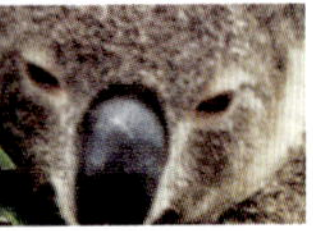

Step-by-step Sleepy Koala

This is a beautiful project. We look at painting a sleepy koala in pure watercolour and then consider alternative ways of enhancing our art using texture products and techniques. I am lucky to have seen these beautiful animals when teaching workshops on tours all over Australia. Their dense fur is a welcome challenge to recreate, and as a subject this animal is extremely fun and appealing. Our goal is to give the appearance of a sleepy animal, and one that seems cuddly, in our results.

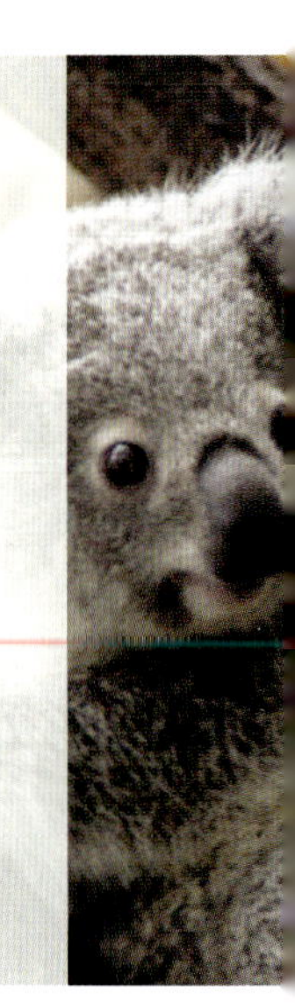

Materials

- Surface: 300gsm (140lb) weight Not surface watercolour paper, 28 x 38cm (11 x 15in)
- Brushes: size 10 and 12 round, rigger
- Watercolour paints: Payne's blue gray, moonglow, amethyst genuine, quinacridone burnt scarlet, quinacridone gold
- Other: toothbrush, white gouache

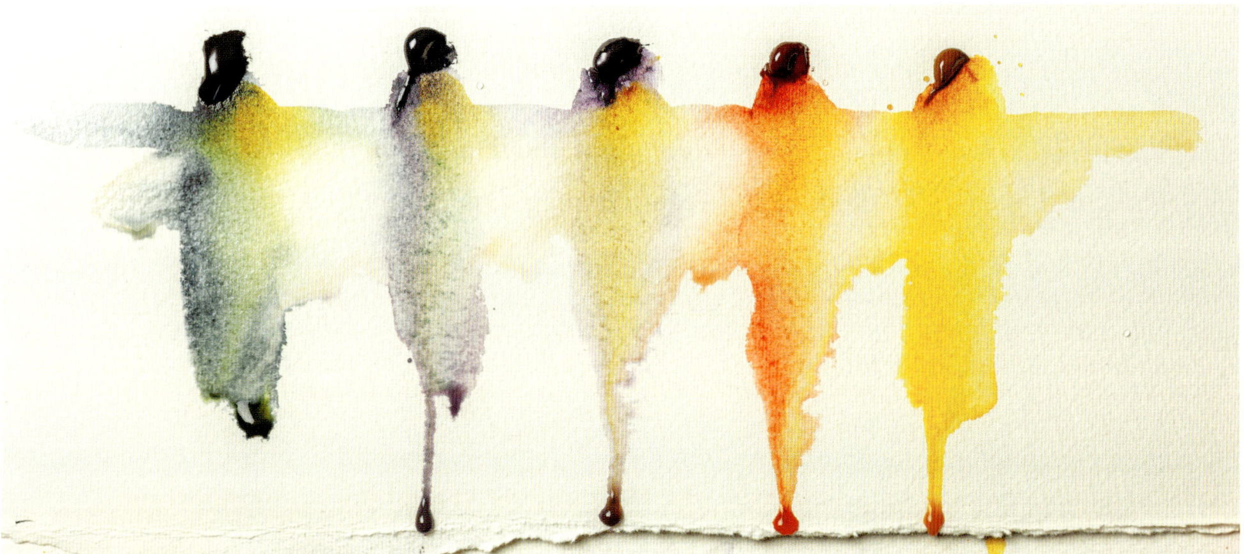

Dancing ladies: colour selection

For this painting, I have selected the following colours from the Daniel Smith range: Payne's blue gray, moonglow, amethyst genuine, quinacridone burnt scarlet and quinacridone gold.

Note that I have taken a touch of quinacridone gold and added it to each of the other colours. A powerful pigment, it adds a burst of sunshine to almost any other paint.

You may find the inclusion of a strong turquoise a rather odd decision. When I paint I deliberately opt for the addition of at least one stand-out colour that will make my painting seem more alive. This way of working, of finding unusual colour combinations, adds great impact to our results. It takes us well away from the 'boring' word and leaps us into the realm of extraordinary, and – dare I say – fantastic!

Tip

Always look for unusual colour combinations to bring your atmospheric art to life with unique and dramatic results.

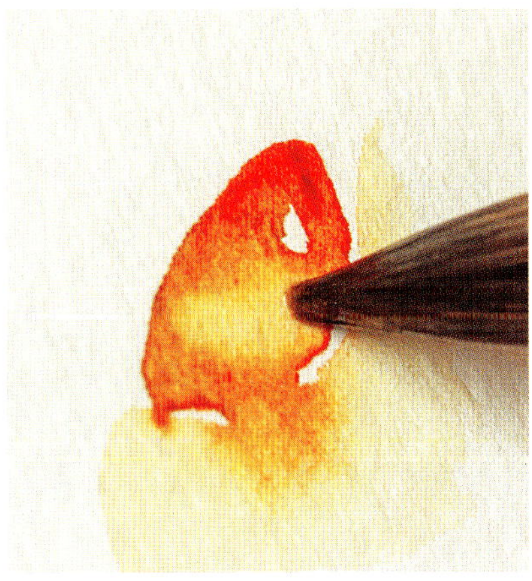

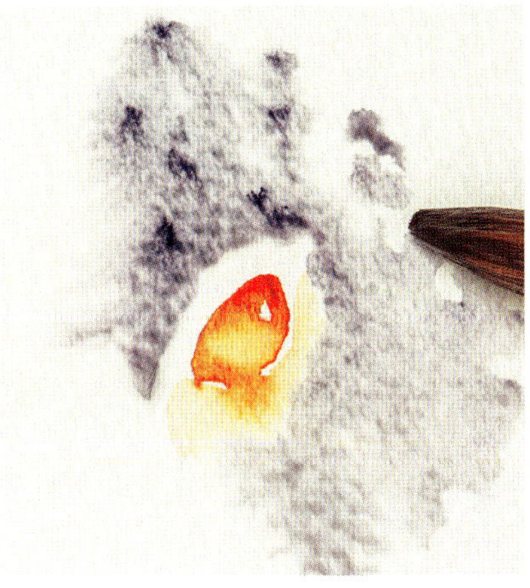

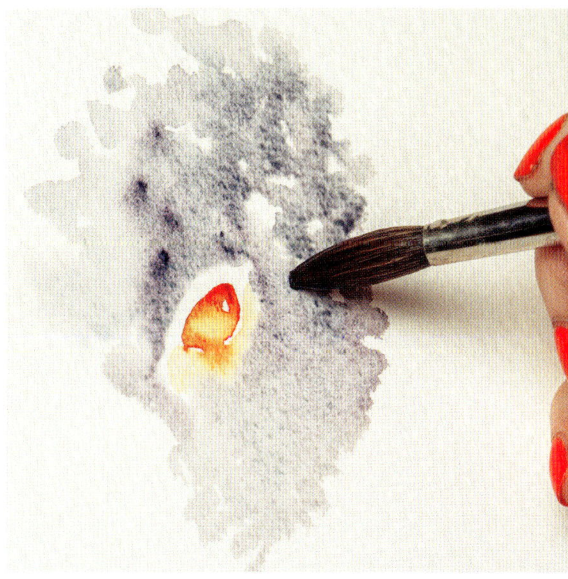

1 I begin by creating the eye. For this project you need to consider where the whole animal will be in the completed painting before making your first brush mark. Leave space around the eye to add the upper ear, head and lower body. Using quinacridone gold and quinacridone burnt scarlet, follow the directions for painting eyes as seen on page 71.

2 Leaving a gap around the eye, I wetted the nearby area with the size 10 round, then started to build up the fur around the eye with Payne's blue gray and hints of amethyst genuine, adding the paint with dabbing touches of the brush tip, rather than sweeping strokes.

3 I next develop the rest of the face surrounding the eye section, leaving a space where the nose will be placed. I use brush work to follow the direction for the fur and face shape. No straight lines!

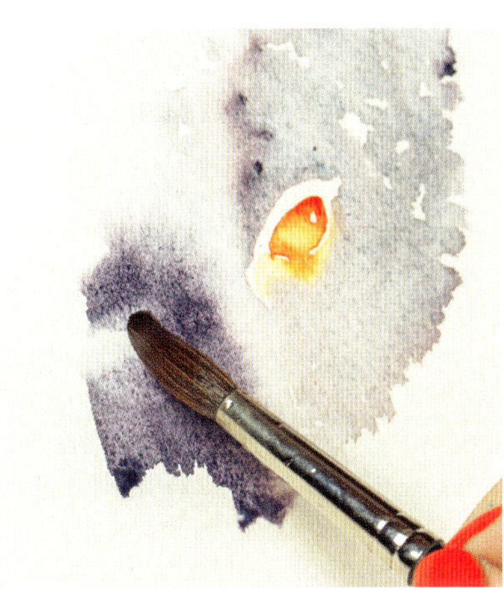

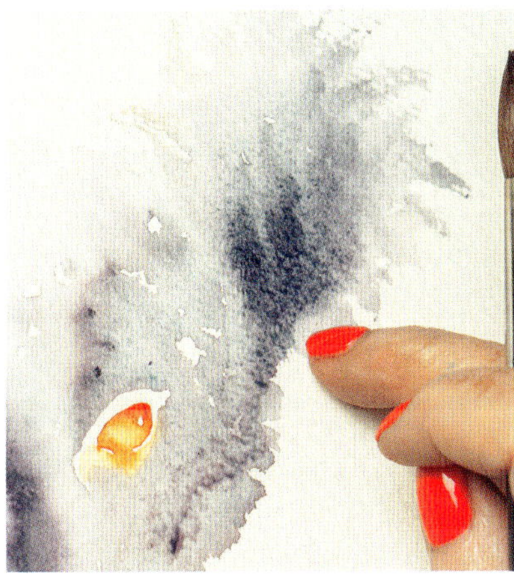

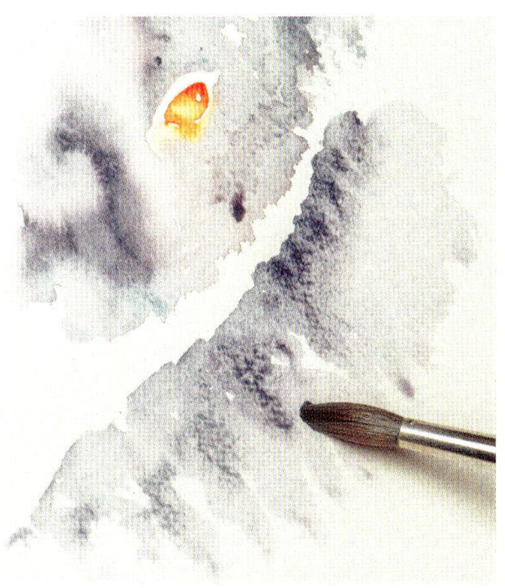

4 The nose of the koala is unique. It almost seems leathery in appearance. Hinting at its shape with moonglow and a touch of Payne's blue gray works very well, using suggestive colour placement rather than a defined 'hard block' of colour.

5 Paint the shape of the ear with moonglow, then add Payne's blue gray wet in wet. Draw out tufts with a clean finger.

6 Once your koala head and ear are painted, begin to add the body by placing colour under the face. Start with the arm, using moonglow and Payne's blue gray. Imagine you are stroking the koala's fur with your brush to create the effect of longer fur.

Tip

If you are uncertain on how to begin painting the nose, try placing a soft shape first and building up colour on it gradually, once you know your nose is in the right position.

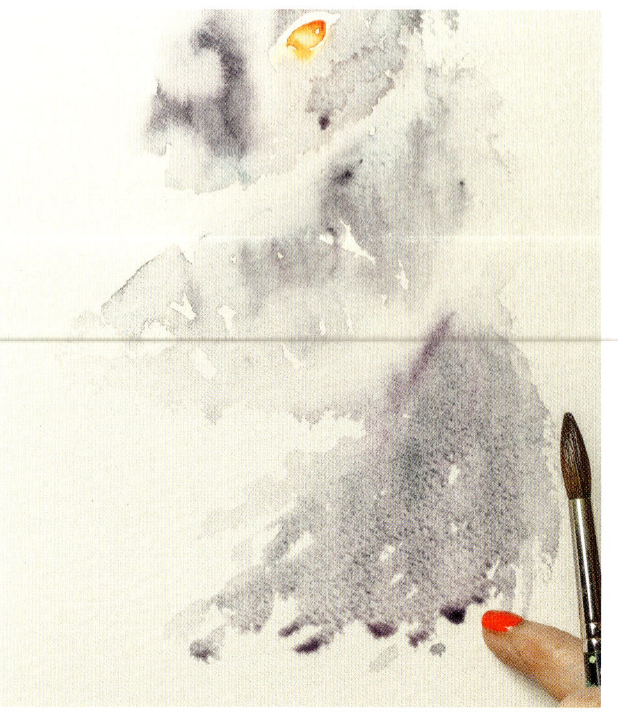

7 Continue working downwards with your brushwork, gradually building up the koala's body. Remember you are aiming for an atmospheric result, so leave sections to the viewer's imagination. Hint at the lower leg rather than paint it completely. Using a clean finger or thumb to brush away colour will give you a wonderful furry effect on the outer edge of your animal.

Trapping the light

Leaving white space between areas of the animal, or between the subject and the background, will give an illusion of sunlight hitting the koala. You can also add an outer edge to the ear in this way.

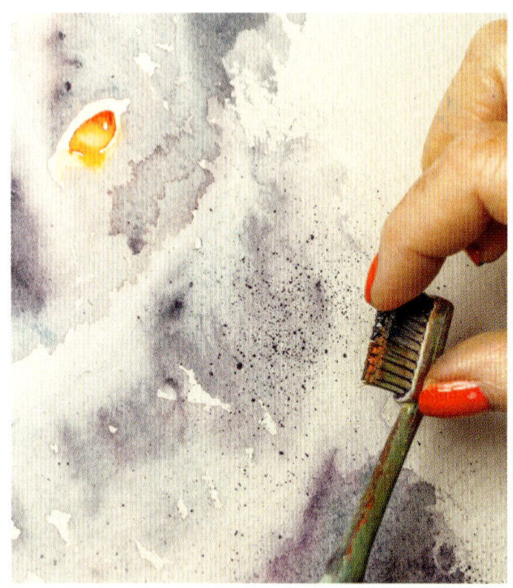

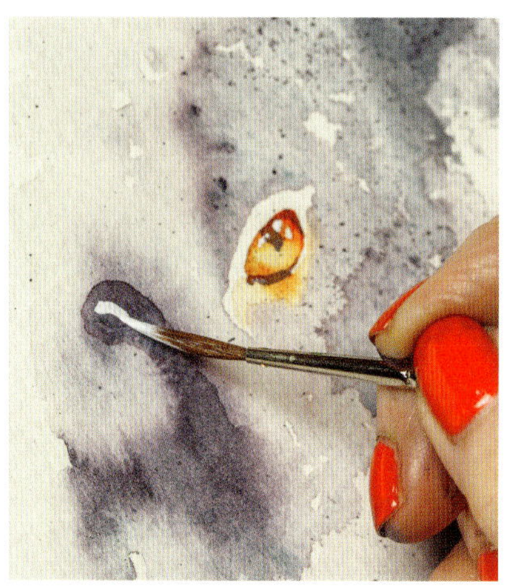

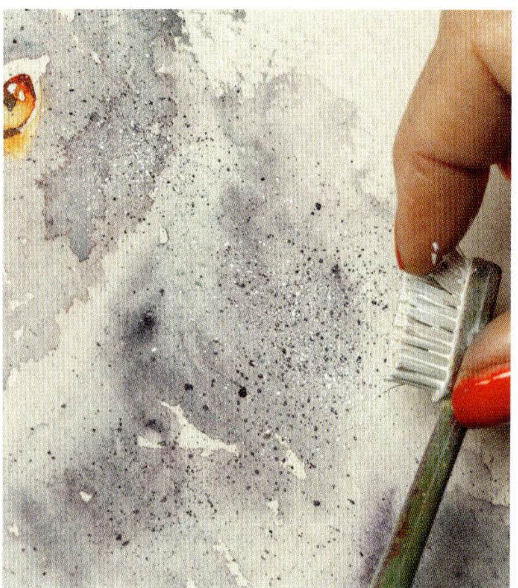

8 Once your koala painting is completely dry, dip the toothbrush in a pool of paint and use the splatter technique (see page 90) to create the dense fur. You can splatter with a variety of colours. I used Payne's blue gray.

9 Detail the eye with Payne's blue gray, using the rigger to add the eyelid and pupil. Swap to white gouache for additional highlights on both eye and nose.

10 When the first splatter application was completely dry, I used a double splatter technique by splattering with a second colour. In this case, I splattered white gouache on top. The combination of white dots on top of dark grey splatter placed on a watercolour base background gives a terrific illusion of dense fur patterns. You can use as many splatter applications as you wish, gradually building up both colour and texture.

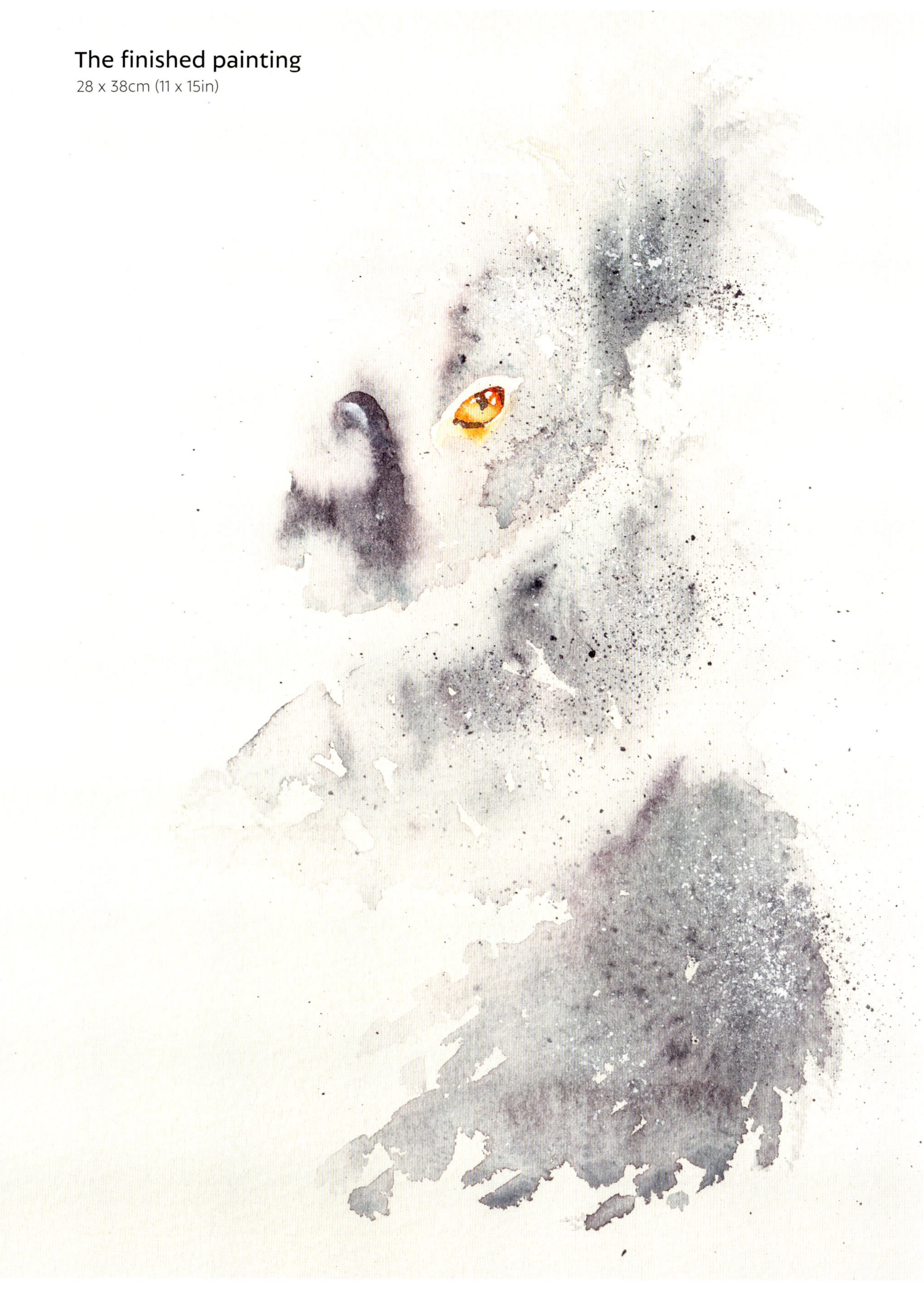

The finished painting

28 x 38cm (11 x 15in)

An alternative option: dense fur texture effect

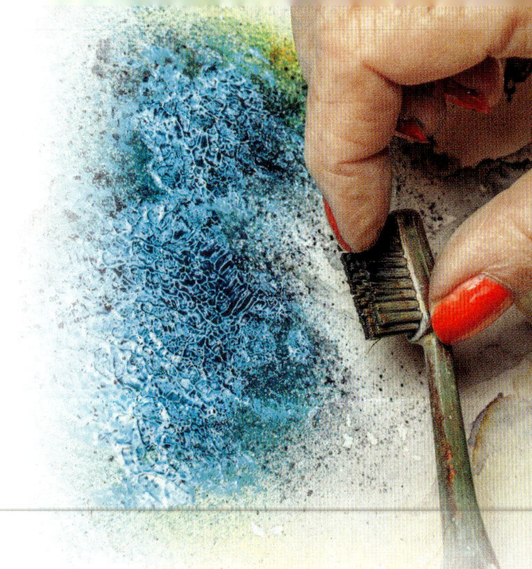

You may love your koala painting as it is at this stage, but in the magical world of watercolour there are always many options to take your painting further in technique. My advice is this: if you love any painting as it is, leave it well alone. If, however, you aren't happy with your work, or simply wish to experiment, you can take your animal paintings further by experimenting with texture products as seen in this next exercise.

Working with any product that isn't strictly watercolour should be considered carefully and used purely to add to the existing composition. I always aim to use these products minimally so that my painting is still a watercolour, rather than a mixed-media painting. This is why I use the term 'enhance'.

Crackle paste

Crackle paste is a white opaque medium that cracks as it dries. This texture effect creates a beautiful pattern that will add life and a gorgeous fur effect to your koala.

It is important to note that you need to leave the texture product to dry for at least twenty-four hours before working further. Crackles will form as the product dries if you apply the paste smoothly, as shown in the detail here. In the step-by-step example, I have gained a patterned effect by simply working with my spatula application to form a highly uneven surface suitable for my subject.

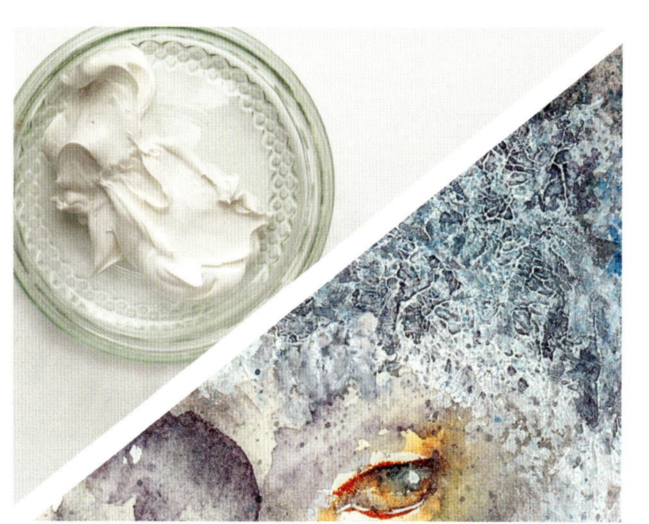

Wet crackle paste, and the finished effect. Paint has been worked over this example, further developing the effect.

Animal meaning: koala

I love the meaning of this animal. It is said to remind us to approach everything with an almost childlike wonder. A perfect thought for the artist who loves to explore and has enthusiasm for all things new and exciting. I know many children worldwide are fascinated with this cuddly bear-like animal – although it should never be referred to as a bear! Koalas are symbols of dreams and magic, so I wish you many magical hours painting them in watercolour.

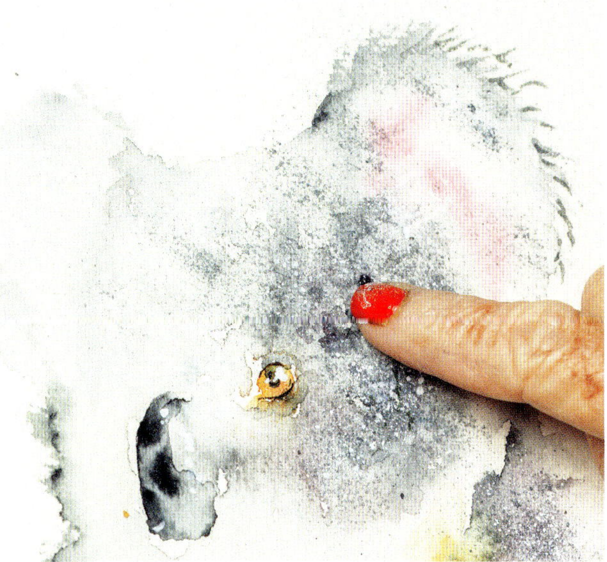

1 Working on a dry, finished painting, I carefully select sections of my subject that I feel could be improved or enhanced. Here, I will start with the fur by the ear.

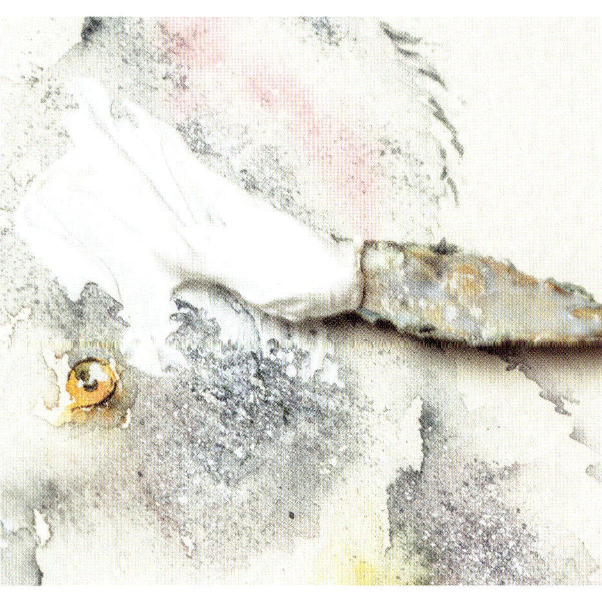

2 Apply a thick layer of the crackle paste to the selected section or sections of your koala. I use a spatula for this.

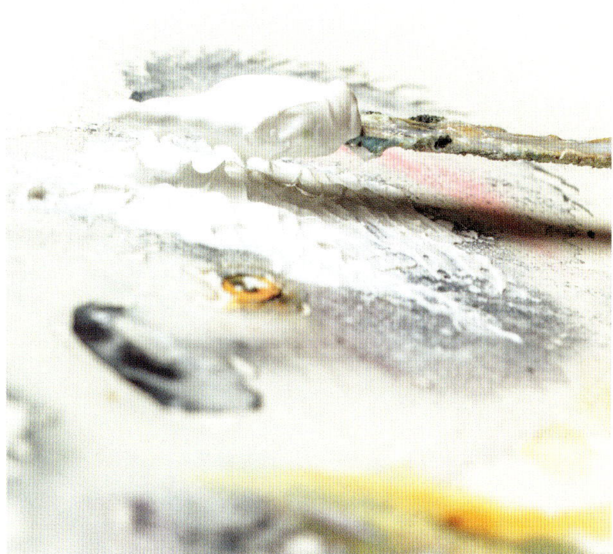

3 'Pat' the wet surface with the flat of your spatula. Doing this during application helps to ensure the product surface is uneven, which will enhance the effect.

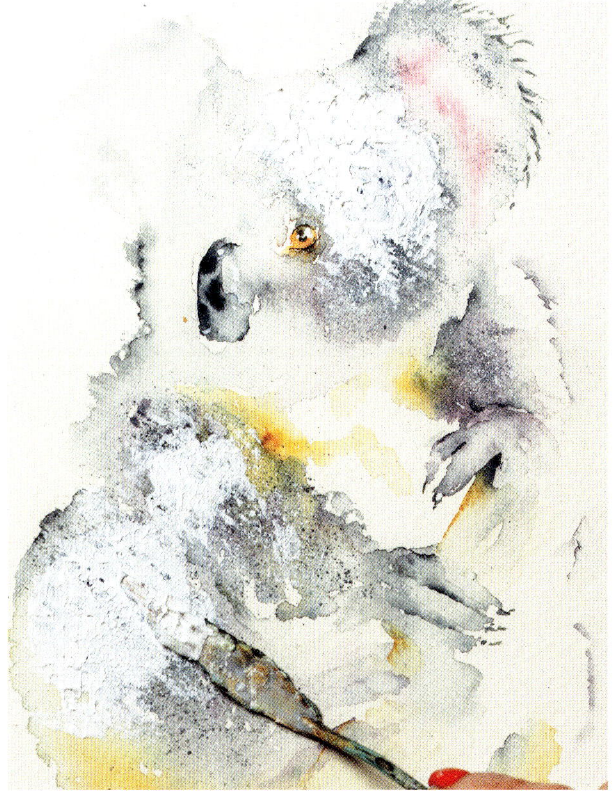

4 Apply the paste to any other areas that you want to.

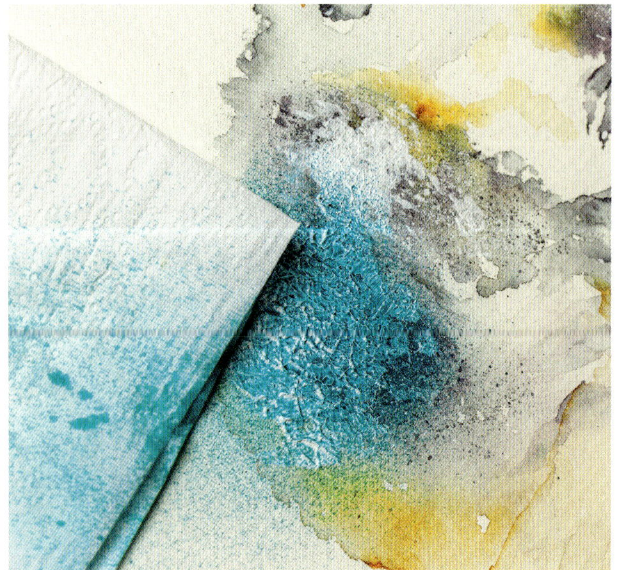

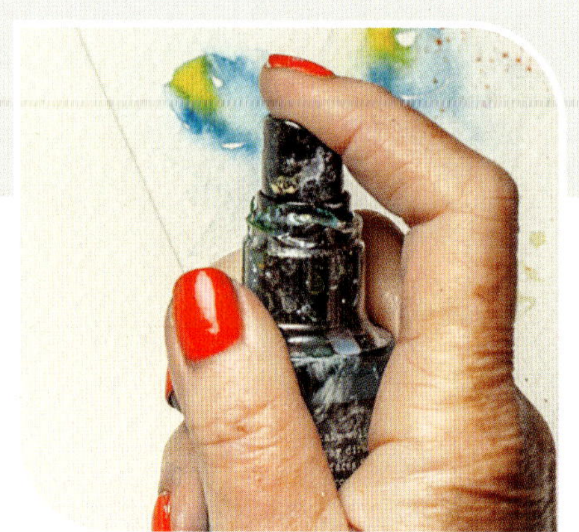

5 While the texture paste is still wet, you can use a spray
bottle to apply colour. This can be an optional choice of
realistic grey shades or something more unusual such as
the turquoise used here. Protecting any areas that you
want to remain clear with kitchen paper, hold the bottle a
few inches from the surface, and spray.

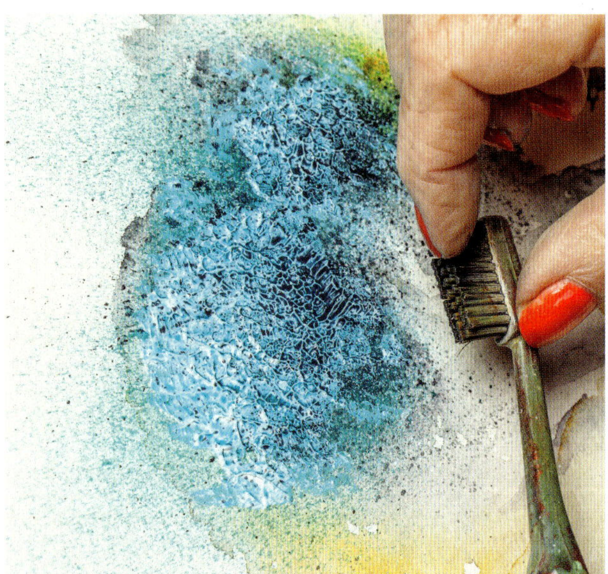

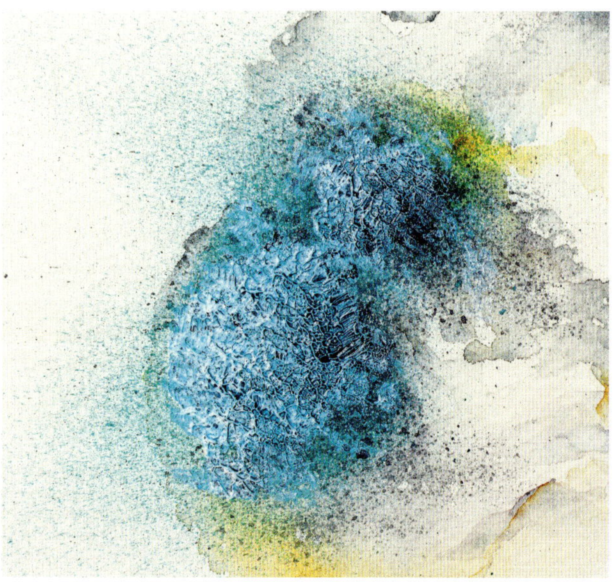

6 Splattering can be used to vary the effect, too. Pick
up paint from a pool of colour on your toothbrush, and
gently draw your finger across to flick the paint onto
the surface. I used Payne's blue gray, moonglow and
amethyst genuine here.

7 Leave the surface to dry naturally for the effect
to develop.

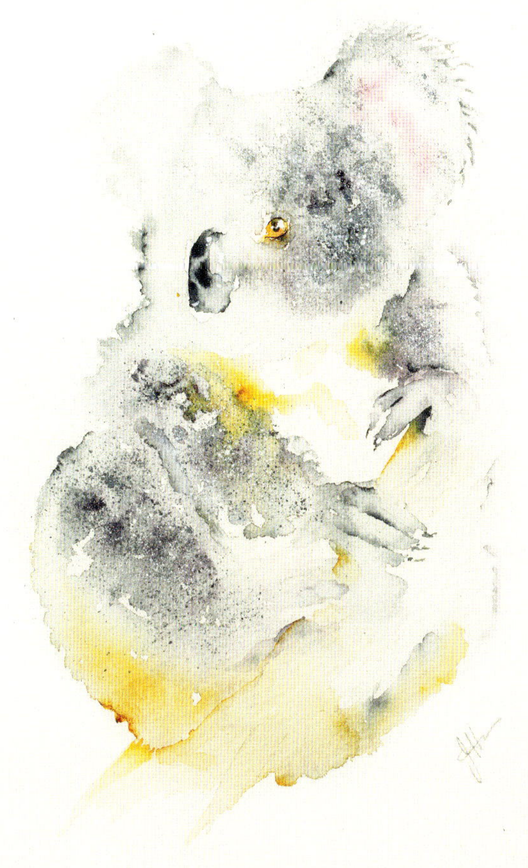 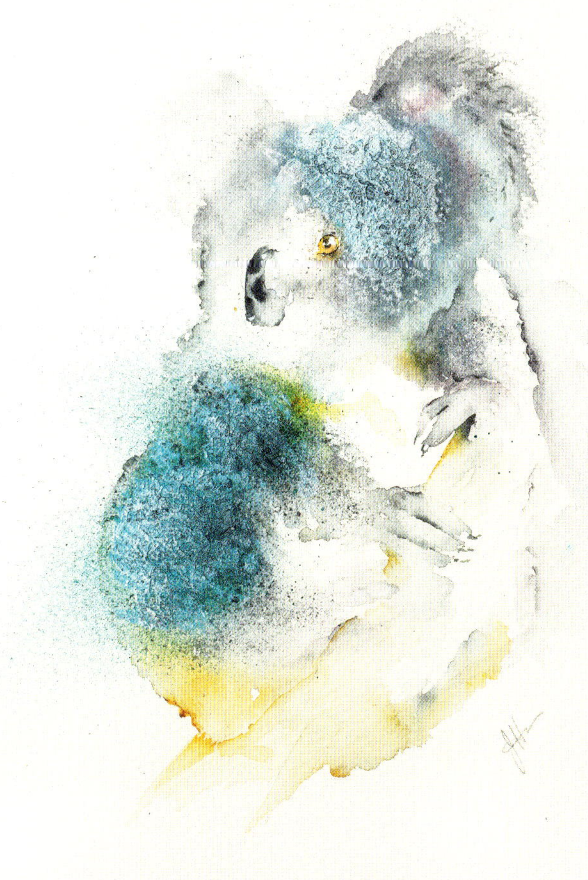

Art comparisons

If you compare these koala studies and the completed painting on page 95, one will likely appeal to you more than the others. If you prefer working in pure watercolour, you may dismiss the idea of working with texture pastes. I find them fascinating and I tend to flit between two ways of working. But my purist watercolourist soul tends to be drawn to art minus texture effects. That is, unless they are used in a subtle or unique manner.

Homework

Find paintings of animals that you are not happy with and experiment with adding texture products to them. Aim to achieve different fur patterns each time you do. You can apply the pastes in different ways to gain a vast variety of fur effects and many tips are included in further chapters of my book showing how to do this.

Experimenting with texture products

Years ago, many artists made their own recipes to create texture in their work. There simply weren't the products around then that are readily available now. I can't recommend highly enough playing with your own ideas to develop personal ways of creating texture. Experimenting can be so rewarding and lead you to amazing outcomes that you never would have expected.

You can buy special mediums to work with watercolour, including bead paste, texture paste or simply buy watercolour ground (see page 50) and add your own items to create unusual patterns. When painting sheep, for example, I have often cut strands of sewing cotton and blended this with my ground before applying it to my painting. The results, which you can see on page 142, have been awesome.

I will be sharing more ideas in the following chapters. Painting animals is fun, and we can learn so much from the textures in each. Let's continue our journey.

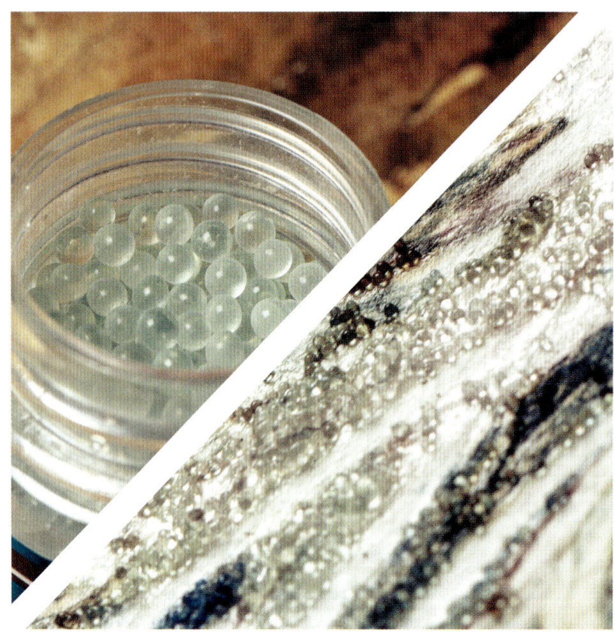

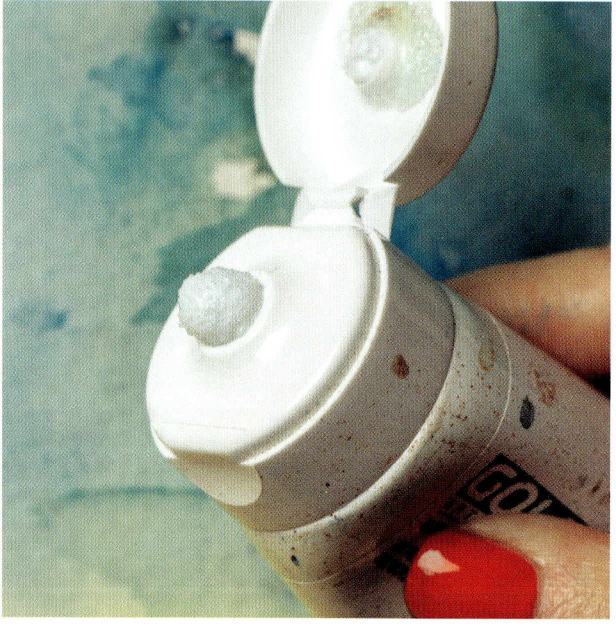

Gel beads

Available in different sizes, these can be dropped into wet paint or watercolour ground. As it dries, it will hold them in place, adding a textural sparkle.

Bead paste

This is a ready-made texture medium of gel beads in a gel carrier. As the carrier dries, the beads are fixed in place. You can mix it with paint when it's wet, or paint over it when dry.

How-to make your own granulation fluid

You may ask 'why make your own homemade materials when so many are readily available to purchase?' Firstly, I have been painting for so long that many texture products weren't available earlier in my career. Secondly, my art background has seen me living in many countries and, as a result, I have painted with lots of different groups of artists over the years; often being introduced to irresistible recipes and formulae for homemade texture pastes like watercolour ground and crackle paste; usually achieved by adding glue to a base that could simply be basic acrylic paint. But I never, at any time, came across a successful homemade granulation recipe.

Until, that is, I invented this one, purely by accident. I had been making a variety of inks as discussed on pages 48–49, and noticed that the simple addition of rust to many of these inks gave me a fantastic granulation effect to which shop-bought products just don't compare. You can add rust to mushroom or any homemade ink. Place some iron items, such as old nails, on their own in a glass jar and top it up with vinegar to encourage rust to develop. Leave the solution for a couple of months for the best effects. The longer the fluid is left the better your granulation will be.

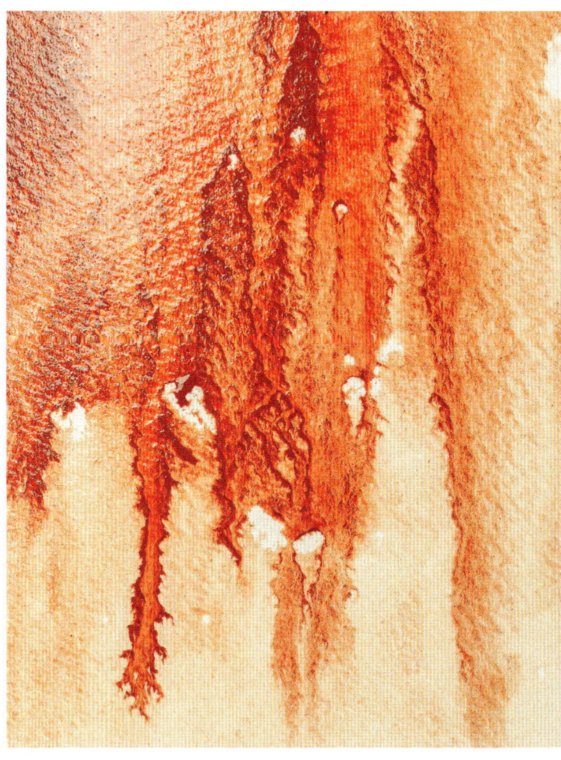

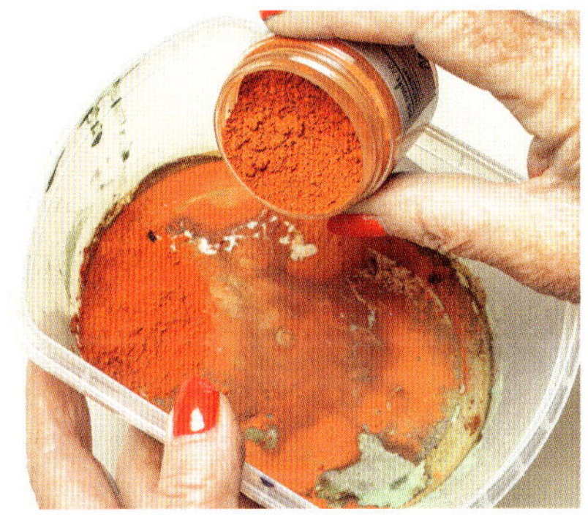

1 Add artist pigment powder to a plastic pot.

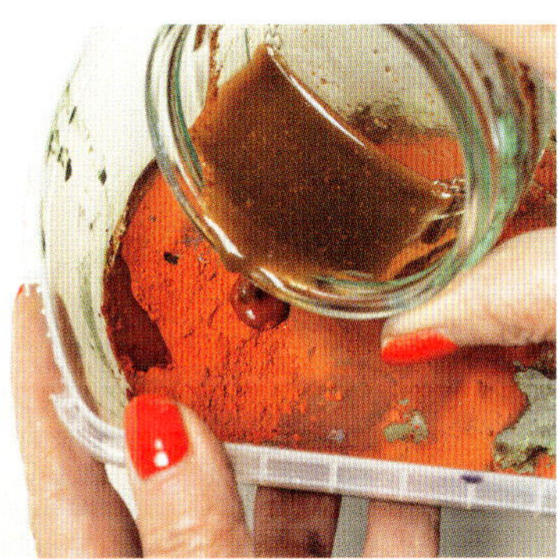

2 Add a few small drops of rust ink (see page 49). Remember – you only need a touch.

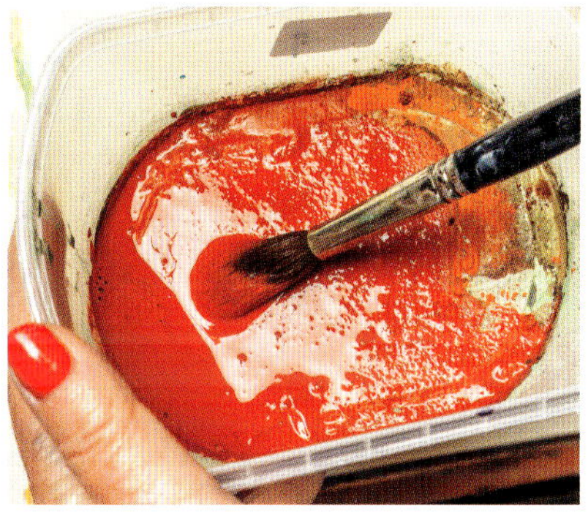

3 Use an old brush to mix it into a paste. This can now be used like a paint.

Rust ink formula

Rust can be added to any home-made ink to create interesting patterns. To create a basic rust ink, just place rusty iron objects in a glass jar and add vinegar to cover it. Leave for a few weeks before use.

Important Only use drops of this solution when mixing it with other products.

I need to point out here that you only need a drop of the fluid combined with raw natural pigment to gain great results. It is the combination of the rust ink with homemade inks or raw pigments that gives magical results: not the rust ink alone. I have been asked if I add this fluid to watercolour shades and, although you can, I find there is no point as many shades granulate naturally without any additional help.

I've been extremely successful with my homemade experiments; from turmeric ink, and texture pastes to my own granulation fluid formula – and you could be too. Just take time out to explore and you may be amazed at what you discover.

As we move to the next chapter, you will see how all these wonderful texture products can be combined to create unusual art.

Under the sea

OUR NEXT SUBJECTS ARE SEA creatures, which, in all their glory, add an extra element of excitement to this book. I have taught workshops in many countries all over the world, and some of the most popular subjects have been the seahorse and starfish. Both are fascinating creatures to paint, with beautiful shapes and colouring. They lend themselves perfectly to texture effects in watercolour. Combined with the other techniques in this book, this can lead to incredible paintings. It just needs a touch of imagination and perhaps ingenuity to get you there, to this point in painting. Just remember that, as mentioned earlier, you have to want to succeed in your art journey. Have fun trying these fabulous subjects and combining techniques to create them.

An atmospheric style

Learning to paint in an atmospheric style is very much like learning a new language. We have to want to learn the new way of thinking and creating if we are to succeed in our chosen art journey. It isn't enough to just look at paintings or demonstrations in a book. It is necessary to practise each exercise, learn every technique, and discover how we can gain the best results from a vast variety of available watercolour products. Mastering all these skills is like putting them, one by one, into a magical treasure chest that we can later open, time and time again, to use what is inside.

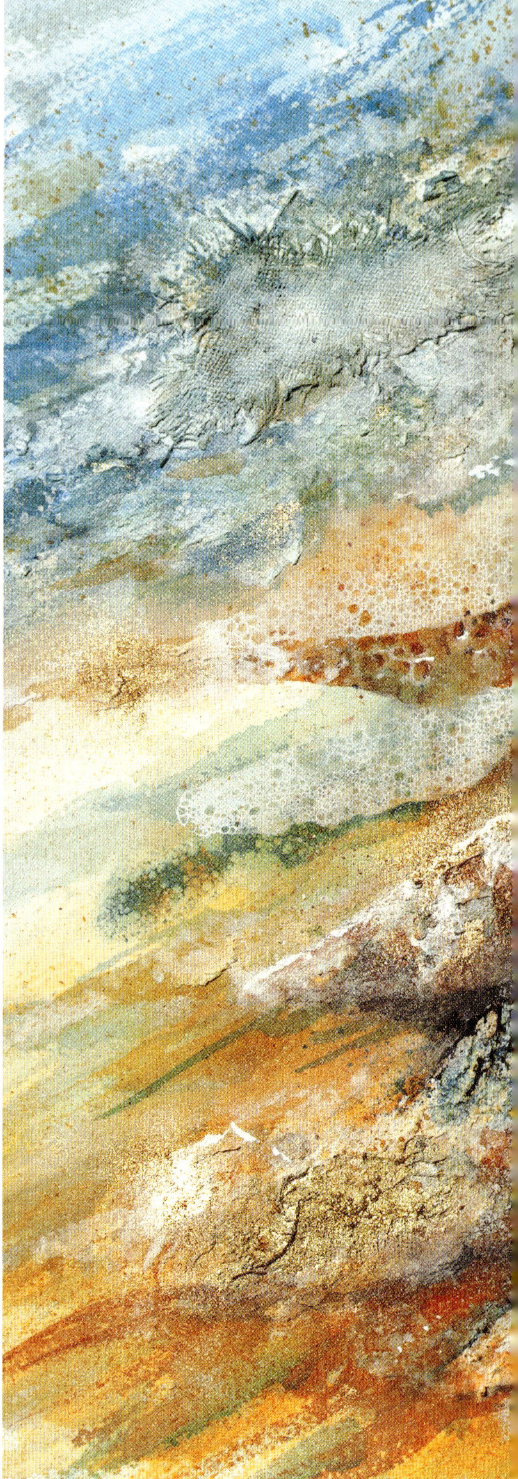

Treasures from the Sea
58 x 38cm (23 x 15in)

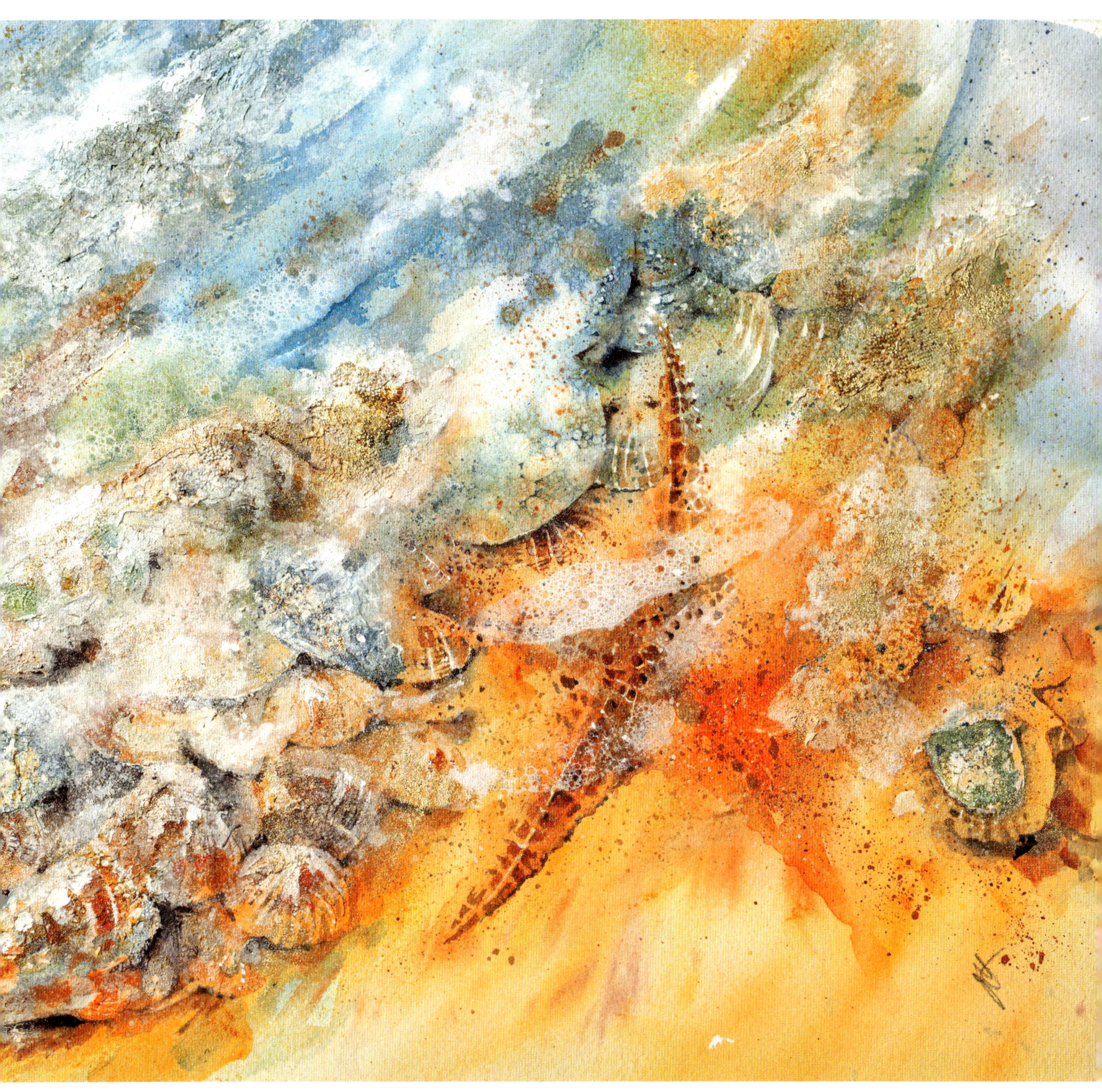

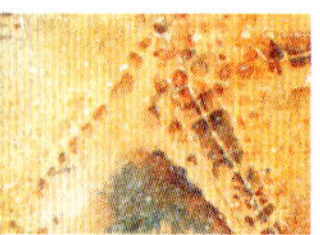

Step-by-step Starfish

If you study my starfish painting, you can see many forms of texture included throughout the composition. This painting was created by forming an initial background, and then working through the following stages.

This project showcases the versatility of using watercolour ground and a variety of different additional mediums to get great effects. There are many more ways that you can achieve them and many other products available, so it is well worth researching and experimenting further.

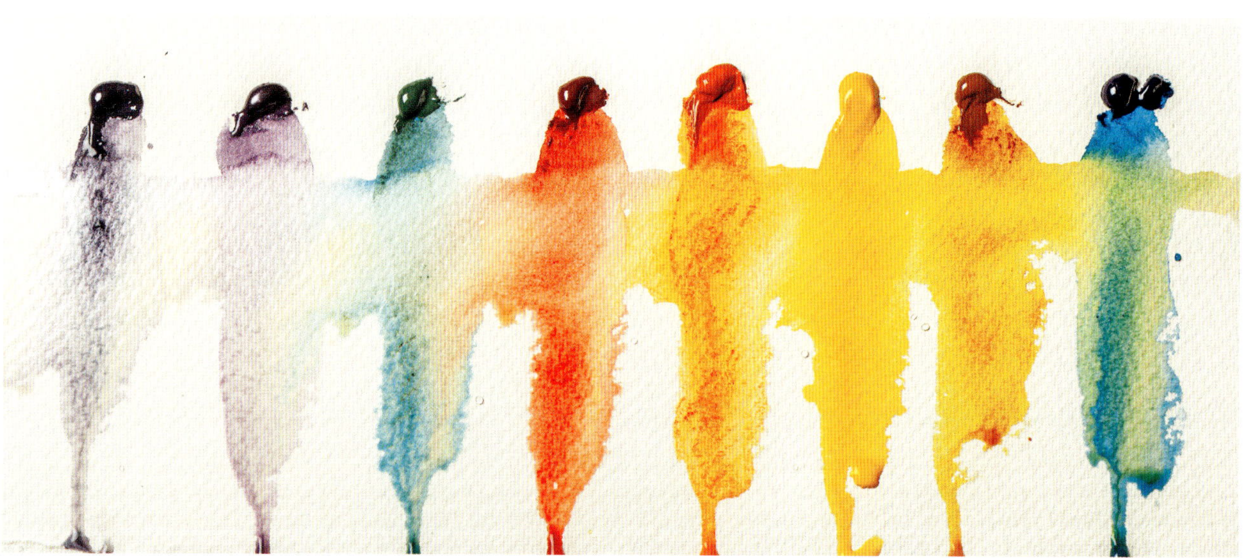

Dancing ladies: colour selection

Choosing the right colours can make a huge difference to the atmosphere and mood of your painting. Here I want to capture a warm beach scene. For this reason I have selected golden shades along with turquoises and violet for shadows. This range will be perfect for sand, shells, the starfish and the sea, as seen in the following step-by-step images.

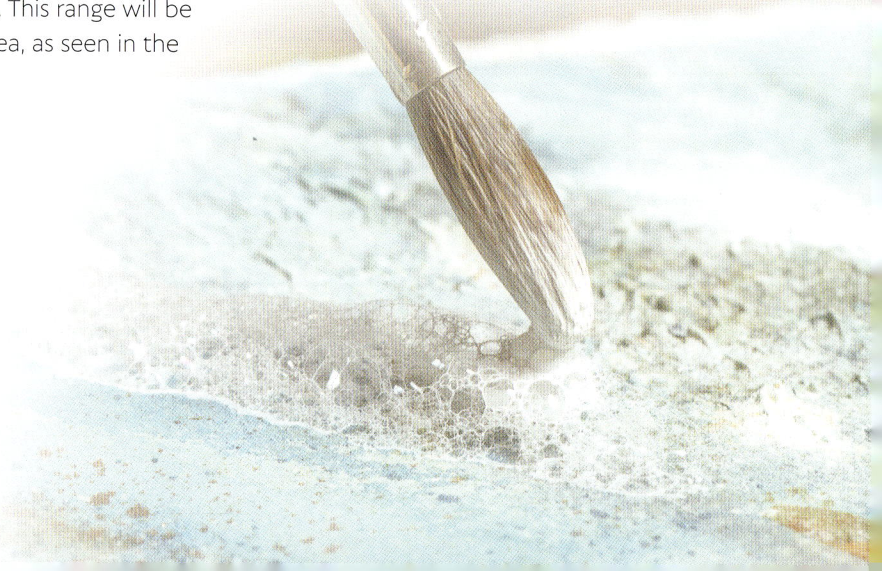

1 I start by painting an initial creative wash (see page 90), placing the main starfish and shoreline in their correct positioning for the composition – phthalo blue turquoise at the top left suggests the sea, while combinations of quinacridone gold, quinacridone burnt scarlet and cadmium yellow make up the beach. The whole story will revolve around this starting point.

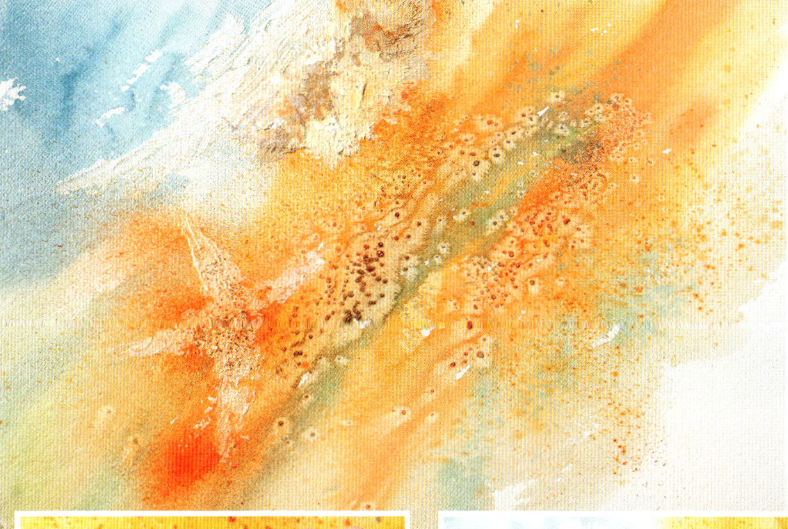

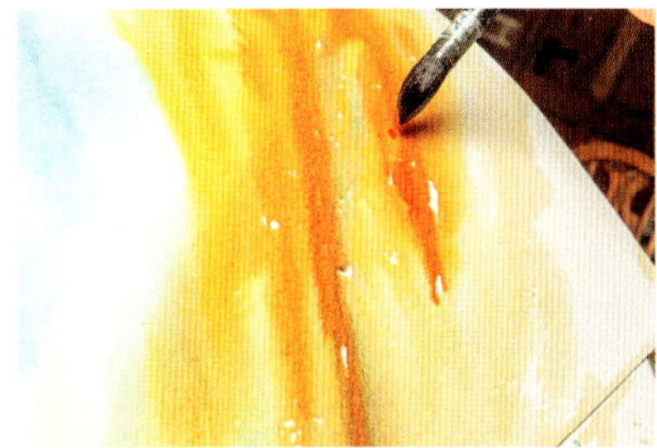

I apply the paint using the large mop brush, with the paper at an angle to encourage the colour to flow.

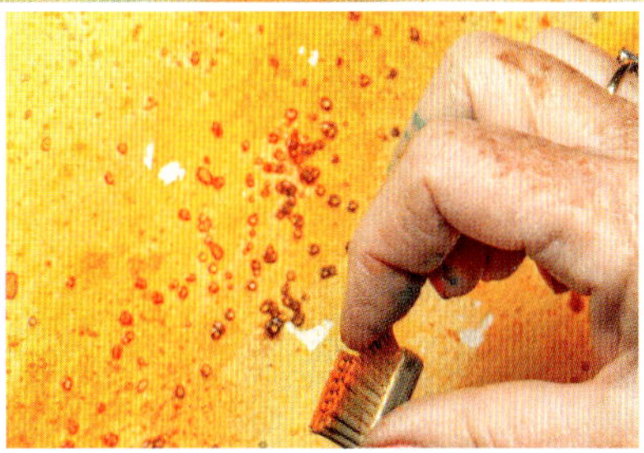

I add salt and splattering while the paint was wet, in order to add texture.

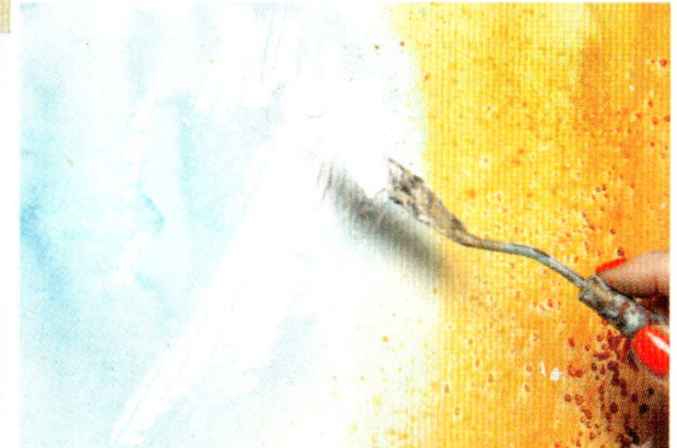

Working on a section at a time I apply watercolour ground to the shoreline using the spatula. I leave this application smooth, to give the impression of a calm scene.

2 Next, I began by adding a focal starfish on the right, picking out details using the rigger to apply a mix of quinacridone gold with a touch of Aussie red gold to each little patterned section on the limbs of the starfish. Start with the central portion and radiate out from this starting point.

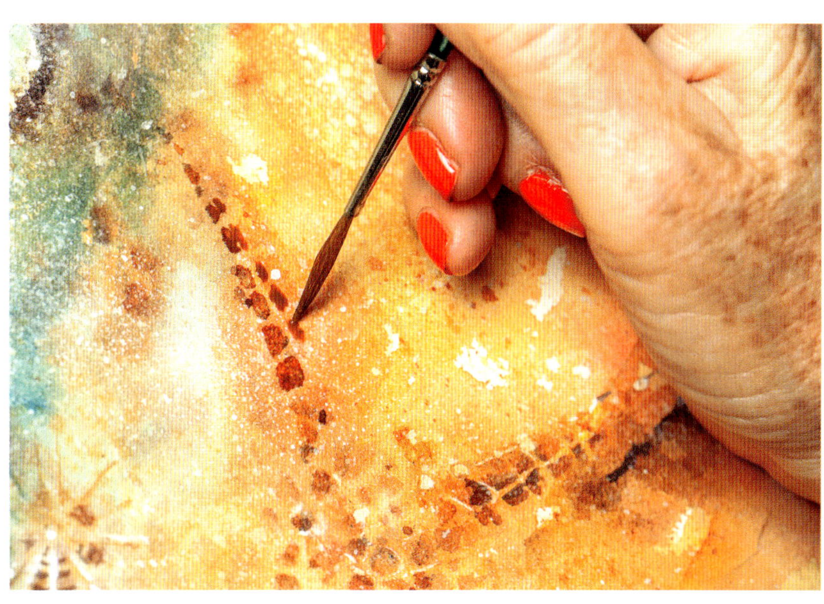

3 Next, I suggest the shape of the starfish further, and begin 'finding' seashells using the negative edge technique with the rigger and a mix of Payne's blue gray and amethyst genuine. I paint around each one, adding dark shadows or partial outlines. For the darkest shadows, I paint on touches of black watercolour ground sparingly. Once my painting has enough shells and the starfish looks pleasing, I move on to adding texture effects.

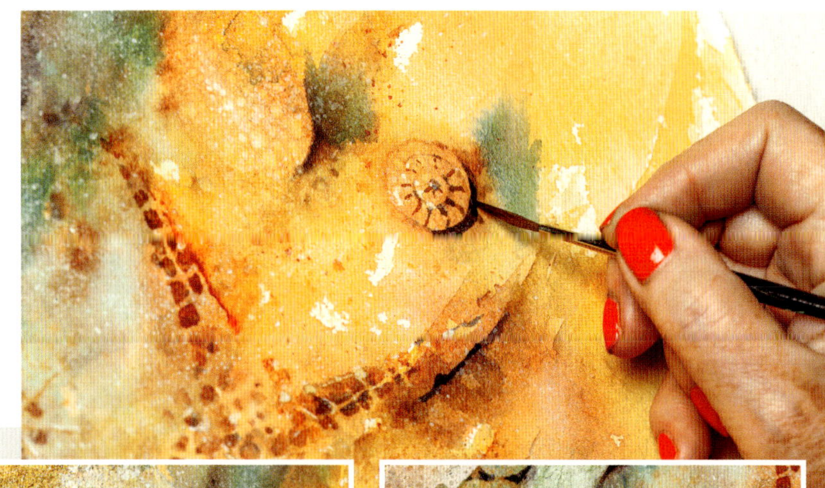

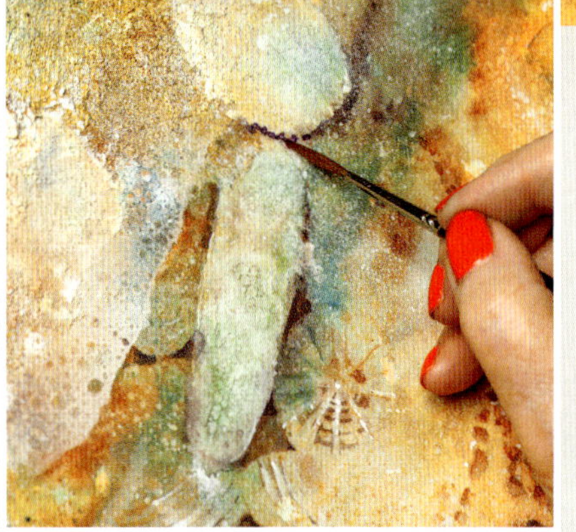

Adding detail to the central shells. Note that most of the shadows are not pure black.

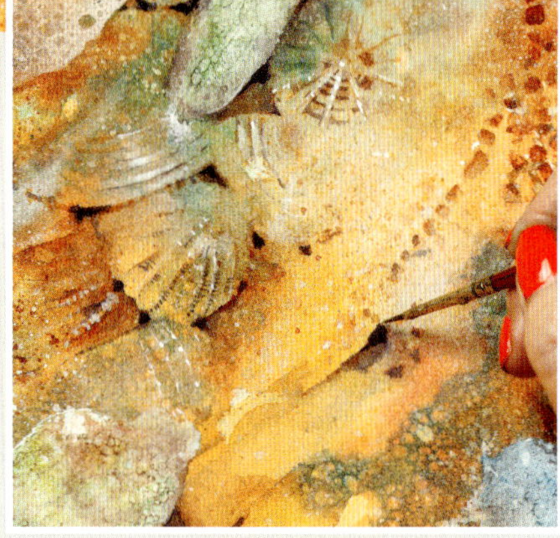

I use black watercolour ground because the result has a slightly satin shimmery quality once dry; not flat and dead like black watercolour paint.

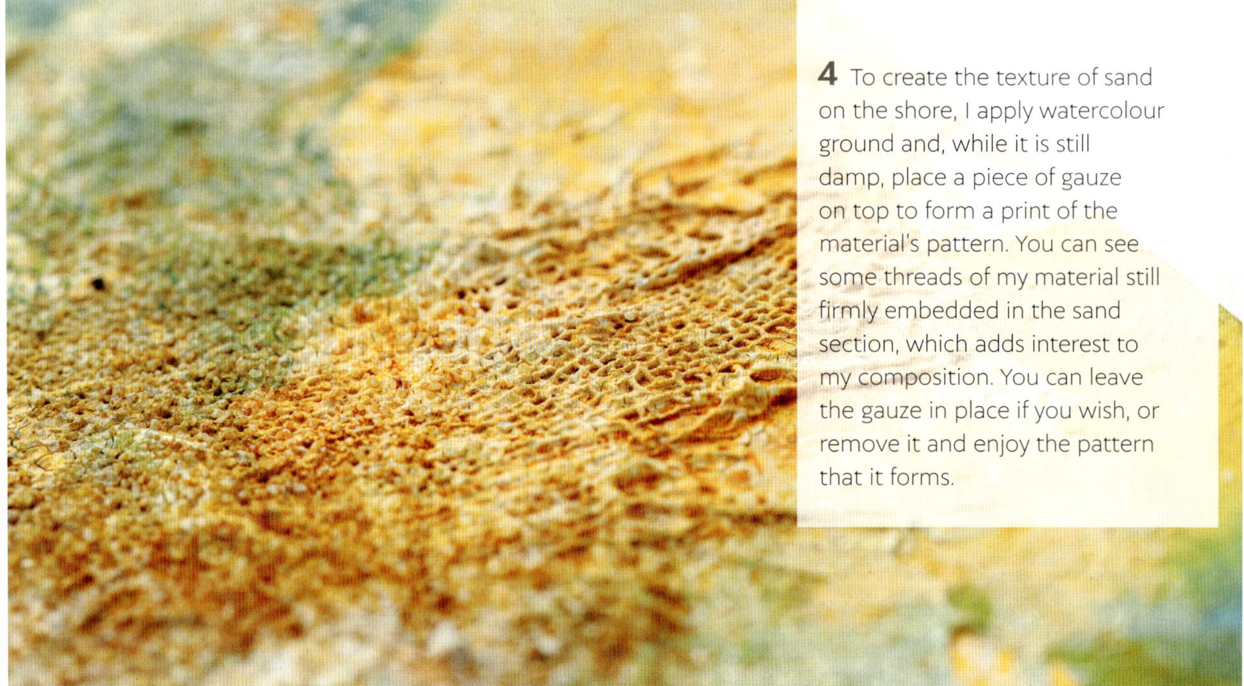

4 To create the texture of sand on the shore, I apply watercolour ground and, while it is still damp, place a piece of gauze on top to form a print of the material's pattern. You can see some threads of my material still firmly embedded in the sand section, which adds interest to my composition. You can leave the gauze in place if you wish, or remove it and enjoy the pattern that it forms.

5 If you observe the second, less important, starfish on the right, it has small gel beads in the surface. These were dropped onto the still-wet watercolour ground to create an interesting pattern.

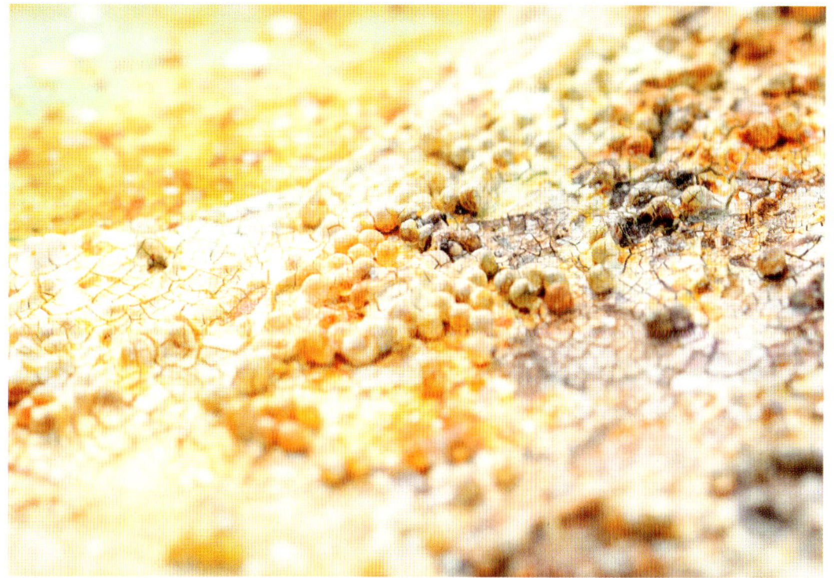

6 To gain the beautiful sea foam effect I used the bubble technique. This is a very old technique; the pictures below show you how to create these intriguing patterns.

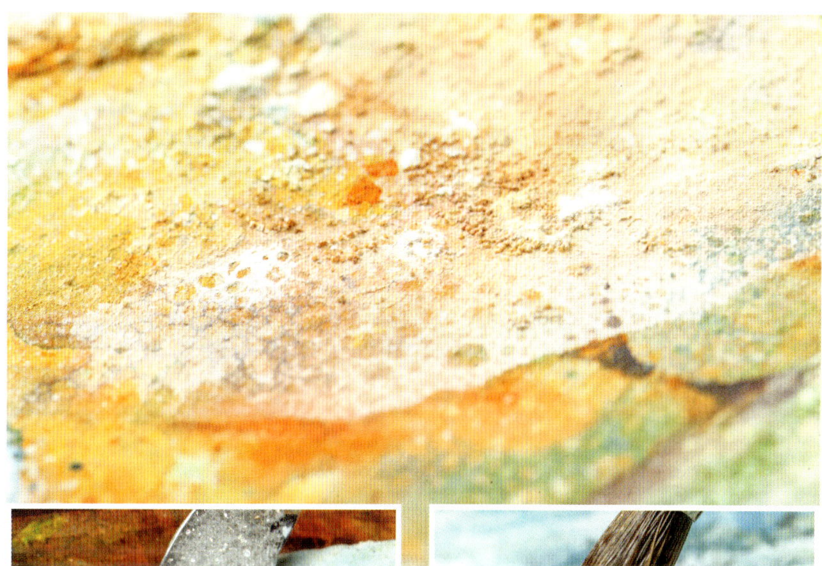

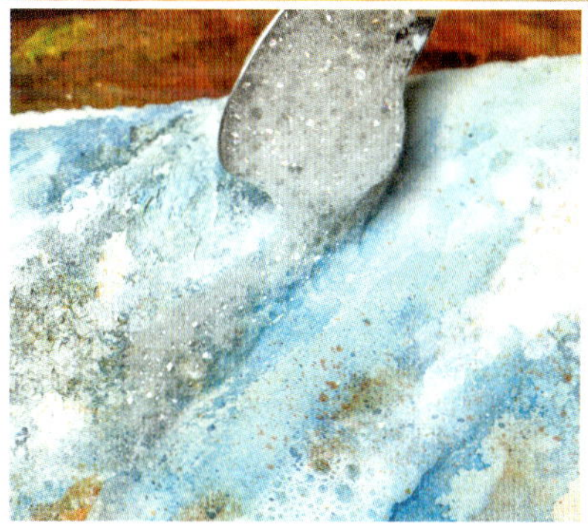

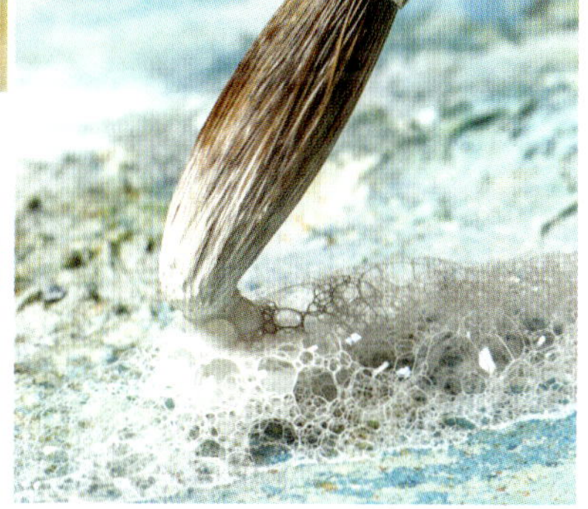

Lay the painting down flat and make sure that it is dry. Mix washing-up liquid with a little water in a small bowl or plastic pot to create a mass of bubbles.

Skim the bubbles off the top with a spoon and gently transfer the foam to the dry surface of your painting.

Load a brush with diluted paint (white gouache in this example) and touch it gently to the bubbles. Be careful not to touch the surface of the paper with your brush.

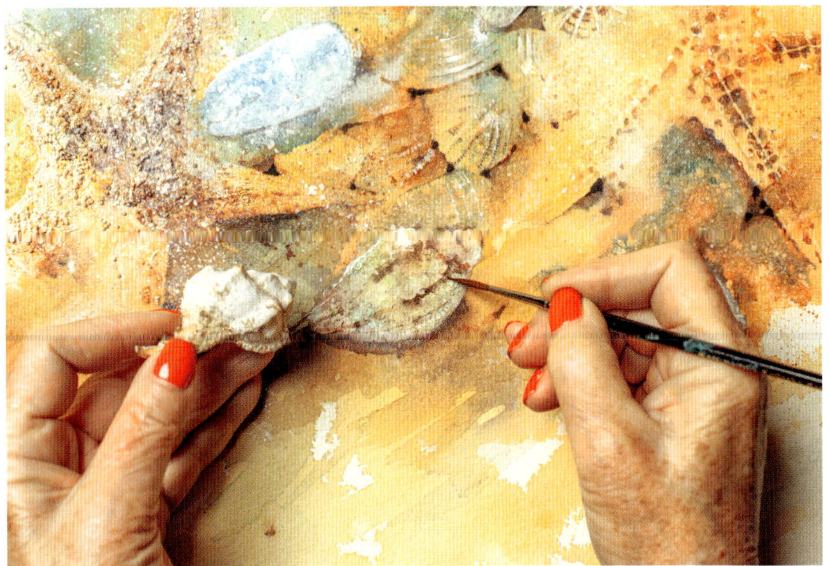

7 Next, I begin to add fine detail with the rigger. Taking my time, I make sure to enjoy every single brushstroke. Paintings like this take time to create as you can add to them continually until you feel your work is complete. Note that I keep my reference close to hand.

> ## Tip
>
> *This piece was created from my imagination. I have shells in my studio, and I used each one for inspiration individually.*

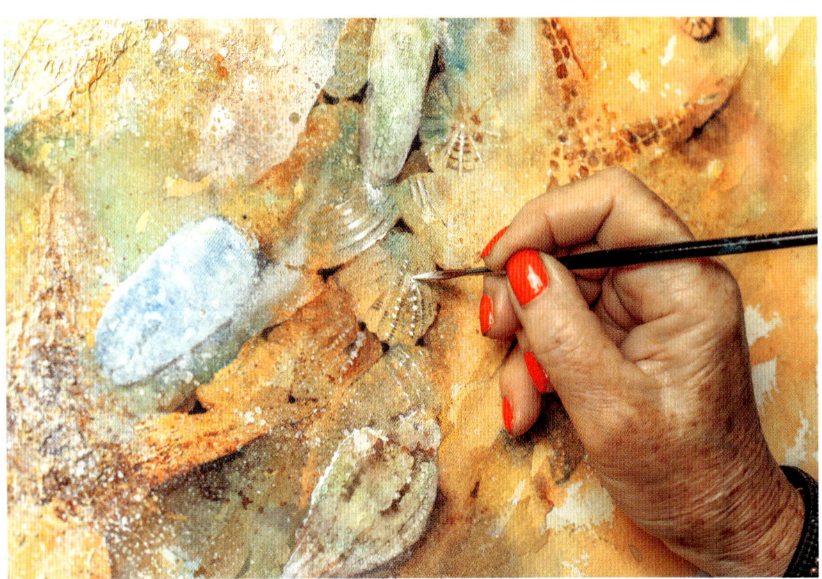

8 To complete my painting, I add highlights with white gouache to make my shells shine as if underwater.

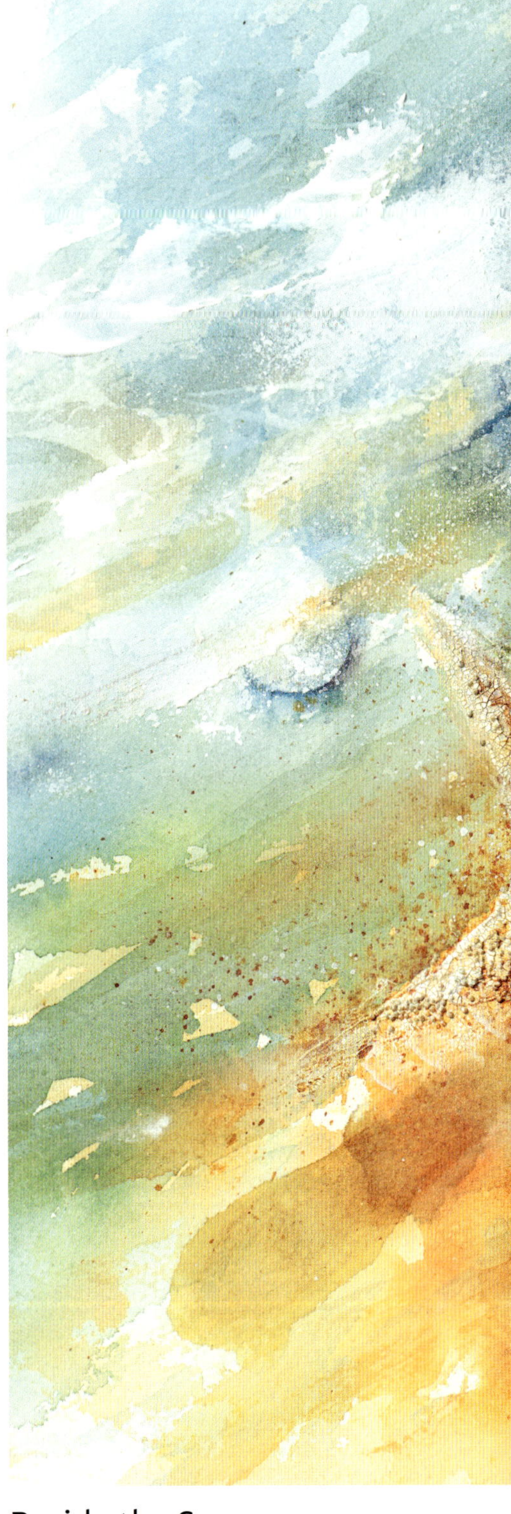

Beside the Sea
58 x 38cm (23 x 15in)

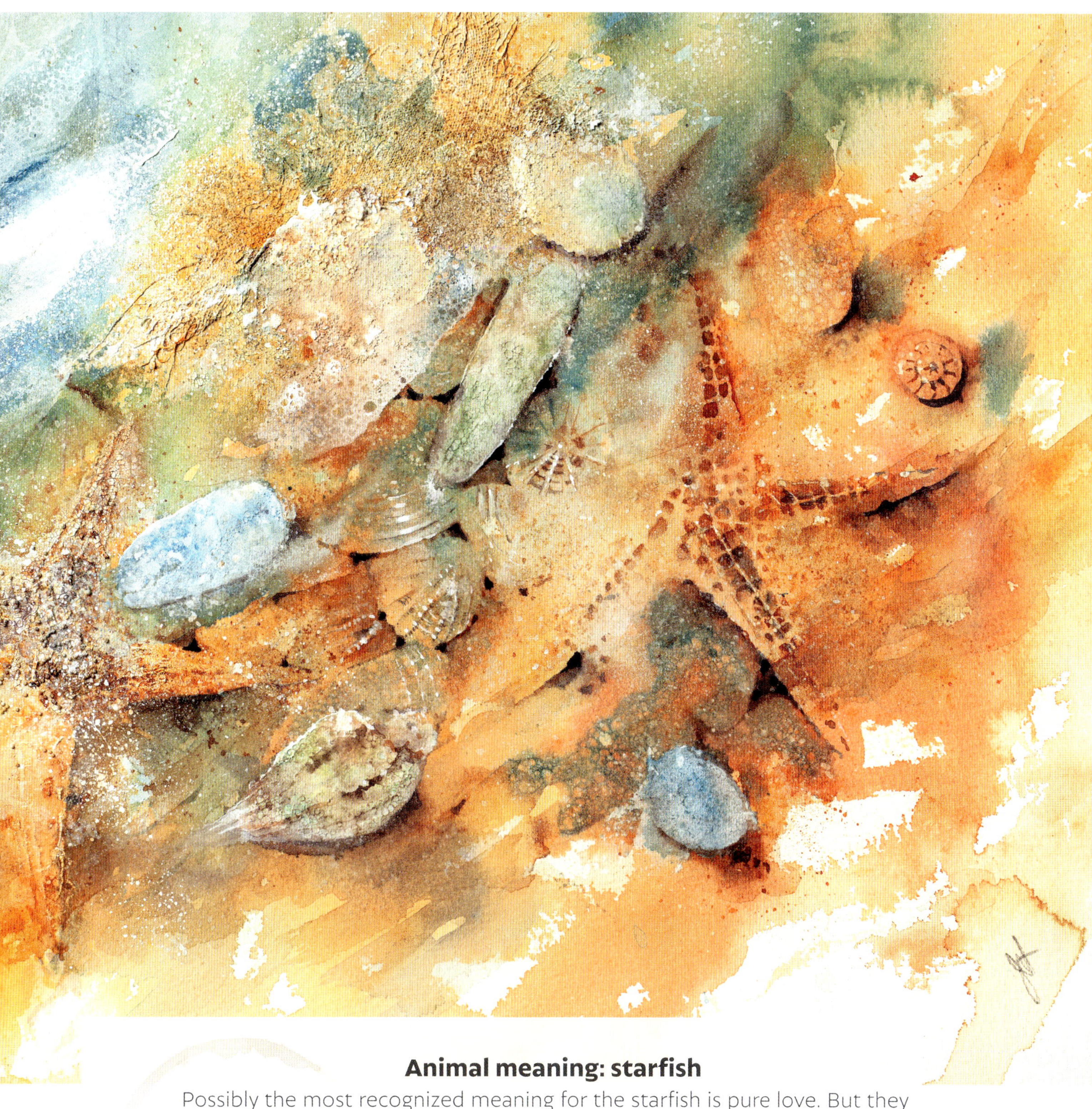

Animal meaning: starfish

Possibly the most recognized meaning for the starfish is pure love. But they also symbolize brilliance, inspiration and intuition. There are so many fascinating starfish species and they make the most wonderful subjects for artists due to their fantastic colourings and incredible formations. Be inspired by undersea creatures and let your art flow.

Follow your instincts

When creating and allowing our inner artist to shine, using our imagination in combination with real subjects can be invaluable. The ability to follow our instincts, placing colour or detail where we feel it is needed, will come over time. Time and practice – and the longing to create animals in watercolour – will get you there. Have faith in your ability and think of learning new techniques as a fascinating adventure that will never have an ending.

When we first set out to paint, we can look at a complex scene like this and feel daunted. It is the sense of adventure that will help us to reach our goal of becoming a great artist.

I am still exploring and learning new techniques today, as shown here. We come now to my next fabulous subject in this chapter: the octopus. What an incredible creature the octopus is! I have always been fascinated by making my own homemade formulas for textural effects, and in this painting (as with my giraffe paintings on page 84–87) a granulation pattern is quite obvious in the centre of my sea creature. This was created by my own magic formula which I invented, as explained on page 105.

Animal meaning: octopus

There are many meanings associated with this creature, but most are connected to its ability to camouflage itself when necessary and its superb timing at getting what it wants. Perhaps to the artist this can be interpreted to mean waiting patiently to reach your goal. You can multitask but don't lose sight of what you are aiming to achieve.

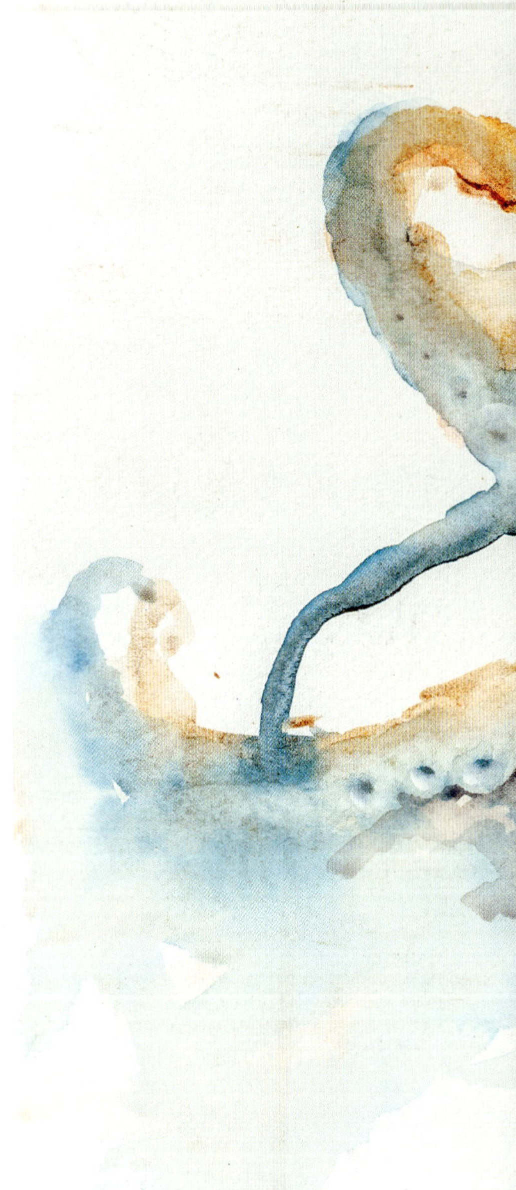

Tentative Tentacles
58 x 38cm (23 x 15in)

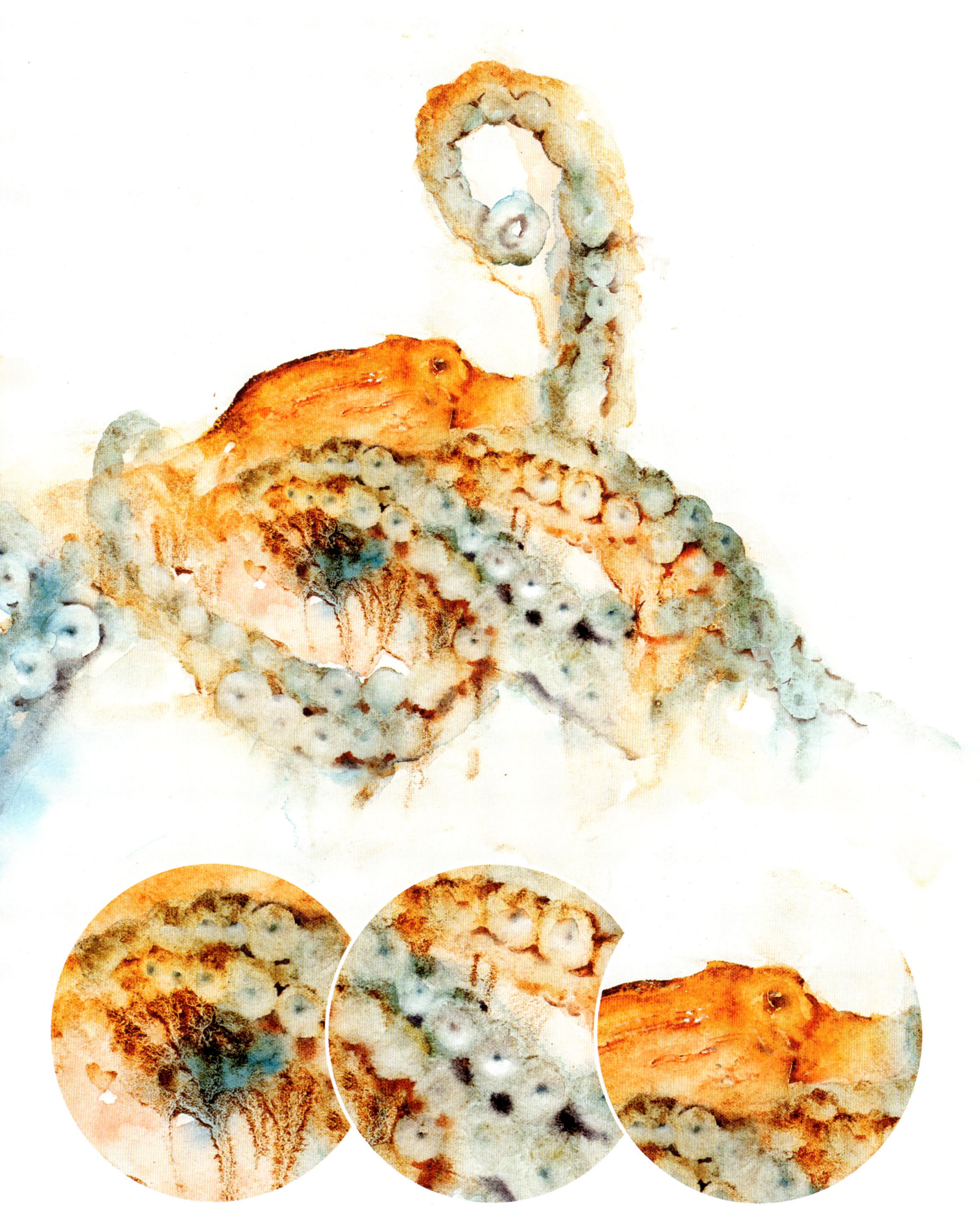

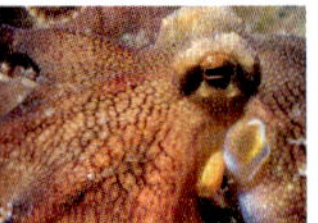

Step-by-step Octopus

I love painting so much that I wish I had the same number of limbs as an octopus, so that I could hold a paintbrush in each one. Imagine the number of paintings I could create then, and the fun I would have! Painting makes me feel so happy, and I really love sharing my passion with you. I hope you are enjoying every chapter of my book.

I enjoy experimenting and making my own pigments and granulation fluid. Here I have combined my own homemade granulation fluid with neat pigment. Pigment as a powder in its raw form can be purchased online from either specialist art suppliers or directly from manufacturers. You can, of course, follow this demonstration using any watercolour shades that you prefer rather than my selection.

"Talent without discipline is like an octopus on roller skates. There's plenty of movement, but you never know if it's going forward, backwards or sideways." H. Jackson Brown, Jr.

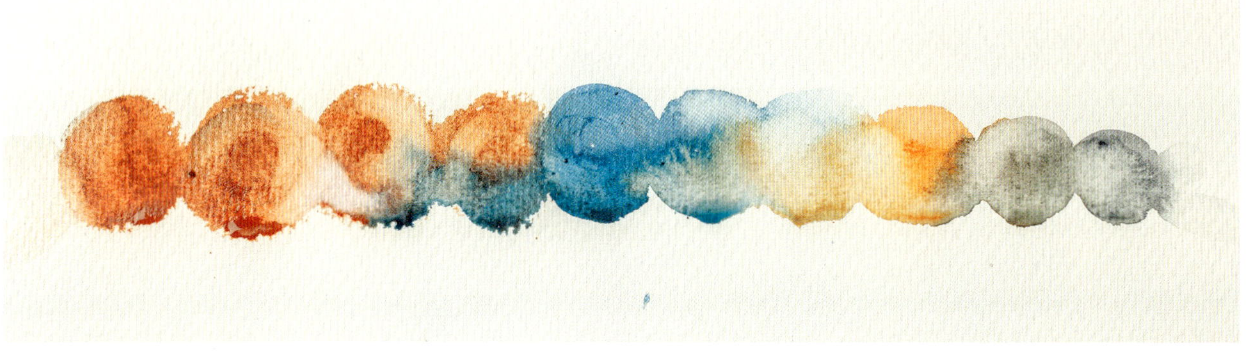

Dancing ladies: colour selection

I usually begin all my paintings with a row of dancing ladies. For fun, I have instead combined the colours I have used for my octopus painting on a tentacle; allowing my chosen shades to run into each other.

I began by creating the first circle of the tentacle using red ochre artist pigment combined with my homemade granulation fluid. As I worked along the tentacle, I added phthalo blue turquoise. I created this colour selection exercise using circular movements with my brush and lifted colour in places to form varying shades for the tentacles. Working on scraps of paper prior to working on a complete painting is a great way to get to know your subject. I kept my colour choice simple and depended on the pigment's interaction with water to give me a unique result.

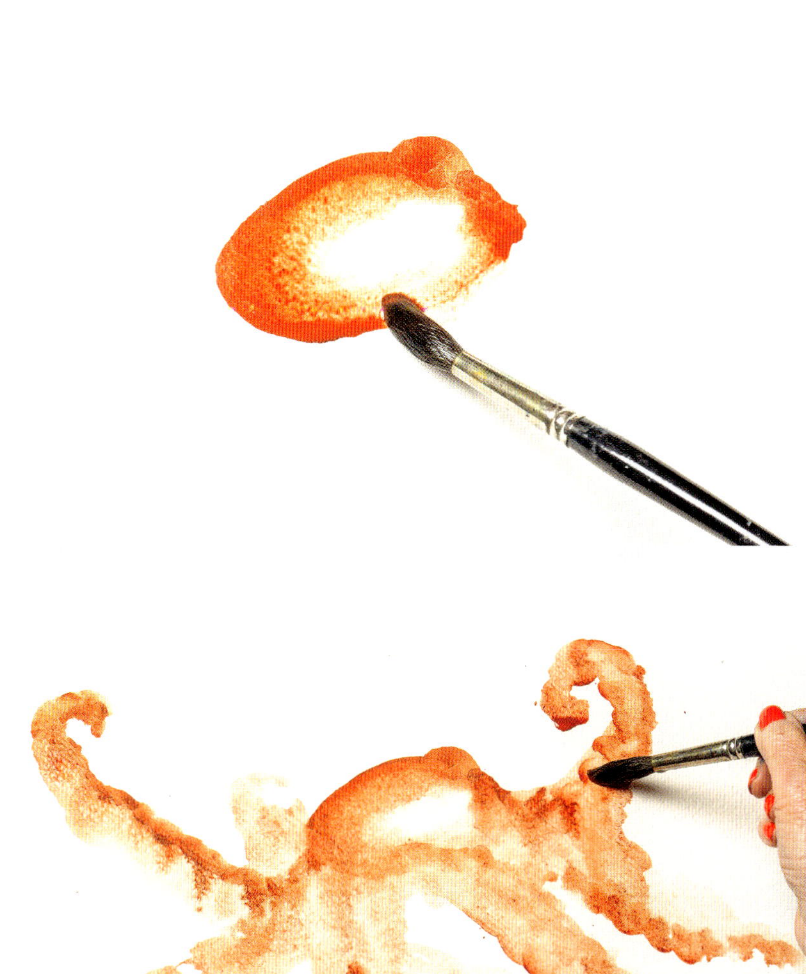

1 I began by painting the main body of the octopus as a shape, using the size 10 brush to apply a mix of rust ink and red ochre pigment (see page 105), making the lower central section lighter by adding a little water. In most of my animal paintings I usually work from the eye as a starting point; but on this animal the eye is so small that it is easier to add later in the creative process.

2 Next, I began to add tentacles. It is worth bearing in mind that these long limbs are extremely versatile in how they can move, so my aim was to demonstrate this with their positioning. I also wanted my subject to look as though it actually was moving – hence the sections omitted from the finished work, left to the viewer's imagination.

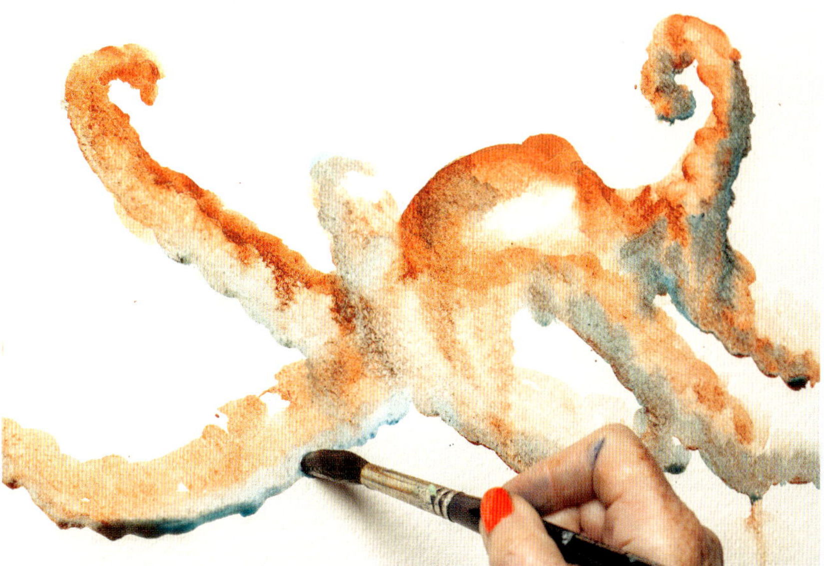

3 At this stage and while my paint was still wet, I used circular brushstrokes to create the tentacle sucker shapes. I introduced the second colour of phthalo blue turquoise along each limb to enhance my colour combinations and use.

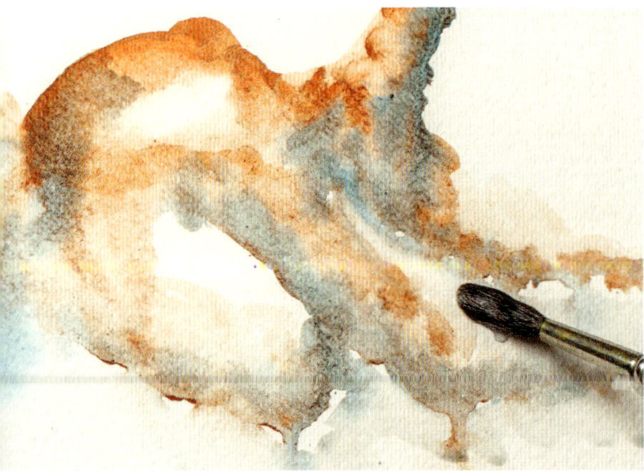 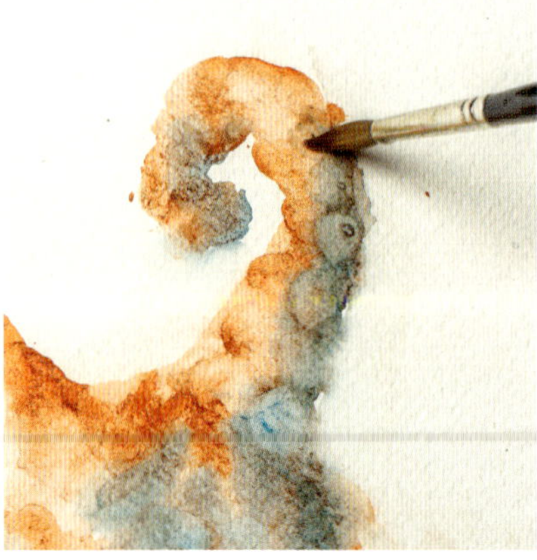 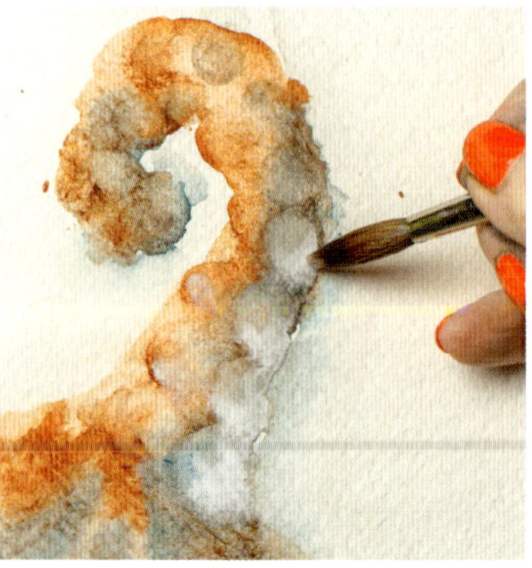

4 I blurred some of the outlines with clean water to heighten the feeling of the limb's movement.

5 While wet, I used a damp size 10 round brush to make rows of small circular strokes on the tentacles.

6 Working quickly, I developed the marks with white gouache, adding it wet-in-wet in small curved strokes at the bottom of the suckers.

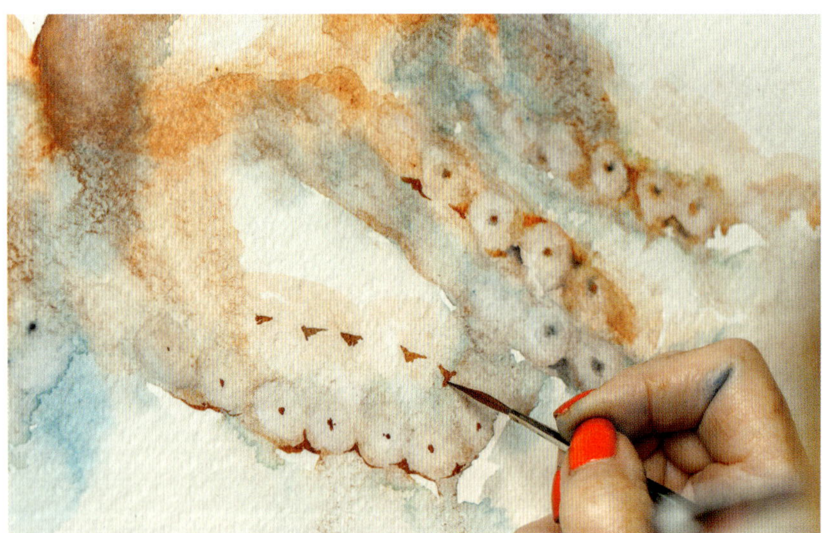 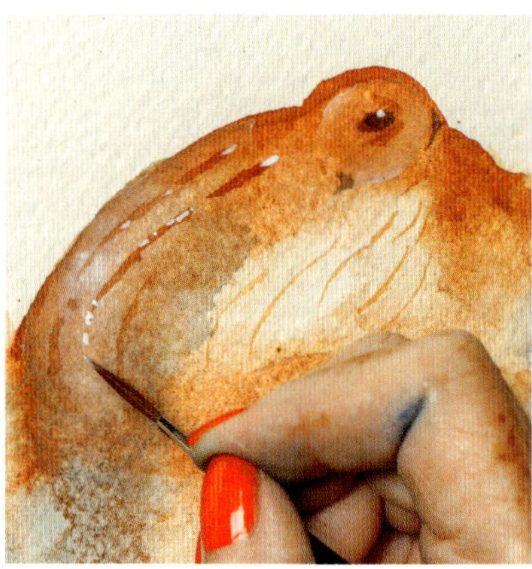

7 I highlighted the body and near the eye with white gouache, then allowed my work to dry completely before beginning to add detail. This was added using my rigger brush. I placed central dots in a few of the suckers and fine shadow lines along the outline edges of some of the limbs.

8 I added a small eye with the rigger and quinacridone burnt scarlet, allowing it to dry before adding a white gouache highlight; then used quinacridone burnt scarlet to add some patterning and markings to the body to finish.

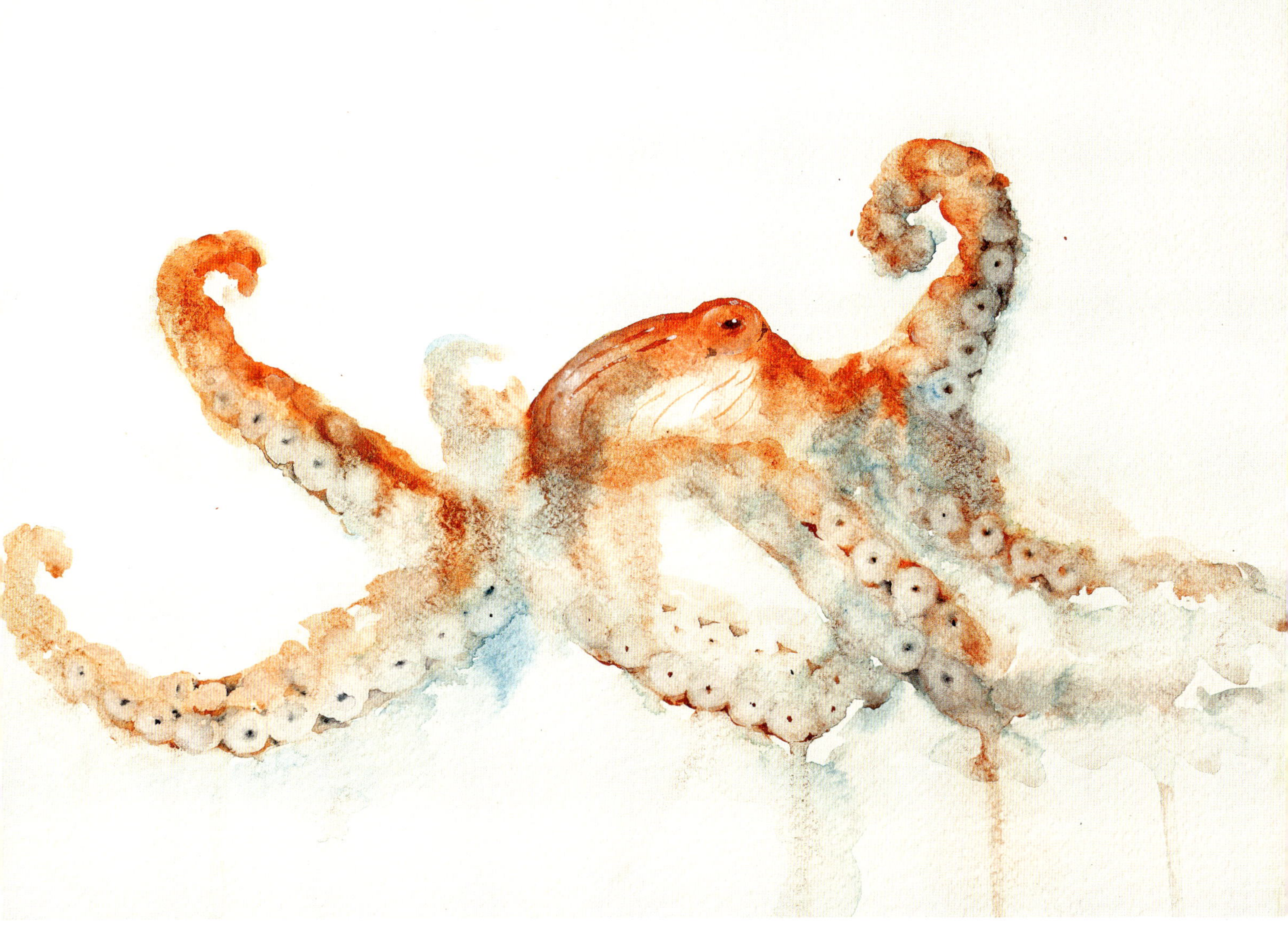

The finished painting

58 x 38cm (23 x 15in)

Homework

Try painting other sea creatures using these techniques. Lobsters and crabs both have beautiful colourings and incredible shells which could be perfect for texture effects. They really are amazing subjects to create in watercolour. Also, try working on larger paper, as single subjects look great in huge sizes against a white backdrop.

Life lessons from the sea

I was painting seahorses non-stop at one period of my life when things were very difficult for me. I shared my paintings online and a lovely artist contacted me to ask whether I was well. Apparently if you dream about a seahorse, or feel the need to paint them repeatedly, it's a sign that things are going to get better. Luckily for me they did. My health recovered and I am absolutely fine now. But I think painting seahorses got me through a very frightening time.

Art can be healing. And I have no doubts that there are spiritual connections to animals. We dream of or feel a need to create them in our art and they often carry a message. Believe it if you wish, or not: I did. There is a magic to the animal world that we will perhaps never fully understand, but for now, let's enjoy its beauty!

Advice from the Ocean

Be shore of yourself

Come out of your shell

Take time to relax and coast

Avoid pier pressure

Sea life's beauty

Don't get tide down

Make waves!

Anonymous

Animal meaning: seahorse

There is a wonderful meaning to seahorses. These tiny creatures carry the message to hold on, no matter what you are going through in life. Due to their ability to hold on to something with their tails, no matter how strong the current or storm, they survive. A great way to use this information is to consider painting seahorses if ever you are struggling at any time in life, or with your art. Imagine how delicate they seem to be and yet they are so strong. Pulling through always; as you will.

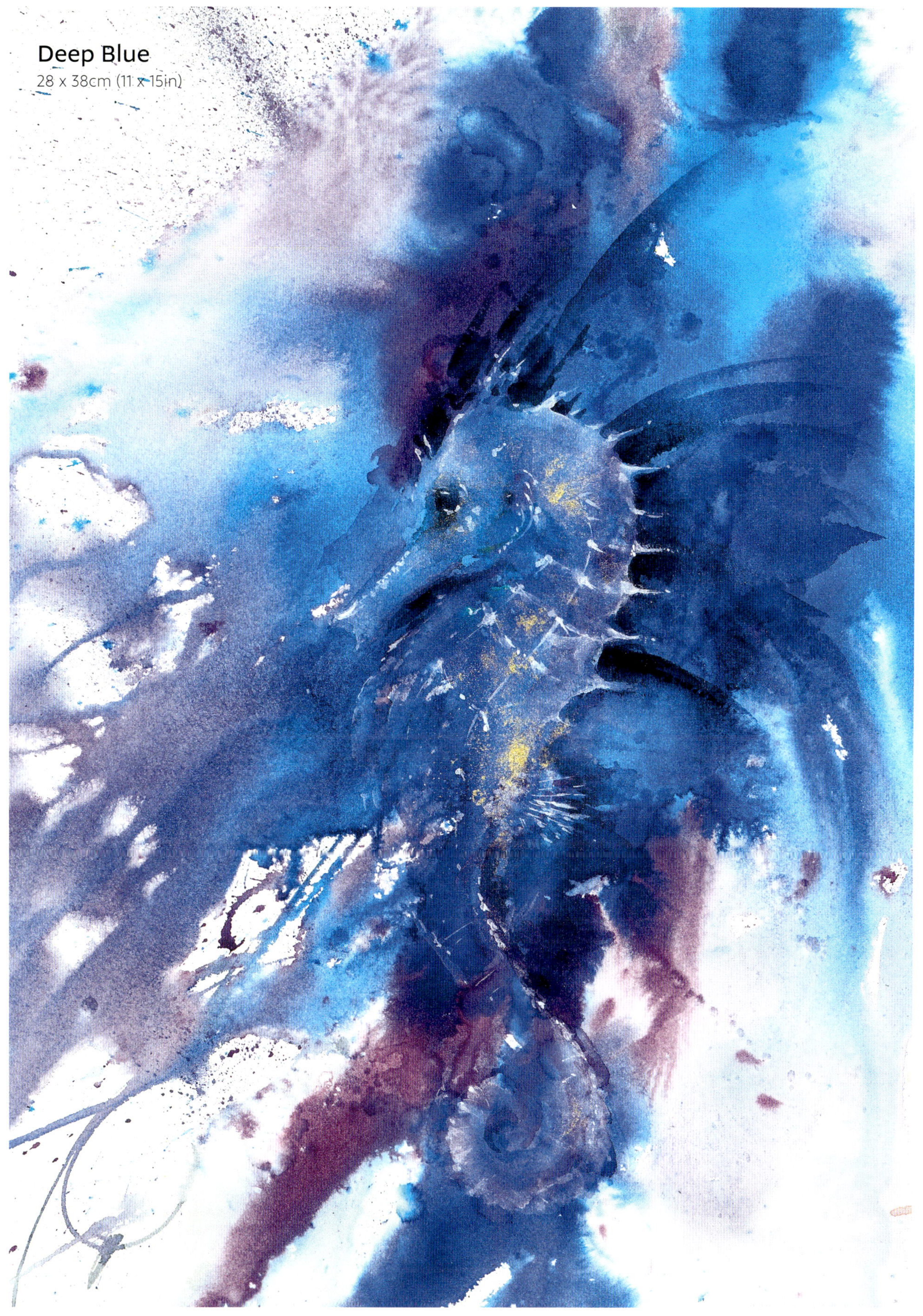

Deep Blue
28 x 38cm (11 x 15in)

A mammoth task

ELEPHANTS HAVE ALWAYS BEEN AMONG my favourite animal subjects. Who doesn't love them? We have looked at them in this book already, but we return to them now because I would like you to imagine that you are just starting out painting and finding your style.

Finding your style

Even if we all painted in an atmospheric manner, our results would be very different, because working with my technique allows you to shine individually as an artist in your own right.

As your style evolves, you will feel instinctively guided to follow a path that pleases you. We aren't copying a set way of painting. There are no preliminary sketch lines to follow. We are guided by colour alone. Due to this way of creating, a strong connection can often happen between the artist and their art; not only by liking your results, but also by finding peace while you are creating.

It is frequently said that the act of creating can be extremely therapeutic. I have certainly found that to be true. I often leave my studio feeling exhilarated and eager to return. It's an escape, a way of life, and something I look forward to as part of my daily routine. However, painting daily can become stale if we repeatedly paint the same thing in exactly the same way. Painting what we know is fine, but inside each of us an explorative artist is often screaming to be allowed to shine.

This is your time to shine. Look at the following paintings, remind yourself of the lessons learned so far, and see if they guide you to a path in your own art journey. They may encourage you to explore new possibilities in watercolour.

Find the right subject, and the right style, for you

To the right you can see a very old photograph that I love creating from. Opposite, you can see one of my older original elephant paintings. As you can see, I have always loved painting with fascinating colour combinations to tell my story. In this chapter I am sharing a variety of elephant paintings in different styles as it shows the versatility of working in watercolour.

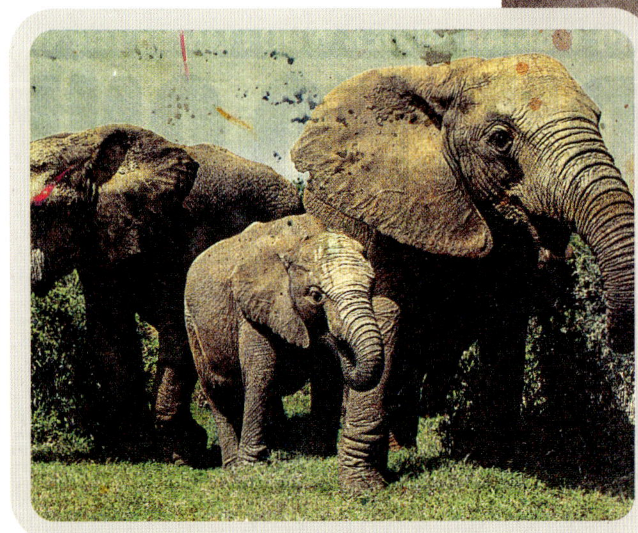

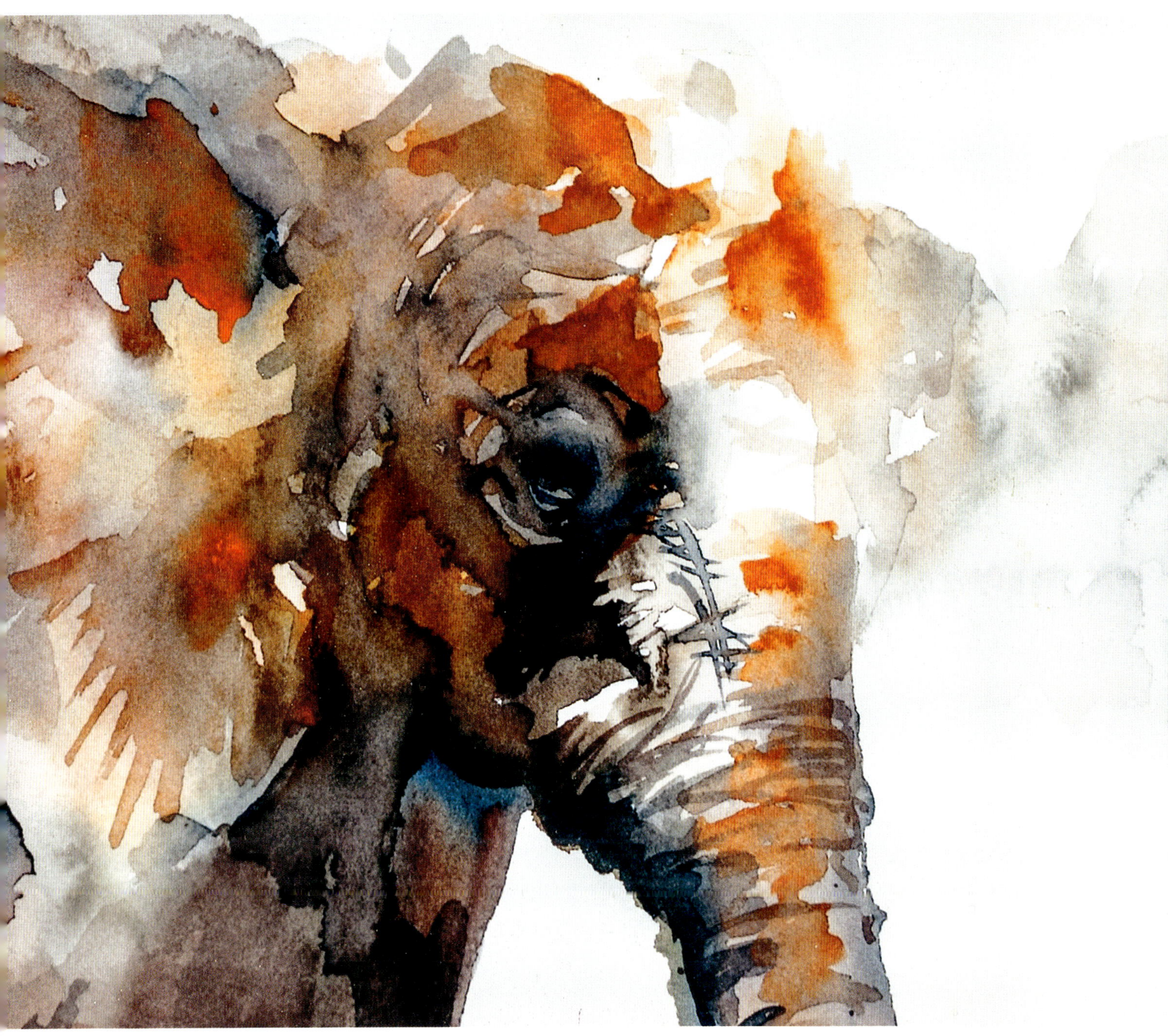

Gold

38 x 28cm (15 x 11in)

A unique interpretation of the
photograph on the facing page.

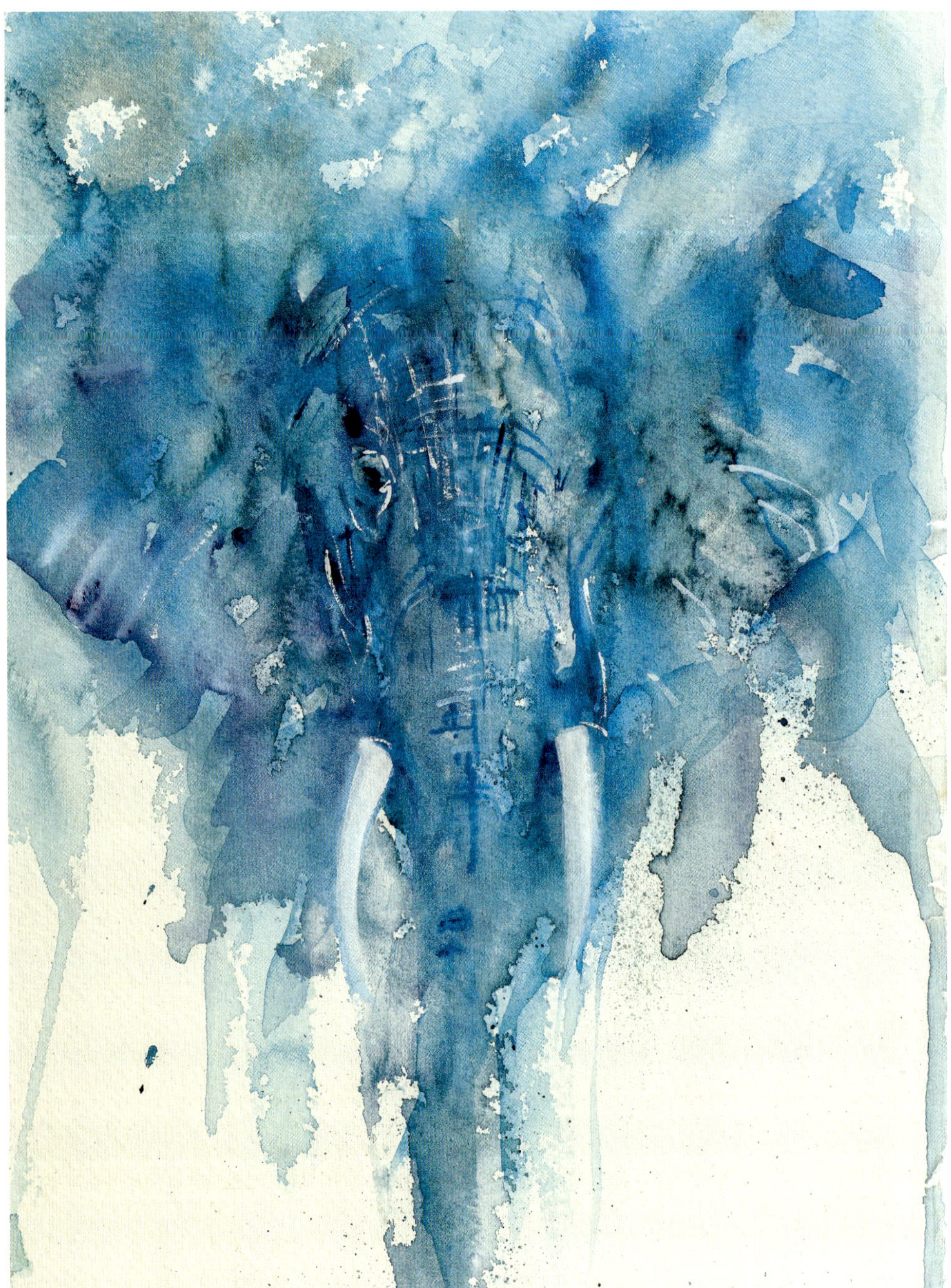

Monochrome elephant: tonal values

Monochrome is very valuable to beginners (see page 30), but it is equally useful as an exercise for the more advanced artist who finds it difficult to add tonal values in their work.

Here I created a simple blue wash and found my subject on top of it. Painting this elephant all in one shade, then adding touches of white gouache for the tusks, was a calming exercise.

Try painting half of a subject on top of a wash using just one colour. Leave out as many sections and details of your subject as you can. The more you practise this exercise, the more atmospheric your results will become. Similarly, the more familiar you are with your subject, the better your paintings will be. Try this with many other animal subjects too!

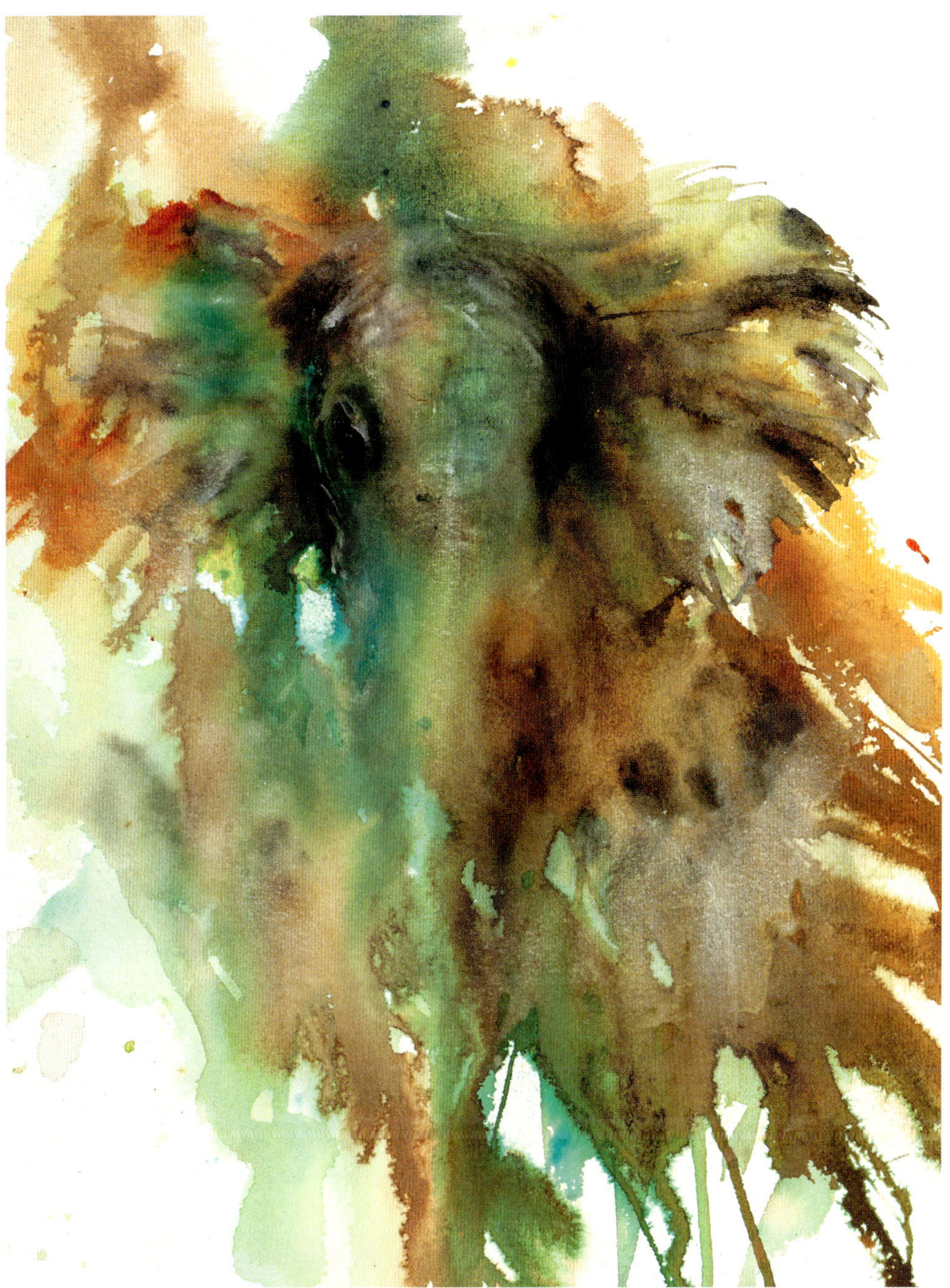

Expressive colour and brushwork

Sometimes we can express ourselves by saying very little in a painting. In this composition I painted a creative first wash (see page 88) using bold, darker colours. I then used expressive, energetic brushwork to bring my elephant to life – but note that in this painting, very little is stated. There is no trunk, and no tusks. So much is missing and yet the story is nevertheless told. I could complete the painting by adding detail, yes. But the feeling of energy in this and that fabulous sense of spontaneity could then be lost.

Try painting half subjects, allowing your own energy and feelings to come through. Stop the minute that you can see what your subject is, and learn from this creative process. As with monochrome, we learn so much from the self-set limit of half-finished work. Working in this way, absorbing information, can greatly improve our skills as artists.

Full composition with detail

This full composition of an elephant may appeal to you more if you like detail. The colours set the stage of the animal being in a warm climate. Touches of gold bronzing powder add a sense of richness to the result. The whole of the head and upper part of my subject are painted. More detail has been added. It is a complete story.

If you prefer this image, it could be that you prefer a less loose and impressionistic style; but you can still create an atmospheric result by blending your animal into the background. A combination of loose and detailed work is magical in a composition and as a style, so try to blend your subjects with detail and see what happens.

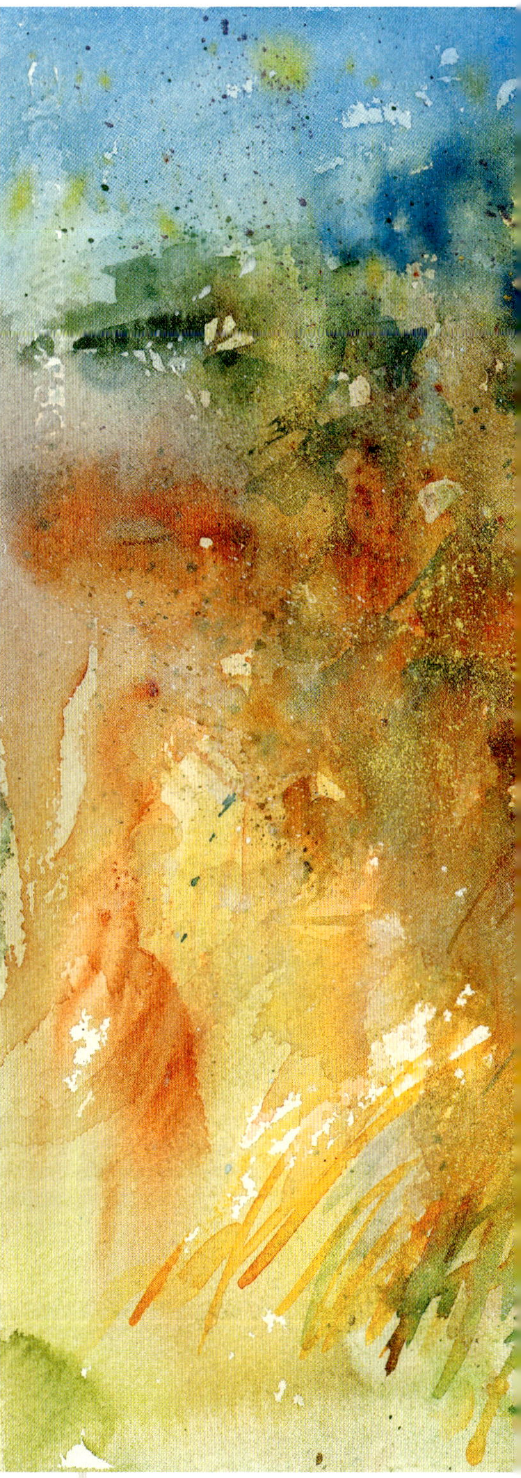

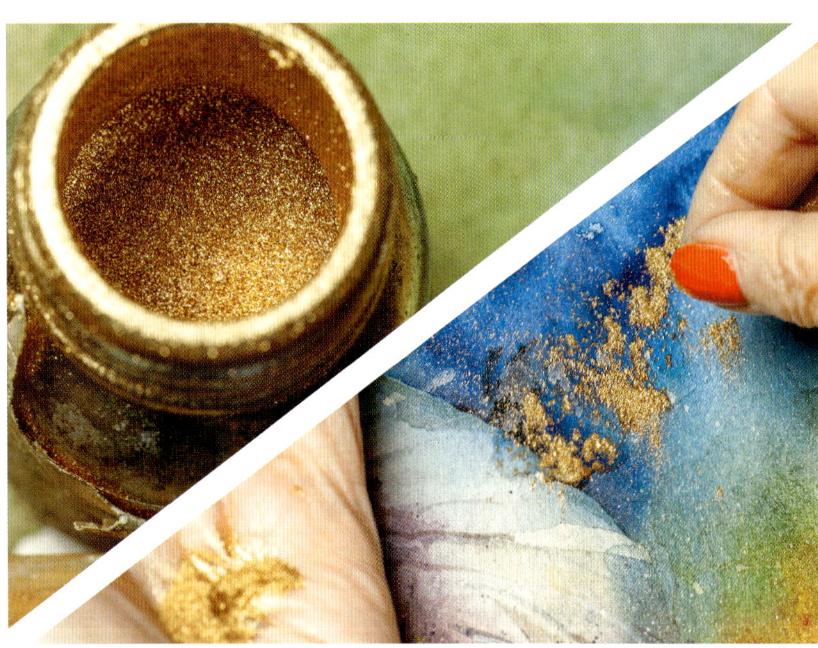

Bronzing powder

When applying bronzing powder, it's important to recognize that it needs to adhere to the paper surface. I tend to apply a small amount of gum arabic first and then pour a little bronzing powder into the palm of one hand. I then sprinkle a pinch of powder on top of the wet gum arabic so that it sets and stays well. Avoid applying too much bronzing powder at once. A fine sprinkle gives you beautiful effects without looking too overpowering.

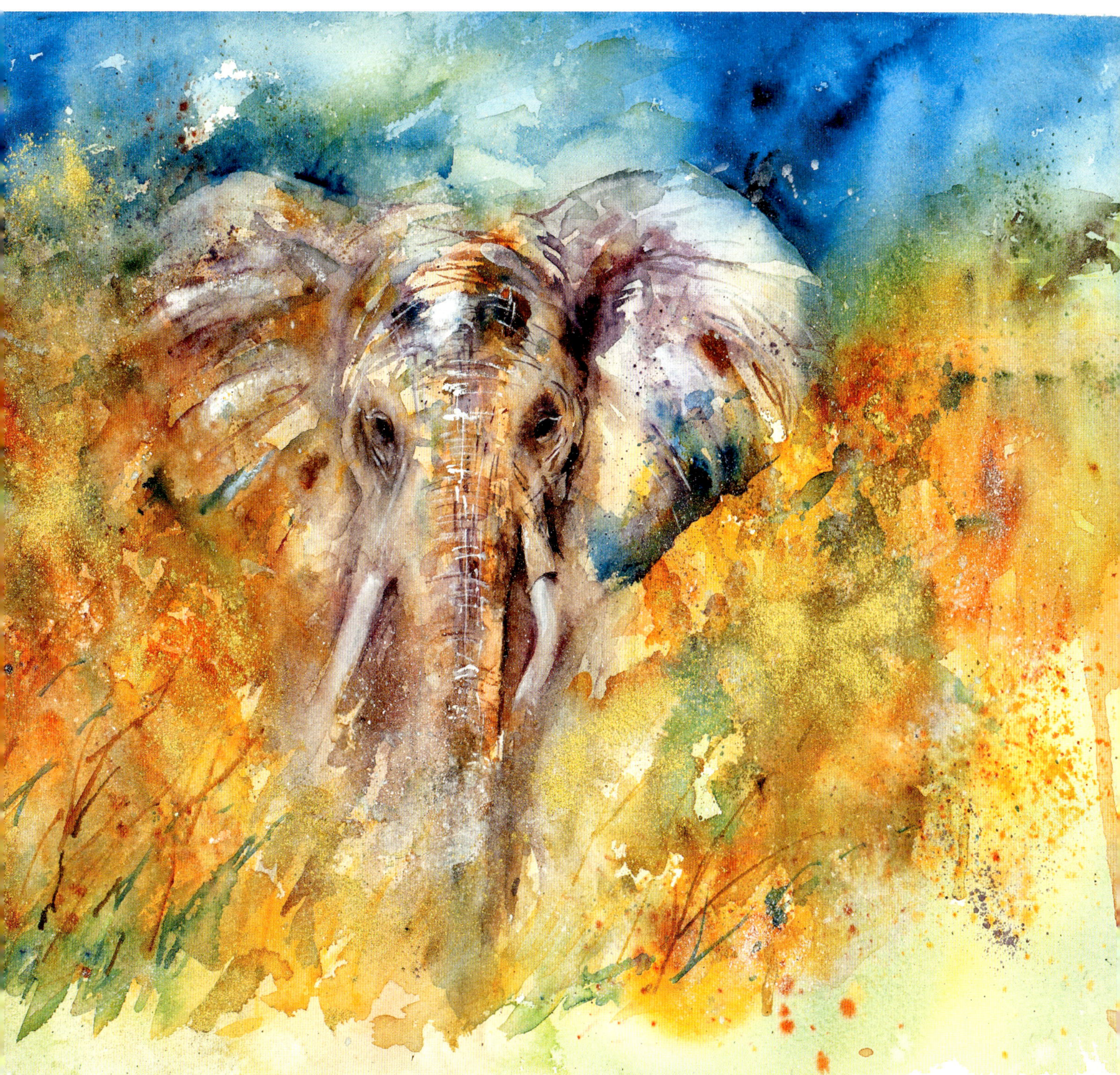

Out of Africa

58 x 38cm (23 x 15in)

Capturing the atmosphere of the country the animal is from, through the colours used in an interesting background wash will not only set the scene, but also add drama to a composition.

Abstract animals

Pushing the limits

Comparing the elephant paintings earlier in this chapter highlights the many ways to paint in a loose style. But if you want to push your boundaries as an artist further, this final painting, which I have taken to the extreme, shows how far you can go.

I started with an initial creative watercolour wash using my preferred Daniel Smith shades (see page 16), which established the whole painting. From here, I drew my texture products to me, and set out exploring. The following pages look at details of the finished painting, and show the results of combining the different products from earlier in the book – together with some new ones!

Spray paint

Spraying gives a more diffuse result than splattering. To spray watercolour, I fill small spray bottles with pigment using a loaded brush, then top it up with water. Alternatively, you can use one of the commercially available alternatives, such as Tim Holtz Distress Spray from Ranger, in colours of your choice.

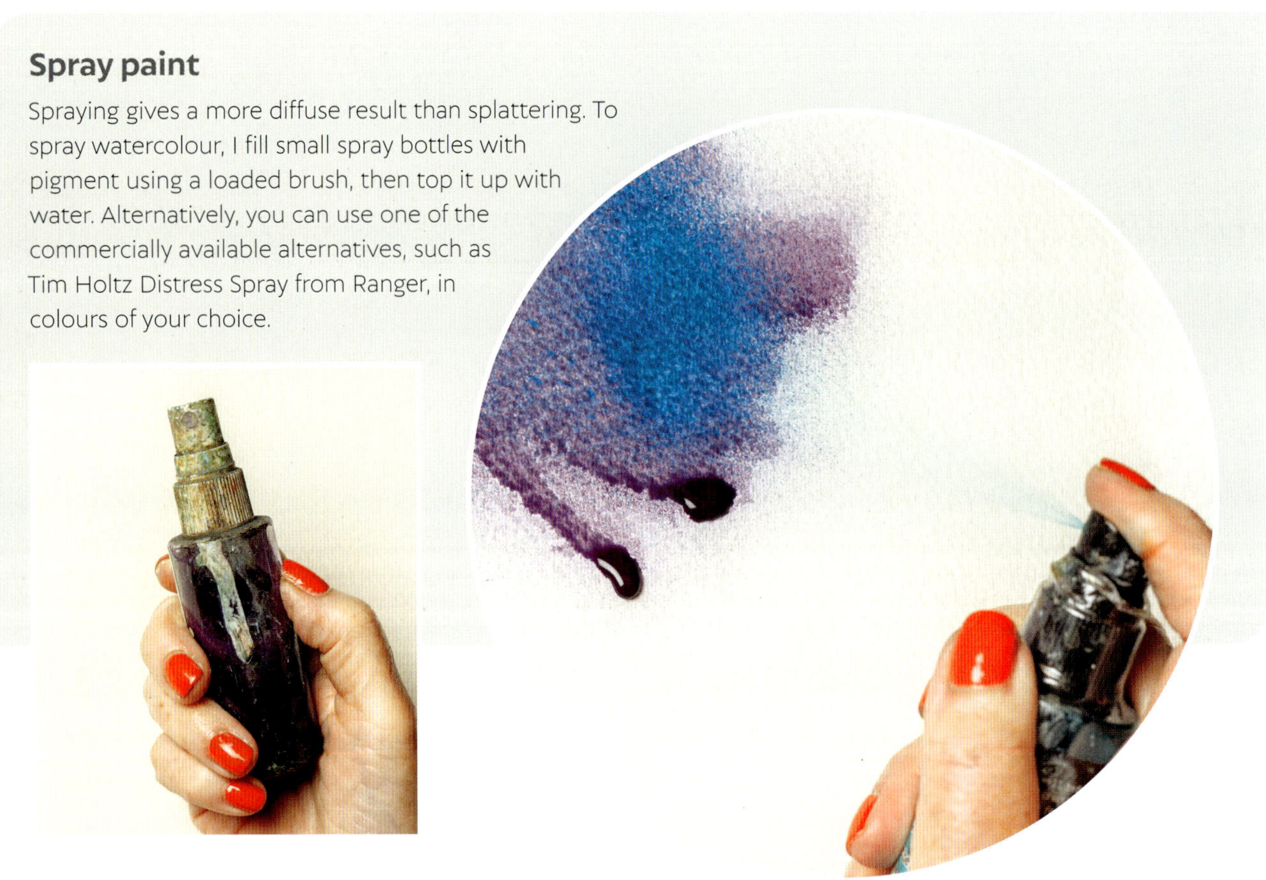

"They say that somewhere in Africa the elephants have a secret grave where they go to lie down, unburden their wrinkled gray bodies, and soar away, light spirits at the end." *Robert McCammon*

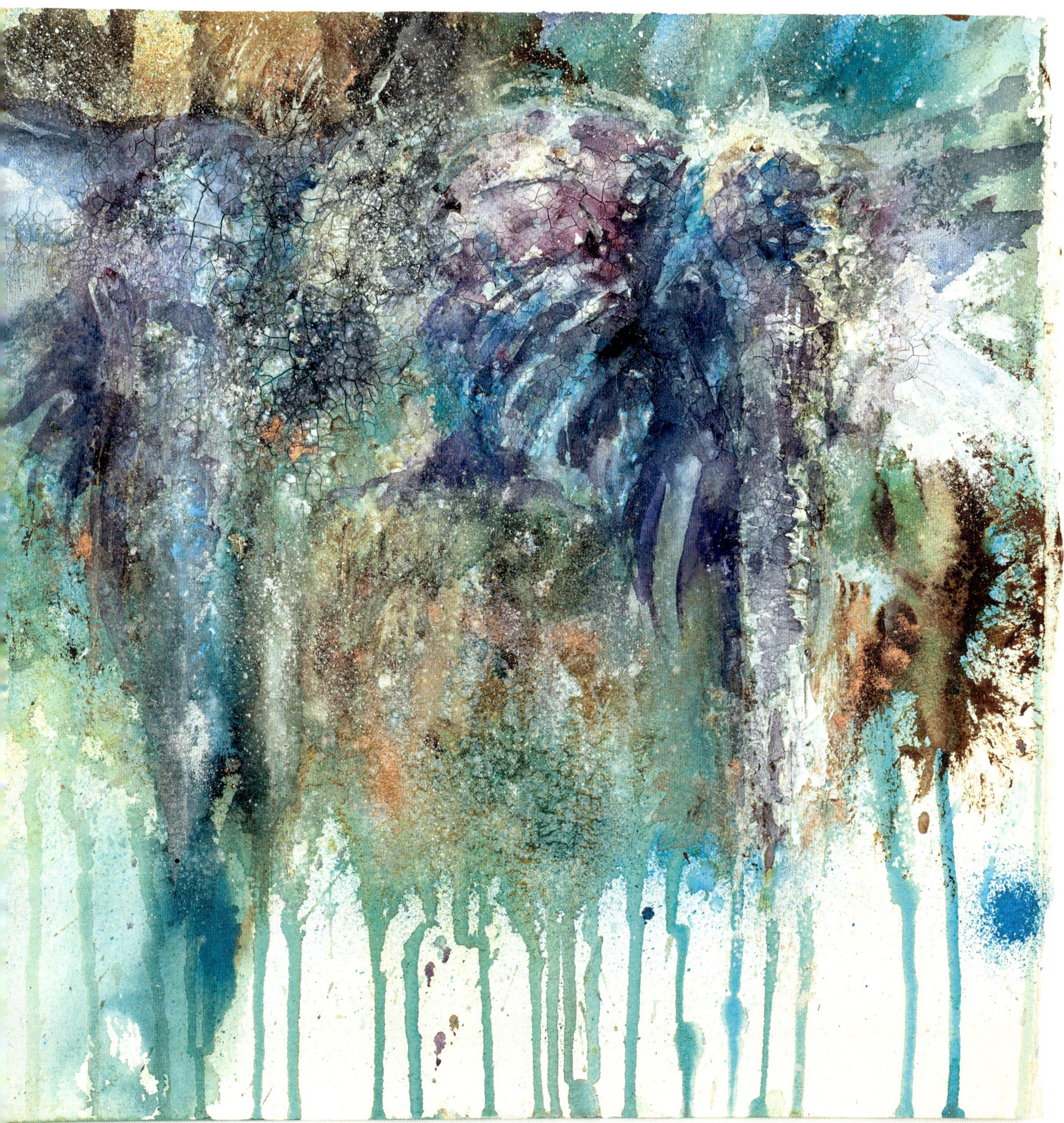

Out of the Blue

58 x 58cm (23 x 23in)
Created with a combination of texture effects detailed overleaf.

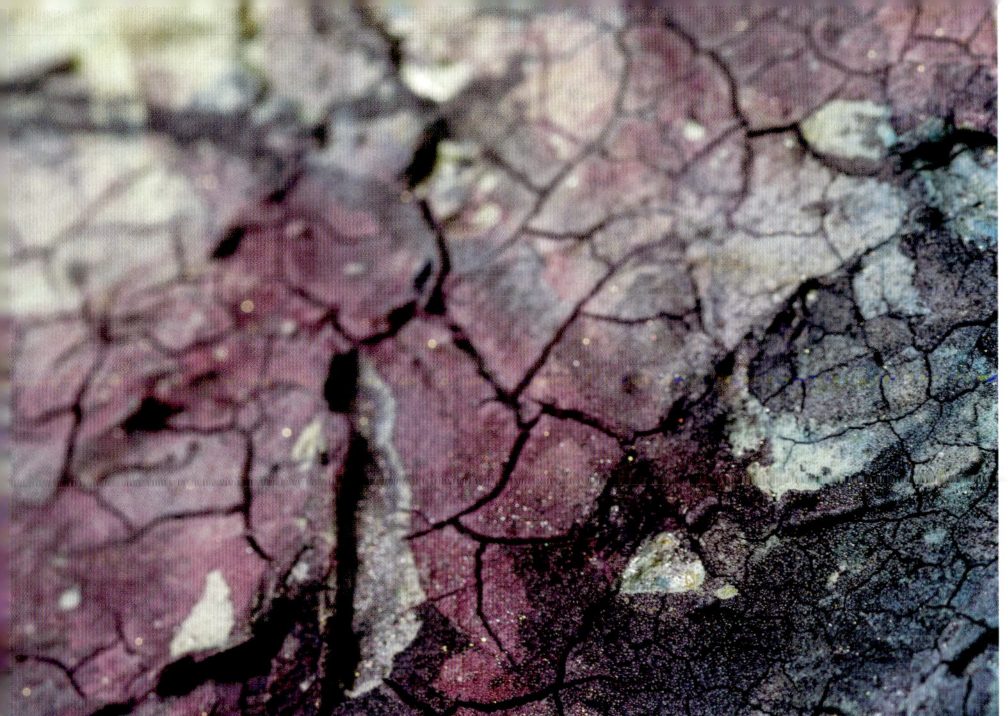

Crackle paste

Applied and left to dry, this forms amazing cracks that you can see in my painting. The cracks develop as the product dries, and the size of the cracks depends on how thickly the paste is added – the thicker, the larger the cracks. In this elephant painting, I applied crackle paste, then, while it was still damp, I sprayed it with watercolour (see page 128).

Gel beads

I dropped medium size beads into the upper sections of my painting while the crackle paste was still wet so they would sit in the paste and remain once dry. These add a contrasting texture shape effect to the lines achieved in the crackle paste.

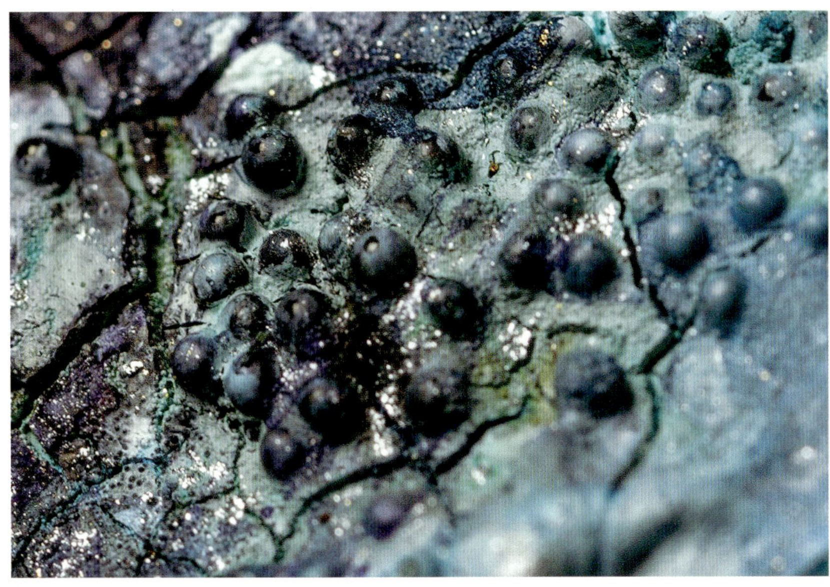

Turmeric ink

This you can see in the lower section of my painting. It creates the most unusual patterns – you can see another example on page 80. Sometimes you can achieve an effect almost like scales, which makes this texture effect perfect for many animals, including fish and snakes.

Bronzing powder

This must be sprinkled on while the pigment and paste are still wet to ensure that it remains in place. It creates a wonderful warm shimmer that catches the light and can enhance many compositions.

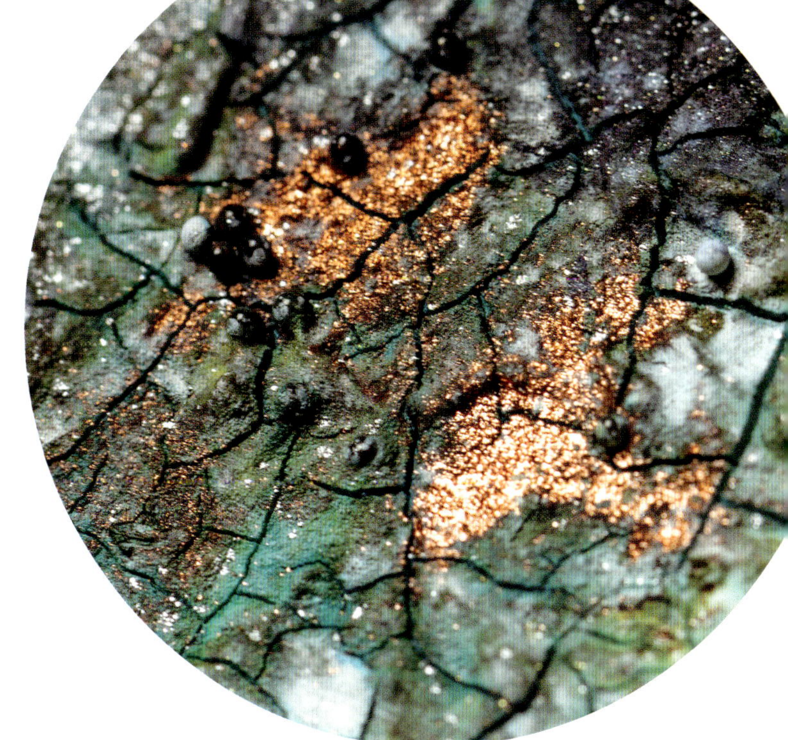

Splattered paint

I have splattered with both watercolour paint and white gouache on the complete painting for this effect. The technique can be found on page 90. Splattering can be an extremely useful technique for breaking up large blocks of dark colour; which is especially useful if you feel you are losing the effects of light.

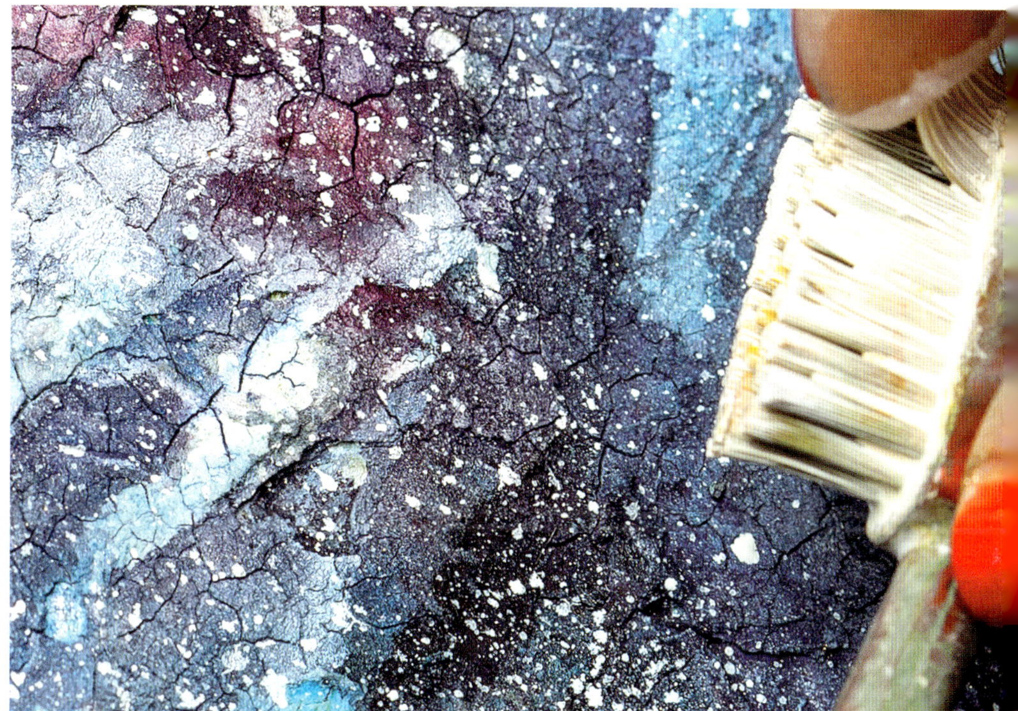

Texture and exploration

This was a fun and wonderful piece to create. I share it as a composition purely to show you how much fun you can have by using texture products. Is this pure watercolour? Certainly not. It does veer towards being a mixed media painting, but, even so, if you used less texture product in a watercolour painting your results could still be really amazing. Always experiment, always look for something new in your artwork. It enriches the spirit and feeds the creative artist's soul.

Seeing double

HARES HAVE ALWAYS BEEN ONE of my most popular and best-selling subjects. Who couldn't fall in love with these fascinating animals that race around stunningly? They are so beautiful to witness in action. Whenever I think of a hare, Aesop's fable of the tortoise and the hare immediately comes to mind. The tortoise, slow and steady, won the race that the hare had expected to win easily. Perhaps the moral of this story is that if we take our time learning techniques and practising as we paint each new subject, our paintings will be far more beautiful than if we race to complete them without thinking at all.

In this chapter we look at a variety of ways to bring a sense of movement into our art. As usual, when painting a new subject, I begin by painting a small study. This way I can avoid any hiccups, such as wrong proportions, that could ruin a larger painting later on. Each time I move my brushes, I am gaining ideas; and I can show you a comparison. Compare my small study, *March Hare,* opposite, with the larger painting of the same animal, *Leaping for Joy*, overleaf.

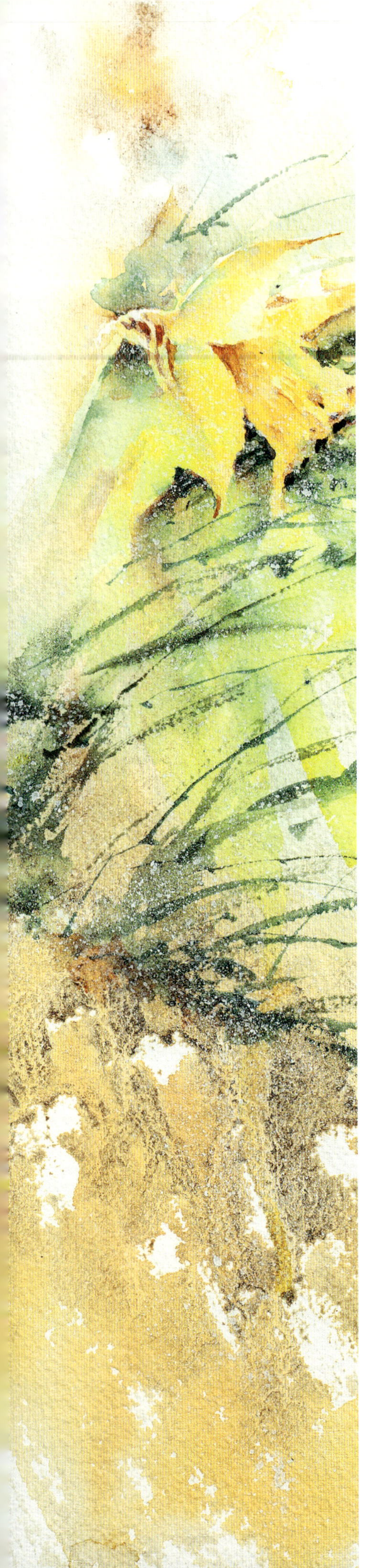

Detail of Spring Flower

Combining seasonal backgrounds with your subjects can bring a greater sense of atmosphere to your piece, and add to the storytelling.

Adding energy

I created the initial small study of this hare by beginning with the eye section, a technique we explored in 'Feline Fine' on pages 68–71. I next painted the face, followed by the ears then finally added the nose. I blended colour away from the face in a directional brushwork movement to hint at the growth pattern of the fur.

Suggesting movement

Adding fine lines for whiskers in a lively way using a rigger can add a sense of movement and character to your hare watercolours.

If you cover the lower part of this painting with your hand, you will see the image as it was in my resource photograph: just a hare sitting in a field. By carefully placing colour randomly at the lower section of this painting, I hinted at a raised paw which could give the illusion that my hare was about to leap or move.

I only discovered this idea from my painting session while playing with colour. This small practice piece led me to a larger painting, which you can see overleaf, where I tried to replicate the idea but in a more planned way.

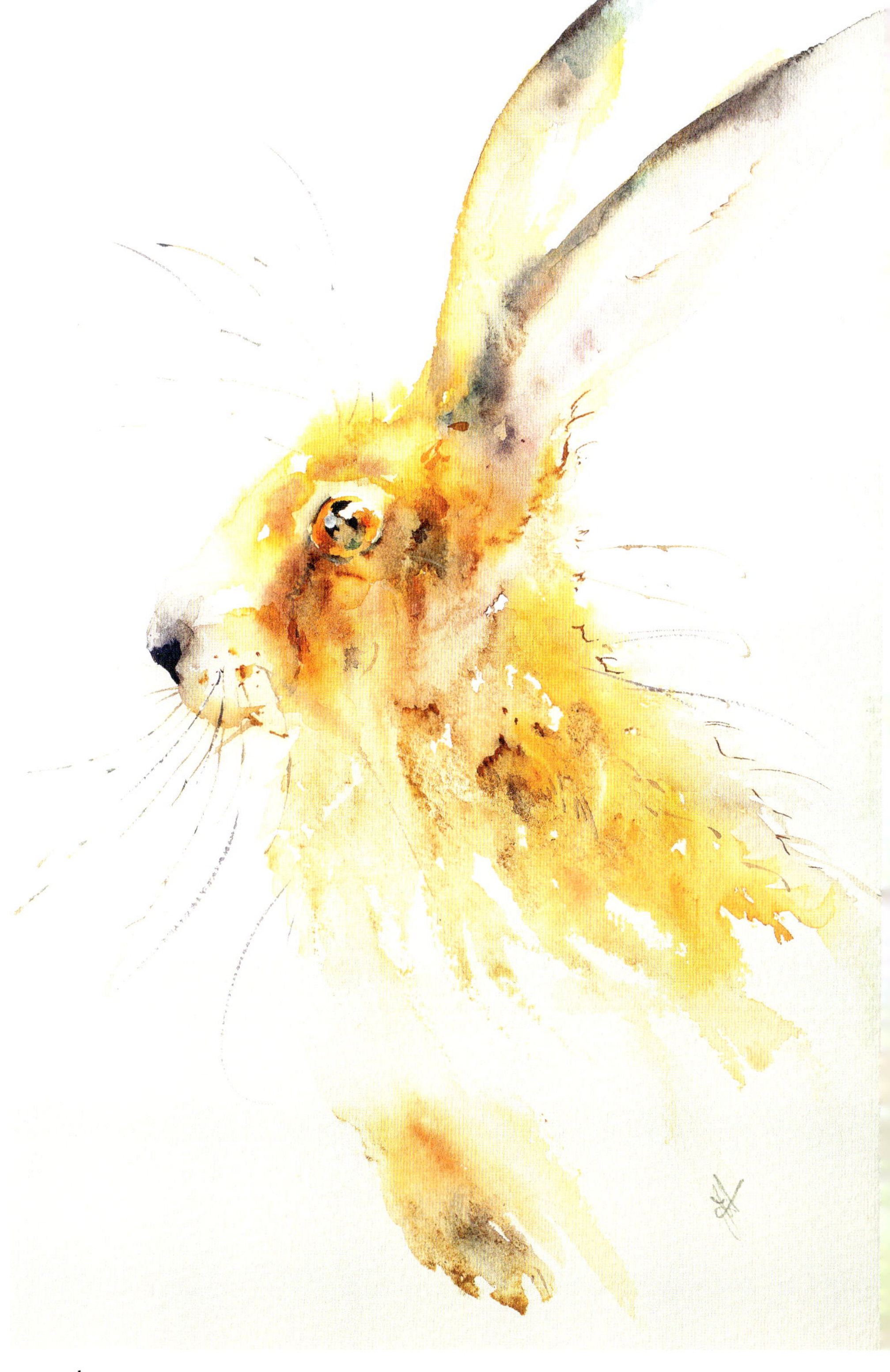

March Hare

28 x 38cm (11 x 15in)

I know we are often eager to begin a painting and, at times, if the subject is familiar to us, our confidence in how we are going to create our composition can be high. Nevertheless, I hope these two paintings will show – and emphasize – how small studies can be valuable in so many ways.

Ringing the changes

Happy with my small hare study (see *March Hare* on the previous page), I moved to a larger piece of paper and began the process again, working from the eye outwards, and taking my time to build up my new painting. Gradually adding the face and ears, I created a section directly under the face adding colour and using brushwork in the direction the fur would be growing in.

This point is where my small study became very valuable, as I now added not one, but two hints of paws towards the lower section of my paper. As I added the whiskers, taking them into the wide-open space of white paper to add energy to my hare painting, I realized that the hare could be twisting as it leapt, so I then added hints of the hind feet. By disconnecting sections of a subject, you are allowing light and energy to become involved in the play of the story behind the painting. By disconnecting segments, you are adding a wonderful illusion of speed.

Both paintings – the small study and the larger composition – carry a different feel to them because each of our watercolours created without a preliminary sketch have a magical sense of life in them that cannot easily be replicated, if at all.

By observing animals, we can learn about shape, colouring and proportions. However, taking into consideration how they move can add a dramatic element of life and movement that can have a really strong impact on our results.

The completed paintings here show how you can capture this magical animal in watercolour simply and effectively.

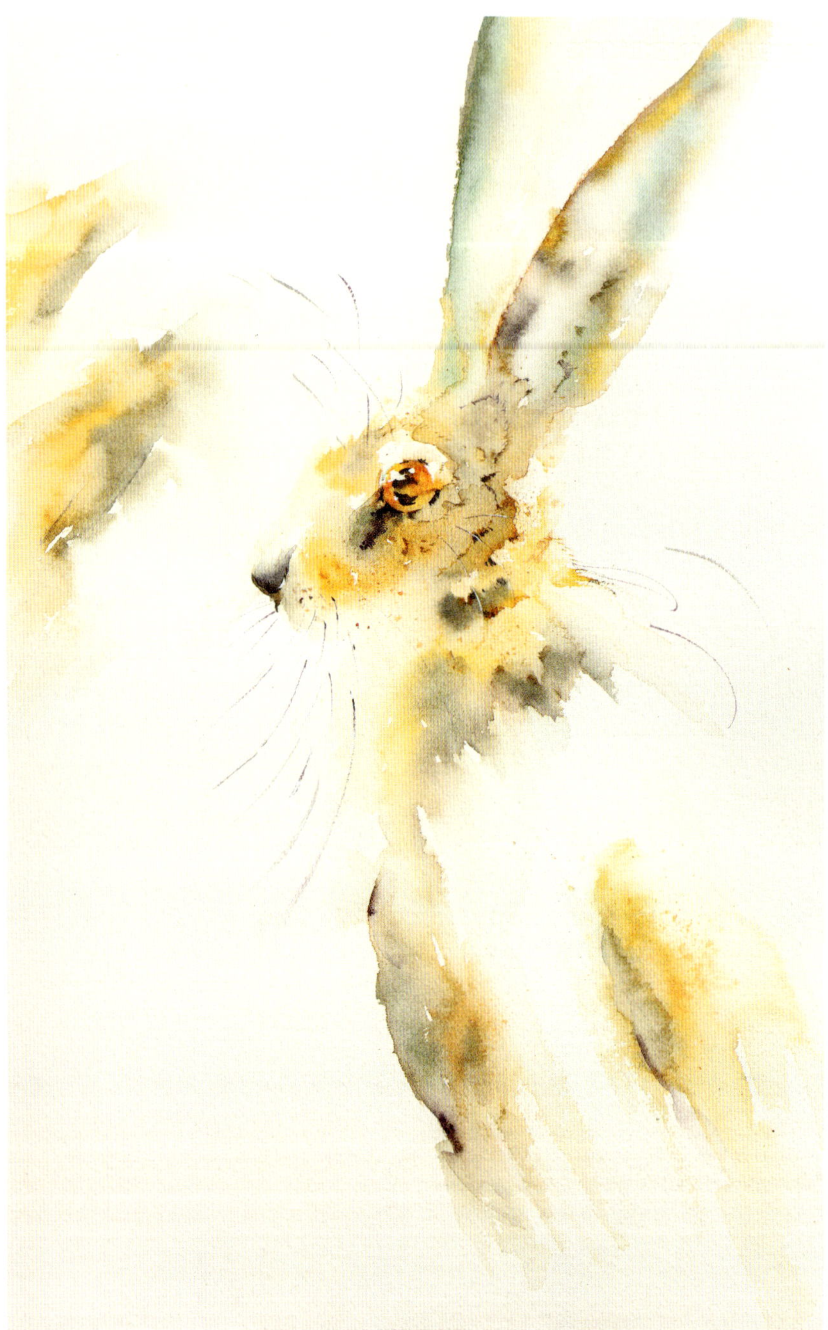

Leaping for Joy
26 x 38cm (10½ x 15in)
Unlike cats, I have yet to paint a sleeping hare, as I always think about them moving; especially in springtime due to the saying 'As mad as a March hare'.

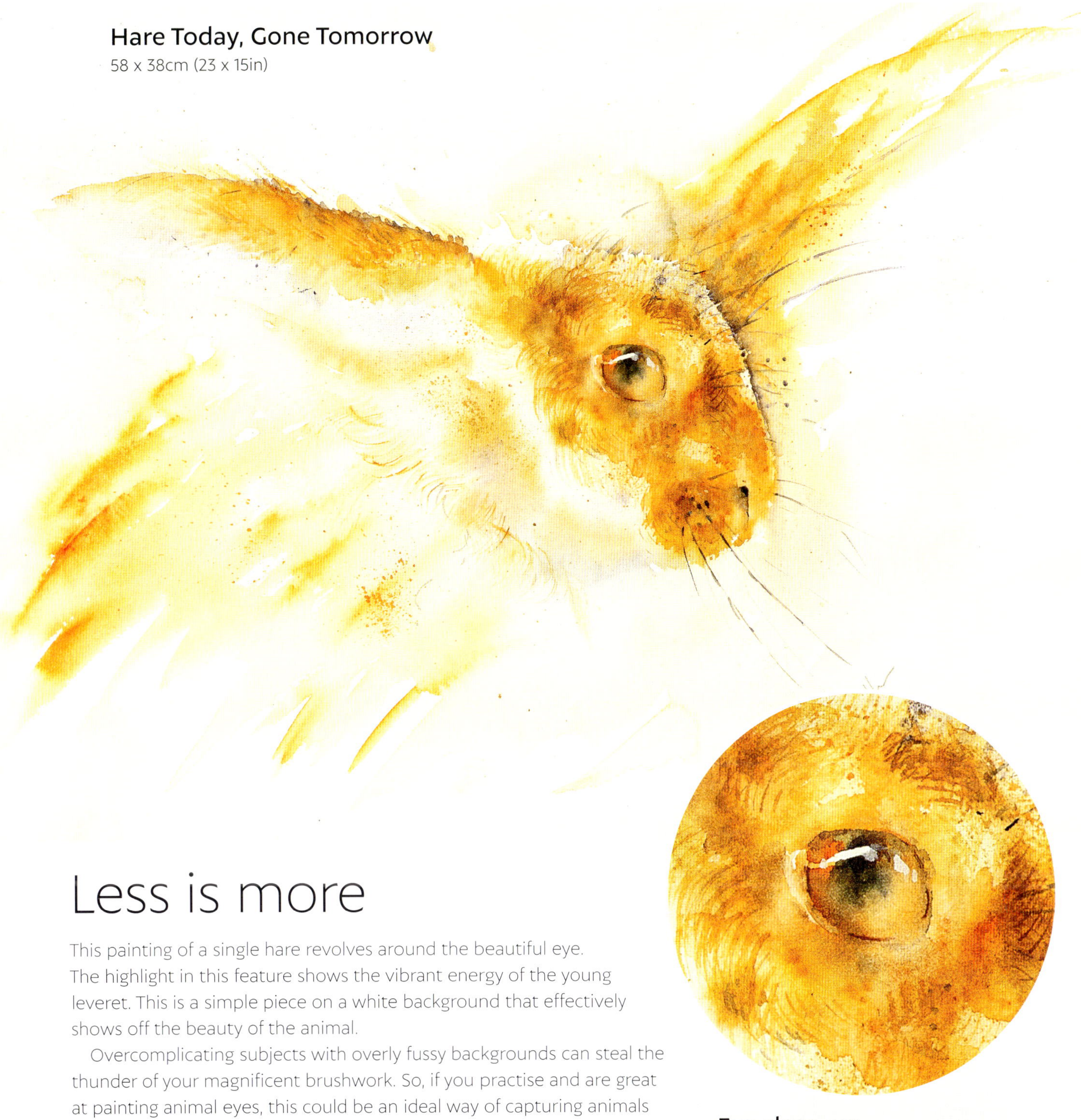

Hare Today, Gone Tomorrow
58 x 38cm (23 x 15in)

Less is more

This painting of a single hare revolves around the beautiful eye. The highlight in this feature shows the vibrant energy of the young leveret. This is a simple piece on a white background that effectively shows off the beauty of the animal.

Overcomplicating subjects with overly fussy backgrounds can steal the thunder of your magnificent brushwork. So, if you practise and are great at painting animal eyes, this could be an ideal way of capturing animals in watercolour. Use your strengths when you paint. Discover what you are amazing at. Maybe you love creating washes, and backgrounds are your favourite way to paint. The elephants shown on previous pages, where we placed a subject on top of a wash, are great examples of this approach.

My advice would be to try all possibilities of developing compositions and, as I have demonstrated on the previous pages, always look for new ways to paint your favourite subjects.

Eye close-up

Getting the eye right is vital to any good animal portrait. Try to avoid defined, heavy, dark black pupils. Keep iris light effects varied by clever use of watermarks, shade variation and softened edges. Note how highlights in the eye can be very different from the popular use of a simple artistic white dot. All these tips can lead to stunning results.

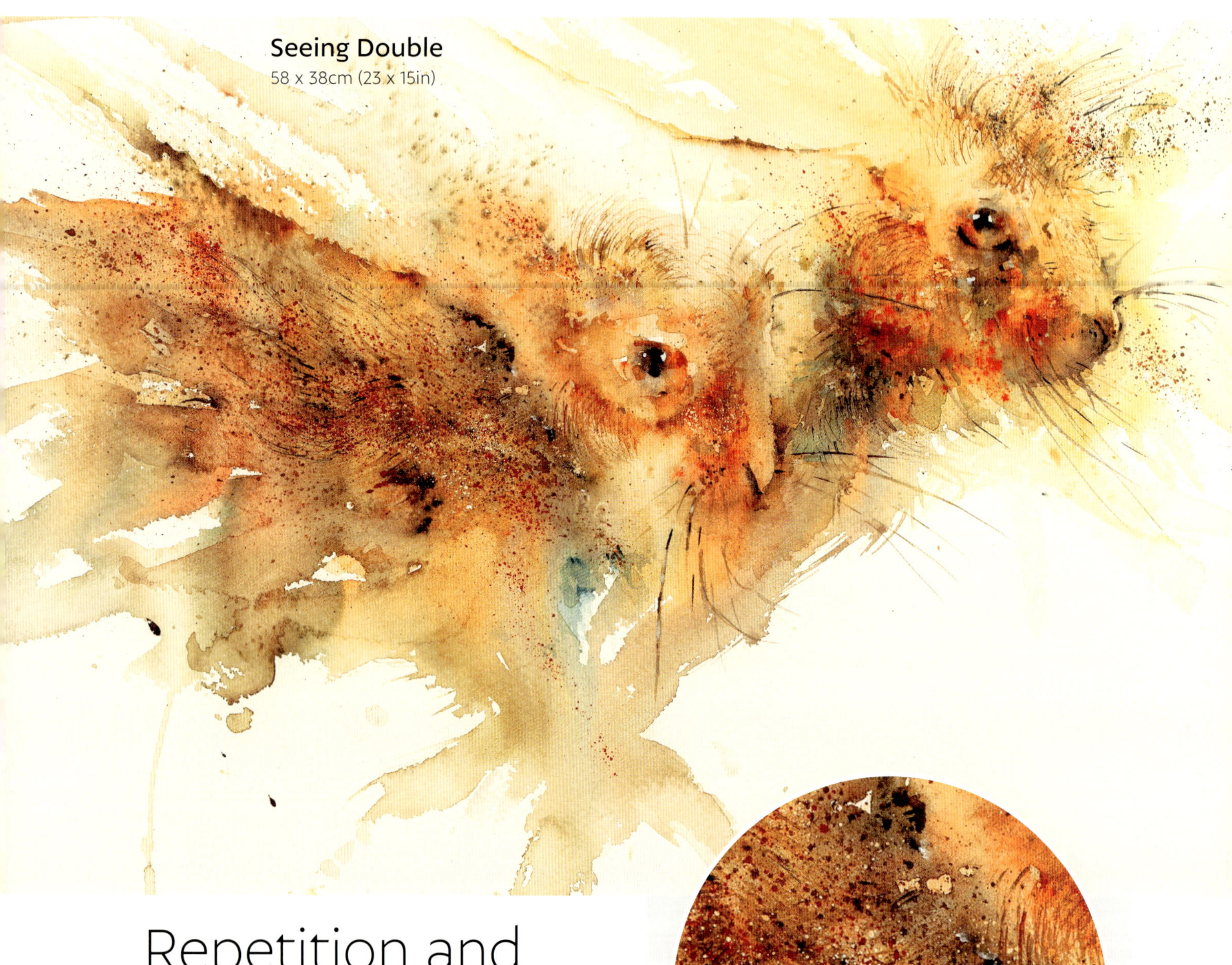

Repetition and rhythm

I love repetition in a composition and it often works particularly well with animals in movement. In *Seeing Double*, above, I took the idea of the first hare and added a second. Again, here I only placed hints of the paws to suggest that both hares were running.

You can have so much fun with painting watercolour animals, working out how to bring their characteristics and personalities into each painting in a new way. I'm happy to sit and watch hares for hours, learning about how they move, before bringing all my newly-found information into my next collection.

Splattering for fur

As a technique, splattering (see page 90) can be invaluable when painting dense fur. Try splattering on top of a block of colour to break it up and gain an appearance of fur texture. A great tip is to splatter with a selection of shades ranging from dark to light, allowing each to dry in between applications. Finish with a light splattering of white gouache to add light to your results.

Suggesting movement

If we watch an animal moving in it's natural setting,
it is often difficult to make out each moving limb
clearly, especially if we are watching from a
distance. In our art, painting suggestions
of legs minus detail can add a wonderful
sense of energy, life and movement.

In this detail, you can see that
suggestive placement of colour
effectively tells the story that my
hares are racing against each other,
but little information is actually there.

Lessons we learn from this chapter

- Don't race to complete a painting.

- Add hints of feet to create the illusion of
  movement; keep these additions less detailed.

- Use whiskers when possible to fill empty white
  space of paper. This not only adds to your animal's
  character, but also adds a sense of fun and movement.

- Disconnect segments of an animal to give a feeling of movement, light
  and life to your work.

- Use repetition wisely to add extra animals – or, when necessary, a
  whole herd!

"An animal's eyes have the power to speak a great language." Martin Buber

Animal meaning: hare

Symbols of luck, fertility and protection, the hare also
represents hope, as these creatures are often seen
as the first signs of spring, bringing with them new
life, freshness and energy. Cupid, the Ancient Roman
god of love, is often depicted with a hare at his feet.
Venus, the goddess of love, is similarly often seen
surrounded by hares.

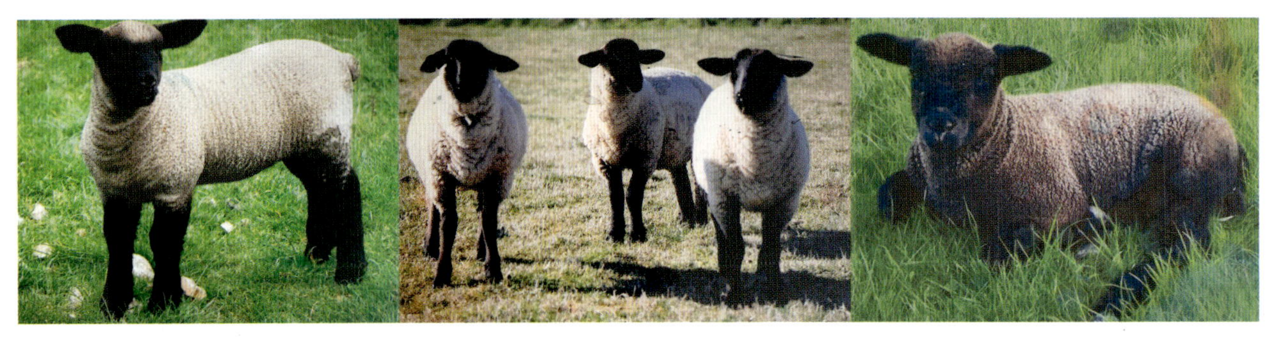

Be unique: sheep

AS A CHILD, I WAS SURROUNDED by countryside and rural scenes, and used to seeing fields filled with flocks of sheep. Every spring I would enjoy seeing the new-born lambs endlessly gambolling and playing – and so joyfully!

As subjects, sheep are beautiful to paint in watercolour and there are many techniques we can use to bring them to life in many unique compositions. And the key word here is unique. In all of my workshops, courses and books, I encourage everyone to find their own style and their own way of working. When we know that we want to achieve an atmospheric effect there are many doors open to us in reaching our goal. If you look back through the subjects and chapters in this book you will see how much pleasure there can be creating in my loose interpretative manner.

As each season passes, we should be growing as artists, developing our skills and style. Let's recap what we have gained so far in my book.

I hope as an artist you become a lion who isn't afraid to roar, by being unique!

1: Find the right subject

The lesson of always falling in love with your subject first will make a huge difference to your art. Painting with a feeling of enthusiasm and eagerness is wonderful. More importantly, if we leave each painting session happy, that element of joy will make us eager to paint again.

Always work from life when possible or from a fantastic resource photograph. Try, whenever possible, to take your own photographs and study each animal well so that you capture them in a pleasing composition, which will help you when you paint them later. As an example, look at the face in my lamb photograph. I already have a pleasing composition to work from and the information regarding the eyes and nose are clearly seen. This made this image very easy to work from. You could paint it too.

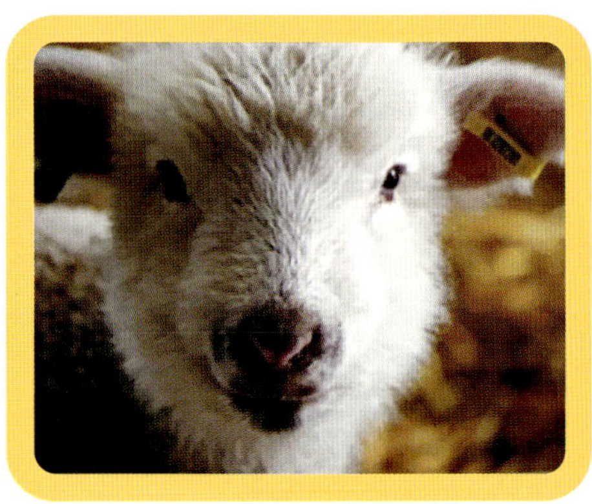

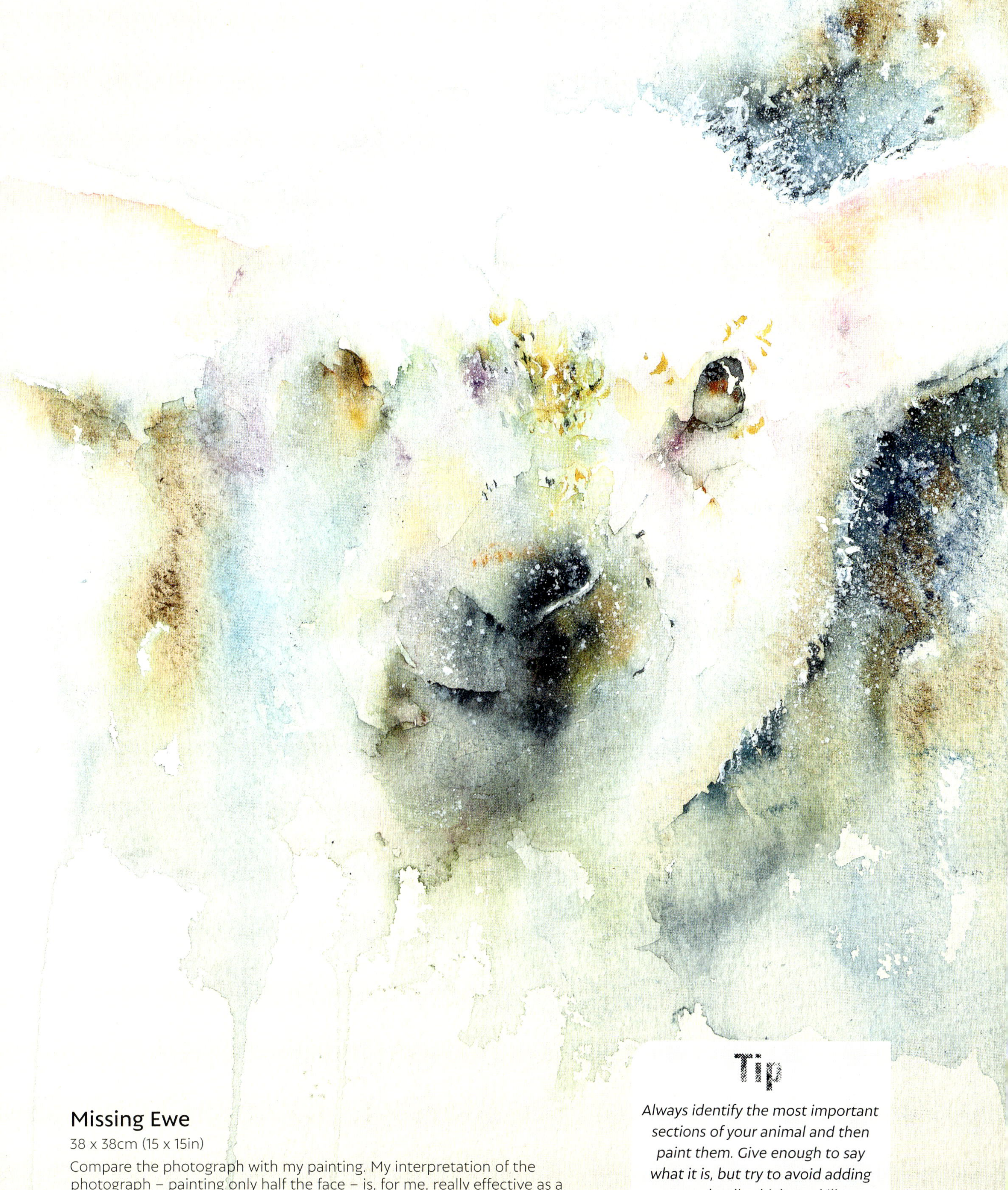

Missing Ewe

38 x 38cm (15 x 15in)

Compare the photograph with my painting. My interpretation of the photograph – painting only half the face – is, for me, really effective as a technique. I spent time first creating a great eye and a soft muzzle. These were the most important sections of the animal in the story I wanted to tell viewers through my finished art. As an exercise, you could paint this lamb using the techniques covered in my previous chapters.

Tip

Always identify the most important sections of your animal and then paint them. Give enough to say what it is, but try to avoid adding every detail, which can kill an atmospheric and free result.

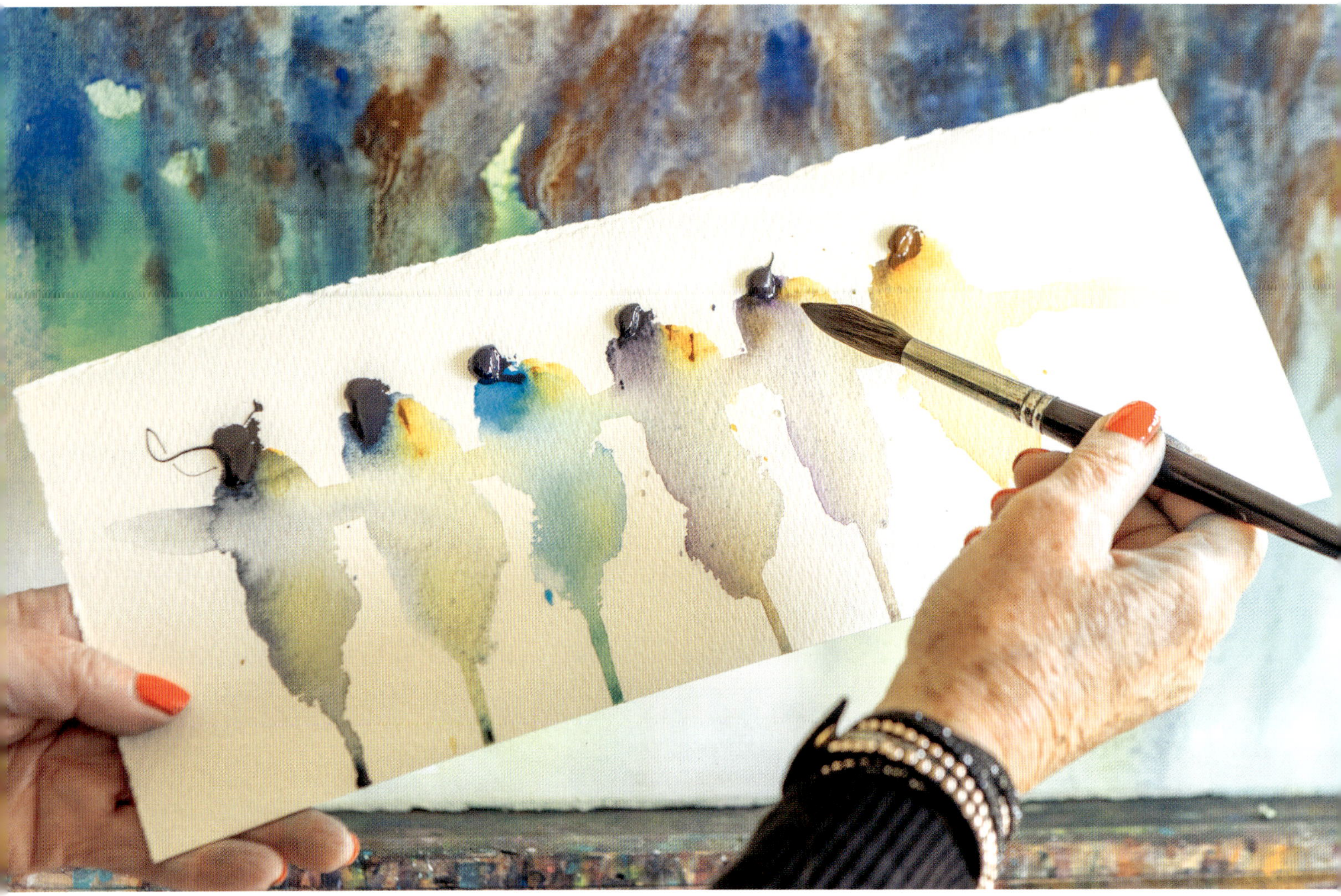

2: Choose the right colours

Throughout this book I have demonstrated how I choose colours for my animal subjects using my invaluable dancing ladies exercises. Please remember that you don't always have to paint the exact colours you see in the subject. You can change them to make your painting more dramatic, more of a fantasy-style piece, or keep your selected shades as realistic as you like. You are the artist, so this is your decision. Make it wisely.

Similarly, you might choose colours that will interact well and give you harmony throughout your composition, or deliberately choose colours that would contrast boldly for a more unusual effect. One of my favourite paintings ever was a pink elephant that someone once asked me to paint in a workshop. It gained so much attention that I have never forgotten it. It also quickly sold because it was so different.

My advice to you as an artist is to always be unique if you can. Stand out from the crowd whenever possible.

The colours I used for the finished painting opposite were: Payne's blue gray, lunar blue, phthalo blue turquoise, moonglow, amethyst genuine, quinacridone gold.

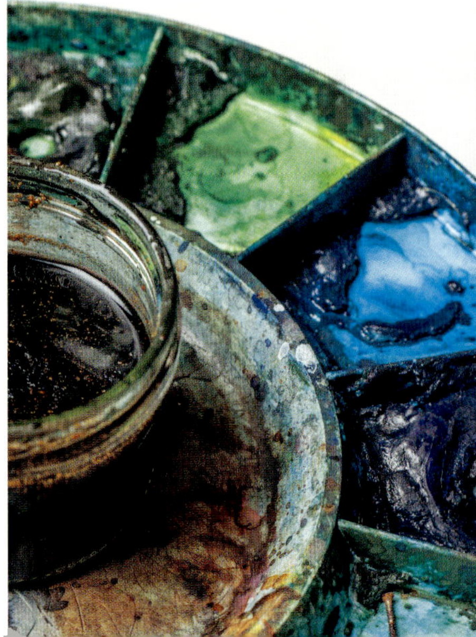

3: Learn about your subject

Avoid leaping into painting a new subject without at least painting one small study first. Getting to know your subject well is never time wasted, because your skill in getting the shape and proportions right will pay endless dividends, and lead to more accurate results.

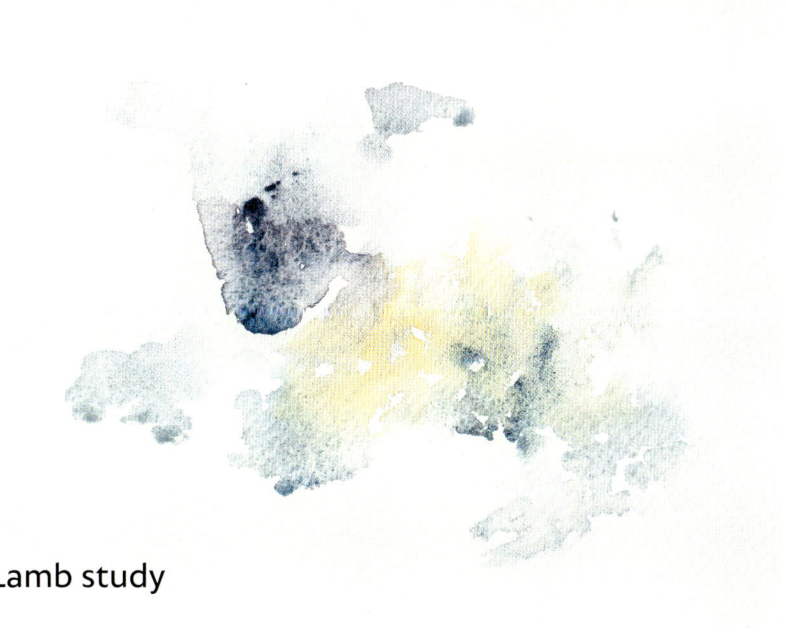

Lamb study

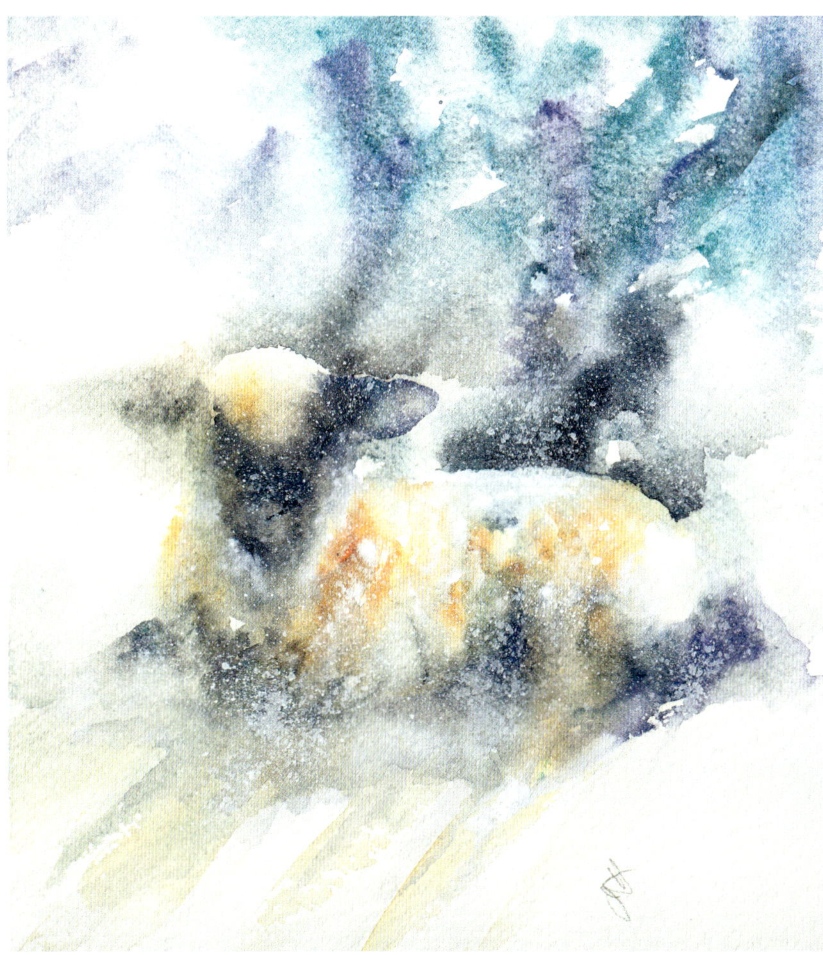

Feeling Sheepish
28 x 38cm (11 x 15in)

4: Gain confidence

Once you are happy with your small practice study, try ringing the changes by painting the same subject again. This time, either add a second animal or experiment with a dark background to give a completely different look.

Compare the sheep paintings in this chapter and notice what I leave out, what information I add and how I use colour.

In the sheep painting here, I splattered white gouache all over the composition to gain a snowy effect, but you could, of course, use a spring green background to give the illusion that your sheep are in fields. The options are endless: it will depend mainly on the strength of your imagination as to how many paintings you can create from one simple study. As you gain confidence, the ideas will flow, and your work will gradually become more fascinating, more interesting and, most importantly, more unique.

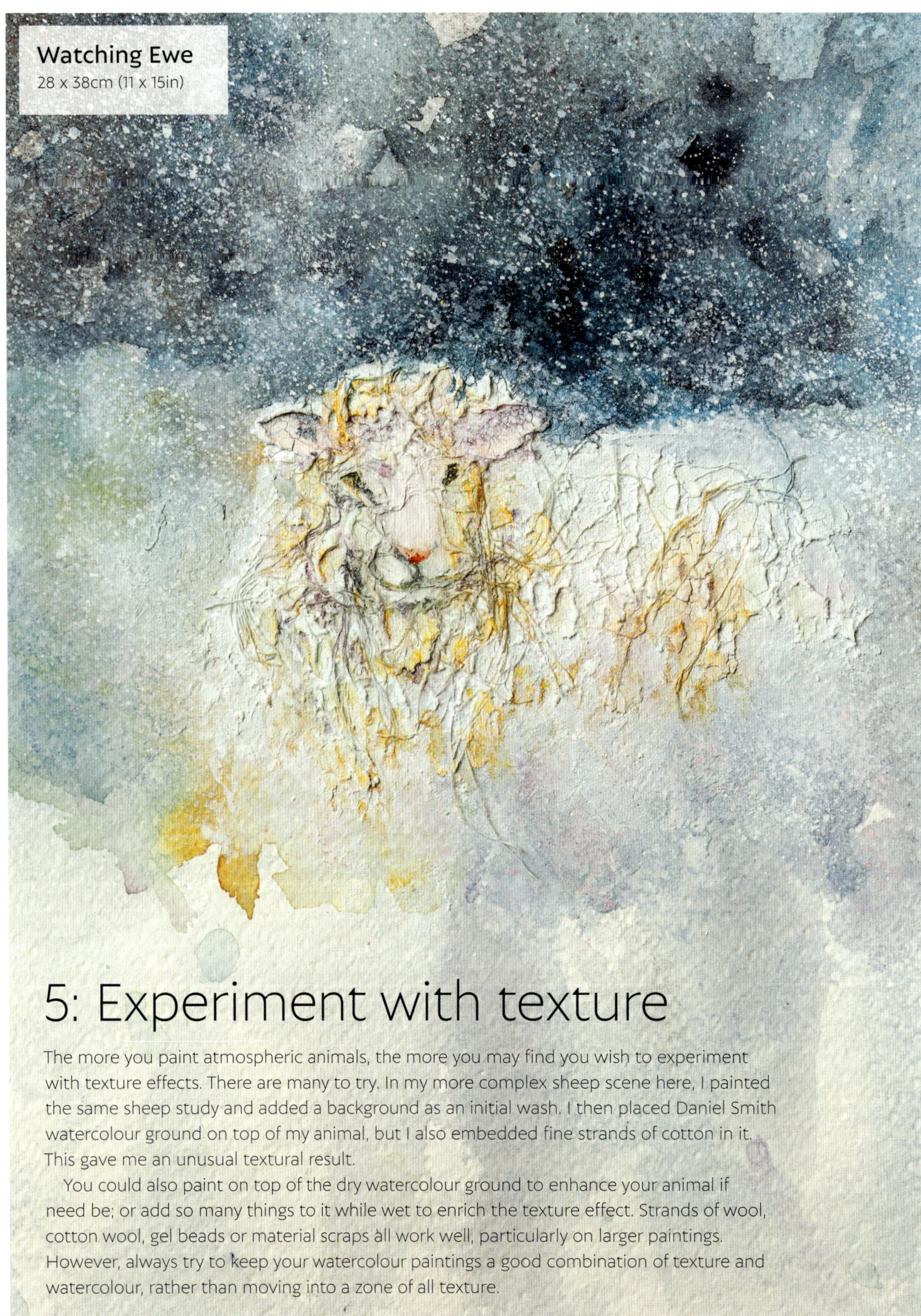

5: Experiment with texture

The more you paint atmospheric animals, the more you may find you wish to experiment with texture effects. There are many to try. In my more complex sheep scene here, I painted the same sheep study and added a background as an initial wash. I then placed Daniel Smith watercolour ground on top of my animal, but I also embedded fine strands of cotton in it. This gave me an unusual textural result.

You could also paint on top of the dry watercolour ground to enhance your animal if need be; or add so many things to it while wet to enrich the texture effect. Strands of wool, cotton wool, gel beads or material scraps all work well, particularly on larger paintings. However, always try to keep your watercolour paintings a good combination of texture and watercolour, rather than moving into a zone of all texture.

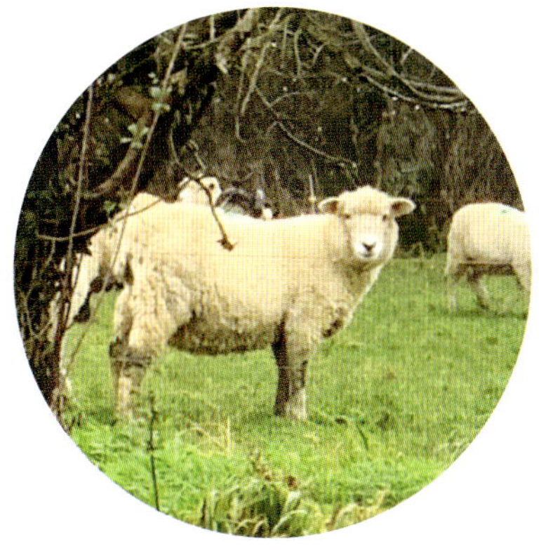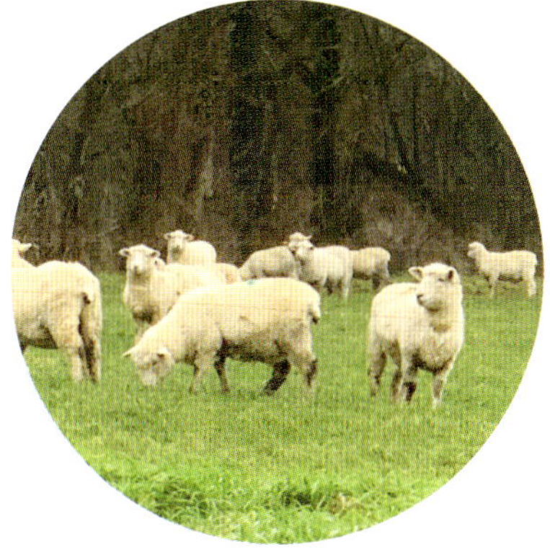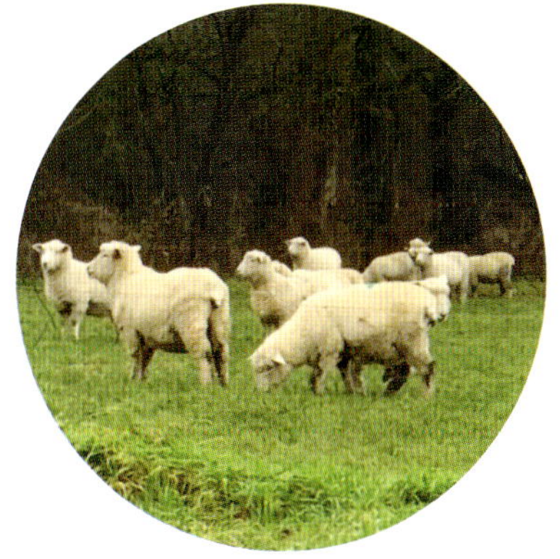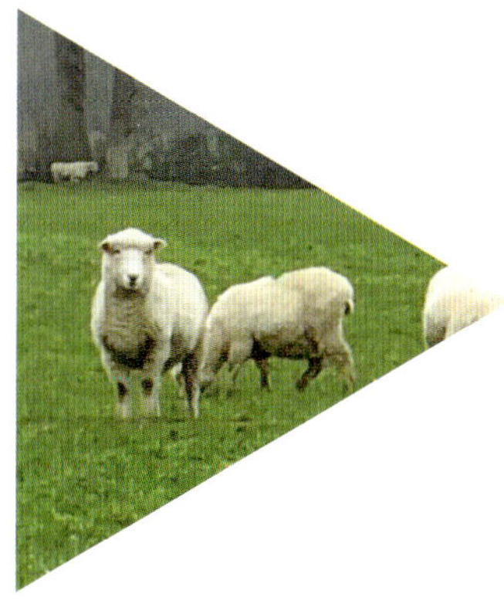

6: Lead, don't follow

The whole point of my way of painting is that there is no end to how any single subject can be approached. Even if I painted the same thing repeatedly, my results would always vary, which makes my art unique – and yours will be too. Remember my own favourite quote for artists:

"Don't be a sheep, be unique." Jean Haines

Animal meaning: sheep

We are used to the idea of sheep being herded as a flock. They are generally known for following the rules, being guided, obedient and going along with everyone else. Sheep are seen as followers rather than leaders. They are said to respect authority. I appreciate that they are also known for being loyal and faithful. I do love the idea that, as artists, we connect worldwide but we are all – unlike sheep – creating on our own unique paths, rather than following constantly where we are told to go!

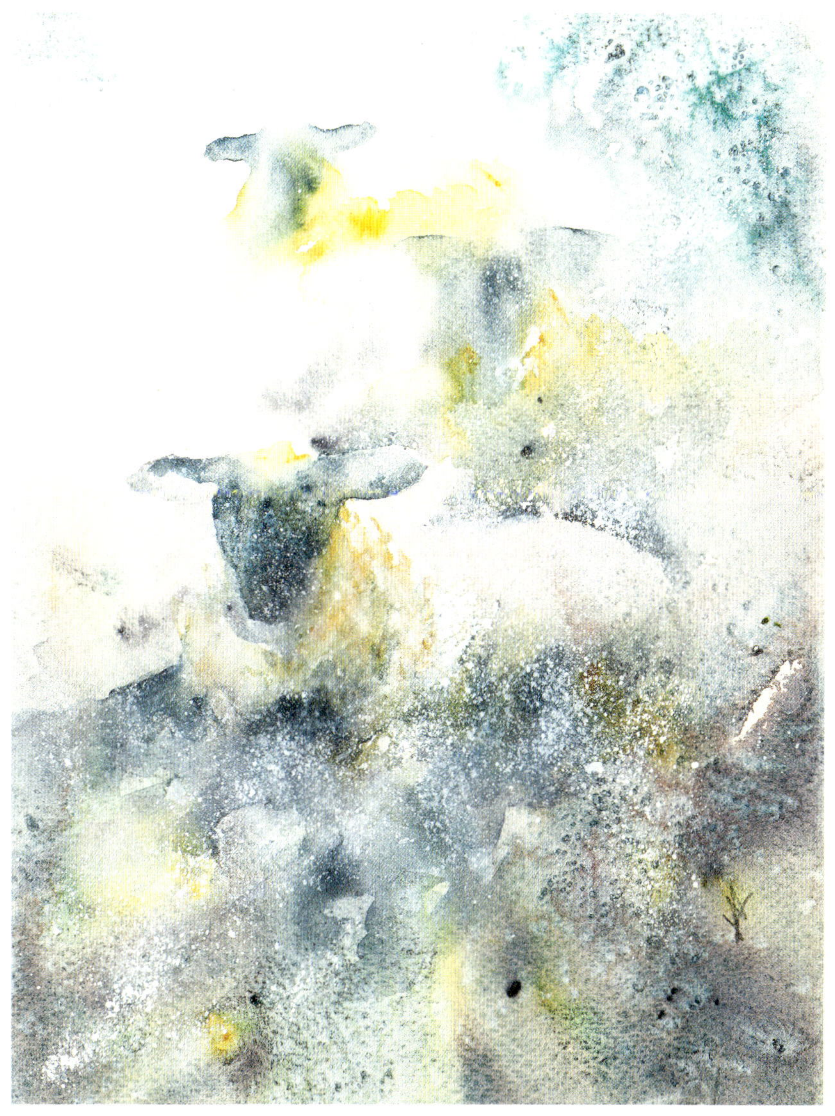

Misty Morn
28 x 38cm (11 x 15in)

Bugs and butterflies

WHEN LEARNING HOW TO PAINT a new subject, technique or style, I always recommend starting small before moving on to larger compositions. The smaller studies as seen throughout my book help us gain confidence in our brushwork, give us knowledge about the products we use, and they can lead us into becoming more experienced artists. It's very tempting to leap into huge compositions long before we are ready in our art journey. The information in this chapter covering painting small subjects can be really valuable as an exercise to cover all the points raised so far in my book.

Enhancing a painting

Insects such as bugs and butterflies can be extremely useful as additions that add interest and drama to existing paintings. If you look at my painting of a rose, which was inspired by a real-life scene in my garden, the simple dragonfly addition turns an ordinary floral painting into something far more pleasing. Now the painting has become unique. And that is what I strive for in my art: a level of fascination in my compositions.

Rather than just aiming to paint exactly what I see as a simple observation, I take the beauty from life and nature and bring it to life in my watercolours; and you can too. Nature is surely the best inspiration for artists of all levels. The sights we see can lead to so many magical paintings. If only we took more time to observe and enjoy the visions before us.

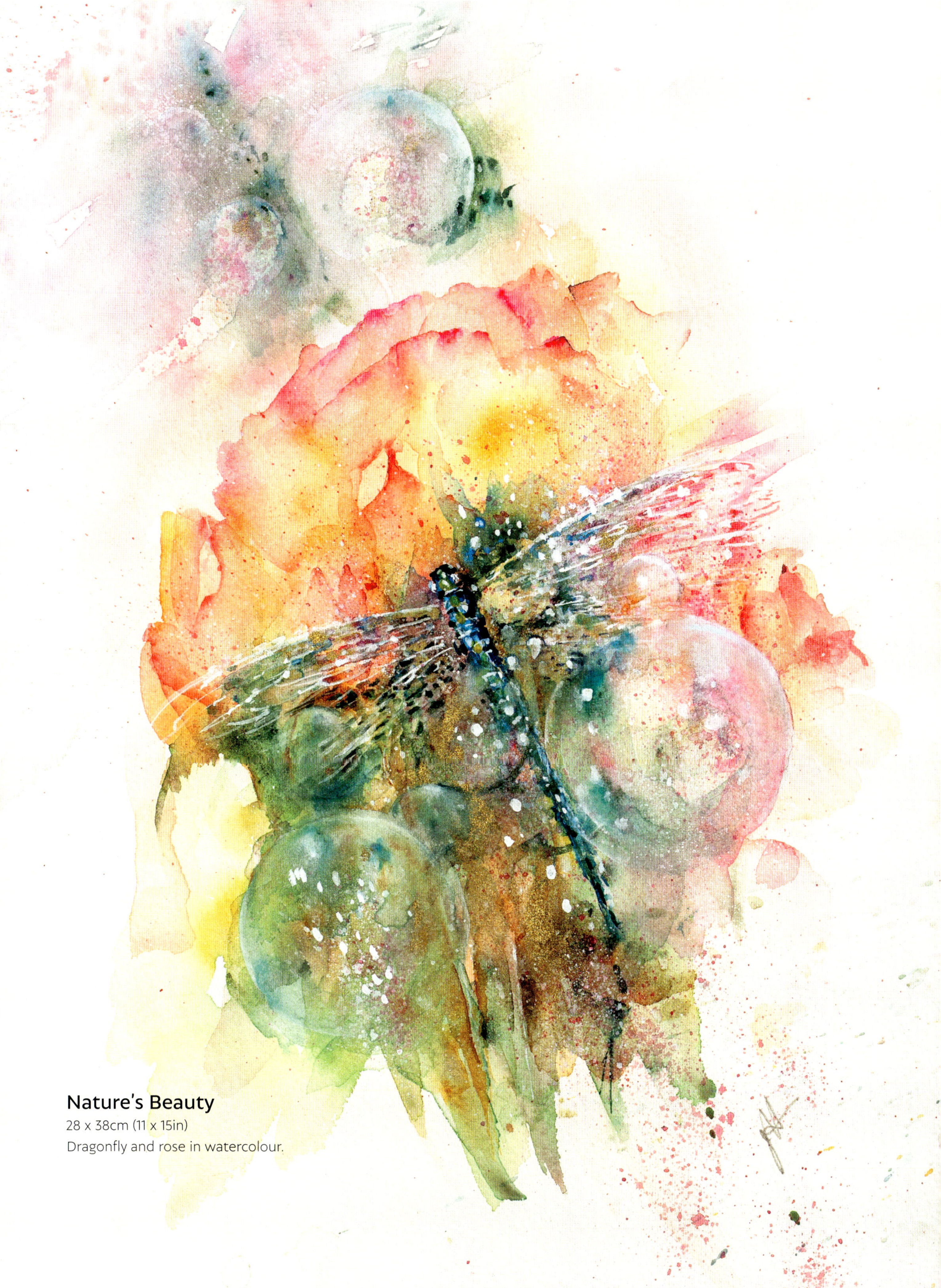

Nature's Beauty

28 x 38cm (11 x 15in)

Dragonfly and rose in watercolour.

Butterflies and bubbles

Producing beautiful atmospheric paintings that include animals relies on use of colour and knowing your subject well. I often observe butterflies in my garden and, as I also love painting flowers, it is no wonder that they appear combined in my art.

I have never been bored when I paint; and I would love for you to feel enthusiastic each time you create too. Experiment to stop your regular habit of painting from becoming routine and dull. I discovered it was fun to paint bubbles. By adding them to my butterfly and floral compositions my art changed. A playful element appeared that had been missing; I began touching on a sense of fantasy but within realistic boundaries. The story in my bugs and butterfly watercolour series became more fascinating with each new piece. Painting bubbles soon became addictive, as I loved how they added a playfulness to my work.

This is a good time to point out that there are no rules in art. As artists we can add what we want and combine no end of ideas to create. The two butterfly and bubble paintings on these pages led to a very successful collection that soon became very popular bestsellers. In large part this was because they were different. The moral of this section is 'always be open to new combinations!'

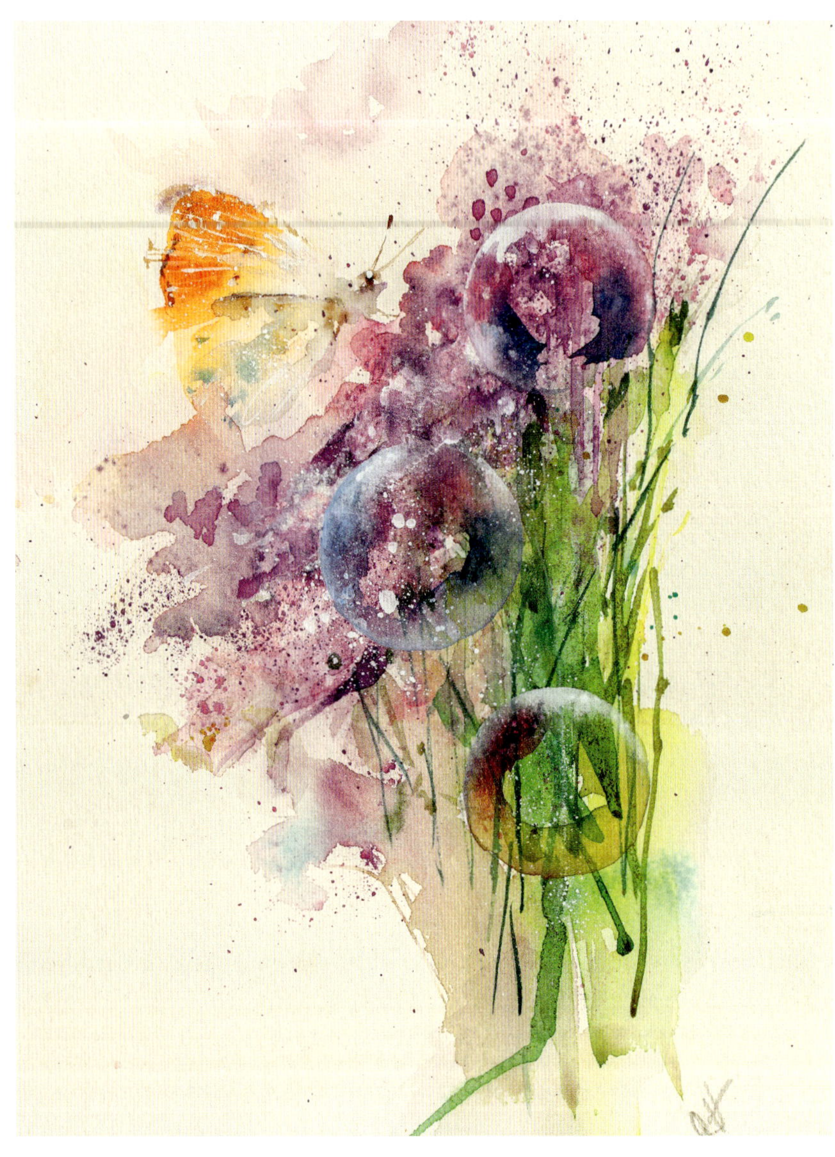

Beautiful World
28 x 38cm (11 x 15in)
Orange-tipped butterfly on floral background.

"Keep your mind open to the impossible when painting; because by creating in this way you never know what will happen. And that is the enviable joy of being a unique creator." The author

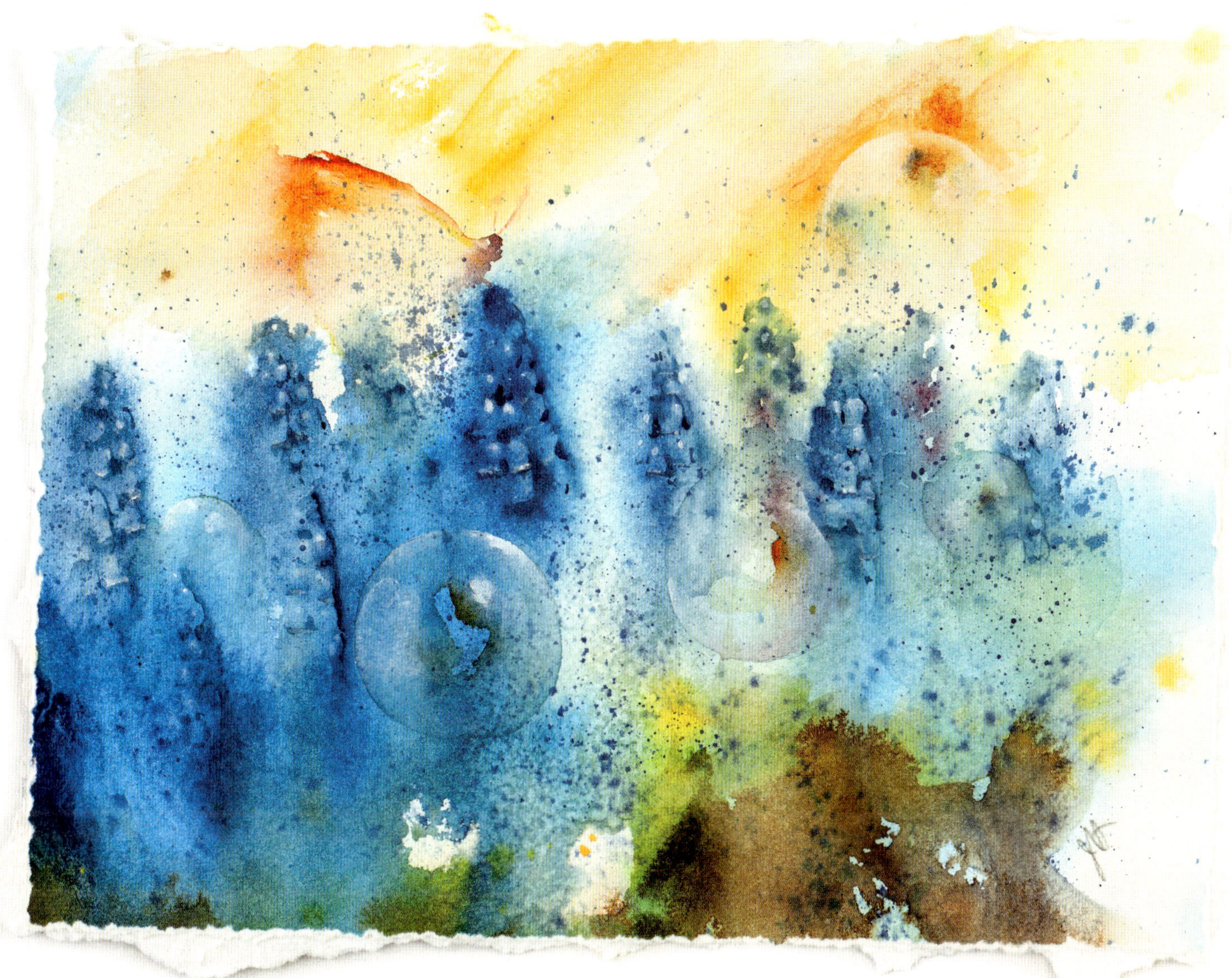

Spring Fantasy

25 x 18cm (9¾ x 7in)
Butterfly on muscari flowers.

Animal meaning: butterfly

Butterflies are associated with change and rebirth. If you
are drawn to painting butterflies, it could be that you are
going through a transformation. Perhaps in your art journey
you are looking for a new style or way of creating. They
are also said to connect to joy in life, happiness, a sense of
playfulness and the yearning to always search for something
new. A perfect subject for the adventurous artist!

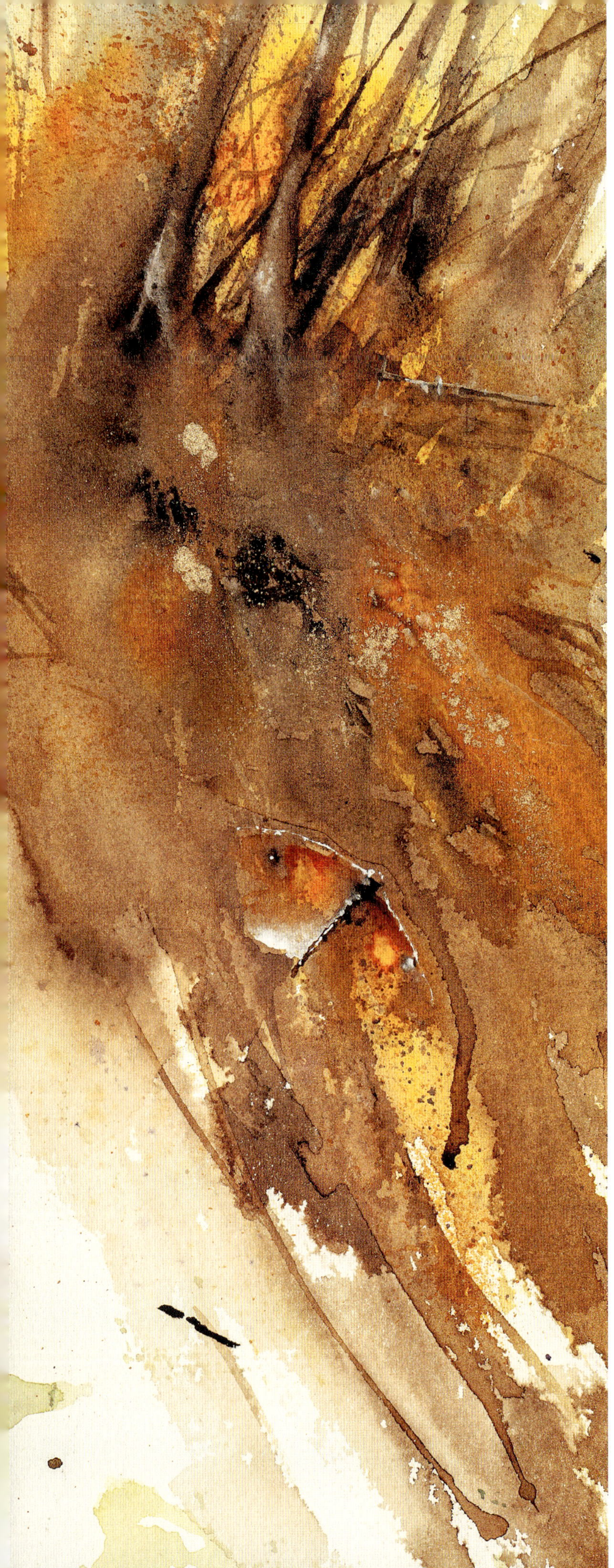

Vital observation

There are many ways to paint small creatures using the techniques previously shown in my book. You can paint the small beings on their own or on top of washes. I highly recommend studying each bug or butterfly before attempting to paint one. Learn about its form and how it moves. This will allow you to bring a believable energy to your work that could be missing if you simply guessed how they looked. I can't stress enough how important it is to study every animal you wish to paint as much as possible before even picking up a brush.

Telling a believable story

It is important to tell the story of how delicate a small subject can be. The butterflies I have painted in this chapter are hardly there in my paintings. I have hinted at them, rather than painted them solidly, to give the impression that they could move.

When studying my art, please notice that what isn't painted is as important as what you can definitely see. To gain atmospheric results we need to leave out sections wherever possible. This gives an air of mystery and can add an ethereal form of beauty to our art. The 'less is more' approach is one I love to aim to master. So, each time you look at a new subject, imagine where you can omit details.

Woodland Wonder
17 x 38cm (6¾ x 15in)
Butterfly in woodland setting.

Creating variety in our art

To paint the butterflies and dragonflies in my series of paintings, I started with a dramatic first wash. The wings will appear on top of this, so the first wash colours should be dynamic so that a fascinating background shows through the wings. Beyond this, you can experiment, so that you create a wonderful varied series of related paintings.

Start with a fabulous background

This is a useful technique for any animal subject, and particularly useful for insects. Select colours that will tell the story of where your animal is from. Opt for a setting that will fit the story you are telling.

For small bugs or butterflies, you could work on top of an almost abstract creative first wash, or add your animal to an existing painting. A landscape could have a butterfly in the foreground, for example, or you might perch a dragonfly on a flower. The idea is to make any ordinary composition become extraordinary.

In the brown wash shown here, I allowed white paper to show in the upper and lower sections to add a sense of light. I placed a strong diagonal of bold colour to gain a sense of direction. My dragonfly or butterfly could then be added on top to echo this direction, creating a form of harmony in the story – and far more powerfully than in isolation.

Add the subject

Once I had painted a suitable background, I added my subject. I started this particular dragonfly by painting its body first. Next, I created the wings. I used a rigger brush to carefully apply fine lines of white gouache, allowing the background colour to show through. This brings the wings to life and pushes the darker background into the distance.

The soft, blurred edges of the background in my creative wash gave a sense of a hazy misty morning. The bubbles were painted next, again using white gouache. The outer edges of the bubbles were painted first, then I blended the white into the centres softly, so there are no defined hard lines. The white from the bubbles harmonizes with the white on the wings. Both the bubbles and the dragonfly were placed in a deliberate diagonal directional position to gain a sense of flow in my work.

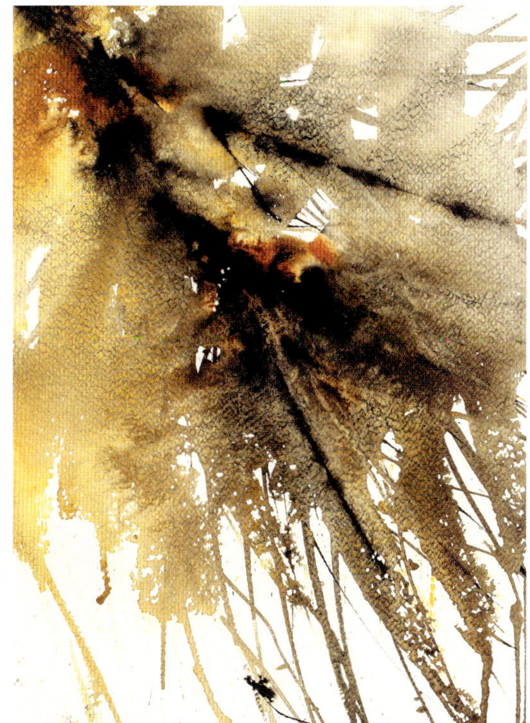

A creative first wash for a butterfly or dragonfly.

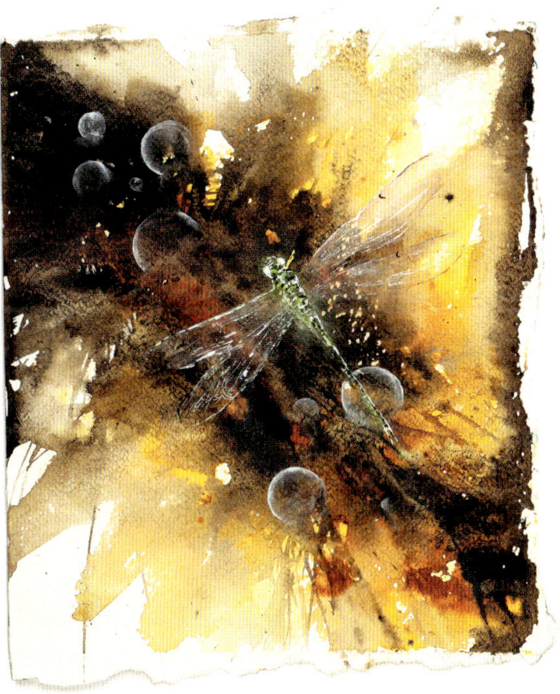

Mystic Morn
28 x 33cm (11 x 13in)
Dragonfly on brown background.

Changing the background colour

A simple change of colour can completely change the story, mood and atmosphere in a painting of a similar subject. Compare *Emerald Flight*, my green dragonfly on a green background, with *Mystic Morn* on the previous page. The composition is similar, but the different colours immediately changes the mood of the piece.

My suggestion is that you try painting this scene with as many different colour combinations as you wish, to see how many variations you can come up with.

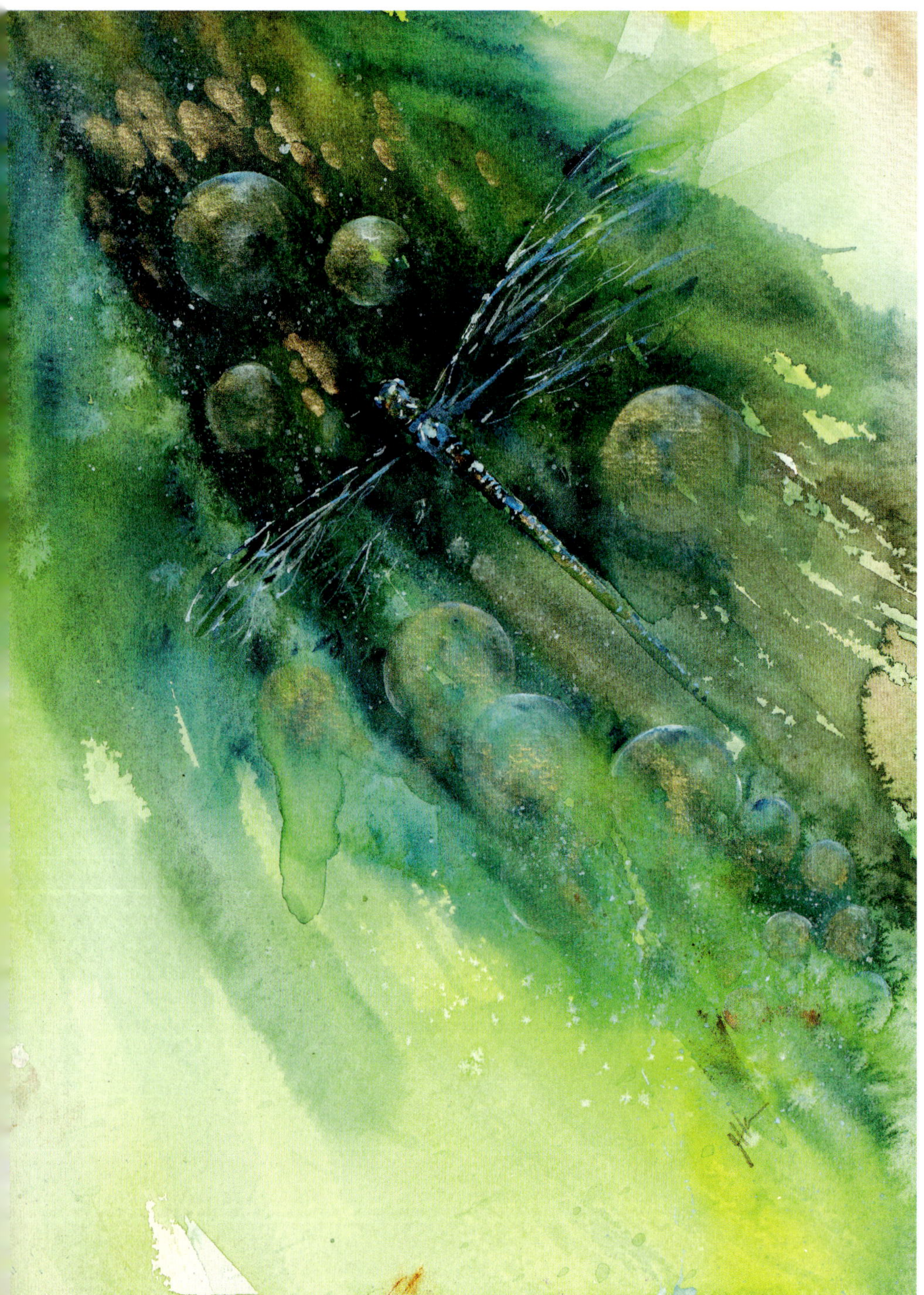

Emerald Flight
28 x 38cm (11 x 15in)
Green dragonfly on green background.

"Magic is seeing the wonder in nature's every little thing, seeing how wonderful the fireflies are and how magical are the dragonflies."

Ama H. Vanniarachchy

Painting on top of ink backgrounds

Experimenting will lead to new discoveries. In painting this series, I discovered a fun and interesting fact. As an experiment, I had painted a strong background using acrylic inks along with my regular watercolours. I added four small dragonflies on top of this wash using white gouache. But as soon as the fresh gouache hit the then-dry paper, each dragonfly changed colour, turning into almost luminous creatures, which was wonderful to observe.

Try experimenting with different products to see how your results could change. This is now one of my favourite discoveries, which I use often in my latest art.

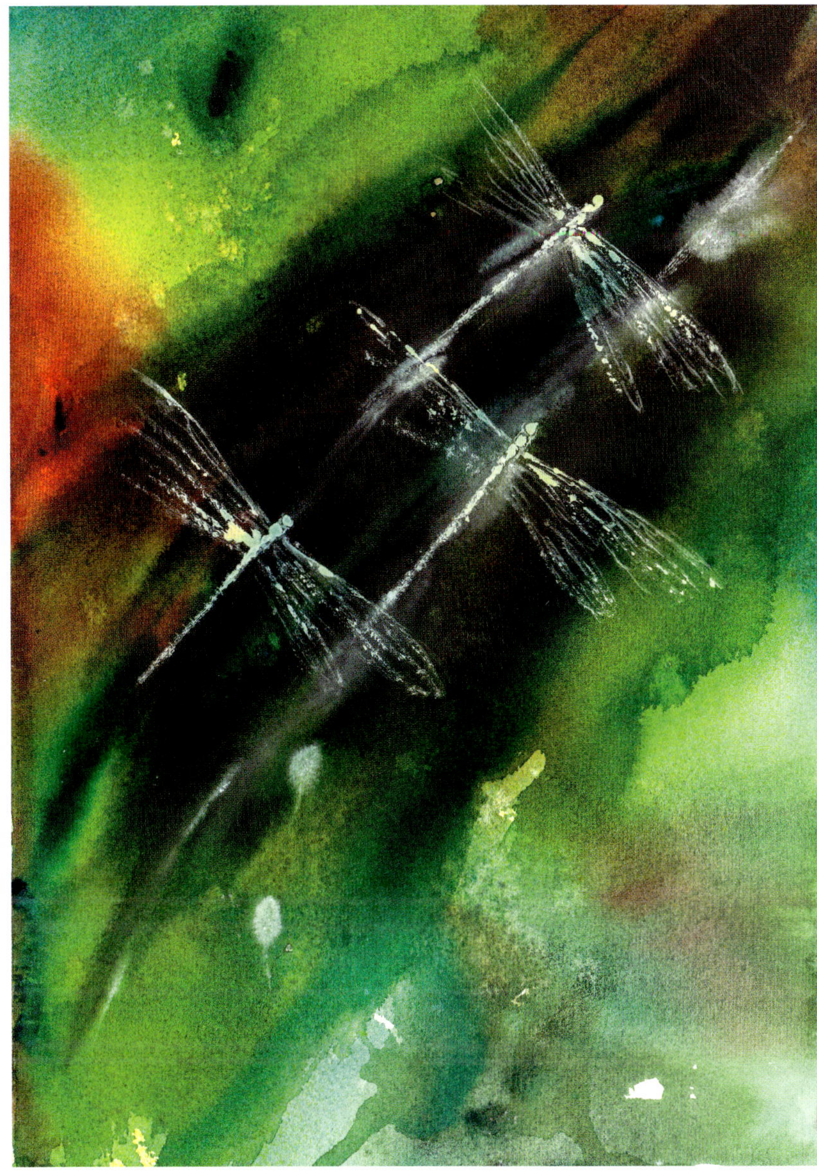

Nature's Jewels

28 x 38cm (11 x 15in)
Dragonflies created on top of a
bold acrylic ink wash.

World of wonder

There is no end to the variety of the smallest of beings that exist on our planet. Each little creature is unique and amazing to create in watercolour. Have you ever considered how beautiful a beetle could be, or how interesting a snail shell would be to paint in watercolour? You could also paint spiders or caterpillars in many different ways. Painting ants on an ant hill could be incredible. All we need is an open mind and a strong imagination when it comes to atmospheric watercolours. The more animals or small beings I paint, the more I want to paint. Creating this way is an addiction – a healthy one from which I never want to recover.

If you have never painted bugs or butterflies before, this really is just the beginning of a new adventure in painting the smallest beings in our animal kingdom. Enjoy your adventure.

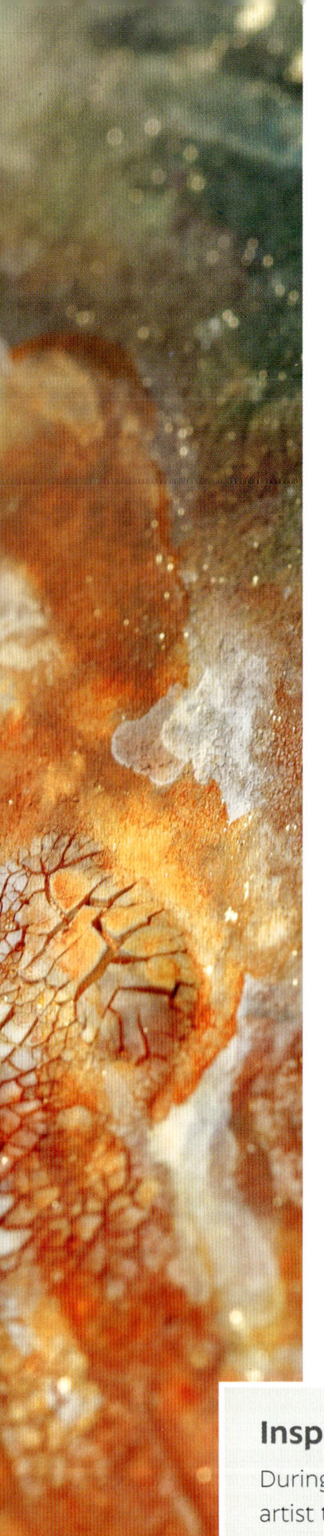

Creative art

PAINTING ANIMALS IS WONDERFUL BECAUSE we can connect with them on so many levels – especially if you love all manner of creatures, large and small. In the previous chapter we looked at bugs and butterflies, showing that size is irrelevant when it comes to creating. But what can we do with our creations once we have mastered techniques and compositions?

There is no end to the ways in which our animal artwork can be used. Pet commissions are always popular, and wildlife is often a bestseller in galleries. One only has to look at the vast number of greetings cards with animal designs in any form to realize how animals make a difference to people's lives; bringing pleasure in so many ways. Animals pull at our emotions. Humans always have been, and always will be, fascinated by the magical world that is the animal kingdom.

Inspirational story

During a wildlife art exhibition in London, a then well-known artist took me aside and told me I would never get anywhere by painting half-animals, which was the entrance into my style at the time. Years later I have travelled the world teaching, written bestselling books on painting with watercolour, exhibited and written for many international magazines. The moral of this story is: always be true to yourself and never let anyone else get you down.

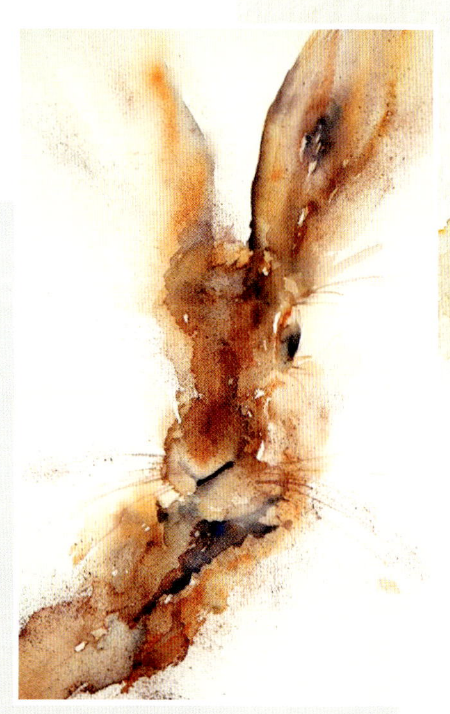

Almost Hare
38 x 28cm (15 x 11in)
Exhibited in the David Shepherd Wildlife Artist of the Year Exhibition at the Mall Galleries in London.

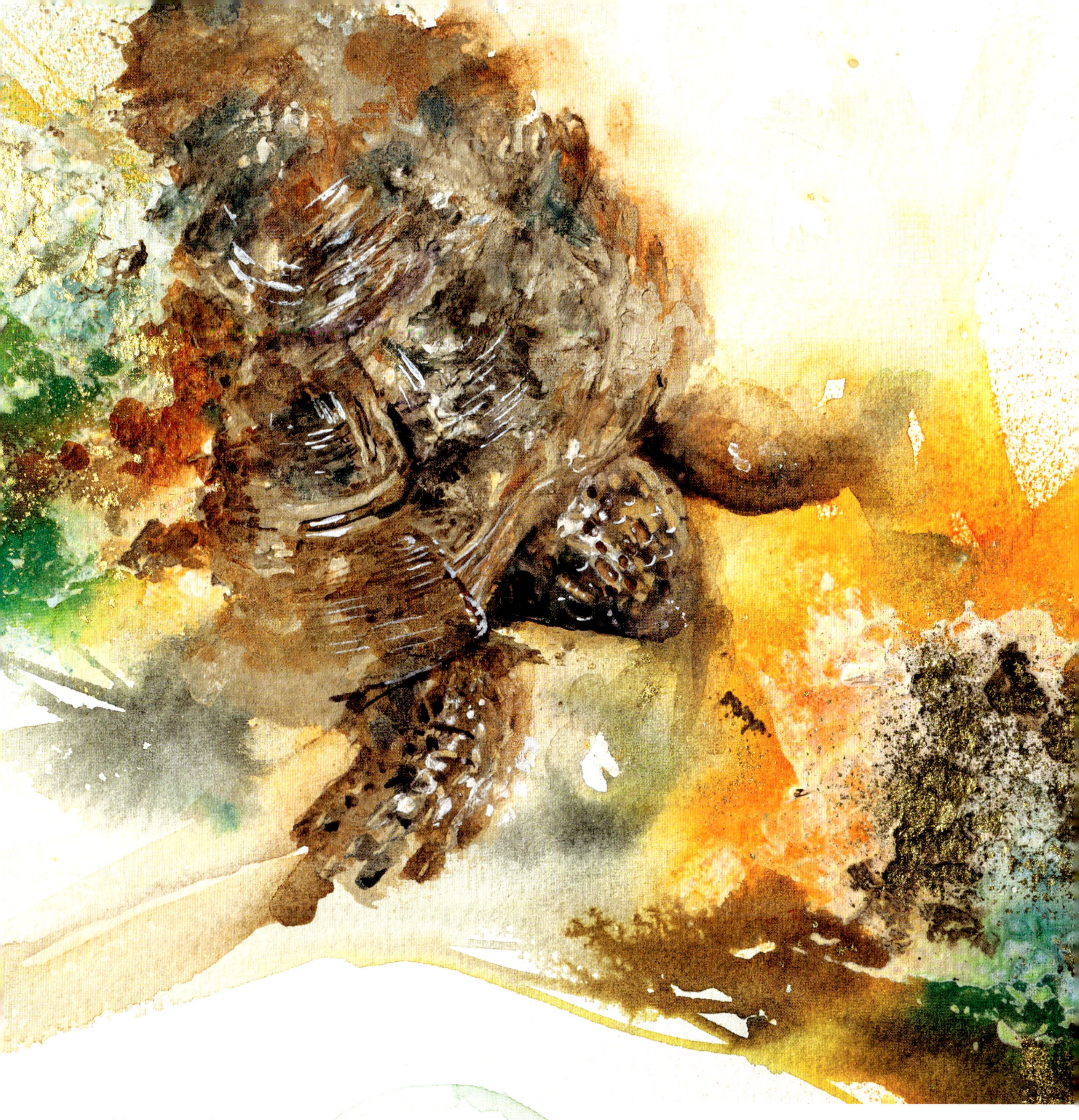

Taking My Time
38 x 28cm (15 x 11in)

Animal meaning: tortoise

The tortoise and the turtle both remind us that at times in life, we need to slow down. For the artist, this is a healthy reminder that we shouldn't rush our paintings. Often, if we do, we miss the beauty in the creative process and the opportunity to work with watercolour's happy accidents.

Fundraising with your art

Over the years that I have been painting I have helped many charities with my art, either by donating original artwork for auction, selling via exhibitions in aid of an animal charity, or by donating my designs to be used as greeting cards. This is such a simple way to do good in the world. Many charities, especially small organizations, love to hear from artists. Rescue centres and rehabilitation centres all value fundraising efforts, so if you feel so inclined, do consider using your art in this way.

   On these pages you can see how I took the initial idea of *Sweet Pup* (see page 56) and turned it into a greeting card simply by adding a Santa hat. I also painted a series of bearded collie dogs in Santa hats for a bearded collie rescue charity. To paint for greeting cards it's wise to follow these tips:

- Remember that your design will need to be clear if it is to be printed, so do add enough detail to tell the story. Your brushwork needs to be defined well.

- Make sure your design is appropriate for the charity.

- Only ever use your own original artwork if it is to be for sale in any way. Never copy other artists' work or paint from photographers' images without their permission, as it could lead to copyright issues.

- Find a way of making your artwork saleable and appealing. For example, use unusual compositions. I have added a few tips in this section for you to consider to help you come up with ideas of your own.

- A simple subject on a white background works very well for printing purposes.

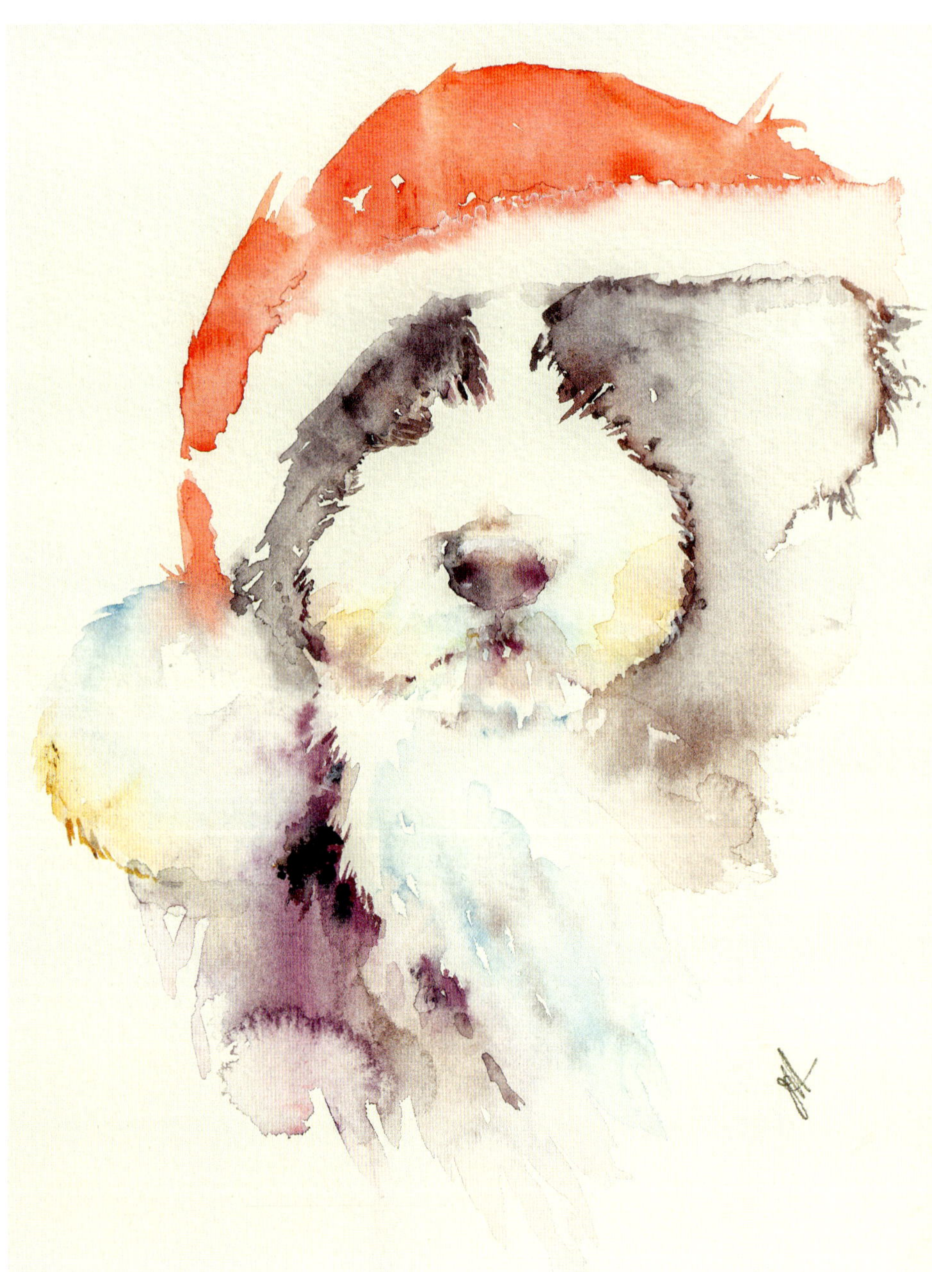

Santa Pup
28 x 38cm (11 x 15in)

38 x 28 cm (15 x 11in)
Bearded collie
with mistletoe.

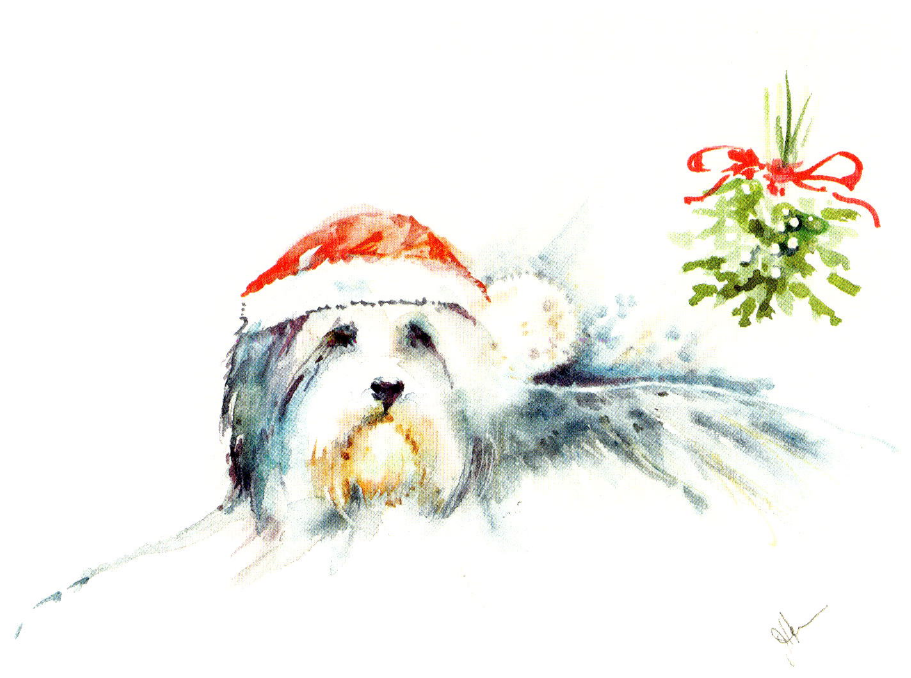

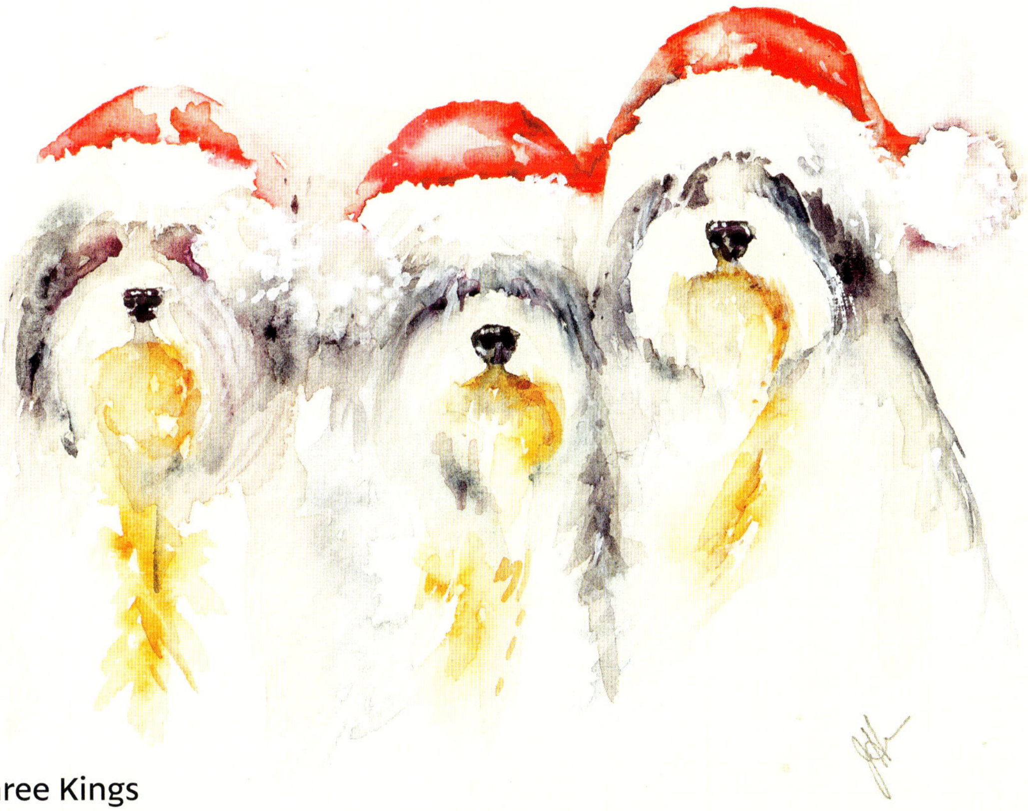

We Three Kings
38 x 28 cm (15 x 11in)
Three bearded collies in Santa hats.

Adding humour

"In a cat's eye, all things belong to cats." *English proverb*

As artists, we can often take ourselves far too seriously. I love adding an element of
fun to my creations; sometimes verging on the side of whimsical, but this is part of
what makes creating enjoyable. Leaping into a completely different genre and smiling
while you paint is a joyous feeling. It releases any stress you may unknowingly be
carrying. You have the uplifting power to make others smile with your artwork too,
and this is a truly magical part of being a creator.

In the previous chapter I added bubbles to my compositions. In *Bubbles Up*, which
you can see below, the bubbles give the kitten something to look at and to focus
upon. The simple addition of the bubbles added to the storytelling in this piece; it
is now fun and not just a painting of a cat. Try to dramatize your work whenever
possible. Find ways to make a simple subject more fascinating and appealing,
especially if you are painting young animals. Aim to make them look playful, which
will help to create a feeling of youth in your results.

Bubbles Up
38 x 28 cm (15 x 11in)
Kitten with bubbles.

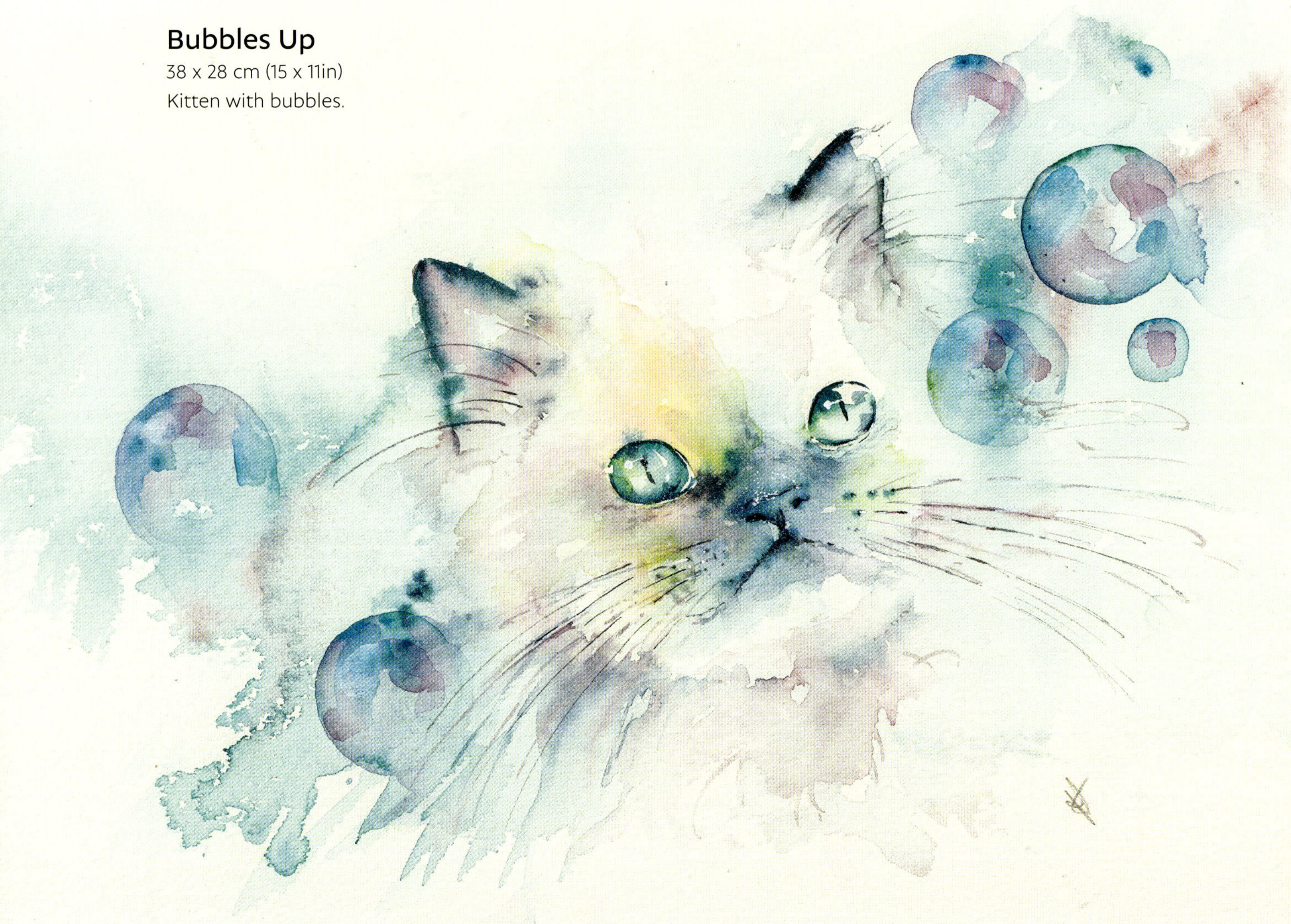

Storytelling in animal art

I pursued this idea of playfulness further in *Buzz Off*, by adding a bee for the black cat to look at in another watercolour. When adding a subject for an animal to look at in artwork, it is important to align the eyes accurately, so that they are looking at the additional attraction.

Here the bee looks as though it is heading towards the cat's nose, and the cat's expression, along with the eye highlight, connects the bee with the cat. The storytelling here is simple and effective.

You could instead try adding a dragonfly or butterfly to your animal paintings. Adding a new smaller subject as an additional focal point to a larger animal painting will bring a fantastic new story to what could otherwise have been a rather dull painting.

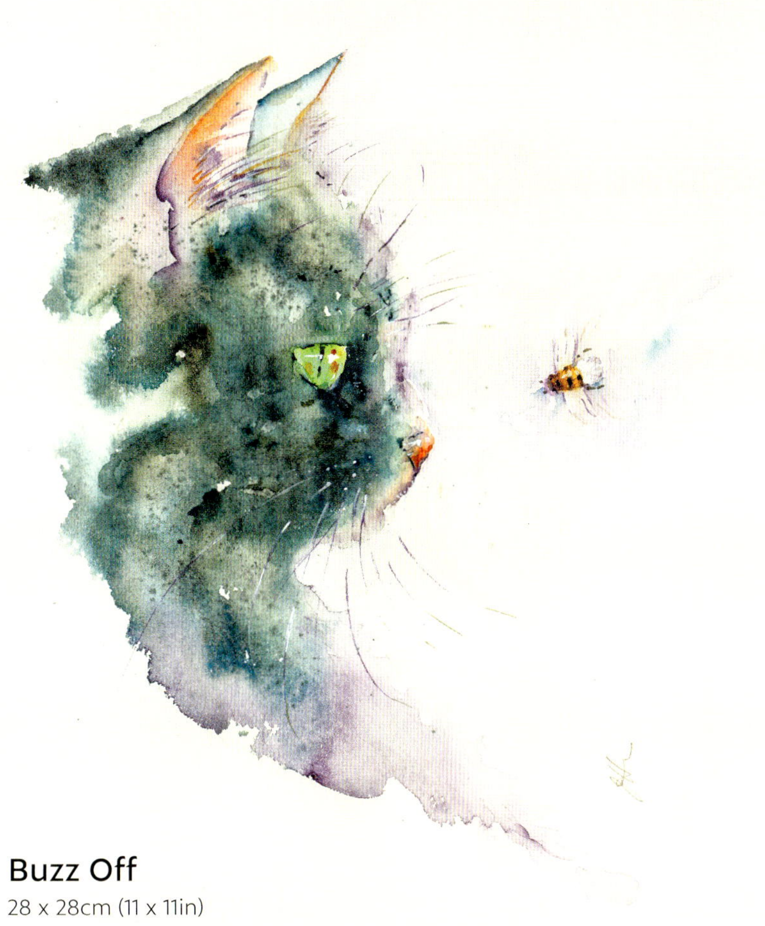

Buzz Off
28 x 28cm (11 x 11in)

"In ancient times cats were worshipped as gods; they have not forgotten this." *Terry Pratchett*

Aim for the unexpected

There are many ways we can create in a unique way. Just because we may look at a dog or cat and see it alone, it does not mean we have to limit ourselves to portraying it that way.

For me, being an artist is all about exploring; understanding my subjects, their personalities and characters; showing if they are fun or comical. I aim to add a strong sense of communication in my work, not only between myself and my painting, but for the viewers of my finished work. If the chosen animals I am painting are more serious, then yes, I keep my work serious. But whatever I am painting, my goal is to be one hundred per cent unique. I love that the unexpected is expected of me.

Breathe energy into your animal paintings

Remember to make your painting time enjoyable, so you can look forward to each time you pick up your paintbrushes. Plan ahead. If you have a composition in mind, imagine how you can improve it or enhance it. Don't fall into a rut of just painting animals as they first appear. Bring them to life. Breathe energy into each brushstroke. Tell stories with your art and, where possible, help animal charities. Together as artists we can do so much good in this world. And the animals on this planet deserve our respect and help.

Never underestimate how well you can paint. Even if you are a beginner. You will find painting animals unites you with other animal lovers. So have fun painting animals, and be the best artist you can be while learning from them.

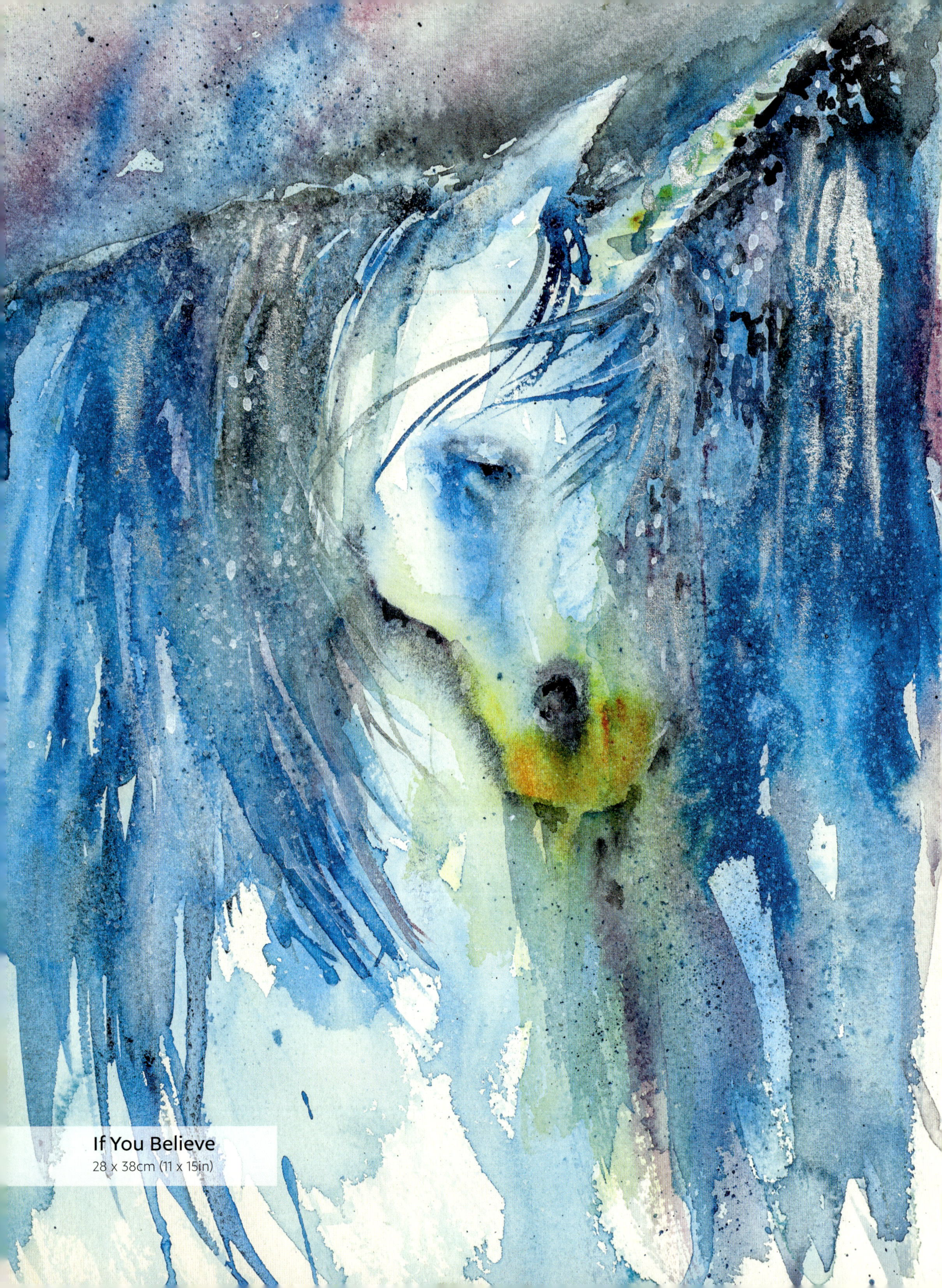

If You Believe
28 x 38cm (11 x 15in)

Magical interpretations

I have loved writing this book and sharing my way of creating animals using my favourite atmospheric watercolour techniques. There are many incredible animals in the world to paint; many animals that inspire us to pick up our brushes and capture them in watercolour. There are also endless techniques, many gorgeous watercolour shades and tempting products to try. Through the pages of my book, my goal has been to inspire you; to encourage you to find your own style, your own voice when painting. I want to help you to create watercolours that aren't just paintings, but something far more: magical interpretations that are undeniably unique.

Painting animals can bring so much pleasure, joy and, as seen in my last chapter, even do good by helping charities. What we need as artists is the confidence to try to be different: the eagerness, the thirst, to consistently search for new approaches to painting familiar subjects – and a belief that magic can happen when we introduce colour to paper. I have always believed that enthusiasm is the key to being a successful artist. When it comes to painting animals, I believe that passion, skill and enthusiasm are a powerful combination.

The unicorn is a mythical creature; a magical being that is popular worldwide, especially with children. It is said to hold magical powers and you are lucky if you see one. To me they represent the idea of searching for the impossible, something that doesn't exist.

I have always loved telling the story that unicorns eat only magical berries, and if you ever see these fruits, a snow-white unicorn will be nearby. Adapting that train of thought to my artwork, I have always believed the next best painting is just about to appear. It will be magical; beautiful. The thought of creating it excites me, so much so that each animal painting I create is never enough. There will always be another one on my mind. That is the joy of being an artist – painting what we love and bringing it to life in an atmospheric style: undoubtedly an enviable ability.

My wish is that this book allows you to enjoy painting animals as much as I do, that you find many ways to bring them to life in watercolour, and that you always have the feeling that the next one is going to be your best ever.

Happy painting, and may you always create stunning atmospheric animals in watercolour.

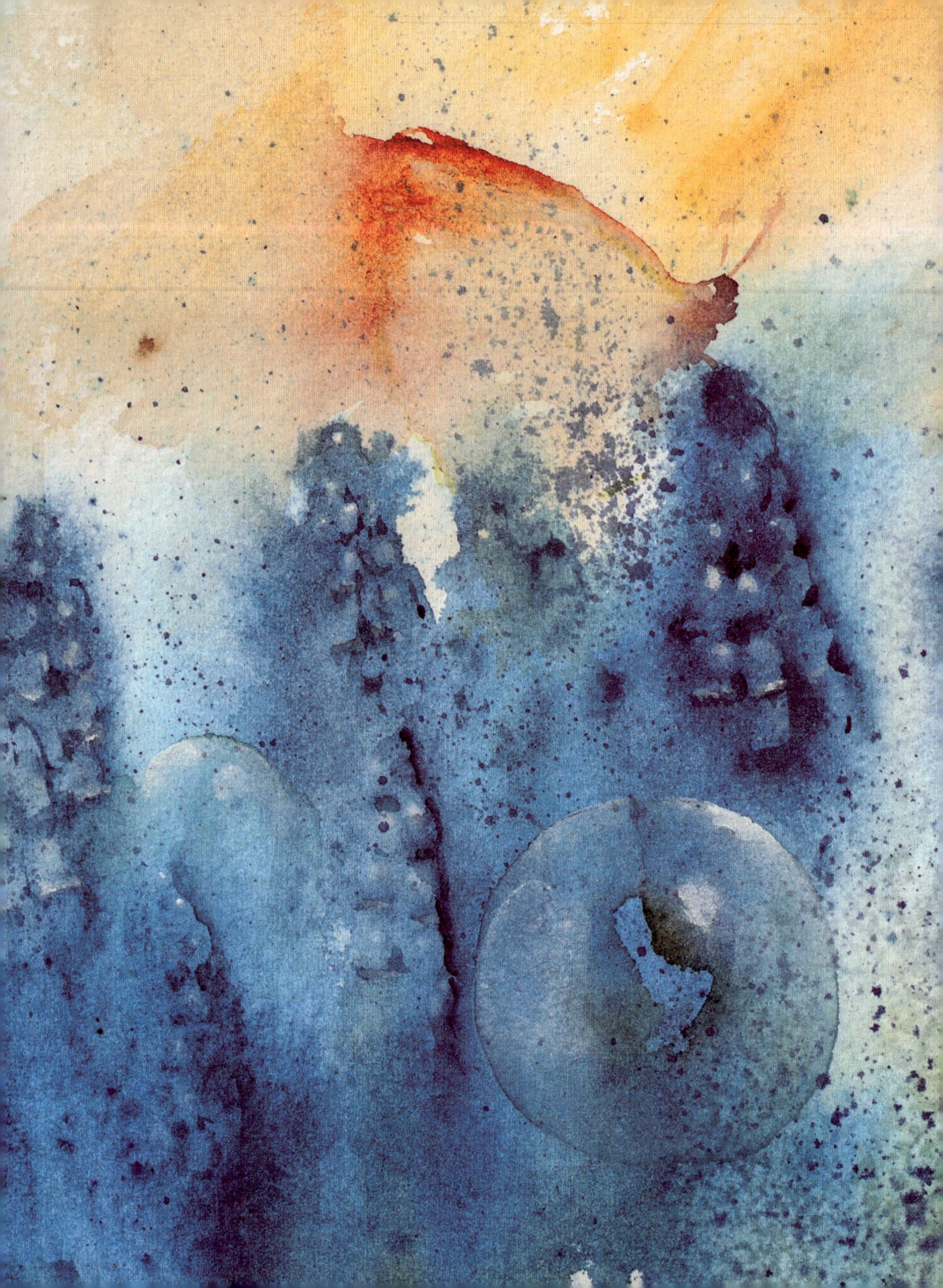